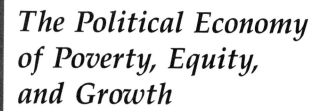

The Political Economy of Poverty, Equity, and Growth

Series editors
Deepak Lal and Hla Myint

A World Bank
Comparative Study

*The Political
Economy of Poverty,
Equity, and Growth*

Costa Rica
and
Uruguay

**Edited by
Simon Rottenberg**

**Country studies by
Alberto Bensión
Víctor Céspedes
Edgardo Favaro
Claudio González-Vega**

Published for the World Bank
Oxford University Press

Oxford University Press

OXFORD NEW YORK TORONTO
DELHI BOMBAY CALCUTTA MADRAS KARACHI
KUALA LUMPUR SINGAPORE HONG KONG TOKYO
NAIROBI DAR ES SALAAM CAPE TOWN
MELBOURNE AUCKLAND
and associated companies in
BERLIN IBADAN

Published by Oxford University Press, Inc.
200 Madison Avenue, New York, N.Y. 10016

Oxford is a registered trademark of Oxford University Press

Manufactured in the United States of America
First printing January 1993

Library of Congress Cataloging-in Publication Data

Costa Rica and Uruguay / edited by Simon Rottenberg ; with
contributions by Claudio González-Vega ... [et al.].
  p. cm. — (A World Bank comparative study. The Political
economy of poverty, equity, and growth)
  Includes bibliographical references and index.
  ISBN 0-19-520883-8
  1. Costa Rica—Economic conditions—1948– 2. Income distribution—
Costa Rica—History. 3. Poor—Costa Rica—History. 4. Uruguay—
Economic conditions—1946– 5. Income distribution—Uruguay—
History. 6. Poor—Uruguay—History. I. Rottenberg, Simon.
II. González Vega, Claudio. III. Series: World Bank comparative
study. Political economy of poverty, equity, and growth.
HC143.C668 1993
339.2'097286—dc20   92-29890
                                                                              CIP

Foreword

This volume is the fifth of several emerging from the comparative study "The Political Economy of Poverty, Equity and Growth" sponsored by the World Bank. The study was done to provide a critical evaluation of the economic history of selected developing countries in 1950–85. It explores the *processes* that yielded different levels of growth, poverty, and equity in these countries, depending on each country's initial resource endowment and economic structure, national institutions and forms of economic organization, and economic policies (including those that might have been undertaken).

The Scope of the Comparative Study

The basic building block of the project is a coherent story of the growth and income distribution experiences of each country, based on the methods of what may be termed "analytical economic history" (see Collier and Lal 1986) and "political economy." Each country study provides both a historical narrative and a deeper explanation of how and why things happened. Each study also seeks to identify the role of ideology and interest groups in shaping policy.

Our comparative approach involved pairing countries whose initial conditions or policies seemed to be either significantly similar or significantly different. Although initial impressions of similarity or difference may not have been borne out on closer inspection, this binary approach offered a novel and promising way of reconciling in-depth case studies with a broader comparative method of analysis.

To provide this in-depth study of individual cases, a smaller number of countries was selected than is conventional in comparative *statistical* studies. We have serious doubts about the validity of inferences drawn from such cross-sectional regression studies about historical processes (see Hicks 1979). Therefore this project, by combining qualitative with quantitative analysis, has tried instead to interpret the nature and significance of the usual quantifiable variables for each country in its historical and institutional context.

To provide some unifying elements to the project, we presented the authors of the country studies with several provisional hypotheses to be considered in the course of their work. These concern the determinant of growth, the importance of historical and organizational factors in determining alternative feasible paths of growth to redress poverty, and the relative roles of ideas, interests, and ideology in influencing decisionmaking.

The following list of the country studies and their principal authors suggests the range of the overall comparative study:

Malawi and Madagascar	Frederic L. Pryor
Egypt and Turkey	Bent Hansen
Sri Lanka and Malaysia	Henry Bruton
Indonesia and Nigeria	David Bevan, Paul Collier, and Jan Gunning
Thailand and Ghana	Oey A. Meesook, Douglas Rimmer, and Gus Edgren
Brazil and Mexico	Angus Maddison and Associates
Costa Rica and Uruguay	Simon Rottenberg and others
Colombia and Peru	Antonio Urdinola, Mauricio Carrizosa Serrano, and Richard Webb
Five Small Economies: Hong Kong, Singapore, Malta, Jamaica, and Mauritius	Ronald Findlay and Stanislaw Wellisz

Many of these volumes will be published in this series by Oxford University Press. In addition, a volume of special studies on related topics, edited by George Psacharopoulos, will also be published.

This Volume

This study of Uruguay and Costa Rica reveals two countries with striking similarities in initial conditions, economic policies, and outcomes. Claudio González-Vega and Víctor Céspedes describe Costa Rica, Edgardo Favaro and Alberto Bensión describe Uruguay, and Simon Rottenberg compares the two countries. The book portrays two countries that have achieved relatively high per capita income through the export of primary products—coffee and bananas in Costa Rica, beef and livestock in Uruguay. Both countries have also followed redistributive policies and were among the earliest to establish welfare states. This occurred after World War II in Costa Rica and at the turn of the century in Uruguay. The result has been a high degree of equity in both countries, both of which have democratic systems of government.

Over time, however, as a result of growing urbanization and the interplay of interest group pressures in democratic politics, redistributive policies have led to explicit and implicit taxation of their most productive source of revenue—the agricultural sector. Entitlements created by the welfare state have been underwritten by an increasing squeeze on the rural sector. This has come about as a result of the growth of public employment and parastatals, discriminatory exchange rate and agricultural price policies, growing trade protection, and inefficient industrialization. Incipient fiscal crises resulted in both countries. In Uruguay this manifested itself as a balance of payments crisis triggered by the large oil price increase of the early 1970s; Costa Rica's plight occurred a decade later, when voluntary lending to Latin America was brought to a halt by the world debt crisis and the rise in interest rates.

The authors chart the twists and turns in subsequent policymaking in both countries. Both countries aimed to liberalize their economies—thereby raising their growth rates by increasing their responsiveness to a more turbulent world environment; both aimed to roll back redistributive entitlements that had become unviable. Their success has been mixed, although Uruguay's spectacular growth in the early 1970s, after initial liberalization, shows the potential for growth flowing from good policies that exists in both countries.

These studies illustrate the feasibility of improving equity through state action; but they also reveal a corresponding danger that state action might produce long-term economic stagnation. This may arise if the policies that have been applied put brakes on the very sector whose surpluses support the redistributive entitlements. The studies also show that many such adverse effects may take a long time to appear, so that there is little incentive for politicians with relatively short time horizons to take the preemptive remedial action. They demonstrate, additionally, that a serious fiscal or balance of payments crisis can be the trigger for the radical change in policies needed to attain a viable long-run growth path.

Deepak Lal and Hla Myint
Series editors

Contents

Preface

Costa Rica and Uruguay exhibit striking similarities in their economic policies and make an interesting pair for a comparative examination.

For much of its history the Costa Rican population has been settled in isolated subsistence farmsteads and villages, and it has experienced an equality of poverty. The growth of the coffee economy, beginning in the midnineteenth century, greatly improved the material standard of living. The country is still much less urbanized than Uruguay, but the San José Metropolitan Area has grown disproportionately in the twentieth century. As in Uruguay, the government is democratically elected.

Uruguay's prospects were sufficiently promising to attract large numbers of European immigrants in the late nineteenth and early twentieth centuries. Although livestock raising was the main activity, the population of Montevideo from the beginning constituted a large proportion of the population. The exercise of competitive private power in rural areas in the nineteenth century gave way in the early twentieth century to a process of accommodation and co-option by a centralized, democratically elected state.

In both countries—in Costa Rica since the late 1940s and in Uruguay since the early twentieth century—government has been instructed by a social democratic perspective. Both countries have developed reputations as archetypal "welfare states." In both, policies adopted by an activist state have regulated economic activity, redistributed income, altered the composition of economic output, and opened opportunities for the privileged use of the state power to capture rents.

Income is more equally distributed in Costa Rica and Uruguay than in much of the rest of Latin America. This has been achieved in part by the application of policies that were explicitly designed to transfer income or that had other purposes but also had income transfer effects. The main beneficiary of these policies has been the urban population.

Economic policy has, however, distorted prices, diminished incentives, and had adverse effects on economic output. The Uruguayan economy has been stagnant since the 1950s. Costa Rica, which lagged behind Uruguay by some four decades in the active administration of redistributive policy, began to experience economic crisis in the early 1980s.

In both countries social security, the protection of industrial activities, and the employment of large numbers of people in public sector institutions have been important policy instruments that have worked to the relative advantage of urban residents. In Uruguay policy has also sought to provide urban consumers with a cheap and abundant supply of beef—an important component of the Uruguayan consumption basket.

Public policy in both countries has often had distorting and disadvantageous distributional effects that have introduced inefficiencies and diminished economic output.

Claudio González-Vega
Víctor Hugo Céspedes

I Costa Rica

Introduction

Compared with other developing countries of similar size and resource endowment, Costa Rica has been exceptional. In the long run this country has been able to sustain an unusual combination of rapid economic growth, substantial improvements in standards of living, political stability, and a strong concern with the wide distribution of the fruits of progress and with the alleviation of poverty. The sharp contrast to other countries makes it clear that these outcomes must have been the result of cumulative, long-term processes that reflect the different and complex historical evolution of Costa Rica. Economic and political development takes time.

During the early 1980s, however, Costa Rica experienced major economic difficulties, including reduced rates of output growth, higher levels of inflation, devaluation, and unemployment, and increased poverty. A central argument of this part of the book is that key features of the historical evolution of the country—centered around dynamic interactions between economic constraints and political demands—explain, to a large extent, both the long-run successes in economic growth and social equity outcomes and the nature, evolution, and extent of the recent fiscal crisis.

The purpose of this part of the book is, therefore, to bring out the unusual, but systematic, relations among political and economic factors that explain the comparatively favorable long-term results with respect to growth and equity and to examine the long-term sustainability of these outcomes.

Successes

Costa Rica's evolution during the 1950–85 period was marked by (a) a successful growth record, (b) unusually good performance of most socioeconomic indicators, (c) moderate income inequality, (d) substantial alleviation of poverty, and (e) sustained political stability and strong democratic institutions.

3

During the period Costa Rica enjoyed a rather satisfactory rate of economic growth. In real terms, gross domestic product (GDP) grew at an average annual rate of 5.0 percent. Since at the same time population was growing rapidly, at 3.2 percent a year, GDP per capita grew at 1.8 percent a year. By the end of the thirty-five-year period the population had tripled and GDP per capita had doubled. The record is even more impressive if the slower growth rates of the late 1950s and early 1980s— regarded by Costa Ricans as "crisis" periods and therefore as unusual—are ignored. Between 1961 and 1979 a GDP growth of 6.5 percent made possible a 3.4 percent annual increase in GDP per capita.

Vulnerability to external shocks, as well as unstable output growth, was as much a part of the period's economic history as the comparatively high average rates of growth. Economic growth was thus compatible with a high degree of externally induced instability. Although the prices and exportable supplies of the traditional crops (coffee and bananas) fluctuated, significant improvements in crop yields contributed to the country's pronounced and sustained comparative advantages and its high returns from exports. Moreover, despite the fluctuations, high average rates of output growth validated Costa Ricans' expectations of continued improvements in real income.

The positive performance of all major socioeconomic indicators revealed a higher quality of life than would be predicted for countries at Costa Rica's level of GDP per capita. In particular, there was outstanding progress in all health indicators (mortality and infant mortality rates, life expectancy, and nutrition), and the already high educational standards improved. In addition, most Costa Ricans gained access to publicly provided services (running water, sewage disposal, electricity, schools, health clinics, and social security assistance), as well as to many modern conveniences (roads, telephones, newspapers, radio, television, movies, and refrigerators).

By 1950 many of these indicators had already reached high levels, and they improved rapidly during the next decades, even within ranges in which marginal improvements became difficult. This reflected the rapid expansion of the country's physical and institutional infrastructure, high educational levels, and explicit public sector policies and expenditures.[1]

In addition to these measurable components of the standard of living, Costa Ricans enjoyed many of the less tangible determinants of the quality of life: freedom, in all its dimensions; social, political, and economic mobility; democratic participation; personal safety; tolerance and peaceful resolution of conflicts; institutional stability; and an efficient legal and judicial framework. Most of these features were already apparent by 1950, and they continued to improve throughout the period as traditions were preserved and institutions and the legal framework were strengthened. Others, however, were jeopardized by the larger size and growing complexity of society.

Inequality was moderate; the Gini coefficient for the distribution of household income was 0.44 in 1971. Income was more equally distributed in 1971 than in the early 1960s, as wider segments of the population shared in the rapid income growth of the period, but the trend toward a more egalitarian distribution slowed somewhat during the late 1970s, and the crisis of the early 1980s led to some temporary deterioration. Income has not been excessively concentrated; the share of the richest 20 percent was only 51 percent of household income in 1971, and the distribution of land, by value, was moderately concentrated. The middle classes have thus enjoyed comparatively large shares of incomes and assets and have played a prominent role in the political arena.

During 1950–85 there was a substantial reduction in absolute and relative poverty, complemented by the development of effective public sector assistance programs for the indigent and for children, old people, and women. Although poverty increased during the crisis of the early 1980s, by the middle of the decade it had returned to its earlier low levels.

Costa Rica has been an example of growth with equity. Its history does not support the hypothesis of an inevitable tradeoff between these goals. On the contrary, there has been a strong positive association between rapid economic growth, a more egalitarian distribution, and the alleviation of poverty. The Costa Rican experience suggests that—given an appropriate political and institutional framework—when growth leads, equity follows.

Costa Rica's sustained political stability, willingness to evolve without abrupt changes, and marked preference for a peaceful resolution of conflicts have characterized the country from its early years as an independent nation. Whereas between 1824 and 1842 in the other four Central American countries there was a total of 97 rulers, 143 battles, and 7,088 war dead, Costa Rica had only 4 presidents, 2 battles, and fewer than 50 war dead. Political stability continued during the twentieth century; only one president was overthrown (González Flores in 1917).

The two-month civil war in 1948 forced the incumbent administration to recognize the results of that year's presidential election and led to the disbandment of the army and the prohibition by the 1949 Constitution of its reestablishment. During 1950–85 scrupulously supervised elections were held every four years, and, except on one occasion, political parties alternated in controlling the executive.

The Crisis

In the early 1980s Costa Rica experienced acute economic difficulties. What came to be called "the crisis" was marked by declining output, shrinking foreign trade, growing unemployment, falling real wages, rapid inflation, and the devaluation of the domestic currency (*colón*), accompanied by a huge public sector deficit and public external debt.

These difficulties were in sharp contrast to the previous record of successful growth.

Some dimensions of the crisis (the fiscal deficit, inflation, devaluation, and the external debt) were more acute in Costa Rica than in other Central American and Caribbean countries, although Costa Rica escaped the insurrections and political instability that have marred the recent history of the region. Indeed, social unrest was almost nonexistent in Costa Rica despite the depth of the crisis and its impact on the standard of living of a people with high expectations of real income growth.

The crisis was generated by both exogenous forces (sharp external shocks and the consequences of unrest elsewhere in Central America) and endogenous factors, including changes in relative factor endowments, the choice of development strategy, macroeconomic management responses to the exogenous shocks, growing institutional rigidities, fiscal inconsistencies, and political-economy conflicts within Costa Rican society.

Costa Rica's successful political and economic development, on the one hand, and the near collapse of the system during the recent crisis, on the other, were two predictable dimensions of the same political-economy processes. Indeed, some of the same factors that explain the singular growth-with-equity outcomes also explain the magnitude and depth of the crisis. The strong investment in human capital and improved institutional framework contributed to growth and equity, but at the same time fueled growing political-economy conflicts and directly unproductive behavior.

Importance of the Initial Conditions

The country's initial conditions in 1950 play a key role in this political-economy story. These initial conditions include several characteristics that set Costa Rica apart from other developing countries and explain a large part of the growth-with-equity outcomes of the 1950–85 period. Six of these conditions deserve brief attention here. Four are related to features of the political system: (a) stability, (b) democratic institutions, (c) mechanisms to prevent or reduce the concentration of power, and (d) a great concern for equity. The other two are the country's small size and the ample availability of unexploited land. Chapter 4 discusses these initial political conditions.

The country's political stability has reflected its long-term capacity for evolving without abrupt change (Dabène 1986). There have been no revolutions in Costa Rica. Major institutional transformations have taken place not violently but according to well-defined rules. This has been reflected in a long tradition of nonviolence and consensus and in a general attachment to legality.

With a few notable exceptions, institutional development has come about by trial and error, through efforts to explore, in miniature, the nature of potential reforms and arrive, on the basis of these experiments, at a consensus on their desirability. By the time ambitious programs and policies were adopted, their feasibility had already been tested. In the meantime substantial debate about the innovation had taken place on the basis of the results of the experiments, and the modifications required for its wide acceptance had been made. These experiments were often initiated by one administration and eventually adopted by the opposition. In other instances, by the time the opposition gained power, it had become impossible to dismantle existing institutions.

Other aspects of this tradition of peaceful evolution have been the abolition of the army, the uneventful transmission of power (frequently from one political party to another, as a result of closely scrutinized elections), and the institutionalization of public dialogue and policy compromise.

Costa Rica is the oldest continuously working democracy in Latin America. The country's institutions have guaranteed not only the orderly transfer of power but also widespread popular participation in the definition of goals and the choice of means. There has always been an active opposition, with ample access to a free press, to question public policies, while a multitude of groups and organizations has represented the interests of almost every segment of society. Participation has been furthered by strong municipalities and a high educational level.

Conflict has been freely expressed in Costa Rica, and both the process of conflict resolution and the actual solutions have frequently been institutionalized. In particular, economic conflicts have been resolved openly in the political arena, under the protection of a well-defined and strongly enforced legal system and efficient courts.

Mechanisms for preventing or reducing the concentration of power have proliferated. Thus, after the 1948 civil war the military—whose influence had declined rapidly after the 1870s—were sent home, and the army was disbanded. The 1949 Constitution forbade the reestablishment of the army. The power of the Catholic Church was sharply curtailed after the liberal reforms of the 1880s, and Costa Rica became one of the most secular societies in Latin America. The 1949 Constitution was designed to check the concentration of political power, and there is a well-defined separation of the branches of government. The judiciary is particularly strong and independent. Reelection of presidents is prohibited, and there has been, in practice, an almost perfect alternation of opposing political parties in controlling the executive. Frequently, different parties have controlled the executive and the legislative. An independent electoral board (Tribunal Supremo de Elecciones) is in charge of organizing and supervising elections. The centers of political decisionmaking are well dispersed. The multitude of autonomous institutions created after 1948 is clear evidence of the efforts to decentralize power. When the commercial banks were nationalized, the four existing institutions were left as separate entities, to promote competition.

There has been a parallel multiplicity of organizations for the promotion of private sector interests. Numerous pressure groups, frequently not organized along class lines, have represented product, sectoral, regional, or communal interests and have actively participated in policy debate. Multiple affiliations are widespread, giving rise to complex cross-associations among the principal actors in the political and economic arenas. During most of the 1950–85 period growth and stability led to the institutionalization of compromise and to the actual neutralization of interests. A stable equilibrium was increasingly solidified, only to be disturbed by the crisis.

Successive administrations of different persuasions have preserved and furthered a strong concern for equity. The preoccupation with equity grew out of a tradition of interdependence and reciprocity that had its roots in the colonial organization of society and was strengthened by the nineteenth-century social contract among coffee exporters, small coffee producers, and farm workers, as described in chapter 4. The organization of production in this small and vulnerable economy, and the social mechanisms for dealing with risk in a homogeneous society, eventually led to the development of a strong egalitarian ideology.

Size was also important as an initial condition. Costa Rica has a small, homogeneous population that is highly concentrated in one small mountain valley. The limited size of the domestic market and a narrow resource base have been among the country's main economic constraints and have explained the high degree of openness of the economy, as well as Costa Rica's dilemmas in choosing a development strategy.

Small size may have also had an important effect on the political system. Costa Ricans have lived in close contact with one another since colonial times. Before the twentieth century most of the population was concentrated in the inner part of the Central Valley, which covers only 8.3 percent of the territory. In 1980, 58 percent of the population still lived there. The extensive road network further facilitated interactions among all segments of the population since, in most instances, travel from one part of the country to another takes only a few hours.

All this facilitated domestic trade and the rapid elimination of subsistence agriculture (particularly in the Central Valley), promoted the integration of the labor market, and allowed the continuous exchange of political views. This intense interaction was furthered by the homogeneity of the population and by the high level of education. The transaction costs of group organization and of political activism became very low. The common experiences of this homogeneous population thus led to a steady development of the common egalitarian ideology that has pervaded most Costa Rican institutions.

From an economic perspective, small size was a critical constraint on diversification and growth based on the domestic market. Growth and structural transformation inevitably led, in turn, to a more complex society, to less personal contact, and to a less commonly held ideology.

In particular, Costa Ricans have found it difficult to extend their earlier voluntary social contract beyond the coffee pact and replicate it in other sectors of economic activity. Instead, they have attempted to legislate institutional, less efficient replicas of the coffee pact, even though the circumstances have been different and the personal bonds have been absent. The resulting conflicts are a main theme of this part of the book.

In 1950 Costa Rica's population occupied only one-fifth of the territory and faced a wide, unexploited agricultural frontier. Through the mid-1970s the steady growth of agricultural output, both for export and for domestic consumption, was to a large extent a result of the expansion of the cultivated area (Céspedes and others 1983a). Rapid population growth during the following decades, however, quickly reduced this favorable land-labor ratio.

This shift in the country's relative factor endowment modified its comparative advantages and worsened the politically sensitive problem of generating sufficient jobs for a rapidly growing labor force. The promotion of land-extensive cattle ranching in the new areas further reduced the opportunities to create employment in the agricultural sector, and protectionist policies discouraged the use of labor in the manufacturing sector.

In sum, by 1950 Costa Rica's economic and political performance was already exceptional. On the basis of these initial conditions, the country's evolution during the following decades reflected the interaction of political and economic phenomena.

Political-Economic Interactions

The interaction of the political and economic dimensions of development is at the core of the explanation of the Costa Rican growth-with-equity outcomes. Sustained political stability promoted economic growth in that it favored investment in physical and human capital, attracted foreign savings, and facilitated the consolidation of an institutional framework that stimulated trade and productive efforts.

Political stability made long-gestation investment in infrastructure and human skills profitable. The comparatively low risks and transaction costs stemming from a peaceful environment and effective legal system also attracted substantial foreign savings that helped finance a relatively high rate of domestic investment. The strong institutional framework permitted a stable definition of property rights and efficient enforcement of contracts.

The emphasis on equity reinforced a heavy investment in human capital (health, nutrition, and training and education), which further contributed to economic growth by creating a mobile and productive labor force. The low cost of the country's defense, in the absence of an army, made it possible to devote the substantial inflows of foreign savings and the available fiscal resources to higher-than-usual public sector expenditures on human capital formation, equity-enhancing programs, and development of infrastructure.

The pursuit of these equity objectives and the availability of the means of enjoying the less tangible dimensions of the quality of life, such as freedom of speech through access to radio and television, were made possible by high rates of economic growth. Growth and inflows of foreign savings also financed the rapid expansion of the infrastructure, further reducing transaction costs and facilitating market integration. Subsistence agriculture rapidly disappeared.

The fruits of growth and their widespread distribution helped to preserve political stability. Economic growth, increasing equality in distribution, and sustained political stability reinforced each other. The final outcome was more than the simple sum of their effects. In this cumulative and interdependent process of political and economic development, Costa Rica used a "technology" of institutional evolution characterized by important "economies of scope" in the joint "production" of economic growth, political stability, and social equity.

The Political Economy of the Crisis

Political and economic developments are an important part of the explanation for the recent crisis, as well. This crisis was not an isolated episode triggered entirely by exogenous forces (such as the unusually negative external shocks after 1973). It reflected, in addition, the consequences of the same political and economic interactions that explain the high standard of living enjoyed by Costa Ricans.

Widespread political and economic participation promoted the formation of a multitude of interest groups, while sustained stability contributed to their growing strength and their influence on policymaking. Education and social mobility, combined with high rates of economic growth and large inflows of foreign savings, fueled rising expectations and increasing demands for freely and publicly provided services, specific subsidies, and a greater share in the national income. These demands, in combination with explicit concerns for equity, led to the institutionalization of numerous entitlements to future income streams and transfer payments. These entitlements were not always sustainable.

Although the emphasis on equity was an important—but not the only—determinant of the increasing number of public institutions and employees, protectionism gave rise to substantial implicit taxes and subsidies that were not formally reported in the country's fiscal accounts. The increasing size of the public sector, coupled with the consequences of a highly protectionist governmental intervention in the economy, was at the root of the fiscal disequilibriums that led to the crisis.

Rent seeking, opportunism, the rigidity in policy management brought about by the need for compromise and consensus, a deadlock of interest group conflicts, and the high costs of the entitlements and equity programs eventually contributed to the stagnation of output and to the fiscal imbalances that led to the crisis. Although the unusual strength of the middle classes guaranteed political stability and increased the level of domestic demand, their low propensity to save and the few entrepreneurial interests of the growing public sector bureaucracy contributed little to economic growth. Purely redistributive efforts that disregarded economic efficiency eventually jeopardized the pursuit of equity.

Organization

This study analyzes the transformation of the initial conditions already present by 1950 through the crisis of the first half of the 1980s. During this period Costa Rica evolved from a system of liberal political and economic institutions, softened by strong voluntary solidarity, toward an interventionist state characterized by protectionism and paternalistic welfarism.

The main turning point occurred at about the beginning of the period, when a social-democratic ideology began to replace the earlier local version of a liberal ideology. Political change was accelerated by external forces, particularly by changes in coffee prices, and by the conflicts arising from the more diversified and complex society that evolved as the relative importance of coffee declined. These economic changes modified the balance of power, gave rise to questions about the earlier policies, promoted the reorganization of coalitions, and reshaped political and economic institutions.

Before 1950 income and wealth came from the exploitation of Ricardian rents and from exports of a "vent-for-surplus" produced by Costa Rica's comparative advantage in coffee and bananas.[2] The technological and economic features of coffee production, combined with the structure of society inherited from colonial times, fostered voluntary solidarism and interdependence in the society that evolved during the century and a half prior to 1950. The foreign banana enclave had little impact on the fabric of society.

By the 1980s the old coffee alliance had been replaced by a coalition of new state-dependent groups whose income and wealth arose from the rent-seeking manipulation of interventionist policies and public sector activities. Many of the new groups were located in state-owned productive enterprises and in highly protected private sector enclaves. Equity concerns had been institutionalized, and bureaucratic enforcement of entitlements had replaced the earlier voluntary reciprocity. These entitlements, which were financed by inflows of foreign savings, became increasingly unsustainable.

Whereas in the past the distribution of rents and of the fruits of trade and development had been mostly governed by market forces and technological and economic circumstances, the distribution of the newly created rents of the post-1950 era took place mainly in the political arena, through both explicit and implicit taxes and subsidies. The new definition of property rights eventually contributed to slower rates of economic growth. When international and domestic circumstances led to the crisis of the 1980s, this unsustainable system was severely tested.

This part consists of chapters 1–8. (A statistical appendix on Costa Rica is at the end of the section.) Chapter 1 presents basic information about Costa Rica. It describes the country's geography and resources, legal system, and government and identifies the political parties, labor unions, and private sector associations that are the principal actors in the story.

Chapter 2, on growth and structural transformation, surveys the main economic outcomes for the period. It describes the evolution of the components of aggregate demand and supply and highlights changes in the degree of openness of the economy. The economy's structural transformation is explored by analyzing the changes in the importance of different sectors of economic activity and in their shares in employment. The chapter includes discussions of population growth, with its implications for demands for employment generation, and of the reduction of real wages, which illustrates the magnitude of the crisis.

Chapter 3 presents outcomes for distribution and the alleviation of poverty. It examines the distribution of household income, functional factor shares, and the effect of taxation and government expenditures on distribution. Available evidence about the characteristics of poverty, fulfillment of basic needs, and other indicators of the quality of life is reviewed.

Chapter 4 explores in detail the formation of the initial political conditions that obtained in 1950. These features were the result of long historical processes with roots in the colonial and postindependence periods. The chapter examines the development of the Costa Rican nationality and its major attributes. It deals with the colonial legacy of equality in poverty and explores the consequences of the introduction of coffee and the establishment of the banana plantations. The egalitarian trend that underlies the country's history is highlighted, and the changing role of the state is discussed.

Chapters 5–8 examine the political economy of growth, distribution, and poverty alleviation in Costa Rica during three subperiods. Chapter 5 deals with the first subperiod (1950–63), which began with the aftermath of the crucial events of 1948 and ended with Costa Rica's entry into the Central American Common Market (CACM). The main themes are the modernization of the state and the earlier attempts at industrialization. Highlights include the initial problems with the implementation of the social security system adopted in the 1940s and the nationalization of the banking system. Fluctuations in the country's international terms of trade were a significant influence on the evolution of events during this subperiod, but as the country's productive structure became diversified, the overwhelming dominance of coffee and banana exports declined.

The second subperiod (1963–73) began with Costa Rica's attempt at import-substituting industrialization within the CACM and ended with the first oil shock (chapter 6). Debate during this subperiod centered on the choice of policy instruments for protecting specific sectors of the economy. Output expansion brought about an improved distribution of income and substantial alleviation of poverty.

The third subperiod (1973–85) began with the country's first inflationary experience, at the time of the international oil shock, and ended with the attempts to stabilize prices and the exchange rate, after a deep fiscal crisis. Chapter 7 describes the country's adjustment to two oil shocks, the coffee boom, and the international interest rate fluctuations. Major questions concerned the appropriate size and role of the state, the tools for macroeconomic management, and the nature and extent of the social welfare system.

This division of the 1950–85 period into three subperiods not only corresponds to important turning points in the choice of development strategy and in policy management but also facilitates the analysis, since the sets of available census data correspond to 1963, 1973, and 1984. The duration of each subperiod (about a decade) makes it possible to describe medium-term trends in the economy.

Chapter 8 presents the conclusions derived from the political-economy story of Costa Rica. From a quasi oligarchy of coffee growers, with ample popular participation in the distribution of the fruits of development and in the political process, the country evolved toward a factional state controlled by a coalition of rent-seekers located in state enterprises and in highly protected private sector activities. In the process the set of liberal economic policies that had promoted output growth for more than a century were replaced by social-democratic protectionist interventionism, and the voluntary interdependence of the coffee social contract was replaced by the compulsory entitlements of a highly developed welfare state. On the basis of the initial conditions already established by 1950, the country continued to experience growth with equity during most of the 1950–85 period. The risk of collapse during the recent crisis raised serious questions, however, about the sustainability of the new version of Costa Rica's successful model of political and economic development.

Notes

This study is the result of several years of collaboration between Claudio González-Vega and Víctor Hugo Céspedes concerning Costa Rica's economic and social problems. It incorporates materials published elsewhere by the authors, as yet unpublished results from earlier research efforts, and new explorations. The authors considered this study, initiated in the 1980s, one more stage in their efforts to better understand the reality of their country.

Several colleagues have been close partners in these efforts, to the point that it is difficult to separate their ideas from those of the authors. In particular, we wish to mention friends at the Academia de Centroamérica, including Eduardo

Lizano, Ronulfo Jiménez, Alberto Di Mare, Miguel Angel Rodríguez, Thelmo Vargas, Jorge Corrales, and many others.

Given the scope of the effort and the multiplicity of the topics explored, the authors drew on many sources, rather heavily at times. It would be impossible to acknowledge all of them, but among major influences were Gary S. Fields (income distribution); Jorge Rovira Mas (economic policies); José Luis Vega Carballo (the formation of the Costa Rican nationality); Mitchell Seligson, Carolyn Hall, and Samuel Stone (colonial economic history and the impact of coffee); Mark Rosenberg (social security); and Lorin Weisenfeld (industrialization law). Some of their ideas were accepted and others were rejected, but in all cases their work was an indispensable source of information for the authors.

The authors are grateful to the World Bank for its support of the project on the Political Economy of Poverty, Equity, and Growth; to the directors of the project for their guidance and patience; and to Simon Rottenberg for his useful suggestions at various stages of the effort.

1. Costa Rica's health and education indicators, which by 1950 were already high in comparison with those in other developing countries, are reported in Ross and others 1988.

2. Hla Myint used the term "vent-for-surplus" to denote the gain to a hitherto isolated developing country on obtaining a "vent" for its surplus productive capacity (Myint 1971, p. 120).

1 Costa Rica: Basic Information

This chapter provides information about Costa Rica's geography, population, resources, legal system, and government organization. It also describes the political parties, private sector organizations, and labor unions that have served as vehicles for the expression of particular political-economy interests.

Geography and Resources

Costa Rica is located in the southern part of the Central American isthmus, the only region in the world that is both interoceanic and intercontinental. With an area of 50,900 square kilometers, this small country contains a complex ecological mosaic and a wide range of natural resources. Its topography is marked by three high mountain ranges flanked by coastal swamps and lowlands (Hall 1985, p. 11). Most economic activity is concentrated in the Central Valley (Meseta Central), an area of 4,218 square kilometers, where the capital city, San José, is located.

Rugged mountains modify temperature and vegetation to produce a complex succession of microclimates. Bleak mountain summits and cool montane climates contrast with hot, humid coastal lowlands. As a result, Costa Rica has a diversity of land use uncommon for a country of such limited area. In the Central Valley rainfall is moderate, whereas in the humid Caribbean and Southern Pacific regions rain is abundant and farmers must adapt to excess water rather than to shortages. These tropical zones were successfully inhabited by the Indians, but they presented difficulties to settlers of European descent and were not colonized until recently. The Northern Pacific area (Guanacaste) is less humid and has a prolonged dry season. There, high temperatures cause heavy evaporation, and many crops require irrigation (Hall 1985, p. 27). Most of Costa Rica has relatively infertile soils that are subject to rapid depletion if poorly managed. Fertile alluvial and volcanic soils are found in less than one-fifth of the territory, mostly the mountains around the Central Valley (Holdridge and others 1971, p. 578).

Agriculture

Costa Rica's large number of ecological zones permits the cultivation of a wide range of crops. The better soils and gently sloping land in the wet lower montane zones can be used for dairy farming and horticulture. Subtropical crops—coffee, tobacco, and pineapples—are cultivated in the premontane zone. The tropical dry zone is well suited to beef cattle ranching. Its most fertile soils can be sown in cotton, sugarcane, rice, corn, sorghum, and cashews. The tropical wet zones are ideal for rice and for tree crops such as bananas, cocoa, coconuts, rubber, and African oil palm (Hunter 1976).

Pre-Columbian Indians created a niche for themselves in the tropical forest ecosystem, living by hunting, fishing, gathering, and primitive cultivation. The native economy was unable to support dense populations, urban centers, or complex political systems. The Indians put up prolonged resistance to European rule, but once they had been subdued, their small numbers and primitive culture doomed them to assimilation into colonial society. High mortality rates, miscegenation, and acculturation reduced the Indian population to an ethnic minority. By the early nineteenth century Indians accounted for less than one-fifth of the population, and today they make up less than 1 percent (Hall 1985, p. 40).

Costa Rica possesses few resources except for its fertile soil. There are no important mineral resources and no oil deposits, but the abundance of water and the topography of the country have allowed the production of hydroelectric power. An extensive power generation, transmission, and distribution network has provided relatively inexpensive electricity. An efficient telecommunication system has also been installed.

Until recently, agricultural expansion was facilitated by the availability of uncultivated land. Increases in the cultivated area were made possible by the well-developed road network. Access to the coastal areas was made easier by the elimination of malaria and by the provision of potable water, sewerage, and electricity, as well as public services in education, health, and nutrition. Provincial towns became important market and service centers that have supported agricultural production in their respective regions. This expansion of infrastructure promoted market integration and the growth of an exportable vent-for-surplus. The agricultural frontier has been rapidly disappearing, however, and has recently been expanded only at the cost of deforestation and the loss of some water resources. Whereas earlier output had been expanded by bringing new areas under cultivation, now increased yields are needed.

Population Growth

In 1985 the population of Costa Rica was 2,562,000. With more than 50 inhabitants per square kilometer, it was the third most densely populated continental country in the Western hemisphere. The population was highly concentrated in a small area; in 1980, 58 percent lived in the inner part of the Central Valley, which covers only 8 percent of the territory, and 28 percent of the total was in the San José Metropolitan Area. The average density was 306 inhabitants a square kilometer in the inner part of the valley and only 20 inhabitants a square kilometer elsewhere (Zumbado and Raabe 1976). Because of its temperate climate and fertile soil, the Central Valley has been the political and economic center of the country since colonial times.

In 1800 the population of Costa Rica was about 53,000. Few Indians were left. Population growth accelerated in the nineteenth century, partly because of immigration but mainly because of the decline in the death rate. The population reached 300,000 inhabitants by the beginning of the twentieth century and surpassed 2 million in 1976. During the first half of this century the population doubled in thirty-three years, but after 1950 the doubling time was only twenty-one years, as shown in table 1-1.

International migration (Spanish, German, Italian, Chinese, and Jamaican) made only a minor contribution to population growth during the second half of the nineteenth century, and after 1925 its contribution was negligible. In 1927 foreigners made up 9.4 percent of the total population; in 1973 they were only 1.9 percent. During this century the banana plantations attracted large numbers of temporary workers from other Central American countries, and in the 1980s about 200,000 refugees from these nations came to Costa Rica to escape political and economic instability. These refugees have been a problem for the country; most are poor, uneducated, malnourished, and sick, and they have not grown up sharing the traditions of respect for the law and peaceful resolution of conflict that characterize the Costa Rican social contract.

Migration—from rural areas to the cities and, in particular, between rural areas—was important, especially after 1950. Formerly, the most important migration was from the rural areas of the Central Valley toward the coasts and other lowlands. The availability of uncultivated

Table 1-1. Costa Rica: Population Growth, 1892–1985

Year	Population (thousands)	Annual percentage change (period average)
1892[a]	255.4	n.a.
1927[a]	489.0	1.87
1950[a]	858.2	2.48
1955	1,023.9	3.59
1963[a]	1,379.8	3.80
1973[a]	1,871.8	3.10
1976	2,017.9	2.54
1980	2,245.4	2.71
1985	2,562.0	2.67

n.a. Not applicable.
a. Census years.
Source: Academia de Centroamérica 1981.

government-owned land that could be claimed as private property was an important incentive for this migration, which increased as basic infrastructure was developed. The expansion of the banana plantations, on both the Caribbean and Pacific coasts, also attracted important migration. More recently, however, migration has led to further concentration of the population in the Central Valley, mostly in the San José Metropolitan Area. Because of the country's small size and high population density, there has been much interaction between the rural and urban populations, particularly in the Central Valley. An extended road network has allowed any rural household access to a relatively important urban center in a matter of minutes. Rurality has thus been a relative rather than an absolute condition.

The demographic transition started in the second half of the nineteenth century with a sustained decline in mortality that accelerated in this century. Birthrates, however, remained high and even increased in the 1950s, when the population growth rate reached 4.2 percent a year, among the highest in the world. Since 1960, as a result of dramatic reductions in fertility, the rate of population growth has generally declined, but the mid-1980s rate of 2.6 percent a year was still far from low.

Birthrates declined to 31 per 1,000 by 1980; they had been 48 per 1,000 two decades earlier. This decline was the result of changes in reproductive behavior. By the late 1970s average family size was slightly less than four children, whereas up to the early 1960s the average was more than seven. The change took place in less than one generation. This decline in fertility, unprecedented in Latin America, affected all sectors of society.

In 1960 families with a higher level of education and the urban population in general showed significantly lower fertility than the rest of the population. These were the groups responsible for the earlier reductions in fertility. In 1960 the average number of children per rural family was between nine and ten; the figure was about four for the middle- and upper-income urban families and six for urban families in general. During the second half of the 1960s the rural population, as well as groups with lower levels of education, also experienced important reductions in fertility. By the late 1970s there were no significant differences among social groups in contraceptive use, reproductive goals, or fertility (Behm and Guzmán 1979).

The decline in mortality meant that whereas in 1866 the life expectancy of a Costa Rican was 30 years, by 1959 it was 56 years and by 1980 it was 72 years. The largest gains took place during the 1930s and 1940s. Marginal gains became increasingly difficult as the country neared the biological limit of 75 years.

Despite this dramatic gain in life expectancy, until 1960 the Costa Rican population was young. At that time 48 percent of the population was 15 years old or less, and only 3 percent was above 65 years of age. The high proportion of young people in the population created a growing demand for public services (education, health, and so on), while the high rates of population increase led to growing demands for jobs two decades later. Both effects had significant fiscal implications.

The decline in birthrates that took place during the following two decades reduced the proportion of children and young people in the total population, but it did not significantly increase the relative number of old people. Whereas the proportion of people 15 years old or less declined to 38 percent by 1980, the proportion of those 65 years old and older had increased to only 3.6 percent.

The Government and the Legal System

Costa Rica was discovered by Columbus in 1502 and was subsequently governed as a Spanish colony. In 1821 it declared independence from Spain and, after a short period as part of the Unified Provinces of Central America, it became an independent republic. Its population is mainly of Spanish and other European descent. The language is Spanish, and the religion of the majority is Catholicism.

The 1949 Constitution provides for separation of powers among the legislative, executive, and judiciary. The Legislative Assembly consists of fifty-seven congressmen (*diputados*) elected as provincial representatives every four years. The president is elected by universal suffrage for a four-year term and is not eligible for reelection. Together with his ministers, whom he freely appoints and removes, the president is vested with all executive power. Judicial authority is exercised by the Supreme Court of Justice and the lower courts. There is a fourth, independent power in charge of the electoral process, the Tribunal Supremo de Elecciones.

The country is divided into 7 provinces, which in turn are subdivided into 81 *cantones* (counties) and 415 districts. Each *cantón* has a municipal government elected by popular vote for a four-year term. There are also many decentralized public sector entities. The most important autonomous institutions are listed in table 1-2. The state enterprises include the oil refinery, the railroads, and CODESA, a holding firm for subsidiaries engaged in production in competition with the private sector.

The financial system consists of the National Banking System: the Central Bank, four state-owned commercial banks, and several private commercial banks, as well as nonbank institutions and a large number of unregulated intermediaries. There is a stock exchange, where a large volume of government paper is traded.

The Central Bank, an autonomous institution created in 1950, performs conventional monetary functions and coordinates the activities of the commercial banks. It lends directly to the central government and the state-owned commercial banks, and through the 1980s it lent to some autonomous institutions. It can set reserve requirements, rediscounting criteria, and interest rates and commissions on loans and deposits. Since the mid-1980s it has allowed interest rates to be determined by the

Table 1-2. Costa Rica: Main Autonomous Institutions

Organization	Function and date established
Caja Costarricense de Seguro Social (CCSS)	Social security, health, and pensions (1943)
Instituto Costarricense de Electricidad (ICE)	Electricity and telecommunications (1949)
Instituto Nacional de Vivienda y Urbanismo (INVU)	Housing and urban development (1954)
Consejo Nacional de Producción (CNP)	Stabilization of basic grain prices and consumer protection (1943, 1948)
Instituto Costarricense de Acueductos y Alcantarillados (ICAA)	Water supplies and sewerage systems (1961)
Instituto Nacional de Aprendizaje (INA)	Vocational training (1965)
Instituto Costarricense de Turismo (ICT)	Tourism (1955)
Instituto Nacional de Seguros (INS)	Monopoly of insurance (1925)
Instituto Mixto de Ayuda Social (IMAS)	Social welfare programs for the poorest (1971)
Instituto de Desarrollo Agrícola (IDA)	Agrarian reform and rural development (1961)
Instituto de Asesoría y Fomento Municipal (IFAM)	Municipal development (1970)
Instituto Nacional de Fomento Cooperativo (INFOCOOP)	Cooperatives (1973)
Patronato Nacional de la Infancia	Welfare of children and mothers (1940)
Consejo de Investigaciones Científicas y Tecnológicas (CONICIT)	Science and technology (1972)
Junta Administrativa para el Desarrollo de la Vertiente Atlántica (JAPDEVA)	Development of the Caribbean region (1963)

market. For a long time it fixed limits on the volume of credit for each economic activity, but this practice was abandoned in the late 1980s. It sets the exchange rate and manages the country's foreign exchange system, as well.

The state-owned banks, which were nationalized in 1948, act as both commercial and development banks. Only they are allowed to accept demand and savings deposits from the public, and only they have access to Central Bank rediscounting. Private banks, which numbered sixteen in 1985, are small institutions that mobilize funds from equity capital, term deposits, bonds, and borrowing abroad. Their relative importance increased during the 1980s as a result of strong support from the U.S. Agency for International Development (USAID).

During the second half of the nineteenth century Costa Rica developed a legal system that carefully defined contracts and the mechanisms for their enforcement and efficiently protected property rights. Coffee exports made possible a significant degree of institutional consolidation. Trade brought new goods and services, new ideas, new migrants, and new opportunities to the inhabitants of the Central Valley. The Constitution of 1871 represented the first mature attempt at government organization, and it lasted for sixty-seven years. This golden age of liberal rule in Costa Rica saw intense legal activity. New criminal, civil, and civil procedures codes that followed Spanish and French models were enacted, as were laws regarding notaries, courts, and the registries for recording contracts and land titles and transactions.

A new constitution was enacted in 1949, after the 1948 civil war. It was a compromise between the two ideologies—liberal and social democratic—that would influence policymaking during 1950–85, and it represented a renewed attempt to limit the concentration of power. The autonomous institutions, created by the constitution as decentralized agencies for specific tasks, multiplied rapidly.

The ideological conflicts that characterized the 1950–85 period were reflected in two contrasting statements in the 1949 Constitution. Article 46 protects freedom of commerce, agriculture, and industry by forbidding any restrictions on them, even restrictions enacted as law, while article 50 authorizes the state to organize and promote production and the most appropriate distribution of wealth. In practice, a flexible interpretation of the constitution has facilitated the development of an interventionist welfare state.

Economic and social legislation has been created ad hoc, making for a large body of disparate laws. These laws, frequently issued under the pressure of current circumstances to solve a conflict or avoid a threat, have not been coordinated into the rest of the legal structure. They have usually reflected a political compromise rather than a clear principle (Gutiérrez 1979).

Political Parties

There are two main political parties: the Partido Liberación Nacional (PLN), which has a social-democratic orientation, and the Partido Unidad Social Cristiana. Before the 1980s the Partido Unidad was an unstable coalition of heterogeneous groups that united under different names in their opposition to the PLN. It has recently been organized as a permanent party with a Christian-democratic orientation. In addition, several very small socialist and communist parties have existed under different names.

Since the enactment of the 1949 Constitution there have been eleven successive, regularly elected administrations, in addition to the eighteen-month government of the Figueres junta that took power after the 1948 civil war (table 1-3). Seven of these twelve governments were under the PLN, and five were under the control of groups associated with Unidad.

Table 1-3. Costa Rica: Presidential Administrations

Year	President	Party	Percentage of votes[a]
1948–49	José Figueres	Liberación (Junta)	n.a.
1949–53	Otilio Ulate	Unión Nacional[b]	55
1953–58	José Figueres	Liberación	65
1958–62	Mario Echandi	Unión Nacional[b]	46
1962–66	Francisco Orlich	Liberación	50
1966–70	José J. Trejos	Unificación Nacional[b]	51
1970–74	José Figueres	Liberación	55
1974–78	Daniel Oduber	Liberación	43
1978–82	Rodrigo Carazo	Unidad	51
1982–86	Luis A. Monge	Liberación	59
1986–90	Oscar Arias	Liberación	51
1990–94	Rafael A. Calderón, Jr.	Unidad	53

n.a. Not applicable.
a. Percentage of valid votes in presidential election.
b. Party related to Unidad.
Source: Jiménez Castro 1986.

Before the mid-1970s the two major political parties alternated in the control of the executive. Perfect alternation was broken in 1974 and in 1986, when the PLN was reelected. The PLN has also enjoyed a majority in the Legislative Assembly since 1953 (with the exception of 1978–82), and it had effective control of the autonomous institutions and of most civil service employees throughout the period. As a result, the PLN agenda moved forward steadily. Its progress was moderated every alternate four years, when the opposition controlled the executive, but since this opposition did not possess sufficient power, there was no turning back.

The Communist party (Partido Comunista) was founded in 1931 and in 1934 elected two *diputados*. The communist vote reached a peak of 16 percent in the 1942 elections for *diputados*. Support came mostly from the banana plantations and San José. President Rafael Angel Calderón Guardia (1940–44) sought the support of the Communists in 1942, when his unstable administration faced much opposition. To take advantage of the opportunity, the Communists disbanded their party and created the Vanguardia Popular. They also requested Archbishop Víctor Sanabria to state that Catholics would be allowed to join the new party. The affirmative answer sealed the alliance between Calderón Guardia, the Church, and the Communists. Together they contributed to the election of Teodoro Picado as president in 1944. His weak administration left him, however, with almost no support except that of the Communists (Rojas Bolaños 1986, p. 19).

In the tense elections of February 1948 Calderón Guardia received 44,438 votes and Otilio Ulate received 54,931 votes. Although Ulate was declared president by the electoral tribunal, the Congress, where

Calderón Guardia and the Communists had a majority of *diputados*, nullified the results of the presidential election. The consequence was the two-month civil war of 1948. The Communists represented the majority of the forces of the incumbent government that fought against José Figueres, the victorious leader of the rebels. Figueres headed a junta that governed by decree from May 1948 through November 1949, when the government was finally turned over to Ulate. The events of 1948 marked the defeat of the coalition of forces that had been in power for eight years (1940–48) and led to the banning until the 1960s of the Communist party, which was declared "contrary to the democratic system."

The PLN arose from a coalition of new, smaller entrepreneurs and urban intellectuals led by José Figueres. Its agenda included the political, social, and economic modernization of the country and the diversification of its productive structure, particularly the promotion of industrialization through import substitution. The PLN has represented the interests of the industrial groups, the growers of food for the domestic market and of new export crops, and the rural and urban middle class, which was swollen by the rapid growth of the public sector (Rovira Mas 1987, p. 18).

An important component of the PLN's explicit agenda has been to diversify the country's productive structure through industrialization and the development of new crops for export and for the expanding domestic market. Protectionist instruments have been preferred for this purpose. Redistributive measures aimed at increasing domestic demand and enlarging the party's electoral base have also been important. To foster political stability, it has been considered essential to strengthen the middle classes, and this has required the widening of the social security system introduced in the 1940s, the modernization of the state, and the strengthening of political institutions—in particular, the institutionalization of the electoral process. All this has implied an increasing government presence in all dimensions of life including, notably, a growing state intervention in economic activities, which has characterized the PLN agenda. This agenda was gradually implemented by the party through seven administrations until it completely dominated the design of economic and social policies in Costa Rica—although compromises were required and some resistance had to be overcome (Rovira Mas 1987, p. 19).

The opposition to the PLN consisted of different parties and coalitions that represented mainly the traditional exporting, commercial, and importing groups as well as other businessmen unhappy with the PLN's interventionist tendencies. Professionals and intellectuals of conservative and libertarian persuasion associated with the Asociación Nacional de Fomento Económico (ANFE) gained increasing influence in Unidad. In addition, the opposition to the PLN enjoyed the electoral support of a large segment of the low-income working class.

The opposition's agenda has emphasized political and economic liberalism and the defense of private enterprise and has opposed the rapid growth of the public sector and of fiscal deficits. Beginning with the Trejos administration, the liberal agenda was complemented by a Christian-democratic (*social cristiano*) emphasis that attacked the "state paternalism" promoted by the PLN and recognized the Catholic Church's "principle of subsidiarity." ("Man is the master of his own destiny, and state action, in attempting to improve welfare, must only be subsidiary and complementary to that of man or his community, in order to achieve his own progress"; Trejos Fernández 1973, vol. 1, p. 18). Until recently, therefore, the identity profile of the opposition to the PLN had been mostly negative: the main interest was in slowing the progress of the PLN agenda. A more aggressive economic liberalization program has been pursued in the late 1980s and early 1990s.

Four communist parties and a coalition of three of them, Pueblo Unido, have operated since 1970, and in 1978–86 their representation reached its high point of four *diputados*. Their proportion of the electorate has recently declined from 6 percent to an even more marginal 2 percent—a loss that many observers have attributed to a reaction to the Sandinista regime in Nicaragua.

Private Sector Groups

Numerous organizations created to represent the interests of their members have had a great influence on policymaking. The usual means of influence had been personal contact between business leaders and government officials, but as society became more complex and these associations grew larger and represented a wider range of interests, the groups incorporated more educated businessmen and used less personal, more modern means of communication.

The Chamber of Industry (Cámara de Industrias) has been the most influential private sector organization. Founded in 1943, by the late 1970s it represented more than 90 percent of all medium-size and large industrial firms. The chamber was deeply involved in Costa Rica's entry into the Central American Common Market (CACM) in 1963, and its members obtained important benefits from regional economic integration. It has been the most sophisticated business association, and it has been active in all issues in which its interests are at stake. Its leaders have been selected on the basis of their reputation and their ability to maintain direct contact with top government officials (Ramírez Arango 1985).

The Chamber of Commerce (Cámara de Comercio) is the oldest private sector association. Its influence declined when the import-substituting strategy for industrialization was adopted, but it gained strength during the crisis of the 1980s. It opposed the high level of import tariffs put into effect as part of the industrialization strategy, and in recent years it has argued with considerable influence against protectionism for either the manufacturing or the agricultural sector and against fiscal disequilibriums.

The Chamber of Agriculture (Cámara de Agricultura), established in 1947, initially represented the interests of the most important producers and was regarded as very influential. As a result of internal divisions, however, it became fragmented during the 1960s and 1970s and lost its previous stature. At the end of the 1970s its organizational basis was weak; its administrative activity was carried on under the sponsorship of the Ministry of Agriculture, which provided it with office space and personnel. Not until 1983 was it able to establish its own offices and to hire its own staff. By then it was composed of eleven chambers of agricultural producers that represented more than 30,000 farmers and 150 agricultural firms of intermediate to large size.

There are many organizations of agricultural producers, by crop and by region. The Cámara Nacional de Cafetaleros brings together coffee producers, processors, exporters, and roasters. Many of its members also grow sugarcane and belong to the powerful Cámara de Azucareros. Also influential is the Cooperativa de Productores de Leche, which by the mid-1960s already included 470 dairy producers. There are at least eight regional chambers of beef ranchers. The Cámara Nacional de Granos Básicos has been effective in influencing basic grain policies and in attracting subsidies, particularly for rice. The Asociación Bananera Nacional has been equally influential on behalf of banana producers.

The relatively weak Union of Chambers (Unión de Cámaras) was established in 1975 by six of the most important private sector associations as the formal top private sector association in Costa Rica. In the following five years it grew to represent about thirty associations. Its resource base has been limited, and it has become involved only in issues of interest to all of its members. All issues have been decided by consensus.

Labor Unions

The degree of unionization in Costa Rica has been low, and until recently labor unions played a minor role. Unions flourished briefly in the 1940s but then became largely inactive. In the late 1970s they were again very active, particularly in the public sector, but they never regained the degree of influence that they had in the 1940s.

The Partido Comunista, created in 1931, organized the General Workers Union (Unión General de Trabajadores). The union's most important activity was the organization of the 1934 strike in the banana plantations, in which about 10,000 workers participated. This success against the fruit company was not replicated elsewhere.

Two important confederations were created in 1943: the Confederación de Trabajadores Costarricenses, which included 125 communist unions, and the Confederación Costarricense de Trabajadores Rerum Novarum, which was promoted by the Catholic Church as an alternative to the communist confederation and which established strong links with the

American Federation of Labor. In the 1940s all unions were forced to affiliate with one of the two confederations. Through their alliance with the Calderón Guardia and Picado administrations, the Communists gained access to the decisionmaking process. With the defeat of the incumbent government during the 1948 civil war, however, they lost this influence. Communist unions were banned and did not operate openly until the late 1960s.

Of the 809 labor unions created between 1943 and 1970, only 235 were still active by 1970; 524 had been disbanded, and 50 were totally inactive. Between 1970 and 1976, 239 new unions were created, but many never operated in a regular fashion. In the late 1970s only about 10 percent of Costa Rican workers were members of any labor union, including unions of technicians and professionals. Increasingly, government employees represented a large proportion—close to half—of union membership. Thus, in the mid-1970s only one in four union members was an unskilled laborer or a farm worker. Most unions were very small; almost one-half of them had fewer than 50 members, about 65 percent had fewer than 100, and only 14 had more than 1,000 (Cuéllar and Quevedo 1981, p. 63).

In sum, the level of unionization has been particularly low for workers in agriculture and manufacturing and high for government employees, technicians, and professionals. In the mid-1970s 43 percent of all public sector employees belonged to labor unions, as against only 5 percent of private sector workers. Today, there is no profession or trade without an association, and there is no ministry or autonomous institution without an association or labor union. Workers in the agricultural and manufacturing sectors have found fewer opportunities to use labor unions in defense of their interests, whereas the middle classes, organized in the white-collar unions of the modern sector, have made effective use of this tool. With the growing importance of the public sector, Costa Rica has experienced the unionization of its middle class.

The low degree of unionization of private sector workers may be explained by a weak demand for union services, in view of the relatively large importance of agriculture and the widespread ownership of land. Only the workers in the banana plantations represent a true rural proletariat. In the Central Valley even the rural population has a middle-class mentality. Also, because of the active intervention of the government, negotiations take place between the authorities and the employers, bypassing the unions. The extensive social security system makes demands for fringe benefits less urgent (Backer 1978, p. 25). In addition, the supply of union-organizing services is hampered by provisions of the Labor Code—for example, employers are able to fire union organizers, and although a large proportion of manufacturing firms has fewer than twenty employees, a minimum of twenty workers is required to organize a union.

Private sector organizations and labor unions have maintained close links with the political parties. Thus, ANFE has had a special relationship with Unidad, and the Chamber of Industry has been a major source of support for the PLN. Several labor unions have been affiliated with the Communist party. These organizations have thus exercised influence not only directly but also indirectly, through their connection with the parties. In turn, they have represented different segments of society and their interests. There has been a trend, however, for both major political parties to include a wide spectrum of groups among their following.

2 Growth and Structural Transformation

Comparatively high rates of output growth were among the outstanding economic development outcomes in Costa Rica during 1950–85. Income per capita increased substantially despite rapid population growth. This chapter reports on these rates of growth, their increasing variability, and the economy's medium-term trend toward stagnation. The effect of international terms of trade movements and of other external shocks is highlighted. Changes in consumption and imports per capita illustrate the impact of the crisis of the early 1980s on standards of living, while the sharp contraction of investment reflects its effect on potential future growth. The dramatic decline in real wages and increased unemployment suggest some implications of the crisis for income distribution.

Growth was accompanied by substantial structural transformation: a sharp reduction in the relative importance of agriculture, a dramatic increase in government activity, and a lesser increase in the relative importance of manufacturing. Despite the import-substituting strategy for industrialization, the openness of the Costa Rican economy increased, in both the current and the capital accounts. Trade and capital flows have been of paramount importance for this small country. The external debt represented, however, a significant constraint on growth during the 1980s.

The Growth Record

Costa Rica's economy grew at a satisfactory pace during most of 1950–85. Growth was not even, however; rates were lower in the earlier part of the period (the late 1950s) and toward the end (the early 1980s). Real GDP grew at 5.0 percent a year for the whole period, but for 1961–79 it grew at a comparatively high 6.5 percent a year.[1]

Exceptionally rapid GDP growth in the early 1950s, mostly fueled by traditional exports to a dynamic world market, was interrupted after the mid-1950s when the international market became less favorable, coffee prices declined, and floods caused a drop in banana production. Growth accelerated again after the formation of the Central American Common Market (CACM) in the early 1960s and as banana production expanded at the end of the decade with the introduction of new disease-resistant varieties. It remained rapid until the mid-1970s, when it was again interrupted by the first oil shock. The coffee boom of 1976 and 1977 generated another burst of growth, which was followed by a sharp decline in output in the early 1980s and by a comparatively poor recovery after the crisis (table 2-1 and figure 2-1).

Since the 1960s there has been a medium-term trend toward a decline in the rate of growth of output. The causes have included diminishing opportunities for import substitution within the CACM, distortions introduced by the protectionist strategy of development, the institutionalization of rent seeking, the excessive growth of the public sector, and changes in relative factor endowments. The annual rate of growth of GDP was 7.0 percent for 1965–70 and 6.0 percent for 1970–75 but only 5.2 percent for 1975–80 and 0.3 percent for 1980–85.

Because of a rapid increase of payments to factors of production abroad, GNP did not grow as fast as did GDP. Its contraction during the first half of the 1980s reflected the increasing burden of interest payments on the external debt; these payments were not sufficiently compensated for by growing unilateral transfers from abroad. Gross national income (GNI), which measures the purchasing power abroad of GNP (after adjusting it for changes in the country's international terms of trade), is an important indicator because foreign goods and services represent a high proportion of aggregate supply. The coffee boom (1976–77) made GNI grow more rapidly than GNP for a while, but later GNI declined sharply. For the whole period GNI grew less rapidly than GNP, as a result of the

Table 2-1. Costa Rica: Growth Rates of Real GDP, Population, and Real GDP per Capita, 1950–85
(annual average percentage change)

Period	GDP (constant 1966 prices)	Population	GDP per capita (constant 1966 prices)
1950–85	5.0	3.2	1.8
1961–79	6.5	3.0	3.4
1950–63	5.3	3.7	1.5
1963–73	7.2	3.1	3.9
1973–85	2.9	2.7	0.3
1950–54	8.9	3.5	5.1
1954–61	3.0	3.9	–0.8
1961–74	6.9	3.1	3.7
1974–79	5.5	2.6	2.8
1980–85	0.3	2.7	–2.3

Source: Statistical appendix tables A-2, A-11, and A-12, based on Central Bank figures.

Table 2-2. Costa Rica: Growth Rates of GDP, GNP, *and Gross National
Income (*GNI*) in Constant 1966 Prices, 1966–84*
(average annual percentage change)

Period	GDP	GNP	GNI	GDP per capita	GNP per capita	GNI per capita
1966–84	4.6	4.2	3.8	1.8	1.4	1.0
1966–74	6.9	6.9	5.7	4.0	4.0	2.8
1974–79	5.5	4.9	6.3	2.8	2.3	3.6
1979–84	0.2	−0.7	−1.5	−2.5	−3.4	−3.4

Note: The periods do not coincide with those in table 2-1 because of the lack of data
before 1966.
Source: Statistical appendix tables A-11, A-12, and A-13, based on Central Bank figures.

long-term deterioration of the country's international terms of trade
(table 2-2).

Manufacturing output grew more rapidly than agricultural output,
particularly in the 1960s (figure 2-1). During 1957–85 the rate of growth
of manufacturing was 6.4 percent a year, compared with 3.9 percent for
agriculture. This reflected changes in factor endowments, as well as the
protection of industry and the penalization of agriculture implicit in the
strategy of development that was adopted.

Before Costa Rica's participation in the CACM, the rates of growth of
agriculture and of industry were very similar (see table 2-3), but subse-

Figure 2-1. Costa Rica: Change in GDP, *by Sector, 1958–86*

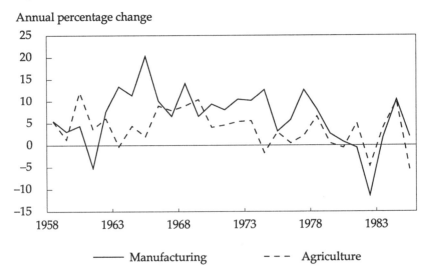

Annual percentage change

                              Manufacturing   - - - Agriculture

Source: Statistical appendix table A-14, based on Central Bank figures.

quently manufacturing grew almost twice as rapidly as agriculture, particularly in the early years of the customs union. This situation was reversed in the early 1980s. Agriculture suffered less from the crisis than manufacturing, which experienced a dramatic decline in growth rate.

High rates of output growth during 1950–85 allowed a GDP per capita growth of 1.8 percent a year (see table 2-1), despite a population growth rate of 3.2 percent. Growth of GDP per capita was slow and even negative in the late 1950s as a result of slow output expansion and rapid population growth, but it accelerated during the first decade of Costa Rica's participation in the CACM. GDP per capita continued growing through the late 1970s, thanks to the coffee boom and to a decline in the rate of population increase that offset the slower growth in output. High population growth rates combined with declining output, however, to bring about a substantial reduction in GDP per capita in the early 1980s (see figure 2-2).

In real terms, in 1982 GDP per capita was lower than in 1973, GNP per capita was lower than in 1971, and GNI per capita was equivalent to its 1969 level. This impoverishment reflected lower growth rates for output, a continued deterioration of the country's international terms of trade, and the need to devote a higher proportion of GDP to servicing the large external debt.

The reduction in standards of living during the crisis was indicated by a sharp reduction in private consumption per capita and imports per

Figure 2-2. Costa Rica: Change in Real GDP and GDP per Capita, Constant Prices, 1951–85

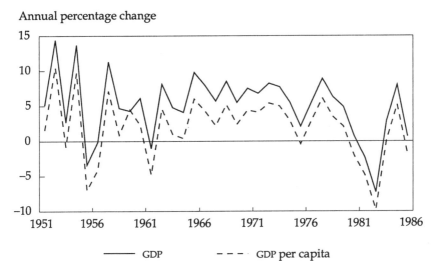

Annual percentage change

GDP — — — GDP per capita

Source: Statistical appendix tables A-11 and A-12, based on Central Bank figures.

Table 2-3. Costa Rica: Growth Rates of GDP, *by Sector, in Constant 1966 Prices, 1957–85*
(annual average percentage change)

Sector	1957–63	1963–74	1974–79	1979–85	1957–85
Total GDP	4.5	7.0	5.5	0.4	4.8
Agriculture	4.6	5.5	2.5	1.6	3.9
Industry	4.7	10.8	6.5	0.4	6.4
Construction	6.3	6.8	10.9	–4.8	4.8
Electricity and water	6.5	12.3	6.6	8.1	8.9
Transport	4.1	9.7	9.6	1.5	6.7
Commerce	3.9	6.2	5.9	–1.8	3.9
Finance	6.9	9.0	8.1	2.5	7.0
Real estate	4.2	3.9	3.5	1.6	3.4
General government	2.7	6.3	4.6	0.4	3.9
Other services	6.4	5.5	3.3	0.1	4.1

Source: Statistical appendix table A-14, based on Central Bank figures.

capita. The 1982 level of real consumption per capita was the same as in 1968, and imports per capita were lower than in 1969.

Determinants of Growth

Between 1950 and 1980 the labor force increased three times, enlarging the domestic market and the availability of human resources for economic development. Rapid population growth, combined with the demands of a younger population, fueled pressures to provide health, education, and other services, thereby contributing to the accelerated expansion of the public sector that has taken place since the 1950s. The increase in the labor force has also made the creation of new jobs an important political-economy issue. Substantial investment in human capital formation has led to rapid growth in labor productivity and to increasing demands for highly paid jobs.

In 1950 the population occupied only one-fifth of the national territory and faced a wide, unexploited agricultural frontier. From 1950 to the mid-1970s agricultural output grew mostly through the expansion of cultivated land. By 1973 farms already accounted for three-fourths of the territory, and since then, growth in agricultural output has been mostly the result of increases in productivity. The expansion of cultivated land promoted both growth and the absorption of the growing labor force. In turn, exhaustion of the agricultural frontier exacerbated the problem of generating jobs.

The steady reduction in unexploited land was compensated by substantial increases in physical yields as a result of intense technological change. Since the early 1950s Costa Rica has experienced a true "green revolution," particularly in coffee and banana production but also in general agricultural practices. Fertilizers and agrochemicals were widely introduced, and there was a major replacement of coffee plants with new varieties. Banana production exploded with the development of varieties resistant to traditional diseases.

Output growth was associated with increasing investment efforts. Between 1966 and 1979 real gross fixed investment increased 10.4 percent a year, twice as rapidly as private consumption. The ratio of fixed investment to GDP increased from 17 percent in the 1960s to 28 percent during the coffee boom of the 1970s. These high levels of investment were increasingly financed with foreign savings. Between 1973 and 1981 net foreign savings amounted to 12 percent of GDP.

Rapid productivity growth was a result of heavy investments in human capital, more capital per worker, major technological innovations, and the transfer of workers from rural low-productivity occupations to jobs in the modern sector. There was, in addition, a high degree of market integration. Even in rural areas subsistence agriculture was negligible. Self-consumption represented only 1.6 percent of household income in the early 1980s, and most farmers sold something in the market. Because of a similar integration of labor markets, salaried workers represented more than three-quarters of the labor force.

Openness and Aggregate Demand and Supply

Two main characteristics of the Costa Rican economy have been its small size and its high degree of openness. With a population of fewer than 2.6 million inhabitants in 1985 and a GNP per capita of CR$45,669 in 1983 (about US$1,000), the economy is very small. Costa Rica has perceived that, given the country's narrow resource base and limiting domestic market, trade with other countries must act as the economy's engine of growth. Much of the impulse for growth during this century has come from the export of agricultural commodities. The development for export of coffee, bananas, cacao, sugar, and beef raised the levels of domestic output and income, increased the country's capacity to import, and yielded many of the dynamic benefits of specialization for this land-abundant country.

Exports accounted for between one-fifth and one-third of GDP during the past three decades. The trend was for this proportion to increase, and it reached almost one-half during the early 1980s. Imports represented between one-quarter and two-fifths of GDP. Their share reached 48 percent in 1974 (during the first oil shock) and in 1981 but dropped to 27 percent in 1982, when imports were severely restricted. A consequence of this high degree of openness has been extreme vulnerability to external shocks.

Costa Rica has exported mainly primary products. About two-thirds of agricultural output was exported in recent times, and these exports contributed about two-thirds of the country's export earnings. Trade also played an important role in the development of the manufacturing sector. In 1963 Costa Rica joined the CACM and adopted a strategy of regional import substitution. Manufactured goods, which represented only 4 percent of exports in 1963, grew to 29 percent of the total in 1979. About four-fifths of these exports of manufactured goods were sold in the protected markets of the partner countries of the CACM.

After growing 5.8 percent a year in the 1970s, real imports declined at an average rate of 7.3 percent a year in the early 1980s as the country's importing capacity was severely curtailed by the loss of access to foreign savings. Exports grew faster than any other component of aggregate supply and demand—the average rate for 1966–84 was 7.0 percent (figure 2-3). The growth of exports was particularly rapid in the early years of the CACM (15.3 percent a year for 1966–70). During the crisis exports declined or stagnated. One reason was that CACM trade was interrupted because of the refusal of the other governments to pay accumulated deficit balances in the Central American Clearing House, the recurrent border closures, and measures restricting trade. Another was the effects on nontraditional products of the antiexport bias that characterized the prevailing development strategy (table 2-4).

Through 1979 government consumption grew more rapidly than private consumption, and it declined less during the crisis (see figure 2-4). By 1982 private consumption was 81 percent of its 1979 level, whereas government consumption had only declined to 93 percent of its 1979 value. This reflected, among other things, political-economy pressures that increased the size of government. Unfortunately, marginal

Figure 2-3.   Costa Rica: Change in Real Imports and Exports, 1967–86
(trade figures measured in constant 1966 colones)

Annual percentage change

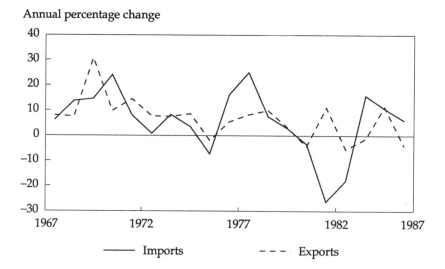

Source: Statistical appendix table A-18.

Table 2-4. *Costa Rica: Growth Rates of the Components of Aggregate Demand and Supply, in Constant 1966 Prices, 1966–84*
(annual average percentage change)

Period	Aggregate supply	Imports	Private consumption	Government consumption	Investment	Exports
1966–84	4.5	4.6	3.4	4.4	4.7	7.0
1966–74	7.6	9.7	5.1	6.8	9.4	12.7
1974–79	6.3	8.3	6.1	6.7	9.0	4.9
1979–84	–1.8	–6.6	–1.6	–1.4	–6.4	0.5

Source: Statistical appendix table A-18, based on Central Bank figures.

social returns to public sector activities were lower than returns to displaced investment in the private sector.

The greatest contraction was in real fixed investment. After growing at 9.3 percent a year during the 1970s—a growth that reflected substantial inflows of foreign savings, since domestic savings did not grow as fast—real fixed investment declined dramatically, during the early 1980s, at an average rate of 9.4 percent a year. As a result, by 1982 gross domestic investment stood at only 50 percent of its 1979 value.

Figure 2-4. *Costa Rica: Change in Real Private and Government Consumption and in Investment, 1967–86*

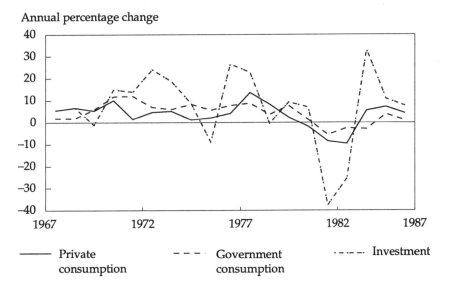

Annual percentage change

— Private consumption   – – – Government consumption   · – · · – · · Investment

Source: Statistical appendix table A-18; based on Central Bank figures.

Mobilization of Domestic Savings

Abundant access to foreign savings may in part explain Costa Rica's relatively unsuccessful effort to mobilize domestic savings. High reliance on foreign savings also explains a good portion of the relatively high rate of capital accumulation and the associated high rates of output growth, despite the poor performance of domestic savings. It may be argued, moreover, that substantial expenditures on education and health, although accounted as government current expenditures, were actually investment in human capital formation and contributed importantly to the growth record. Clearly, inflows of foreign capital, together with human capital formation, made possible domestic investment well above the rate of domestic savings.

The ratio of gross (fixed) domestic investment to GDP increased steadily, from 18 percent for 1960–64 to 26 percent for 1975–79, at the time of the coffee boom. This reflected the growth of real investment, which was 9.1 percent a year between 1966 and 1980. During the 1960s about three-quarters of this investment effort came from the private sector, but the proportion declined to about two-thirds by the late 1970s as public sector involvement in production and investment increased (see table A-18 in statistical appendix).

Domestic savings contributed a higher proportion of gross domestic investment during the 1960s than during the 1970s. In effect, the ratio of domestic savings to gross domestic investment declined from 82 percent in 1958 to 29 percent in 1980. Even during the coffee boom, the contribution of domestic savings was lower than in the late 1950s and early 1960s. Foreign savings were particularly important during the first oil crisis (1974), when they financed 78 percent of gross domestic investment, and during the second oil crisis (1979–81), when they contributed two-thirds of investment. The reasons for the comparatively poor domestic savings performance have not been explored sufficiently. Relatively easy access to foreign savings may have weakened the need and willingness to make a stronger domestic effort, and the ample provision of social security services may have diminished the precautionary motives for accumulating reserves. The financial policies of the nationalized banking system may have been partly responsible for the comparatively weak savings performance, which may have also reflected the rapid expansion of the middle classes and, in particular, the growth in the number of public sector employees. These bureaucratic middle classes have been consumption oriented, more interested in the stability of their jobs than in entrepreneurship, and more concerned with wages than with profits. Lacking the desire to engage in productive activities, they were not attracted by potentially high returns in entrepreneurship, and the financial system did not offer them sufficiently attractive rewards. Instead, they tried to copy the consumption patterns of the upper classes. Highly protected by social security and with ample access to all kinds of social services (including education), they did not need to be much concerned with savings (Lizano Fait 1975).

Structural Transformation

Because of changes in relative factor endowments, the growth of productivity in agriculture, and the protectionist strategy of industrialization, Costa Rica's economy experienced important structural changes. The contribution of agriculture declined substantially, whereas that of other sectors, with the exception of commerce, increased. Most dynamic were manufacturing, personal services, and general government. The most significant transformation took place before the 1960s. In current prices, the share of agriculture in GDP declined from 41 percent in 1950 to 26 percent in 1960. This reduction was slower in the 1960s— agriculture's share stood at 23 percent of GDP in 1970—but accelerated during the 1970s. By 1980 the share of agriculture in GDP was only 18 percent.

The share of manufacturing in GDP only increased from 13.4 percent in 1950 to 14.2 percent in 1960, despite efforts to promote industrialization. Thus, the decline in importance of agriculture during the 1950s was the result not of the expansion of industry but rather of the growth of other activities, particularly the public sector—general government, public utilities, transport, and banking and finance. The expansion of these other sectors reflected the consolidation of the organizational framework for economic and political activity. The share of general government grew from 5 percent in 1950 to 9 percent in 1960.

The share of manufacturing increased most rapidly in the 1960s during the early, easy stages of import substitution, after Costa Rica joined the CACM. Between 1960 and 1970 this share increased from 14 to around 19 percent. Once the early gains from replacing imports of final consumer goods had been obtained, however, manufacturing only managed to maintain a constant share of GDP. Again, most of the decline of agriculture during the 1970s was the result not of the expansion of industry but rather of an increase in the share of general government, from about 11 percent in 1970 to 15 percent in 1980 (see table A-15 in statistical appendix).

When these shares are measured in real terms, a somewhat different picture emerges. The share of agriculture in real GDP declined slightly, from 24.4 percent in 1957 to 24.1 percent in 1970. Thus, while this share, measured in current prices, kept diminishing, it was fairly constant in real terms during the 1960s. The nominal decline was mostly caused by the deterioration of the domestic terms of trade of agriculture, particularly as a consequence of the adoption of the protectionist strategy of industrialization. Whereas the prices of agricultural products were 11 percent lower in 1971 than they had been in 1957, the prices of manufactured goods were 38 percent higher. The index of the terms of trade of agriculture with respect to industry declined 36 percent between 1957 and 1971, the early period of the CACM. As a result, during the 1960s in real terms there was a smaller degree of structural transformation than the nominal figures suggest.

A significant reduction in the importance of agriculture, in real terms, took place during the 1970s, when the share of agriculture in GDP declined from 24 to 18 percent and the share of manufacturing increased from 19 to 22 percent. Thus, the important periods for structural transformation in Costa Rica were the 1950s and the 1970s, not the 1960s. Although the domestic terms of trade of agricultural products with respect to manufactured goods improved in the second part of the 1970s as a result of the coffee boom and of policies that increased the price of specific domestic crops (such as rice), the contracting share of agriculture also reflected the urban bias of the protectionist strategy of industrialization.

The most conspicuous improvement was in the domestic terms of trade of general government, which increased two and a half times between 1957 and 1979. This explains why the share of general government in GDP in real terms declined from 12 percent in 1957 to 10 percent in 1980 whereas, when measured in current prices, it increased from 7.5 percent in 1957 to 15 percent in 1980. Although during the three decades the contribution in real terms of general government to the GDP remained fairly constant, the expenditures required were almost three times larger. The growth of this sector reflected increases in the wages paid to general-government employees. Moreover, the total expansion of the public sector was not fully captured in the share of general government in GDP, given the increasing importance of the autonomous institutions, where wages were comparatively higher. The deterioration of the terms of trade of agriculture, therefore, worked to the benefit of the government bureaucracy more than of industry.

Evolution of the Labor Force

The age profile of Costa Rica's population is changing. In 1960 people of working age accounted for 50 percent of the total population; by 1985 the proportion had increased to 60 percent. The rate of growth of the labor force accelerated from 2.8 percent (1950–63) to 3.7 percent (1963–73) and to more than 4 percent a year in the late 1970s. This reflected the increased participation of women, which more than compensated for reductions in male participation. Between 1963 and 1980 the annual rate of growth of the female labor force was 6.8 percent, more than twice the 3.2 percent rate of growth of the male labor force.

Changes in participation rates were in part the result of expanding educational opportunities at the high school and university levels. They also reflected increasing incomes, which helped to keep family members in school and delayed their entry into the labor force. The increasing incomes and the expansion of social welfare and the pension system also allowed earlier retirement from the labor force. Modernization of the economy and changing attitudes toward female employment opened up employment opportunities for women, and the reduction in the number of children per family increased women's interest in taking advantage of these new options.

The urban population grew more rapidly than the national population. The proportion of urban dwellers in the total population increased from 34 percent in 1950 to 49 percent in 1984. The reduced availability of uncultivated land, the increasing urban-rural wage differentials, and the decline in the importance of agriculture were reflected in growing rural-urban migration and the declining share of agriculture in employment. Whereas 55 percent of employed persons worked in agriculture in 1950, only 27 percent did so in 1980. Moreover, between 1963 and 1973 agriculture generated only 11 percent of the new jobs in the economy, as against 35 percent between 1950 and 1963, and in the late 1970s absolute employment in agriculture actually declined. By 1980 the reduction in employment in agriculture was greater than the increase in employment elsewhere in the economy. This trend was reversed with the crisis. Those who could not find jobs in urban areas returned to their families in rural areas, and the share of agriculture in total employment increased (table 2-5).

A decade after Costa Rica joined the CACM, the share of manufacturing in total employment had increased little—from 12 percent in 1963 to 13 percent in 1973. It then grew faster, to 17 percent in 1983. The other large employer in addition to agriculture was the personal services sector, the share of which increased from 18 percent in 1950 to 24 percent by 1980. But it was commerce that grew most rapidly as a share of employment— from 8 to 18 percent between 1950 and 1980. The growth of employment in services reflected the expansion of the public sector. The share of public sector workers in the labor force increased from 6 percent in 1950 to 20 percent in 1980, and most of the expansion took place in the autonomous institutions. The share of central government employment increased only from 7.3 percent (1973) to 8.7 percent (1980), while that of the autonomous institutions increased from 7.9 to 11.0 percent.

The expansion of employment in the public sector was one of the implicit policies for preventing the rise of unemployment—particularly that of skilled and professional workers—in the presence of commercial and factor price policies that reduced the incentives to hire workers in the modern private sector. This expansion, however, helped to bring about the fiscal deficit that was at the root of the financial crisis of the 1980s. The importance of wages in total government expenditures made it politically difficult to reduce public spending, and the concentration of workers in large public institutions facilitated unionization. Almost one-half of public sector workers were unionized in the mid-1970s, compared with a national average of just above 10 percent. These public

Table 2-5. Costa Rica: Employment of the Labor Force, by Sector, 1950–83
(percent)

Item	1950	1963	1973	1976	1978	1980	1983
Composition of employment							
Agriculture	54.7	49.7	38.2	34.8	30.3	27.4	28.3
Manufacturing	11.3	11.7	12.9	14.6	15.2	16.3	16.7
Construction	4.3	5.5	6.9	6.5	7.4	7.8	5.1
Basic services[a]	4.0	4.8	5.5	5.6	6.1	6.6	5.6
Commerce[b]	7.9	9.9	14.7	16.3	17.8	18.1	18.2
Personal services[c]	17.8	18.4	21.8	22.2	23.2	23.8	26.0
Annual growth rate (period average)							
Agriculture	n.a.	1.8	0.9	−1.2	−1.1	−2.9	3.4
Manufacturing	n.a.	2.8	4.6	8.8	8.1	5.7	3.0
Construction	n.a.	4.5	6.0	2.4	13.1	4.8	−11.1
Basic services[a]	n.a.	4.0	5.0	5.1	10.6	6.2	−3.0
Commerce[b]	n.a.	4.3	7.8	8.1	10.7	3.0	2.4
Personal services[c]	n.a.	2.8	5.4	5.1	8.3	3.4	5.3
Total	n.a.	2.5	3.6	4.4	6.0	2.1	2.2

n.a. Not applicable.
a. Includes electricity, water, gas, transport, communications, and storage.
b. Includes wholesale and retail trade, restaurants, hotels, and financial institutions.
c. Includes personal services and general government.
Source: Céspedes and others 1983a, 1984a.

sector unions have been the strongest in the country and have kept wages in the public sector above private sector wages for similar occupations (see table A-29 in statistical appendix). They have also opposed reduction of the size of the public sector.

As a consequence of the fiscal constraint caused by the crisis, the capacity of the public sector to create employment declined. In combination with the slower growth of private sector employment, this led to increasing rates of unemployment. In 1978, thanks to the coffee boom, the rate was a comparatively low 4.5 percent, but the crisis drove it to 8.7 percent in 1981 and to 9.4 percent in 1982. Subsequently, unemployment declined slightly. When visible underemployment—which reflects the unemployment equivalent for those persons who are looking for full-time jobs but can only find part-time work—is added, the unemployment rate increased from 7.5 percent of the labor force in 1977 to 16.4 percent in 1982.

Prices, Exchange Rates, and Wages

Before the 1970s inflation was practically unknown in Costa Rica. The annual rate of change in the wholesale price index (WPI) between 1950 and 1970 was 1 percent. During the same period the consumer price index grew 2 percent, and the GDP deflator increased 1.8 percent a year.

Double-digit inflation did not appear until 1973, with the onset of the first oil shock. As a consequence of increased fuel costs and rapid credit expansion, the WPI increased 38 percent in 1974—the first inflationary experience for several generations of Costa Ricans. The coffee boom and the use of ample international monetary reserves, however, made it possible to reduce the rate of price increase, although inflationary pressures continued to accumulate during the second half of the 1970s and exploded in 1981. In 1978 and 1979 Costa Rica lost US$147 million in reserves and borrowed an additional US$564 million to avoid inflation and devaluation. In 1981 however, access to international borrowing was lost, and the WPI increased 117 percent. In 1982 it grew another 79 percent (figure 2-5). After fiscal control was regained, in 1983, and the expansion of domestic credit slowed, the rate of inflation was brought under control.

The exchange rate followed a similar evolution, governed by the availability of international monetary reserves and access to foreign borrowing. Abundant reserves made possible a uniform, fixed exchange rate, which was modified only in 1961 and in 1974. Inflationary pressures caused by lack of fiscal discipline and rapid expansion of domestic credit,

Figure 2-5. Costa Rica: Changes in Wholesale Price Index and in Total Liquidity—M₂—(Percentages) and Weighted Average Exchange Rate (Colones per U.S. Dollar), 1951–85

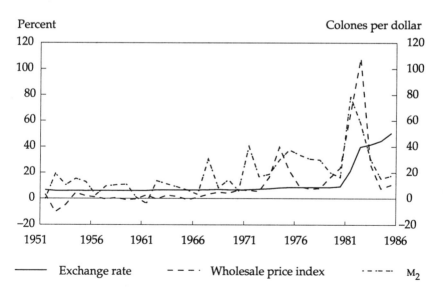

Note: WPI (1978:100).
Source: Banco Central de Costa Rica, Crédito y Cuentas Monetarias.

however, led to the collapse of the exchange system in the early 1980s. Although the official rate was set at CR$8.60 per U.S. dollar, the free-market rate increased from CR$19.30 in June 1981 to CR$62.40 a year later. After June 1982 the two rates converged, and the Central Bank began a new system of slowly devaluing the colón along a passive crawling path.

As a consequence of declining output and accelerating inflation, real wages declined dramatically. The real wage in July 1982 was only 46 percent of its March 1979 level. It increased slowly afterward, but by November 1984 it was still only 67 percent of the March 1979 level. Thus, for 1978–84 real wages declined at a rate of 6.3 percent a year (see table A-30 in statistical appendix). The loss of purchasing power was proportionately larger—6.5 percent a year—for public sector wages than for private sector wages, which declined at a rate of 4.5 percent a year. Thus, whereas during the 1970s Costa Ricans spent more than their incomes, in the early 1980s they were forced to "endure about as much austerity as most other peoples are willing to endure" (Adler 1981).

Note

1. It has been claimed that between the end of World War II and 1980 the trend rate of growth of GDP for Costa Rica was 6.8 percent a year. This rate was surpassed only by Brazil among the Latin American countries (Ground 1986, table 5). The figure confirms Costa Rica's exceptional growth record.

3 Income Distribution and Poverty

Throughout 1950–85 income inequality in Costa Rica was moderate, and substantial progress was made toward alleviating poverty and its consequences. The Gini coefficient of 0.44 for the distribution of household income in 1971 was at about the midpoint for developing countries as a whole, but it was low by Latin American standards (Fields 1980, p. 185). The share of household income going to the richest 20 percent was only 51 percent. Thus, the rich did not capture too large a share of income, the middle classes enjoyed a much larger share than in most developing countries, and the proportion of the population below a given poverty line was lower than elsewhere in Latin America.

Although the surveys that provide information about the distribution of household income are not strictly comparable and suffer from several deficiencies, all show that substantial improvements in the distribution of income and in the redress of poverty took place during the 1960s but that some worsening may have occurred between the early 1970s and the early 1980s (Céspedes and Jiménez 1988).

Between 1961 and 1971 the economy grew at an exceptionally high rate, and social and occupational mobility led to absolute income improvements for large segments of the population and to a more egalitarian distribution. By the late 1970s, however—even before the crisis began—there were signs that inequality was no longer diminishing. When the crisis finally struck, income distribution apparently became more unequal. In comparison with the mid-1970s, poverty increased sharply during 1982–85. By 1986, however, the macroeconomic stabilization program and efforts to alleviate the impact of the adjustments on the poorest had already reversed the negative trend, and the proportion of the poor in the total population had declined to traditional levels. The effects on income distribution of the crisis and of the associated adjustments have not yet been well documented.

Between 1961 and 1971 households with intermediate incomes increased their share in the total, mainly at the expense of the share of those with the highest incomes. The result was a less concentrated distribution.

Moreover, among Latin American countries Costa Rica had the highest rate of growth of employment in modern nonagricultural activities and the highest rate of labor force absorption, despite very rapid population growth. Labor markets thus served as vehicles for distributing widely the fruits of growth.

The alleviation of poverty followed a similar evolution. The proportion of the poor in the total population declined from approximately 50 percent in 1961 to between 20 and 25 percent in the mid-1970s. In about a decade and a half, therefore, poverty was substantially reduced. This successful performance was reversed after 1979. During the worst three years of the crisis, output per capita declined 17 percent, unemployment rates doubled, and inflation rates reached three digits. Between 1980 and 1982 real wages declined at least 40 percent, and consumption per capita dropped 27 percent. Thus, in the middle of the crisis the proportion of poor in the population increased to about 30 percent. This increase, however, was not long-lasting.

Between 1971 and 1983 real average household incomes increased much more in rural than in urban areas. The rural areas may have benefited more from the coffee boom and the programs for self-sufficiency in agricultural products that were implemented in the second half of the decade, while the urban areas were hurt more by the oil crises and the breakdown of the CACM. In the early 1980s real incomes in rural areas declined for only the poorest 10 percent of all households, whereas in urban areas all but the 10 percent richest urban households suffered declines. This suggests a generalized urban impoverishment as a consequence of the crisis but a less negative impact in the countryside. Not surprisingly, the direction of rural-urban migration was reversed, and the share of agriculture in GDP increased.

Distribution of Household Income in the 1960s

The distribution of household income changed significantly during the 1960s. The available evidence suggests that concentration—and, in particular, the share of the richest 10 percent—declined during the decade. If it is assumed that the surveys for different years are comparable, in 1961 the 10 percent richest households received 46 percent of total income, but in 1971 they received only 34 percent. This large change may reflect both measurement errors and an actual improvement in the distribution. The 1971 survey was specifically designed to measure income distribution and is the most reliable source for the whole period; the 1961 estimates are much weaker.[1] The share of urban, as compared with rural, households may have been overestimated in 1961, and such a bias would increase the degree of concentration shown by the distribution. What seems more plausible, however, is that income distribution was indeed more concentrated in 1961 than ten years later but that the extent of the implied improvement was less than these figures suggest.

As one would expect, in 1961 inequality was already comparatively moderate in Costa Rica. As table 3-1 shows, while the share of the poorest 10 percent remained unchanged, in 1971 the intermediate households (those in the fifth through the ninth deciles) accounted for 51 percent rather than 40 percent of total household income.

During the 1960s the middle portion of the distribution was considerably strengthened. As shown in table 3-2, the difference between average household income at the top 10 percent of the distribution and at the bottom 10 percent diminished. Households with intermediate incomes increased their participation mainly at the expense of those with the highest and, to a much lesser degree, of those with the lowest incomes. The result was a less concentrated distribution of household income in 1971, as reflected in the reduction of the Gini coefficient from 0.52 to 0.44, as well as in the Lorenz curves for 1961 and 1971, shown in figure 3-1.

Distribution, Poverty, and Structural Transformation

In addition to improvements in income distribution, the 1960s saw a substantial reduction in poverty. The proportion of families below an absolute poverty line of 250 constant colones (about US$50) a month fell from about 20 to 10 percent between the early 1960s and the early 1970s. If the poverty line is drawn at 500 constant colones (about US$100), the decline is even more marked, from approximately 65 to 30 percent. Thus, absolute poverty was alleviated, and alleviated rapidly (Fields 1980, p. 189; Piñera 1978).

Table 3-1. Costa Rica: Distribution of Monthly Household Income, 1961 and 1971

Household characteristic	1961	1971
Number of households	223,621	313,144
Household size (average number of persons)	5.8	5.6
Household income share		
Top 10 percent	0.460	0.344
Middle (5th–9th) deciles	0.402	0.509
Bottom 10 percent	0.026	0.021
Bottom 40 percent	0.138	0.147
Household income (1971 colones)		
Average	855	1,175
Bottom 10 percent	222	248
Top 10 percent	3,933	4,104
Top 10/bottom 10 percent	17.7	16.5
Top 10 percent/average	4.6	3.5
Bottom 10 percent/average	0.260	0.211

Source: Piñera 1979; Céspedes 1973.

Table 3-2. Costa Rica: Changes in the Distribution of Monthly Household Income, 1961–71

Households, by decile	Share of income, 1961	Share of income, 1971	Increase in real income, 1961–71
Poorest	2.6	2.1	11.6
2nd	3.4	3.3	32.1
3rd	3.8	4.2	50.8
4th	4.0	5.1	76.3
5th	4.4	6.2	94.0
6th	5.5	7.5	91.2
7th	7.1	9.3	78.7
8th	9.3	11.7	73.3
9th	14.0	16.2	58.3
Richest	46.0	34.4	4.3

Source: Céspedes 1973; Economic Commission for Latin America 1970.

According to Chenery and others (1974, p. 12), 10.8 percent of the population of Latin America had incomes below US$50 a year in 1969. Figures for seventeen countries ranged from a low of 2.3 percent of the population, for Costa Rica, to a high of 37.0 percent. Only in Uruguay was the proportion (2.5 percent) close to Costa Rica's. When the poverty line was raised to US$75, the proportion of the Latin American population below that threshold increased to 17.4 percent, ranging between 5.5 percent (Uruguay) and 58.5 percent. Costa Rica ranked second, with only 8.5 percent of the population below this poverty line.

According to Fields (1980, p. 194), the poor benefit from economic growth by becoming employed in higher-income activities in the modern sector. There is evidence of considerable enlargement of the modern sector in Costa Rica. Most of the poor still live in rural areas, but between the early 1960s and the early 1970s, when the labor force grew by 48 percent, the number of farmers and cattlemen grew by only 11 percent. The share of the labor force employed in agriculture fell from 50 to 38 percent during this period. The workers released from agriculture did not become unemployed or underemployed but went into better-paying sectors of the economy (Fields 1988, p. 1495). In effect, the highest-paying sectors were those that exhibited the highest rates of increase in employment. The number of professional and technical workers increased by 126 percent, the number of managers by 88 percent, and the number of office staff by 62 percent. All nonfarming occupational groups showed above-average gains in employment. "Because these are better-paying occupations, this provides one piece of evidence that the Costa Rican economy grew by expanding the share of modern sector workers in total employment, the essence of modern sector enlargement growth" (Fields 1980, p. 194).

During the 1950s and 1960s labor productivity in agriculture increased substantially. The contribution of agriculture to real GDP fell only

Figure 3-1. Costa Rica: Lorenz Curves, 1961 and 1971

Percentage of income

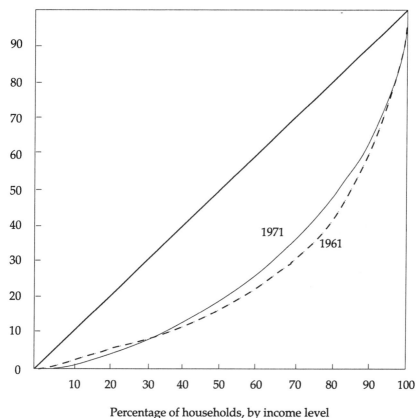

Percentage of households, by income level

Source: Céspedes 1973.

slightly, from 24.4 percent in 1957 to 24.1 percent in 1970, but the proportion of the labor force in agriculture declined from 54.7 percent in 1950 to 38.2 percent in 1973. This mainly reflected increased yields. During the 1960s Costa Rica emphasized investments in infrastructure and agricultural extension, and although participation in the CACM promoted industrialization, there was a rapid expansion and diversification of agricultural exports. Coffee, bananas, sugar, and beef exports grew at rates that were among the highest for the postwar period. During 1965–69 the volume of exports grew by 9 percent a year for coffee, 22 percent for bananas, 12 percent for beef, 13 percent for sugar, and 25 percent for other exports, both agricultural and nonagricultural (Céspedes, Di Mare, and Jiménez 1985, p. 175).

Among Latin American countries Costa Rica had the highest rate of growth of employment in modern nonagricultural activities. During 1950–80 such employment increased, on average, 4.1 percent a year for Latin America but 5.5 percent a year for Costa Rica. For 1950–70 these rates were 3.7 percent for Latin America and 5.1 percent for Costa Rica. Thus, whereas in 1950 the formal nonagricultural labor force was 29.7 percent of the total in Costa Rica and 30.6 percent in Latin America, by 1980 this proportion had increased to 54.2 percent in Costa Rica but only to 47.7 percent in Latin America. The two countries that had the greatest reduction in underemployment and in the total subutilization of the labor force were Costa Rica and Venezuela—the countries that, at the same time, experienced the largest increases in their aggregate and urban labor forces. In Costa Rica the labor force increased at an annual rate of 3.4 percent during 1950–80, compared with 2.5 percent for Latin America (García and Tockman 1985, pp. 49–65).

The share of wage earners in total employment increased from 66 to 74 percent, with equal declines in the proportions of nonremunerated family workers and of the self-employed. While the number of workers with no education declined from 15 to 10 percent of the labor force between 1963 and 1973, the number of those with four to six years of education increased by 88 percent, the number of secondary school graduates by 166 percent, and the number of university graduates by 185 percent. "In short, the Costa Rican economy grew, creating more modern sector job opportunities and educating the skilled labor force needed" (Fields 1980, p. 194).

The share of labor in factor payments increased from 57 percent in 1960 to 63 percent in 1971 and to 68 percent in 1980. There was a close relationship in the 1960s between the steady increase in the share of labor in factor payments and the increase in the share of household income accruing to the middle groups of the distribution—the deciles that included most wage earners. Since this improvement took place during a period when the government did not have an explicit wage policy, it was mainly the result of the general growth of the economy, the process of modernization and integration of the labor market, and the structural transformation that occurred during the period (Lederman and others 1979).

Distribution of Household Income in the 1970s

Although problems of data comparability are more acute for this period, the evidence suggests that concentration actually increased during the 1970s. The share of the richest 60 percent of households improved, and the position of the poorest 40 percent deteriorated (table 3-3). These changes were not as pronounced, however, as those experienced during the 1960s.

Table 3-3. Costa Rica: Distribution of Monthly Household Income, 1971 and 1977

Household characteristic	1971	1977
Number of households	312,830	411,530
Household size (number of persons)	5.7	5.0
Household income share (percent)		
Top 10 percent	34.4	37.4
Top 20 percent	50.6	54.7
Middle (5th–9th deciles)	50.9	51.7
Bottom 40 percent	14.7	10.9
Bottom 10 percent	2.1	0.7

Source: Céspedes 1973, 1979.

The share of income going to the 10 percent richest households increased slightly, from 34.4 percent in 1971 to 37.4 percent in 1977, while the share of the poorest 10 percent declined from 2.1 to 0.7 percent. This result may reflect measurement errors, as the 1977 survey did not report the imputed rents from housing and farm self-consumption, which are important for low-income households.

Between 1973 and 1980, 180,600 new jobs were created. Of these, 47,800 were in the industrial sector and 59,300 in the public sector, mostly in the growing autonomous institutions. All were relatively well-paying jobs. In the meantime, agriculture, the lowest-paying sector, lost 9,100 jobs. Unemployment and underemployment declined substantially through the end of the decade. Real wages fell by 13 percent during 1972–75 as a result of the oil shock and inflation, but they grew by 30 percent during the rest of the decade in response to the coffee boom (Fields 1988, p. 1998).

Rural and Urban Household Income Distribution in the 1970s

In the early 1970s there was a more egalitarian distribution of income among rural than among urban households. The Gini coefficient was 0.43 for urban households but 0.37 for rural households. For households in the San José Metropolitan Area, which comprised 24 percent of the total population, concentration was even greater; the Gini coefficient was 0.44 for this area, whereas for the other urban areas it was 0.39 (table 3-4).

Household income in the San José Metropolitan Area was 2.3 times the rural average. For the poorest 10 percent of households, income was only 1.8 times greater than the comparable rural figure; for the richest 10 percent it was 2.9 times greater. Households with monthly incomes of CR$200 or less (US$30) accounted for 37 percent of urban households and 77 percent of rural households. Per capita income was CR$318 (US$50) a month in urban areas and less than half of that—CR$138, or US$22—in rural areas (Céspedes 1979).

Table 3-4. Costa Rica: Distribution of Monthly Household Income in Urban and Rural Areas, 1971

| Households, by decile [a] | National | Urban | | | Rural |
		Total	San José Metropolitan Area	Other urban	
Poorest	2.1	2.1	2.1	2.3	2.8
2nd	3.3	3.4	3.2	3.9	4.1
3rd	4.2	4.3	4.2	4.8	5.1
4th	5.1	5.3	5.2	5.7	6.1
5th	6.2	6.4	6.4	6.6	7.2
6th	7.5	7.8	7.6	8.2	8.4
7th	9.3	9.5	9.4	9.6	10.1
8th	11.7	11.9	11.6	12.5	12.3
9th	16.2	16.4	15.8	17.2	15.8
Richest	34.4	32.9	34.7	29.1	28.2
Bottom 20 percent	5.4	5.5	5.3	6.2	6.9
Next 30 percent	15.5	16.0	15.8	17.1	18.4
Next 30 percent	28.5	29.2	28.6	30.3	30.8
Top 20 percent	50.6	49.3	50.5	46.3	44.0
Gini coefficient	0.44	0.43	0.44	0.39	0.37

a. Ranked according to total household income, independently for each region.
Source: Céspedes 1973, 1979.

Distribution of Household Income in the 1980s

A comparison of household income distributions for 1971 and 1983 reveals an increasing inequality; the Gini coefficient rose from 0.44 to 0.47. The change was more pronounced in urban areas, particularly in the San José Metropolitan Area. The Gini coefficient increased from 0.44 to 0.49 in that area, from 0.39 to 0.44 in other urban areas, and from 0.37 to 0.40 in the rural areas (table 3-5). The increased concentration seems to have been particularly associated with the larger share of the 10 percent richest households in the urban areas (Trejos and Elizalde 1985).

Household income for the poorest 10 percent was less than 15 percent of the national average in 1983, as against 21 percent in 1971 and 26 percent in 1961. Household income for the richest 10 percent was 3.7 times the national average and almost 25 times the income of the 10 percent poorest households. (It had been 16.5 times the income of the poorest 10 percent in 1971.)

Whereas 66 percent of the households in the bottom 10 percent of the distribution lived in rural areas, only 46 percent of all households were rural, and only 12 percent of those in the top 10 percent lived in the countryside. The San José Metropolitan Area was the place of residence for 19 percent of the households in the bottom 10 percent, for 31 percent of all households, and for 55 percent of those in the top 10 percent.

Table 3-5. Costa Rica: Distribution of Monthly Household Income in Urban and Rural Areas, 1983
(percentage of income)

Percentage of households[a]	Total	Urban	San José Metropolitan Area	Other urban	Rural
10.0	1.5	1.5	1.4	1.6	1.9
10.0	3.0	3.0	2.8	3.4	3.6
10.0	4.1	4.1	4.0	4.4	4.7
10.0	5.2	5.0	4.8	5.3	5.9
10.0	6.3	6.1	5.6	6.7	7.3
10.0	7.5	7.5	6.9	8.2	8.7
10.0	9.2	9.0	8.6	9.5	10.3
10.0	11.4	11.4	11.1	11.9	12.2
10.0	15.1	15.3	15.7	15.0	15.9
10.0	36.7	37.1	39.1	34.0	29.5
Bottom 20 percent	4.5	4.5	4.2	5.0	5.5
Next 30 percent	15.6	15.2	14.4	16.4	17.9
Next 30 percent	28.1	27.9	26.6	29.6	31.2
Top 20 percent	51.8	52.4	54.8	49.0	45.4
Gini coefficient	0.47	0.47	0.49	0.44	0.40

a. Households ranked according to total household income, independently for each region.
Source: Trejos and Elizalde 1985.

Sixteen percent of the poorest, 24 percent of the total, and 33 percent of the richest lived in urban areas outside the San José Metropolitan Area.

It appears that households in rural areas were better able to adapt to the crisis. The domestic terms of trade of agriculture improved, the agricultural-nonagricultural wage differential decreased, and rural unemployment rose less than did urban unemployment. In 1981 and 1982 open unemployment remained stable in rural areas. Thus, the rapid increase in unemployment took place entirely in the urban centers, particularly in the San José Metropolitan Area.

Nonagricultural wages were 65 percent above agricultural wages in 1979 and only 54 percent higher in 1982. The terms of trade of agriculture increased from 98.9 in 1980 to 122.0 in 1982. Urban areas, in contrast, experienced a generalized impoverishment, except for the households at the top of the distribution. The reduction in real income was particularly acute for urban households in the bottom 20 percent of the distribution, especially in the San José Metropolitan Area. The concentration of most social programs for the indigent in urban areas, however, has helped to relieve the distress there.

The crisis also led to increased poverty. Open unemployment more than doubled, from 3.0 percent in November 1979 to 8.7 percent in November 1981. The corresponding figures for March were 4.6 percent in 1980 and 9.5 percent in 1982. Whereas in 1979 job losers accounted for only 66 percent of unemployment, by 1982 this proportion was 86 percent. Moreover, between 1979 and 1982 real wages fell by 40 percent. "It is a tribute to the democratic tradition of Costa Rica that the political system remained intact after so severe and widespread an economic deterioration among the masses" (Fields 1988, p. 1500).

The Components of Earnings Inequality

Bourguignon's (1986, p. 22) decomposition analysis of earnings inequality by sector of employment suggests interesting conclusions. A comparison of the distribution of earnings according to the 1963 and the 1973 censuses showed an equalizing trend over the period, whereas a reversal of this trend was observed by the early 1980s. The part of total inequality explained by intersectoral differences in mean earnings decreased from 20 percent in 1973, as measured by the Theil coefficient, to only 10 percent by 1980. The main reason was the reduction in the differentials between mean earnings, when agriculture was compared with the rest of the economy. Inequality between these two sectors, as measured by the Theil coefficient, fell from 0.046 in 1973 to 0.020 in 1985.

Occupational status did not explain much of the total inequality. For 1980 differences in mean earnings among wage earners, the self-employed, and employers explained 8 percent of total inequality, as measured by the Theil coefficient. Isolating the government from the rest of the service sector led to a significant gain in explanatory power. The public sector employed almost 20 percent of the labor force, at wages 50 percent above the national average. This contributed substantially to the overall dispersion of earnings. The difference was largely attributable to the educational levels of public sector employees but also reflected the monopoly power of public sector labor unions and the fact that government agencies were not profit maximizers but conflict minimizers.

Bourguignon (1986, p. 25) ran regressions on eighty-four groups in the labor force, classified by sector of economic activity and occupational status. Education was an important determinant of overall income inequality. It accounted for approximately one-half of the variance among groups, which itself represented a little more than one-third of total inequality, and it explained a substantial part of the inequality within those groups. In terms of the coefficient of variation, education explained a little more than 50 percent of the average inequality within sector of activity and occupational group. Such a contribution is large in comparison with other countries, especially taking into account the high average educational level of Costa Ricans, by developing country standards. The influence of education may also reflect low levels of inequality in the distribution of nonlabor factors of production. Baldares (1985) reported education as the most important determinant of inequality of earnings among Costa Rican workers.

At least 75 percent of the labor force was salaried and was covered by the social security system—an exceptional proportion for a developing country. Land distribution did not have a major effect on income inequality, but there was a pronounced income difference between landless agricultural workers and owners of land. The data indicate a relatively high concentration of landownership, but this inequality was not reflected in the distribution of income—perhaps because landed property rights do not accurately represent income potentials. The concentration of land was particularly important in banana production, but in this case the largest part of the profit was taken by foreign companies and was not reflected in the domestic earnings distribution. The distribution of valuable land, such as coffee plots, was only moderately concentrated.

The substantial difference between workers and employers in the nonagricultural sector, after controlling for education, may have reflected the distribution of capital in this sector. Agricultural workers earned additional income from the cultivation of small parcels of land, which improved the rural distribution. Education did not entirely explain the higher earnings of the service sector, which is dominated by the government. This suggests the possibility of noncompetitive behavior in this portion of the labor market. All in all, Bourguignon concluded that the distribution of earnings in Costa Rica resembled that in high-income countries. Given the atypically high proportion of wage earners and salaried workers, the main determinant of inequality seemed to be the distribution of skills within the labor force. Other factors of production had a much smaller effect, partly because only a minor proportion of income originated in the agricultural sector. The reduction of the proportion of the labor force in this sector over the period was a major equalizing factor. Another important characteristic was the great importance of the public sector (Bourguignon 1986, p. 27).

The Effect of Taxation and Public Expenditures

Herschell (1977) presented tentative estimates of the effect of taxation on the 1974 income distribution. His main finding was that whereas the tax burden was strongly regressive, the incidence of public expenditures was strongly progressive. Low-income groups, with monthly household incomes below CR$1,750, accounted for 52 percent of all households and received 21 percent of total income. Their share of total tax payments was larger than their share of income, but so was their benefit from public expenditures; their benefits (55 percent of public expenditures) were about twice as large as their taxes (27 percent of total tax payments). This had a favorable redistributive impact.

Middle-income households, with monthly incomes between CR$1,750 and CR$5,000, made up 39 percent of the total number and received 43 percent of total income. Although their share of tax payments (41 percent) was similar to their share in income, their share in the benefits from public expenditures (29 percent) was much lower. High-income households (monthly incomes above CR$5,000) represented 8 percent of the total number but received 36 percent of total income. They paid taxes in a smaller proportion (32 percent) than their share in income and received an even smaller proportion (17 percent) of the benefits from public expenditures (Herschell 1977).

Whereas tax payments represented 32 percent of household income for the low-income groups, the benefits from public expenditures represented 74 percent. Taxes of middle-income households represented 24 percent of household income and benefits represented 19 percent; for high-income households the corresponding figures were 22 percent for taxes and 14 percent for benefits. Tax payments were regressive, but benefits from public expenditures were progressive.

After adjustment for taxes and public expenditures, the total income of the low-income groups increased by 43 percent, whereas total income declined by 4.5 percent for middle-income groups and by 8.3 percent for high-income groups. This meant that the share in total income of low-income groups increased from 21 to 29 percent, while the share of middle-income groups declined from 43 to 39 percent and the share of high-income groups declined from 36 to 32 percent. Herschell (1977) concluded that income redistribution efforts by the state have made possible a transfer from high-income groups to low-income groups.

Standards of Living and Access to Publicly Provided Services

The evolution of most socioeconomic indicators during 1950–85 confirms the trend toward increased equality in income distribution and substantial redress of poverty. Most salient among the indicators in table 3-6 is the reduction in infant mortality rates from 67 per 1,000 live births in 1970 to 21 per 1,000 a decade later. This gain was the result of better control of infections, through sanitation, immunization, and other improvements in child care, prenatal care, and family planning services (Rosero Bixby 1985, p. 129). The table reports equally dramatic improvements in access to water and sewerage, electricity, telephones, and other determinants of the quality of life.

Since the early days of the republic, education has had a high priority. In 1869 education was declared free of charge, compulsory, and a main responsibility of the state. Free education was expanded to the secondary level in 1949. The illiteracy rate was reduced from 69 percent of the population ten years old and older in 1892 to 30 percent in 1912—a proportion that is low for a developing country even by today's standards. The illiteracy rate declined to 21 percent in 1950 and to 10 percent in 1973 (table 3-7). Differences in literacy between the sexes have been practically nonexistent, and the gap between the rural and urban populations was rapidly closed. Enrollment in primary school is universal,

Table 3-6. Costa Rica: Social and Economic Indicators, 1950–80

Indicator	1950	1960	1970	1980
Population with water supply (percent)	53	65	75	84
Population with sewage disposal (percent)	48	69	86	93
Households with electricity (percent)	40	51	65	79
Households with a radio (percent)	—	47	70	95
Households with a television (percent)	0	0	20	79
Telephones (per 1,000 population)	11	12	23	70
Automobiles (per 1,000 population)	9	22	43	63
Life expectancy (years)	56	63	65	73
Infant mortality rate (per 1,000 live births)	95	80	67	21
Physicians (per 1,000 population)	3.1	2.8	5.6	7.8
Births in hospital (percent)	20	49	70	91
Population with health insurance (percent)	8	15	39	79

— Not available.
Source: Rosero Bixby 1985.

Table 3-7. Costa Rica: Education Indicators, 1950–73

Indicator	1950	1963	1973
Illiteracy rate			
Total population 10 years old and older	21.2	14.3	10.2
Males	20.9	14.1	10.2
Females	21.6	14.5	10.3
Urban	8.1	5.2	4.4
Rural	28.5	19.7	14.7
Urban male	6.5	4.0	3.7
Urban female	9.4	6.2	5.1
Rural male	27.8	19.2	14.6
Rural female	29.2	20.1	14.8
Women 15–59 years of age in school	7.9	19.9	36.4
Women 20–24 years of age in school	1.5	5.2	14.9

Source: González-Vega 1985.

with no significant differences between the sexes. The enrollment rate for secondary school (number enrolled as a proportion of the relevant age group) rose from 21 percent in 1960 to 48 percent in 1980, and the enrollment rate for higher education increased from 5 to 26 percent during the same period.

Trejos and Elizalde (1985) attempted to estimate the degree of access of various groups of the population in 1983 to several publicly provided services: education, health and social security, water and electricity, home loans, and food and nutrition. Education has been the most important component of expenditures on social programs. The result is a high degree of access by all segments of the population (see table 3-8). Of children 7 to 12 years old, 92 percent were attending school in 1983, as were 59 percent of those 13 to 17 years old and 23 percent of those 18 to 24 years old. More than 95 percent of primary and high school students and at least 90 percent of those at the preprimary and college levels were registered in public institutions. Access to and demand for education were lower in rural areas: of children 7 to 12 years old, 88 percent were in school; among those 13 to 17 years old, 59 percent were attending high school; and of those 18 to 24 years old, only 10 percent were in college. Evidence was found for a regressive effect at the university level: 72 percent of the students came from the richest 40 percent of the households, and 42 percent were from the 20 percent richest households.

Access to health services through social security programs was high in 1983. On average, 75 percent of the population had access to these services, without important rural-urban differences. Those in the bottom 20 percent of the distribution, however, had less access than the rest of the population. Access to hospitalization did not show significant differences.

Home ownership is important in Costa Rica: 58 percent of urban and 54 percent of rural households owned their homes in 1983. Ownership was common only among middle- and upper-income groups in urban

Table 3-8. *Costa Rica: Distribution of Those with Access to Education, Health, and Social Security, by Household Income Group, 1983*
(percentage of those with access)

| Income class | Education | | | Health | Social security |
	Basic	Middle	University		
Bottom 20 percent	34.7	18.6	4.1	30.0	9.3
Next 20 percent	27.3	26.7	13.3	18.9	9.5
Next 20 percent	19.1	20.8	10.6	21.0	15.7
Next 20 percent	11.7	22.5	30.3	16.9	33.1
Top 20 percent	7.2	11.4	41.7	13.2	32.4
Total	100.0	100.0	100.0	100.0	100.0

Source: Trejos and Elizalde 1985.

areas but was widely distributed among income classes in rural areas. Whereas 87 percent of home owners in urban areas received credit to buy their homes, this was the case for only 45 percent of rural home owners. Those with access to home loans in urban areas belonged to the middle and upper classes. Public sector financing was available to 81 percent of the borrowers in the metropolitan area, whereas elsewhere private sources of financing were most important. Thus, the subsidy implicit in state financing of housing was concentrated in the middle- and upper-income groups in urban areas. Subsidized housing programs have had a regressive effect on income distribution.

Access to water and electricity was widespread and homogeneous. About 99 percent of urban households and 81 percent of rural households had access to potable water, which was provided by the public sector in 100 percent of the cases in urban areas and in 60 percent of the cases in rural areas. Access to electricity was universal in urban areas; electricity reached 78 percent of the rural households and 90 percent of all households. Access to these services was similar and was independent of income level.

Food and nutrition were provided by the public sector through school lunches and through distribution of food to households. School lunches benefited the poorest, in both urban and rural areas; most of the beneficiaries were from rural areas. These food programs were perhaps the most progressive of the social programs, but although they were designed for the poorest, members of more affluent households also benefited from them.

Alleviation of Poverty

About 1961, close to 50 percent of the population was thought to live in poverty (Piñera 1979). This proportion had declined to between 20 and 25 percent by the mid-1970s (Céspedes and others 1977; Fields 1980; Piñera 1979; and Trejos 1983). Over a decade and a half there was a substantial reduction in poverty. In 1982, during the crisis, poverty increased to touch about 30 percent of the population (Altimir 1984), but by 1986 this proportion had declined to 25 percent.

Poverty has been more prevalent among rural than among urban households. The proportions reported by several studies undertaken between 1967 and 1977 were about 32–34 percent for rural households and 14–17 percent for urban households. By 1982 urban poverty was estimated at 25 percent of the population (Pollack 1987). The crisis had a disproportionately negative effect on the urban population.

A study by the Academia de Centroamérica measured poverty on the basis of the 1973 population, housing, and agricultural censuses. The proportion of the poor in the urban population was less than that in the rural population. Three of four of the poor lived in rural areas. Among the rural poor, the share of poverty among nonfarming households was twice that for farming households (Céspedes and others 1977).

Whereas urban poverty appears to be closely associated with such characteristics of the household as education, labor supply, illness, and old age, rural poverty also reflects the relationship between the household and the environment. Lack of infrastructure and communications, limited markets, poor land quality, and other deficiencies of the environment led to pockets of generalized poverty.

The dispersion of the population characteristic of poor districts means that the provision of infrastructure and of public sector services is expensive, and transaction costs reduce the net returns to producers. Distances to any important urban center are substantial. Markets are small, and little division of labor is possible. Most of these poor districts are areas of recent colonization.

In the 1980s one-third of the number of farms and 45 percent of the area of farms in Costa Rica were located in these poor districts. Average farm size was larger than elsewhere: 40 hectares in the poor districts as against 19 hectares in the nonpoor districts and 30 hectares for the country as a whole. Only 4.3 percent of the farm area was devoted to permanent crops in the poor districts, as against 10.5 percent in the nonpoor areas. In the poor districts only 64 percent of the value of agricultural production was related to export crops, whereas in nonpoor districts 83 percent of output was export crops. With a few exceptions, the areas devoted to export crop production were not classified as poor. These observations bear out the strong connection that seems to exist between the alleviation of poverty and production for the international market.

Note

1. The methodology for estimating the 1961 distribution is described in Economic Commission for Latin America (1987). The methodology for the 1971 survey is described in Céspedes (1973).

4 The Development of Costa Rica before 1950

By 1950 Costa Rica presented an unusual constellation of initial conditions, particularly in comparison with other developing countries of similar size and resource endowment, such as those in Central America and the Caribbean. Prominent among these conditions were Costa Rica's social structure, political system, and strong concern for equity. These features were key determinants of the growth-with-equity outcomes of the 1950–85 period. They gave shape and color to the ideologies and expectations of the various segments of society. They both created opportunities for and imposed limits on the attempts by different groups to influence the adoption and implementation of policies. These characteristics, already well established by 1950, were the result of long historical processes with deep roots in the colonial period and in the early decades after independence from Spain in 1821.

The Colonial Legacy of Equality in Poverty

The roots of Costa Rica's political stability and democratic traditions go back to colonial times, when the isolated farmers of the Central Valley—lacking Indians to enserf or a surplus of precious metals to export—worked their own land (Wesson 1984, p. 213). Almost all sources agree that throughout the colonial period social divisions in Costa Rica were minimal. This feature has been associated with the crushing poverty of colonial society.

When the Spaniards arrived, there may have been between 17,000 and 80,000 Indians (Stone 1976, p. 33; MacLeod 1973, p. 332). The Indian population dropped sharply during the early years of colonization as a result of epidemics and relocation. The colony's isolation from the outside world added to the problem of population decline. The Central Valley was cut off from the Atlantic and Pacific oceans by high mountains, and there were few roads and no ports. The lack of gold, a small and shrinking Indian population, and geographic isolation led to the development of what Seligson calls a strong yeomanry.

Given the realities of poverty, the colonists turned their attention to farming. Each new settler found himself a plot of land and began to work it. The colonists did not settle in villages. Rather, they preferred to set up homesteads which were isolated from the other settlers. Each homestead gave birth to a yeoman farmer, independent, self-sufficient, and poor. (Seligson 1980, p. 6.)

As a result of a dispersed pattern of colonization and limited trade with the outside world, farms developed as self-sufficient units. "In such isolation the colonial economy completely disintegrated, and it became in the fullest sense of the term a subsistence economy" (Sáenz Pacheco 1969, p. 16). During several periods food was acutely scarce because of low-yield technologies, the small scale of operation of the farm households, a limited division of labor, and high risks. Production was at the mercy of natural events (González García 1984, p. 143). Little trade, little division of labor, and low productivity also characterized the Indian economy, which did not generate a surplus beyond the Indians' own subsistence for feeding the Spaniards.

By 1720 the Spanish population was little more than 3,000, and the Indians in the Central Valley numbered fewer than 1,000 (MacLeod 1973, p. 332). Since African slaves were expensive and there was no activity profitable enough to justify their use, there were fewer than 200 of them in the colony. Even the black slaves who worked in the cacao plantations on the Atlantic coast had to be granted special incentives: they were scarce, expensive, and relatively independent, isolated in a dangerous area, subject to pirate attacks, and distant from their absentee landlords in the capital, Cartago (Churnside 1985, p. 80).

Because of the shortage of Indians, land was not very valuable. The small farm was the dominant form of land tenure; the settlers had no incentive to acquire more land than they could cultivate, as that would have subjected them to taxation. Traditional Spanish law recognized the right of peaceful, continuing possession as a means of gaining title to a parcel of land (Salas Marrero and Barahona Israel 1973, p. 200).

Land was viewed as essentially limitless in supply, while the demand for it made by the tiny colonial population was almost nonexistent. As a result, there was simply no market for agricultural land, and possession was denied to no one. (Seligson 1980, p. 8.)

In summary, the scarcity of labor, the abundance of land, and the limited opportunities for trade led to the prevalence of family units, to self-sufficiency, to independence, and to the dispersion of economic decisionmaking, despite mercantilistic regulations. Because of the dominance of the farm household, the society of 1600–1800 has been described as a rural democracy, with no class distinctions of any kind (Monge Alfaro 1980, p. 169).

Costa Rican society thus developed differently from that in neighboring countries. Not even the colonial authorities in Cartago were immune to poverty. In 1719 the governor reported that he had to do his own sowing and reaping and that, with no produce markets of any kind, it was not possible to buy anything. The little trade that did exist was conducted under the barter system, and cacao beans were the only accepted medium of exchange (Jones 1935, p. 56; Facio 1975, p. 47). In this generalized poverty, patterns of inequality existed only in miniature.

The Impact of Coffee

There has been much controversy about the effect of the introduction of coffee cultivation in Costa Rica in the early nineteenth century. For some authors, particularly those with a Marxist perspective, the introduction of coffee destroyed the egalitarian society of the colonial period. In their view coffee represented the first permanent capitalist mode of production and led to the concentration of landholdings, to the accumulation of surpluses and political power, and to social distinctions and the formation of a rural proletariat. In the 1940s this thesis was adopted by the ideologists of the new social democratic forces that brought about the formation of the Partido Liberación Nacional (PLN) and challenged the political power of the coffee exporters (Facio 1975). The new forces justified their political platform as a return to the roots of the egalitarian colonial society, which had presumably been destroyed by coffee.

Others have maintained that the economic circumstances surrounding coffee cultivation had helped to consolidate the democratic institutions that characterized Costa Rica by 1950. In particular, coffee's technological requirement of labor intensity and its high profitability even on small plots of land were compatible with and consolidated the existing pattern of small landholdings.

Having failed to find gold, the Spanish in the early days turned their attention to producing a cash crop with a high return that did not require large numbers of workers. Cacao was planted in the Atlantic region in the seventeenth century with the help of a few black slaves and Indians. The colonial government sought to stimulate cacao production by granting land and dispensation from taxes to anybody who would start a plantation (Lindo Bennett 1970, p. 13). Cultivation reached a peak in the eighteenth century, with 200,000 trees planted, but constant pirate and Indian raids discouraged production. Eventually cacao plantations in Nicaragua began to produce large amounts at a lower price, and by 1790 the Costa Rican effort was in full decline.

Tobacco represented another attempt to generate a surplus. Although the crop was first exported in 1638, it was difficult to increase production because of its labor intensity. Moreover, the Costa Rican leaf was of low quality. The lion's share of tobacco profits went to the Crown. In 1787 Spain granted Costa Rica a monopoly for tobacco cultivation, but in 1792 the Audiencia in Guatemala removed Costa Rica's tobacco export rights (Fallas 1972, p. 61).

Costa Rica was the first Central American country to have a flourishing coffee production. Guatemala and El Salvador—more developed at the time than Costa Rica—did not begin growing coffee until fifty years later. Coffee production grew rapidly from the early days after independence from Spain in 1821 and became the engine of the country's economic growth. The timing of its introduction partly explains this positive effect. At independence, most of the country was uninhabited and its land unexploited. A population of about 50,000 people, concentrated in the Central Valley, occupied about 2 percent of the territory (Hall 1982, p. 14). Coffee exports, which began only after independence, were not limited by mercantilist regulations or subject to heavy taxation.

The efforts of the new nation were immediately devoted to creating a physical infrastructure and an institutional organization for promoting the new crop while preserving the existing social structure. By the middle of the nineteenth century coffee production had lifted the country well above the misery of its colonial poverty, and it eventually allowed Costa Rica much greater economic prosperity than elsewhere in the isthmus. Timing and the crop's technological characteristics made it possible to build the country's sociopolitical system on the productive structure of the new crop.

Coffee and Economic Development

Before 1820 coffee production expanded slowly. Its cultivation was an unknown skill, no transport system existed, and there was no assured means of marketing the crop. Lack of capital made the required long-term investment difficult in an economy plagued by risk (Seligson 1980, p. 14). In 1821 the San José town council offered free state land and coffee seedlings to anyone who agreed to plant coffee. This was the first in a long chain of steps taken by local authorities to stimulate coffee production (Soley Güell 1947, p. 40).

The Central Valley turned out to be particularly favorable for coffee growing, and no other crop could compete with coffee in potential profitability (Hall 1982, p. 35). There was, however, no domestic market for the product, and the infrastructure required for exports was almost nonexistent. Few Costa Ricans had any experience with commercial agriculture, few had any foreign contacts, and almost none had credit. Coffee was therefore the key factor in the development of Costa Rica's infrastructure, institutional organization, and productive structure.

Young Costa Ricans established small import-export houses, and regular exports direct to Liverpool began in 1844. As the first profits began to roll in, attention turned to making the improvements in the primitive road network that were necessary for processing and shipping (Seligson 1980, p. 17). In 1843 the largest coffee producers founded the

Sociedad Económica Itineraria to promote road development. A tax of one real per 46 kilograms, levied in 1841, allowed the society to build a road from the Central Valley to the Pacific port of Puntarenas. The road, which was finished in 1846, ensured producers permanent access to the port and stimulated production in new areas along its length (Araya Pochet 1971, p. 80). Private interest, initiative, and participation in building the country's infrastructure characterized most of the century.

The main source of government revenues was the import duties levied on goods brought by the returning coffee ships. Iron stoves, windows, porcelain, steel hoes, plows, shovels, saws, axes, corn mills, new clothing, books, medicines, and tools for agriculture and construction were rapidly introduced. With the cargo came a few immigrants—doctors, lawyers, engineers, and educators—seeking to share in the new wealth. Many children of prominent families were sent in the same ships to study in England. Both the returning students and the new migrants contributed to the formation of Costa Rica's liberal ideology (González Flores 1933, vol. 1, p. 30).

The Coffee Social Contract

A correct understanding of the impact of coffee is critical for the explanation of why Costa Rican society developed differently from that of neighboring countries. The debate has been intense. Stone (1976, p. 23), for example, claimed that commercial cultivation of coffee was initiated by a small group of farmers—descendants of the early Spanish aristocrats (the *hidalgos*), to whom the Crown had granted exclusive access to political, judiciary, and administrative positions. The members of this group were closely linked by strong family connections and formed a political elite from the conquest to independence. In the generalized poverty of colonial times, these *hidalgos* had lost their economic supremacy but not their political power. According to Stone, the economic power obtained from exports allowed the coffee growers to become the most important among the descendants of the *hidalgos* and gradually to monopolize the political power that the whole class had enjoyed. Costa Rica's population at that time was very small, however, and because migration was limited, a large portion of the country's inhabitants were inevitably descendants of the founders or had become related to them through marriage. It is not surprising, therefore, to find that the first coffee growers were related to those earlier conquerors.

Others have claimed that the rapid economic improvement of the earlier coffee growers gave them the opportunity to buy the lands most appropriate for the new crop. Seligson stresses that the increase in land prices was "a strong incentive for the peasant to sell his land. This was particularly true of young men, who had to choose between earning a good wage on the plantation and eking out a living on a small inherited plot" (Seligson 1980, p. 24). Many of what some Marxist authors have called land "expropriations," however, were nothing more than voluntary exchanges of land. Speculation fueled by the rapid increase of land prices in the best coffee areas led to sale of land there, but the seller then used the small fortune thus gained to purchase new plots on the agricultural periphery or to participate in the auctions of state lands and so to become a small entrepreneur (Vega Carballo 1982, p. 26).

Since land in Costa Rica was divided among all the sons and daughters in a family, many parcels were small and nonviable. In these circumstances, sales followed by purchases of new plots improved the welfare of the smallholder. Although plots in some of the best coffee areas were sold to larger growers, small landholders appropriated for themselves a portion of this rent, and a society of small rural proprietors was preserved. "Smallholdings predominated in the Central Valley still in 1935, a century after the introduction of coffee" (Hall 1982, p. 83).

Urbanization, population growth, and inheritance led to the subdivision and fragmentation of already small farms, but it was possible for very small farmers to cultivate coffee profitably. It was not unusual for a coffee grower to cultivate several separate parcels. Many land transactions, therefore, represented consolidations that were agreed on among members of the elite as well as among smaller farmers, rather than a massive transfer of property from the peasants to the large coffee growers. In any case, land was comparatively abundant and easily accessible for all in Costa Rica.

By the time of independence, only a minuscule portion of Costa Rica's territory had been settled and cultivated. Churnside (1985, p. 76) reports that only about 89,614 hectares of land—1.5 percent of the country's territory—were legally appropriated between 1584 and 1821. Of this total, 77,487 hectares were purchased and 12,127 hectares were grants. Land had also been privately occupied without legal title in many cases, but it is clear that land was abundant in relation to the population. After independence, an important mechanism for the acquisition of land was the privatization of state or communal lands, rather than purchase of already private parcels—84,889 hectares of state lands were sold between 1822 and 1850. Coffee cultivation facilitated these transactions.

Gudmundson (1983) claims that rather than being a repressive influence, the introduction of coffee created a mass of small, independent farmer-proprietors that had not existed in colonial times. After independence, coffee production accelerated the privatization of land and consolidated the country's rural democracy. In the pre-coffee era access to land was restricted by communal rights, which were controlled by the aristocracy. The search for new lands for coffee production actually increased social mobility and contributed to a more egalitarian economic development. Because of coffee, land became valuable, and in an egalitarian society this early definition of individual property rights contributed to both growth and equity. A national land registry was established in 1867, and the speed with which thousands of Central Valley peasants claimed legal rights over their small farms indicated their eagerness to protect their titles (Gudmundson 1983).

Stone recognizes that the smallholders survived side by side with large growers and were strengthened through their connection with them.

> The formation of the large exploitations did not destroy the small property. The members of the elite, on the basis of their relative economic predominance and political power, managed to gradually absorb many small plots and create the large plantations. Family links made possible the self-financing of the purchases, an indispensable requirement in a plantation community without banks. Side by side with the *haciendas,* however, coexisted the minifundia, owned by those who did not belong to the ruling class. They managed to survive because their crop was indispensable for the large grower to be able to satisfy the increasing demand in the British market. The *beneficio* (the hullery where coffee is washed, dried, and packaged for export) became the link between the small and the large farms. Only the larger plantations owned a *beneficio*, given its very high investment cost. (Stone 1976, p. 102.)

In 1843, to satisfy the first important demand for direct exports to the British market, Santiago Fernández, an important coffee producer, had to buy more than one-sixth of the country's total annual crop from other producers. At that time, coffee was still cultivated mainly by small producers, several of whom possessed primitive *beneficios*. As the London demand for Costa Rican coffee rapidly increased, the first exporters were forced to buy coffee from the smallholders. They mixed the purchased coffee with their own to obtain a standard quality for export (Stone 1976, p. 107).

Although the mechanization of the *beneficio* freed a portion of the labor force for coffee picking, labor shortages remained a serious problem at harvest time. To some extent, foreign credit helped to alleviate this problem. London buyers paid the exporters in advance for their crop to guarantee delivery the following year. The large growers in turn offered a portion of this credit to the small producers as *adelantos*—partial advance payments for their crop. The small producers used the advances to attract hired labor during the harvest. "Since, however, the majority of peasants at this time were landed, few were available for picking. In order to encourage more people to enter the labor force of pickers, extraordinarily high wages were offered" (Seligson 1980, p. 20).

Seligson adds that "the system of high wages, coming as a direct result of the mechanization of coffee production and the availability of foreign credit, was eventually responsible for a massive proletarianization of the Costa Rican peasantry" (Seligson 1980, p. 23). High wages reflected, however, the country's abundant land supply and labor scarcity and actually contributed to a more equitable distribution of the value from coffee exports. Even today, many workers on coffee plantations grow the export crop on small plots of their own. Moreover, coffee harvesting, which requires additional manpower, has been a seasonal activity that occupies landed peasants and, in particular, other members (women and children) of their families and allows them to complement their farm income.

The *beneficio* system, as it developed in Costa Rica, enabled exporters to realize important economies of scale in preparing for export a large volume of high-quality coffee and also made it possible for both large and small producers to sell all their coffee in the same markets, at the same price. The system provided opportunities for risk sharing, as well.

As a result of these technological and economic constraints, a strong mutual interdependence developed in the coffee economy (Stone 1976, p. 108). The small producer depended for the processing and sale of his coffee on the large grower, who owned the *beneficio* and exported the crop, while the large producer depended on the small landholders not only to satisfy demand but also to achieve a better-quality product by mixing the beans. This technological-marketing interdependence was reinforced by the financial connection.

A similar kind of interdependence developed between the wage laborers and the owners of the coffee plantations. The workers lived on the plantation, in housing provided by the employer, and earned their living there. The owner depended on them for their labor, since even today it has proved impossible to mechanize coffee cultivation. The *hacienda* owner has always been aware of the implications of this technological constraint, which makes substantial labor inputs essential during the coffee cycle. For all of the participants, therefore, the success of their enterprises, large and small, has depended on cordial and respectful relationships among the various participants.

The coffee social contract developed from the voluntary contracts among large exporters, small growers, and farm laborers. As explained below, it led to the formation of a strong, common egalitarian ideology. By the time of the Great Depression of the 1930s, however, the economy had become very vulnerable to the fortunes of coffee exports. Coffee accounted for more than half of total export earnings; the other half was from bananas. The 25,000 farms that cultivated coffee represented 25 percent of the country's population. The National Association of Coffee Growers, created in 1930 mainly by larger producers who did not own *beneficios*, pressured for government intervention in the relationship between producers and exporters. It achieved success in 1933, when the government for the first time decided to intervene in the coffee industry. The Junta de Liquidadores (Settlement Board) was established to fix the price that each *beneficio* was to pay the producer, on the basis of the quality of the coffee. The board set the maximum profit for the *beneficio* at 12 percent of sales (Seligson 1980, p. 36). The voluntary social contract of the coffee pact was thus institutionalized.

Bananas and Labor Conflicts

The evolution of coffee exports and the development of the banana industry show many contrasts. Whereas coffee was fully integrated into the domestic economy, banana cultivation developed as an enclave. Whereas coffee was completely in the hands of Costa Ricans and of a few foreigners who settled permanently, banana plantations were owned by multinational firms. Landless workers, including a substantial number from other Central American countries and Jamaicans brought to build the railroad, were hired by the capital-intensive banana complex to work in isolated regions of the country. Rather than giving rise to a social compact, the banana plantation was the scene of the most important labor conflicts in the country's history.

"Bananas are a historical by-product of the coffee industry in Costa Rica" (Seligson 1980, p. 49). During most of the nineteenth century coffee was carted to the Pacific port of Puntarenas and shipped around Cape Horn. A route to the Atlantic would reduce the time of the trip to England by almost three months. In 1871 Henry Meiggs Keith contracted to build a railroad, financed with loans from London, from the Central Valley to the Caribbean port of Limón. Constructing this railroad was not an easy task, and the project was not completed until 1890. The work was interrupted several times for lack of financing. Of 3.4 million pounds raised in London, only 1.3 million reached Costa Rica, and of these 400,000 were spent in lawyers' fees to obtain the rest (Seligson 1980, p. 51). In 1884 Minor C. Keith absorbed the English debt and promised to finish the remaining 52 miles of the railroad's 142 miles. In return Keith was granted a ninety-nine-year lease on the railroad, 800,000 acres in state lands (where Keith planned to grow bananas, already a promising crop), exemption from taxes on the land for twenty years, and exemption from import duties on all construction materials used to build and maintain the railroad (Seligson 1980, p. 52).

Hundreds of Italian and, later, Jamaican and Chinese workers were hired to build the line. Most foreign workers stayed afterward, but Jamaicans and Chinese were not permitted to migrate to the Central Valley. Between 1881 and 1891 nearly 10,000 Jamaican Negroes arrived in Costa Rica. By 1927 there were 19,136, representing 4.1 percent of the total population, at work in the banana plantations and on the docks (Hall 1982, p. 67).

In 1879 Keith exported the first bunches of Costa Rican bananas. His Tropical Trading and Transport Company and the Boston Fruit Company merged operations in 1899, and the United Fruit Company was born (Stewart 1964, p. 144). The operation was successful, and banana exports skyrocketed. Until 1910 banana exports paid no taxes. Except for providing employment and stimulating the development of the regional infrastructure, banana cultivation had little effect on the rest of the economy. National debate over the issue was intense. President Ricardo

Jiménez, in particular, fought a continuing battle to tax the company (Seligson 1980, p. 60).

Since 1925, the company had been losing its battle against the Sigatoka and Panama diseases of bananas. With the Great Depression, exports fell sharply. By 1933 the company had only 870 hectares under cultivation, as against the 20,000 it had cultivated in 1913. Production dropped even lower in 1934, large numbers of workers lost their jobs, and labor discontent reached new heights (Seligson 1980, p. 68). The Communist party had been founded in 1931, and one of its members, Carlos Luis Fallas, set out to organize the banana workers. After several petitions for improved labor conditions were rejected, a strike was declared on August 9, 1934. Within a few days more than 10,000 workers had walked off the job. When the strike was in its third week, the government intervened, and an agreement was signed. Over the years a long series of strikes characterized the banana enclave, where nothing equivalent to the coffee social pact existed.

In 1938 the company, defeated by the banana diseases, abandoned its plantations on the Atlantic coast and moved to the Pacific side. The black workers, prohibited from moving to the new area, were left behind to fend for themselves and took up cacao cultivation. The departure of the company destroyed the economy of the region (Meléndez and Duncan 1985, p. 74). One year after the move, the first strike on the Pacific coast was called, and labor conflicts continued into the 1980s (Seligson 1980, p. 73). The company began to shift to the cultivation of African oil palm and pineapples, which were less labor intensive and less vulnerable to prolonged strikes, and in the 1980s it abandoned banana cultivation on the Pacific coast.

The Egalitarian Trend

An important constant in the history of Costa Rica is a sustained egalitarian trend. This trend was more than a reflection of the ethnic homogeneity emphasized by several observers, and it even included the assimilation of minority ethnic groups. Thus, the black population of the Atlantic coast has enjoyed, since the 1950s, a noticeable improvement of its access to the benefits from the country's economic and social development. All of this took place through a generalized process of integration of the labor market, in the presence of a high demand for labor and a steady widening of the channels for political participation (Vega Carballo 1982, p. 21).

The introduction of coffee in a system of small farms created a delicate equilibrium that imposed norms of reciprocity among the various social groups. The actors in this balancing act were the firms that combined farming, processing, and exporting (the *beneficios*) and the small and medium-size proprietorships based on family labor. In exchange for stability, protection, and employment, the *campesino* provided loyalty, labor, his production surpluses, and a degree of political subordination (Vega Carballo 1982, p. 25). All this facilitated the consolidation by the middle of the nineteenth century of the coffee pact—the implicit contract developed by the large exporters and smaller producers. In part, this pact was feasible because Costa Rica had a small territory with a small population concentrated in the Central Valley, where economic units were in close contact with one another and all faced the same adversities and risks. The implicit contract was a social mechanism for dealing with these risks and overcoming the shortcomings of small size.

By working part time in the large *hacienda* and in the *beneficio*, the small farmer reduced the risks associated with cultivating his own land. The large exporter provided the credit and marketing services to which the small farmer had little access because of high transaction costs. The development of the implicit contract, in turn, guaranteed a politically stable distribution of export revenues. This contract reflected high reservation wages that were the consequence of the relative scarcity of labor, the relative abundance of land, and the prevailing system of small property holdings. It also reflected the economic dominance of interlinked markets that characterized the coffee pact. The *beneficios* gave *adelantos* to the smaller producers, who agreed to sell the crop to that particular exporter. The British merchants provided links to London financing and to international marketing.

This model of interdependence was institutionalized in 1933, and the same relationships were formally regulated by the state, at a time when the tensions introduced by the Great Depression threatened the destruction of the delicate balance. This institutionalization of social and economic conflicts into apparently successful solutions, with the state as arbiter, became a model that would later be used in other areas of economic and political activity.

These economic arrangements not only reduced transaction costs and risks but also had important implications for the development of Costa Rica's political system. From the beginning, both the large coffee producer-processor-exporter and the small producer-and-part-time-worker became indispensable partners. After the middle of the nineteenth century it became evident that the coalition in power could not completely exclude from political participation any of the important partners in this social division of labor. The power of the large coffee exporters thus required a continuous legitimization from below. The politically dominant group was always vulnerable to pressures from the other partners in the coffee pact, whose demands became particularly explicit after 1890. Eventually new social groups, in addition to the participants in the coffee complex, were added (Vega Carballo 1982, p. 28).

As Vega Carballo (1982) explains, since the 1830s the rural middle class had imposed limits on the economic power of the ruling coffee exporters, and particularly after 1890 they played a key role in democratization and the opening of the political arena to widespread participation. This rural middle class continued to expand as economic diversification and structural transformation progressed, and it played a substantial political role after 1950. It established close associations with the PLN.

Starting in the last years of the nineteenth century a growing middle class made up of small trade and manufacturing entrepreneurs, artisans, professionals, teachers, technicians, white-collar employees, and managers began to participate actively in the political dialogue. As state interventionism increased after 1940, these middle classes acquired an unprecedented amount of political power. Dependent on state employment, they channeled in their favor most of the benefits of the social reforms and of the activities of the large number of government agencies created after 1950.

Ideology, Institutions, and the Role of the State

The social relationships implicit in the coffee pact gradually led to the emergence of a national ideology that validated the participation of the small producers and of the landless workers not only in the distribution of the economy's product but also in the political arena. This led to Costa Rica's version of the liberal state, which stemmed from the need to create a sphere of public activity in which the interests of the different sectors could be democratically expressed. As noted by Vega Carballo (1982), the ruling groups realized that in circumstances of relative equality, the direction of the system had to be delegated to an impersonal source of universally applicable rules. Management of the state was thus transferred to a governing elite, specialized in educational and political affairs, which exercised power with class neutrality and much formal rationality. This contributed to the establishment and the acceptance by all segments of society of an egalitarian ideology and to the generation of institutions and legal codes that promoted both the growth of economic activity and a democratic society. It is this widespread ideology that explains why even today Costa Ricans resist class differentiation and the concentration of power.

The pyramidal structure of society has been permeated by the intricate web of negotiations that the dominant groups must undertake to promote their interests, by the multitude of resistances and counterresistances that have so much enriched political debate, by the internal fragmentation of the bureaucracy and the relative autonomy of the multitude of sectors and interest groups, and by the many pluralistic efforts to reduce the power and influence of dominant groups. Vega Carballo (1982) noted that struggles to control the public sector in the middle of the nineteenth century led to a loss of internal cohesion among the elite and threatened the orderly progress of economic activity. The country required what he called "structural pacification"—that is, an end to the political wars among the various economic factions and a concentration on the protection of national integrity, which was threatened by the chaos and disorganization that prevailed in the rest of the isthmus.

In 1856 Nicaragua was invaded by William Walker, an adventurer from the United States who sought to incorporate the Central American countries as slave states in a confederation with the American South. Walker became president of Nicaragua, causing great concern in Costa Rica. In March President Juan Rafael Mora led an army of Costa Rican farmers into Nicaragua and, two years later, to victory over Walker. The war, which consolidated nationalistic sentiment, was followed by a cholera epidemic that killed 9,000 of the country's 108,000 inhabitants. Both the war and the epidemic accentuated the labor shortage that characterized the cultivation of coffee and thus indirectly strengthened the coffee pact.

The war, however, also strengthened the army and, consequently, the influence of the military. Military intervention in political affairs conspired against the desired stability. The politically more mature society that developed by the end of the century managed to attenuate, if not destroy, this military intervention, transforming the state into a protector of property rights and a manager of the basic social relations implicit in the coffee pact. By the end of the century the Costa Rican state had managed to guarantee a high degree of domestic security, order, and progress, which local politicians constantly compared with conditions prevailing elsewhere in Central America.

The liberal governments carefully administered the resulting reciprocity and interdependence. At the same time, they created a legal framework that protected individual and property rights and guaranteed market freedom. Thus, the political consequence of the economic division of labor implicit in the coffee pact was a system of social coordination with multiple limits and counterbalances which, in turn, consolidated the national state. These mutual agreements and balance of forces would provide, in the middle of the twentieth century, an exceptional springboard for launching the welfare state (Vega Carballo 1982, p. 46).

A history of respect for elections and ample political participation began with the popular insurrection of 1889. The right to participate in elections, originally reserved to those who owned property, had gradually been granted to those with education and human capital. The aim was to allow the electoral market to operate freely without interference from the state. The role of the state was viewed as that of a guardian of the social contract, ready to guarantee that the relations of power prevailing in the civil society could be expressed through the elections. Confrontations were redirected toward the electoral arena and were subjected to institutional rules (Vega Carballo 1982, p. 61).

The decisive influence of a new elite of educators, lawyers, writers, and journalists consolidated the liberal gains. Trained in the best schools of European liberalism, they gave the Costa Rican state a pluralistic character as well as the paternalistic attitude that was a result of the unusual social contract. They were the architects of the democratic and politically stable institutions that characterize Costa Rica.

The Social and Economic Reforms of the 1940s

The 1950–85 period was characterized by the struggle between Costa Rica's liberal ideology of the preceding one hundred years and a new social-democratic ideology that became increasingly dominant after the 1948 civil war. The events of the 1940s were a turning point and had a significant effect on the outcomes of the period. New dimensions were added to the social contract, and important shifts in ideology began. Since then the political arena has been dominated by the actors and the struggles of the 1940s.

Rafael Angel Calderón Guardia, who was elected president in 1940 by a landslide, was one of the most controversial figures in Costa Rican history. On the one hand, he accomplished major reforms in only a few years; on the other, he made major mistakes that eventually led to the civil war of 1948 (Aguilar Bulgarelli 1983). Among his main achievements was the establishment, in 1941, of the University of Costa Rica. The old Universidad de Santo Tomás had been closed in 1888, and only a few professional schools (law, pharmacy, and agriculture) had operated during the first part of the century. The president repealed the laws of 1884 and 1894, which prohibited religious instruction in schools and the presence of religious orders in Costa Rica, and accorded state recognition to private Catholic schools. This gave him the support of the Catholic Church.

In 1941 Calderón Guardia created the social security system (Caja Costarricense de Seguro Social). In 1943 a labor code was enacted and a chapter on social rights (*garantías sociales*) was written into the Constitution. This social legislation weakened Calderón Guardia, and other actions brought him strong criticism from several quarters. The state monopoly on gasoline distribution was eliminated, opening the doors to foreign participation, and a contract with a foreign electric company was negotiated under terms and conditions that some considered unfavorable for Costa Rica. Several groups began to consider overthrowing the president.

The Centro para el Estudio de los Problemas Nacionales (Center for the Study of National Problems), created in 1940 by a group of young professionals and intellectuals, was an important source of opposition to the Calderón Guardia administration. Its members played key roles in the political events of the following decades, and their ideas were the seeds of a new ideology that would gradually replace the liberal legacy of the previous century. They were interested in finding scientific and pragmatic solutions to national problems. The group included the first graduates from the newly created university, who were eager to apply their knowledge to policymaking (Aguilar Bulgarelli 1983, p. 78).

The Center defended the creation of the social security system but attempted to protect it from political interference. Other problems in which its members were interested included land-tenure patterns, agricultural credit, inflation and real wages, fiscal management, and the large external debt accumulated during World War II. Recommended policy reforms included agricultural diversification, expansion of bank credit, scientific management of the government budget, and the creation of a civil service. The Center was particularly concerned about the problems of monoculture and strongly promoted industrialization. It was extremely critical of foreign investment, represented by the United Fruit Company, the Standard Oil Company, and the electric company.

Eventually the Center attempted to create a permanent ideological political party. Until then, elections had been fought around individual candidates who organized parties that were often disbanded after the elections. In 1945 the Center joined forces with Acción Demócrata, a new party of small entrepreneurs and industrialists, to create the Partido Social Demócrata. This party attempted "a combination of measures to raise the standard of living and to guarantee the rights of the workers and the *peón*, to strengthen the small proprietor and to create new ones, to defend the small industrialist, the small merchant, the professional, and the public employee, while at the same time promoting a general economic reactivation" (cited in Aguilar Bulgarelli 1983, p. 111). This enumeration of goals explicitly identified the new constituencies represented by the social democrats, in potential conflict with the participants in the coffee complex. The social democrats' expanding power and presence became a major feature of the post-1950 political arena.

In 1944 an alliance that included the Communist party and the Catholic Church elected Calderón Guardia's official candidate, Teodoro Picado. The following years were characterized by extreme political instability that culminated in the civil war of March–April 1948, when the Picado government refused to recognize the election of Otilio Ulate as the new president. A new group of young politicians, mostly from the Centro para el Estudio de Problemas Nacionales and from the short-lived Partido Social Demócrata, under the leadership of José Figueres, won the civil war. There followed the eighteen-month period of governance by the Junta Fundadora de la Segunda República, led by Figueres.

Significant economic and political reforms were introduced during this period. The army was abolished; the banking system was nationalized; a 10 percent tax on all forms of property was levied; the Instituto de Defensa del Café was nationalized; the United Fruit Company was required to pay a 15 percent income tax; land and inheritance taxes were sharply increased; a price stabilization institution was consolidated; a national power-generating parastatal was created; and the first steps were taken toward import-substituting industrialization (Rovira Mas 1983, p. 47).

A new social-democratic group of professionals, small rural and urban entrepreneurs, and white-collar employees of middle-class origin came into power with Figueres's PLN. These groups adopted and strengthened the social reforms of the 1940s and so consolidated the welfare state. The 1950–85 period was the historical arena in which the new class attempted to use the power of the state to eliminate the economic power of the old coffee groups and to seek the rents implicit in the protectionist strategy of import-substituting industrialization and the paternalistic welfarism of the social security system. In the process Costa Rica began to abandon its liberal economic tradition and to replace it with an increasing protectionism. The political-economy dynamics thus generated led to a major fiscal crisis.

In 1950 Costa Rica possessed unusual initial conditions, including a high degree of political stability and a strong democratic tradition. Participation by the state in economic activities was increasing, and the beginning of a welfare system was in place. A new constitution incorporated conflicting liberal and social democratic rules concerning the role of the state and of private enterprise. The 1950–85 outcomes were significantly influenced by these contradictions.

The country's long-term historical evolution explains the dispersion of political power and of the decisionmaking centers, the neutralization of social classes, and the development of a political system based on interdependence, reciprocity, and compromise. During 1950–85 no social class exercised a marked hegemony, decisionmaking was fragmented, and political parties were neutralized. This was facilitated by the free expression of conflict and its resolution in the electoral arena. The state accepted the role of arbiter of conflicts, within a system of highly formal legality, and eventually institutionalized the balance of forces implicit in the social pact.

5 *The Modernization of the State: 1950–63*

In 1950 Costa Rica was a small, rural, very open economy that exported two crops, coffee and bananas. The public sector was still comparatively small, despite the reforms introduced in the 1940s. Social indicators (especially those concerning education) had already reached exceptional levels. Political stability was reaffirmed when, after ruling by decree for eighteen months, Figueres's junta turned over the government to President Ulate, who had been elected in early 1948. Indeed, by 1950 Costa Rica still resembled the simple country of the first half of the twentieth century more than it did the complex nation of 1985. The 1950–63 period, which was strongly influenced by the consequences of the 1948 civil war and by the institutional innovations introduced by the 1949 Constitution and the new coalition in power, ended with Costa Rica's entry into the Central American Common Market (CACM), after a vigorous debate about the choice of development strategy.

This chapter examines some of the principal debates and policy decisions of the period, including the nationalization of the banks, the early expansion of social security, the first efforts at industrialization, the conflicts surrounding adherence to the CACM, and the creation of numerous government agencies and autonomous institutions as part of the process of modernization of the Costa Rican state after 1949.

The Initial Conditions

Costa Rica has always been a very small economy. In 1950 its population numbered 858,200, GDP per capita was 1,685 colones (about US$250), and total GDP was 1,446 million colones (about US$217 million). The country was experiencing rapid population growth, at a rate of 3.4 percent a year. The median age was 18 years and the growing numbers of young people had already created substantial demands for public services. This small population occupied only one-fifth of the country's territory. Indeed, a wide agricultural frontier was still unexploited by 1950, and the rural population had easy access to land, even to the most profitable lands devoted to export crops such as coffee. By 1973, although farms accounted for three-quarters of the country's area, only two-fifths of the territory was being exploited.

Although the distribution of privately held land was somewhat concentrated, there was not a parallel concentration of the distribution of cultivated land or of land values. Whereas some of the largest holdings were in remote, inaccessible regions or belonged to the multinational banana companies, which cultivated only a small portion of their total holdings, ownership of small but very valuable coffee plots was widespread. A large part of the land was in government hands and would be colonized in later years on the basis of homestead legislation.

The rural sector was large, and its influence pervaded Costa Rican society. The rural population accounted for two-thirds of the total, and rural workers were almost two-thirds of the labor force. Agriculture contributed 41 percent of GDP but employed 55 percent of the labor force—a difference that reflected the low productivity of labor in agriculture. The sector included the prominent banana and coffee export activities, which would realize large increases in yield in the following decades, as well as a multitude of small farmers who produced low-yield food crops for domestic consumption. Manufacturing contributed only 13 percent of GDP and employed 11 percent of the labor force. The remaining 34 percent of the employed population worked in the public and private service sectors, which accounted for 46 percent of GDP. General government contributed 5.4 percent of GDP.

Exports, valued at US$56 million, were one-quarter of GDP and imports, at US$46 million, were one-fifth of GDP. In 1950 there was a trade surplus of about 6 percent of GDP. This surplus survived through the first half of the 1950s but did not occur again until 1984, when Costa Rica was forced to generate a small surplus to service its external debt. Exports were highly concentrated; bananas accounted for almost two-thirds and coffee for almost one-third of total exports, whereas other products accounted for only 3 percent. Coffee and banana exports amounted to one-quarter of GDP and two-thirds of value added in the agricultural sector. The public external debt in 1950 was US$129 million.

The central government collected revenues equivalent to 9.5 percent of GDP, and its expenditures were 8.8 percent of GDP. Only 6 percent of the employed worked in the public sector, which consisted essentially of the central government. Total employment represented 32 percent of the population, and the open unemployment rate was 4.2 percent of the labor force.

The Ulate administration (1949–53) was preceded by the deep political and social changes of the 1940s. The Calderón Guardia administration (1940–44) was marked by major social reforms, by fiscal difficulties, and by inadequate efforts to face the consequences of World War II. Under the Picado administration (1944–48) inflation, social unrest, and political instability accelerated, leading to the 1948 civil war. In contrast to Ulate's

conservative presidency, during 1948–49 the junta led by Figueres introduced numerous institutional reforms, including the nationalization of
the banks. Ulate's primary goals were to achieve fiscal balance and to
maintain a constant external value of the colón. His cautious policies
easily reached these objectives, with the help of good coffee prices and
the expansion of the international economy in the early 1950s.

The institutional reforms introduced by the junta and by the 1949
Constitution slowly but steadily began to change the size, role, and
organization of the government during the 1950s. This modernization of
the state, which was prominent in the agenda of the Partido Liberación
Nacional (PLN), was an important feature of the period and was accelerated by the election of Figueres as president. His administration (1953–
58) was followed by that of the conservative Echandi (1958–62), who
undertook major policy and institutional reforms, although he did not
have control of the Legislative Assembly and had to deal with the
deteriorating conditions produced by a sharp drop in coffee prices.

By 1950 the illiteracy rate had been reduced to 21 percent of the
population 10 years old and older, but 84 percent of this age group still
had not completed primary school. As a consequence of its emphasis on
education, Costa Rica already had a comparatively skilled labor force,
and its investments in health had helped increase life expectancy to 56
years. (Infant mortality, however, remained high, at 90 per 1,000 live
births.) About one-quarter of the labor force and one-eighth of the
population were covered by social security.

Infrastructural development and the provision of public sector services were heavily concentrated in the Central Valley, where population
density was high. Except for the highway to Puntarenas, the railroad to
the two main ports, and roads between the main towns in the Central
Valley, there were only dirt roads, some of which were not passable
year-round. The Caribbean lowlands could be reached only by train or
by air: there was no road to Limón until 1968.

Despite comparatively favorable social indicators, a high proportion
of what Costa Ricans would today consider basic needs were not being
satisfied in 1950. Most rural people did not wear shoes; it would be hard
to find a person without shoes in Costa Rica today. Many rural houses
were wood huts with palm roofs (*ranchos*), and many urban houses were
made of adobe with tile roofs. Most rural transport was by horseback,
and goods were moved by ox carts; hotels in most villages offered stables
and blacksmith services.

Malaria had not been eradicated from the lowlands. Many villages did
not have a school building, and many teachers had finished only primary school. Most villages lacked street lights, bank branches, and even
running water. Milk, delivered every morning by milkmen on horseback, was not pasteurized. Sugar water (*agua dulce*) was the most popular
beverage. Markets would not have met today's hygienic standards and
did not reflect the high degree of specialization of today's excellent

installations. Refrigeration was hardly available, but ice sales were substantial. Newspapers reached only the principal towns. The 1950s and 1960s witnessed a great expansion of the infrastructural and organizational framework needed for a modern economy.

The characteristics of rural Costa Rica reflected a generalized poverty, by today's standards. Perceptions at the time were different, however, particularly when Costa Ricans compared their situation with that in the rest of Central America, where per capita incomes were less than one-half the Costa Rican level and where the distribution of the fruits of export-led development had not been as wide.

During the following decades, massive public investment went into developing infrastructure that benefited most Costa Ricans. With large amounts of foreign assistance, the country built an impressive network of highways and feeder roads, electric power grids, and telecommunications systems. Today there are high schools in all medium-size villages. The lives of rural people were transformed by roads and buses; by water, electricity, and telephones; by agricultural extension, health, and sanitary services; by reliable mail delivery; and by newspapers, radio, and television, which steadily found their way into most rural homes. As shown in table 3-6, the proportion of the population with potable water at home increased from 53 percent in 1950 to 84 percent in 1980, and the proportion with sewage disposal rose from 48 to 93 percent. The percentage of homes with electricity grew from 40 to 79 percent, and by 1980, 95 percent of all households had a radio and 79 percent had a television set. During 1950–80 the number of telephones per 1,000 persons grew from 11 to 70, the number of automobiles per 1,000 population increased from 9 to 63, and daily newspaper circulation per 1,000 population rose from 85 to 118. Although the main beneficiaries were the swelling middle-income groups, the poor increasingly shared in these benefits of growth and development.

The Nationalization of the Banking System

The most important decision in the recent political-economy history of Costa Rica was the nationalization of the banking system in 1948. This interventionist choice represented a significant attempt by new social groups to take economic and political power away from the traditional exporting groups, which also controlled the banks, and to modify the country's economic policies and productive structure to the new groups' advantage.

The 1948 civil war gave a new group of social-democratic leaders a chance to control the government under exceptional circumstances. The junta exercised both executive and legislative power, and it boldly took the opportunity to restructure the country's institutions. The nationalization of the banking system reflected the junta's *dirigiste* ideology.

Thus, the civil war allowed the representatives of the middle classes to gain power and reorient the country's economic and social policies in their favor (Rovira Mas 1983, p. 40).

The junta included representatives of the Centro para el Estudio de los Problemas Nacionales, made up of young professionals and university professors, and of the short-lived Partido Social Demócrata, a political party of small and medium-size entrepreneurs and professionals. The former, despite their university training, lacked direct connections with the country's productive structure, and they sought to create new economic opportunities for themselves. They had been trained at the newly created University of Costa Rica in disciplines for which the traditional export sector generated little demand. They were eager to use their new knowledge to influence policy. Costa Rican society, simple and narrow as it was, offered few opportunities for new entrepreneurial adventures.

Rodrigo Facio, who was to become rector of the University of Costa Rica, summarized the Center's ideology.

> The objective of economic policy must be to increase and diversify the country's output; the preeminence of coffee must decline and so the nation's dependency on external markets. The new policies must take into account the structural characteristics of the country's political system; side by side with growth outcomes are necessary equity outcomes. The latter must reflect the minifundia that characterizes land tenure patterns, the nation's homogeneous ethnic composition, the individualism of its people, the liberal political tradition, and the material welfare of the majority of the population. Thus, the increase and diversification of the national output must be arrived at through the stimulus, defense, and organization of small property. . . . Small property must be promoted, defended, and strengthened through cooperative organizations and through scientific state intervention. (Facio 1982, p. 168.)

The new ideology was also concerned with the need for strong government intervention, particularly in the development of infrastructure (electricity and transport), and with the creation of autonomous institutions. These institutions were to be decentralized public agencies, presumably free of the influence of political parties and placed in charge of specific services to promote economic development while avoiding the concentration of power.

The 1948 civil war provided Figueres and his followers with a unique opportunity to gain early control of the government. Before 1948 they had not amassed any electoral support, and even after winning the civil war, their electoral power remained weak. In December 1948 they managed to elect only four of the forty-five delegates to the Constitutional Assembly. From the junta, however, they began to introduce major institutional reforms that, in time, would improve their own social and economic position. Again and again they would look for the support of the middle groups—the urban middle classes and the small and medium-size farm owners—where the PLN message sank its deepest roots.

On June 19, 1948, the junta suspended constitutional guarantees. That same evening, in a radio speech, Figueres announced the surprising news that the junta had decreed a 10 percent tax on assets and was nationalizing the banking system. On June 21 the minister of finance ordered that 10 percent of all bank deposits be frozen, and Decrees 70 and 71 were published.

Decree 70 stated:

Considering: (1) that in the organization of a modern national economy, all agricultural, industrial, and commercial activities depend on bank credit, the allocation of which determines the progress or stagnation of the country; (2) that economic functions of such a magnitude should not be in private hands but represent, by their own nature, a public function; (3) that the private banking business not only lends the shareholders' own resources but mobilizes the national savings and the financial resources of the country, in the form of deposits from the public; (4) that it is not fair that the large profits of the banks, guaranteed by the state and the social order, be earned by the shareholders, who represent a minimal portion of the capital mobilized, but should become national savings and their investment should be directed by the state; therefore, the junta decrees: (1) Private banking is nationalized. Only the state will be authorized to mobilize, through its own institutions, the deposits of the public. (2) The shares of the Banco de Costa Rica, Banco Anglo Costarricense, and Banco Crédito Agrícola de Cartago are expropriated for reasons of public convenience. The state, through its Ministry of Economy, will take over the banks immediately. The form and conditions for payment of the shares will be regulated afterward. (3) The Ministry of Economy will provisionally keep the present form of organization of the banks and will appoint the boards of directors and the managers.

This measure attempted to take political and economic power from the traditional exporting groups. Since almost all the members of the new emerging groups lacked financial resources, "the banks would become, from then on, their most loyal friends" (Gil Pacheco as quoted in Rovira Mas 1983, p. 50).

The decree was issued without prior debate and consultation, contrary to deeply rooted Costa Rican political traditions. Analysis and debate came after the fact and have not ceased even today. While the Confederación de Trabajadores Rerum Novarum and university professors and students applauded the measure, the private sector chambers did not oppose it. *La Nación*, the main conservative newspaper, opposed the measure, claiming that private enterprise, not nationalization, promoted development. It complained about the failure to consult public opinion and feared that this nationalization would place in the hands of the state, and thus of those who controlled it, all the power of credit, which could at any time be used as a political tool. Víctor Guardia, one of the lonely dissenting voices, asked why, if the nationalization of the banks was such a good idea, few other countries had attempted it. In his view the state was a poor credit manager and would allocate credit according to political, not economic, criteria. He feared that businessmen who opposed the government would not have access to loans (Gil Pacheco 1985, p. 259).

Gonzalo Facio, a member of the junta, responded to the critics of the decree:

> A reform that promotes private property cannot be a communist measure. The nationalization of the banks is not pro-Soviet, it does not go against private property, in its good sense, and it does not penalize private initiative; on the contrary, it promotes it. The nationalization of credit will enormously promote private initiative, since anyone willing to produce will have loans at very low interest rates. (Quoted in Gil Pacheco 1985, p. 249.)

The purpose, according to Gonzalo Facio and other members of the junta, was to redistribute credit, to promote new businesses, to create new entrepreneurs, to stimulate private activity, and to avoid, through a careful allocation of funds, the concentration of resources in a few hands.

After the nationalization the junta left the staff of the banks, who had been loyal to Figueres, in their old jobs. The banks were simply redirected toward new economic activities. In practice, there had merely been a change of owner: the banks continued to operate as private commercial institutions. Under the 1949 Constitution, the four banks became autonomous institutions. In January 1950 the Central Bank was created, and it began to exercise a strict control over the nationalized banks.

Financing Social Security

The social security system, one of the boldest of the pre-1948 institutional innovations, was to become a permanent feature of Costa Rica's equity-oriented policy framework, despite the defeat of its original designers during the civil war. It was organized as a system of forced contributions by the state, the employers, and the workers, with the purpose of providing health and maternity care, old age pensions, and death benefits. A new agency, the Caja Costarricense de Seguro Social (CCSS), was created in 1941 to administer the system. The process of achieving universal coverage of the population was long and slow, expansion of services was poorly organized, and institutional innovations originated from the anticipatory initiatives of individuals rather than as responses to organized pressure (Rosenberg 1983).

Before the 1940s mechanisms for the protection of workers were limited and consisted of a few schemes for on-the-job accident insurance that benefited privileged urban workers, mostly in the public sector. Most protection efforts were related to ad hoc pension plans. The first to receive these benefits were teachers (1886) and the military (1888), followed by telegraph and telephone (1918), postal (1923), railroad (1935), judicial (1939), and customs (1940) workers. These plans provided diverse benefits to specific groups, but there is no evidence that they were created in response to organized pressure. They reflected, instead, the political importance of the beneficiaries, as was clear in the case of the teachers and the military, or the patronage of prominent politicians. The plans were essentially a method used by the state to protect "its own"— groups of people working in the public sector, who were becoming increasingly dependent on their wages (Rosenberg 1983, p. 44).

Calderón Guardia had been influenced by the social doctrine of the Catholic Church during his training as a medical doctor in Belgium in the 1920s. Mario Luján and Guillermo Padilla, who had also studied in Belgium, joined his administration in 1940. Padilla was quietly sent to Chile to study that country's social security system. After his return the president asked three prominent citizens to react to draft legislation, prepared by Padilla, for a social security system. Only one was against it—Tomás Soley, who wrote that "Costa Ricans value individual freedom more than they value their wealth and health" and who also questioned the financial viability of the proposed system (Rosenberg 1983, p. 57).

There were no basic objections to the project in Congress. The commission's report claimed that "nobody questions the importance, need, or urgency of the different social security services." The debate focused on three main issues: the financing of the system and the administration of its funds, the determination of the beneficiaries, and the nature of the services to be provided. Those with salaries above a ceiling of CR$300 would not be forced to join, but if they wished to participate, their contributions would be computed on the basis of CR$300. Low-wage workers were not given this choice, on the grounds that they needed the system the most.

Since social security was a new tax, to be used for something that up to that time had been given away as charity or solved ad hoc through voluntary social solidarity mechanisms and the patriarchal benevolence of employers, the wage ceiling was a mechanism for reducing the incidence of the tax. Nevertheless, a large proportion of the labor force came under the plan.

Rosenberg has shown that the introduction of social security was not a response to organized pressure. There was little interest among the masses in the project, and newspapers from that time show no evidence of public mobilization or explicit support. The Centro para el Estudio de los Problemas Nacionales reluctantly acknowledged that the innovation was a good idea. The lack of interest may have stemmed partly from the climate of fear and uncertainty caused by World War II and partly from the efforts of the proponents of the new legislation to avoid a generalized debate. In fact, the administration did not want to appear overambitious, and many Costa Ricans may not have realized the scope of the reforms. The design of social security was the task of a few men rather than the effort of organized beneficiaries (Rosenberg 1983, p. 65).

During the following decades the financing and coverage of the CCSS became a major policy issue. A permanent job was a requirement for eligibility for the system. Salaried workers were in a better position than the self-employed because of their employer's contribution. Thus, the system was designed for an urban, industrial economy characterized by salaried workers with permanent jobs. It offered no protection to the unemployed, and the expected benefits for the self-employed and for the rural population were limited. Furthermore, although the authorities justified the ceiling as a way of guaranteeing that services would be provided to the low-income population, the ceiling became an avoidance tool for higher-income groups.

In 1942 Calderón Guardia sent to Congress a bill to give the CCSS autonomy. No longer was the decision in the hands of a few, however. Organized groups, once they realized the scope of the institutional innovation, began to raise questions and to force an open debate. The Banco de Seguros, which had had a state monopoly on insurance since the 1920s, had become concerned about competition from the CCSS. It now opposed increasing the ceiling wage because it feared losses for its private insurance program. Thus, two different state agencies were fighting for the same clientele. The Chamber of Industry opposed the reforms. It asserted that the new taxes designed to finance the contribution of the state would be disastrous and that, in fact, firms were being asked to finance not only their own contribution as employers but also that of the state through the new taxes. The Chamber claimed that this would reduce Costa Rica's international competitiveness. Thus, for the first time a private business association stated that social security might be an obstacle to the country's economic development. In addition, the decision to establish a CCSS pharmacy was seen as a governmental invasion of a field reserved for private enterprise and provoked strong protests. Doctors now realized that their profession was going to undergo a deep transformation, and some feared that these were the first steps toward the socialization of medicine in Costa Rica. Nevertheless, the CCSS obtained its autonomy, and the wage ceiling was raised to CR$400. The CCSS was authorized to decide the who, what, when, and how in providing its services (Rosenberg 1983, p. 77).

Between 1946 and 1958 the CCSS slowly expanded its services to meet the demands of a rapidly growing population. The number of workers included in the system increased rapidly at first as the urban populations of the Central Valley were easily incorporated into the program. After that, the rate of expansion began to decline. A unilateral decision by the CCSS in 1946 to eliminate the ceiling, on the grounds that everyone had an obligation to contribute, was followed by a bitter political debate that culminated in a physicians' strike—the first in a long series of strikes by white-collar public sector employees. The ceiling was reintroduced and was not revised until 1958 (Rosenberg 1983, p. 103).

Another critical problem was the state contribution, which had not been paid since 1946. The *junta* paid this debt, but it started to accumulate a new debt right away because it did not have an explicit policy regarding social security. By 1957 the state's debt, accumulated mostly during the Figueres administration, amounted to CR$16 million. Another reason for the slow expansion of CCSS services was the wage ceiling, which had declined substantially in real terms. Faced with increasing costs, the CCSS had either to raise this ceiling or to increase the contribution from those already in the system. An increase in the wage ceiling, moreover, represented an increase of about 50 percent in the amount of the state's contribution. The CCSS claimed that the state should accept its share of social responsibility. Thus, the CCSS was in the middle of a struggle for public funds and had to fight for its financial survival. The institution claimed that the Figueres administration was favoring other autonomous institutions that had been created by the PLN. This was not surprising, since the establishment of these new agencies was the PLN war-horse for the coming elections.

The CCSS also faced serious threats from the powerful teachers' union, which wanted its members to be exempted from the CCSS system so that it could establish its own, more attractive pension system. Despite strong pressure from the CCSS, Congress, with the help of PLN leader Daniel Oduber, approved the teachers' request toward the end of 1958. The CCSS was fighting too many battles, but raising the ceiling was crucial for its future.

The Echandi administration sent to Congress a bill to raise the wage ceiling and another that would force the autonomous institutions to pay their part of the contributions, which had so far been covered by the central government. The new wage ceiling of CR$1,000 was approved, but Oduber opposed the second bill—since the PLN wanted to protect its "own" institutions—and the bill was never approved (Rosenberg 1983, p. 125).

The adoption of the new ceiling by the CCSS was followed by public protests from both blue-collar and white-collar worker organizations. Employees of the nationalized banks and of other autonomous institutions organized a movement to request exemption from the system, claiming that their existing pension plans were adequate and more efficient. Oduber presented a resolution to Congress questioning the CCSS's "violent" implementation of the new law. Minister of Labor Franklin Solórzano convinced Congress that the CCSS was correct in implementing the new ceiling immediately. Oduber withdrew his motion for a revision of the law, and the request of the bank employees did not prosper. The CCSS had won this battle.

Toward Industrialization

Despite the traditionally negligible role of the industrial sector, there were some early efforts to encourage it. In 1940 the Calderón Guardia administration secured passage of the New Industries Law, which granted limited tariff and tax benefits to new manufacturing endeavors. Its main inducement was a five-year privilege to import raw materials unavailable in Costa Rica free of duty, provided that they constituted no more than 25 percent of the raw materials used, and a five-year exemption from duties on capital goods and oils and lubricants. The law was in effect for nineteen years and benefited about sixty firms.

The main voice for manufacturing interests was the Chamber of Industry, organized in 1943. By 1953 it included about one hundred entrepreneurs and was already very influential. The adoption of legislation in Guatemala and El Salvador to promote industry and the initial proposal of the United Nations Economic Commission for Latin America (ECLA) regarding the formation of a Central American Common Market, which began to circulate in 1951, led the chamber in 1953 to submit to the Ministry of Agriculture and Industry a draft of an industrial promotion law. This proposal envisioned the encouragement of any processing industry, regardless of its dependence on domestic or foreign raw materials. Benefits were restricted to a protective tariff, protection from dumping, and privileged access to credit from the nationalized banks. The executive sent the proposal to Congress, where the commission considered that beneficiaries should be restricted to industries that used at least 50 percent domestic raw materials (Weisenfeld 1969).

Coffee prices were exceptionally high in 1953, and the bills were allowed to die in commission. In addition to the increase in agricultural exports during the early 1950s, other factors explained the lack of enthusiasm for an industrialization law. These included attitudes that seem to have been characteristic of Costa Rica for generations. Foremost was the country's self-definition as an agricultural economy. By 1950 the majority of the population still owed their livelihood directly or indirectly to coffee, bananas, and a few other crops. Costa Ricans were proud to point out that the nation's agricultural production had provided them with the highest standard of living in Central America. The Chamber of Foreign Manufacturers' Representatives stated:

> Other Latin American countries, likewise predominantly agricultural, were subjected to industrialization and have been suffering serious economic crises for many years. This should serve as a warning to us. We are an eminently agricultural nation, and our strong economy has depended on agriculture throughout the years. Let us strengthen what we already have, and let us not try to create a fictitious economy based on industry. (Weisenfeld 1969, p. 8.)

There was a marked sentiment that nothing of consequence could be produced in Costa Rica. Existing manufacturing enterprises were small, family-owned, and concentrated in traditional consumer goods; food processing, beverages, tobacco, textiles, shoes, and clothing accounted for about 75 percent of industrial output. Local preferences favored imported goods, and Costa Ricans were quick to point to early attempts at industrialization that had failed conspicuously.

In 1955 Rodrigo Madrigal Nieto, president of the Chamber of Industry, created a working group to prepare a draft proposal for a new law, considerably broader in scope than the 1953 bills, which deleted the requirement of 50 percent of domestic value added. The simplicity of the assembly process and the near monopoly of the local producers made import-intensive industries a low-risk, high-profit investment, in comparison with those based on domestic raw materials. The distinction between high-value-added activities, which used domestic raw materials, and assembly plants, which used imported inputs, became an important issue.

The Chamber of Industry launched an active campaign to promote passage of the bill, but it was unable to generate sufficient interest. A new version, released in December, mobilized the importers for the first time. A letter to Congress from the Chamber of Commerce, the National Association of Foreign Manufacturers' Representatives, and the Union of Importing and Retailing Merchants predicted serious setbacks to the economy: "We cannot accept measures which, under the pretext of aid to the industrial sector, will undermine the country's economic structure, to the evident harm of the consumer." They warned that the bill would create a privileged class of industrial aristocrats at the expense of the working class and that higher wages in industry would draw needed farm labor from the countryside. Moreover, "due to the country's small population and the impossibility of competing with foreign production, industry will not make a substantial contribution to the national income. Too small plants will lead to expensive products or cheap products of low quality" (Weisenfeld 1969, p. 18).

Despite constant pressure, however, President Figueres did not send the draft to Congress. Although his administration clearly favored an industrial promotion law and the president publicly supported it, according to Weisenfeld, "he never gave the bill concrete support and never pushed it in the legislature. He seemed to be afraid to take the steps necessary to have the bill translated into law." Figueres's hesitancy may have reflected his belief that one of the consequences of granting fiscal exemptions would be "to hand wealth on a silver platter to the great American trusts," which were prepared to swoop down and seize the benefits. His minister of finance also believed that it would be unwise to grant tax exemptions before the fiscal problem was solved (Weisenfeld 1969, p. 20).

In 1958 Oduber introduced a new bill which reflected the idea that industrialization should be based on the use of domestic raw materials. Applicants were to be granted a full slate of incentives including, for the first time, exemption from income tax and from national and municipal taxes on invested capital. It became evident to the Echandi administration that support for some form of legislation to promote industrialization was growing—stimulated by the continued downward trend of coffee prices, from US$68 in 1953 to US$43 in 1958 and US$38 in 1961. Under pressure to find an alternative to coffee, and fearful that Oduber might eventually win support for his industrialization bill and claim a PLN victory, Echandi elected to incorporate the bill into his program. The draft he sent to Congress was shaped into law six months later. This significant attempt to modify relative prices was prompted, therefore, by changing coffee prices.

The campaign to place an industrial promotion bill before Congress had lasted more than six years. Between 1953 and 1959 seven different industrialization proposals were prepared, and three were formally introduced in the legislature. All three were based on a program of fiscal incentives. Presidents of political ideology as diverse as Figueres's state interventionism and Echandi's liberalism were equally reluctant to press for the passage of this legislation. On the issue of industrialization the emerging class of small-industry entrepreneurs were lined up against the established class of coffee growers and importers of finished goods. In time, the PLN became associated more and more with the new industrialists, while the traditional exporters opposed the increasing protectionism that the PLN promoted.

The Chamber of Industry, as a main proponent of legislation to promote industry, drafted two of the proposals and was highly influential in shaping four of the remaining five. It was no accident, therefore, that the Chamber's views prevailed on two key points: the law's benefits were to be offered to all industrial applicants, regardless of the extent of domestic value added, and the law would gradually replace the limited incentives offered under the old law with a complete set of customs and tax exemptions, the scope and duration of which increased with new drafts. It is doubtful that the Chamber would have been able to generate sufficient interest to bring this bill to the Legislative Assembly had it not been for the confluence of two factors: the drastic decline in the world market price for coffee and the growing momentum of the Central American integration movement.

With the help of ECLA, the Central American nations had been exploring the feasibility of a common market. The first concrete steps in this direction had been taken with the signing in 1958 of the Multilateral Treaty on Free Trade and Central American Economic Integration by Costa Rica, El Salvador, Guatemala, Honduras, and Nicaragua. The countries were to begin intraregional trade liberalization immediately and to establish mechanisms leading to a common external tariff. The treaty went into effect for El Salvador, Guatemala, and Honduras in 1959. True to its tradition of aloofness, Costa Rica sent observers to the integration conferences and, although it signed the treaties and protocols, delayed formal ratification until much later. Most analysts, however, believed that entry into the CACM was eventually inevitable (Weisenfeld 1969, p. 28).

During 1958 the question of industrialization had been discussed intensively in PLN caucuses and, at the urging of Oduber and Hernán Garrón, the PLN voted to support the industrial promotion bill, although it had been sent to Congress by the Echandi administration. The bill was sent with the justification that there was a pressing need to create urban employment, given the high rate of population growth.

Weisenfeld, in his analysis of the congressional approval of the law, claimed that

> the actual text of the bill that reached the Assembly floor was the work of very few men, acting as representatives of their professional or class interests. The legislative committee with which they met and which rendered the floor report was, consequently, mostly a conduit for the viewpoints of the emerging class of industrialists. The debates were characterized by a conspicuous lack of objective information and of original thought on both sides of the industrialization issue and, similarly, by a failure to bring forth from the generalized Prebisch or anti-Prebisch arguments specific focus on the particular problems of a nation such as Costa Rica.[1] In fact, there was little theoretical discussion of any kind. The bill was enacted partly because of the skill of the representatives of the Chamber of Industry and of its floor proponents and managers, but more importantly, because of two factors: the fall in coffee prices and the resultant pressure to find substitute income and foreign exchange sources, and Costa Rica's commitment to stay in the Central American Common Market. The passage of such a significant piece of legislation did not involve all the groups or interests likely to be affected by it. For example, there was no participation of labor. Hence, no broadly based social dialogue took place, in spite of the openness of the Assembly debates and attendant newspaper coverage and publicity. At no time was there any in-depth evaluation of the likely effects of the key provisions of the bill. The bill was debated, but not analyzed. (Weisenfeld 1969, p. 104.)

The Assembly never challenged the necessity for a complete slate of fiscal incentives. The assumption, strongly supported by the Chamber of Industry since 1955, that ample customs and tax exemptions had to be granted to encourage investment in Costa Rica's industrial sector was accepted without objection.

On August 21, 1959, the bill was overwhelmingly approved. In the rather euphoric words of a key congressmen, "As of the time of enactment of this statute, Costa Rica is an industrial country."

Joining the Central American Common Market

In addition to the debate about industrial promotion, one of the most important policy conflicts of the period was the reluctance of the Echandi administration to sign the General Integration Treaty adopted by the other countries in 1960 and to join the CACM. The industrialists had to wait for the victory of the PLN and the Orlich administration (1962–66) for Costa Rica to join the common market.

For about seven years (1951–58) two administrations of different ideological persuasion had participated in the discussions promoted by ECLA concerning the need to foster industrialization at the regional level through a widening process of economic integration. During those years the different social groups that would be favored or hurt by the process did not devote much attention to the issue. Somehow, regional integration seemed to be something remote and of slow gestation. The industrialists, in particular, were more immediately concerned with domestic legislation to promote their interests. The external shocks of the late 1950s, however, forced the country to consider explicitly the role of traditional exports and import substitution in its development strategy. The resulting debate and policy reforms provide a clear example of how changes in the country's terms of trade influenced the relative strength of different social groups in the political arena and of the effect that exogenous shocks have had on the design of policies and strategies.

The sharp drop in the price of coffee when African producers entered the international market seriously hurt the Costa Rican economy. Moreover, banana exports dropped sharply between 1957 and 1959. After the trade surpluses of the first half of the 1950s, the authorities had to face increasing trade deficits. In reaction, the Echandi administration sent to the Legislative Assembly a bill providing for a Plan de Fomento Económico (Economic Promotion Plan), designed mostly by the minister of agriculture and industry, Jorge Borbón, who was also the president of the board of directors of the Oficina del Café (Coffee Office).

The main components of the plan were the establishment of a fund through contributions from several state agencies, to be used by the nationalized banks for agricultural credit and the promotion of rural cooperatives; the creation in the nationalized banks of mortgage departments, financed with bond issues, to lend to agricultural and industrial borrowers in financial distress; the establishment of credit lines for handcrafts and family industries; and the creation of the industrial sections of the nationalized banks. Although several of these measures attempted to promote industry, the Echandi administration devoted its greatest attention to agriculture, and particularly to coffee.

This emphasis on promoting agriculture was reflected in Echandi's statement to Congress:

> The government has arranged for the rescheduling of agricultural loans owed to the banks, to make them correspond to the lower returns being obtained by the farmers. We cannot eliminate this important source of output for the sake of a total diversification of our economy. The government understands that diversification is necessary, but this will have to be achieved without, in the process, leading to bankruptcy or removing the protection of those who have for so many years been the main support of the national economy.

He also related how his administration planned to use, particularly for small farmer loans, funds to be borrowed from U.S. commercial banks; these were, at that time, the largest loans ever received by the government.

The Chamber of Industry lobbied unsuccessfully for a change in the implicit allocation of funds. In their words,

> An economic promotion plan cannot successfully achieve its objectives if its incentives are denied to some basic sectors of economic activity. The disproportionate allocation of funds to small farmer credit is inappropriate. A similar treatment should be offered to manufacturing.

Minister Borbón responded:

> It is essentially the agricultural activities which face the greatest difficulties, and, therefore, they deserve the greatest attention from the central government. We are essentially a country of farmers, and only an agricultural boom can sustain a manufacturing boom. If the majority of Costa Ricans, who are farmers, are left to their fate, we cannot expect much from the opportunities for the industrialists.

During the late 1950s Costa Ricans were thus engaged in an intense debate about the relative importance of agriculture and manufacturing for the country's economic development and about the appropriate policy instruments for promoting growth. It was in this context that the country had also to decide whether to join the CACM. Jorge Borbón, by then minister of finance and economy, explained his position against participation at a roundtable organized by the Asociación Nacional de Fomento Económico (ANFE), one of the country's most influential organizations. ANFE had been created in 1958 as an ideological association for the dissemination of liberal ideas, the promotion of private initiative, and opposition to interventionism. Its members included prominent professionals and intellectuals, in addition to businessmen.

At the ANFE workshop in 1961 Borbón indicated his opposition to participation in the CACM. He feared that the process of integration was going too fast, and he considered this acceleration dangerous. He believed that a progressive reduction of the differences in the political, economic, and social structures of the Central American countries was needed in order to avoid too large a fiscal effort, and he therefore favored a more gradual process of integration. He pointed out that the Central American economies were competitive, not complementary, and that few gains and many costs could be expected from free trade among the common market partners. In the end, he believed, few firms would be able to survive in the small market, and incipient entrepreneurs would disappear. He insisted on the relative strength of the Salvadoran and Guatemalan businessmen and the weakness of Costa Rican manufacturers. He was concerned about the much higher level of wages in Costa Rica, as well as the much wider set of social security

benefits and their effect on production costs and the country's competitiveness. He perceived that Costa Rica would become increasingly dependent and subordinated to the economic interests of the other
countries. He was particularly concerned about the fiscal losses implicit
in the tax holidays and other exonerations to be granted to protected
firms (Asociación Nacional de Fomento Económico 1968).

Another participant in the roundtable, Manuel Jiménez, president of
the Chamber of Sugar Producers (himself an important coffee and sugar
producer), expressed concern about competition from other Central
American countries in agribusiness activities. These representatives of
the traditional export sector understood that the process of industrialization and economic integration would create new centers of power and
disturb the existing balance of influence on policymaking.

The PLN representative at the workshop, Raúl Hess, who had been
minister of finance in the Figueres administration, argued in favor of an
increasing diversification of the country's productive structure. He believed that the old agroexporting model was exhausted, as reflected by
the fall in coffee prices. Costa Rican agriculture was characterized, in his
view, by low yields and was not competitive in international markets.
New agricultural exports could not be counted on as a growth pole. The
only path open to the country was industrialization. But industrialization would be extremely costly within the confines of the small Costa
Rican market. Participation in the CACM was thus a golden opportunity
to overcome the constraints of small size (Asociación Nacional de
Fomento Económico 1968).

The Chamber of Industry, still under the leadership of Madrigal
Nieto, joined forces with the PLN to lobby for participation in the CACM.
Ratification of the treaties became one of the PLN's most important
presidential campaign issues in late 1961. In July 1962 the new Orlich
administration announced its commitment to integration. It took another year, however, for the Legislative Assembly to ratify the treaties.
Costa Rica did not formally join the CACM until November 1963. Pressure
from the United States, the urging of President John F. Kennedy in San
José in March 1963, and accession being made a precondition for Alliance
for Progress assistance contributed to this inevitable result.

The Modernization of the State

In 1950 the Costa Rican public sector was small and was basically
restricted to the central government. Except for the social security system, created in the early 1940s, its functions were limited to those of a
traditional laissez-faire state. This situation changed drastically after the
1948 civil war. Numerous institutions were created and were granted
increasing interventionist powers.

By the end of the nineteenth century there were fifty-six public institutions, including numerous municipalities. During the 1940s a few
ministries were added to the executive branch, and the University of

Costa Rica and the CCSS were founded. The process of institutional innovation accelerated after the civil war. Twenty-five new institutions were established in 1948–57, twenty-eight in 1958–67, and sixty-six in 1968–77. Two-thirds (seventy-four institutions) were created during PLN administrations. By 1980 there were 185 public institutions in the country (Jiménez Castro 1986, p. 16).

The most important change, however, was not quantitative but qualitative, and it involved a widening participation of the government in different activities. This enlargement of the public sector was facilitated by the 1949 Constitution. Whereas the traditional political groups favored a revision of the 1871 Constitution, with its liberal, individualist, and presidentialist orientation, the social democrats of the *junta* wanted to modify the legal and institutional foundations of the state in order to increase the degree of state intervention in the economy. With this purpose in mind, the junta appointed a nine-member committee to prepare a draft for a new constitution. When the Constitutional Assembly was elected in December 1948, very few social democrats won a seat. The Assembly rejected the committee's draft, but numerous ideas incorporated in it were adopted.

The new constitution represented a major attempt to decentralize power. The greatest loss was suffered by the executive and, in particular, by the president, but the legislature was also subjected to constraints. Both lost their roles in the administration of elections, which was entrusted to the Tribunal Supremo de Elecciones. The civil service was established, limiting the president's authority to appoint and dismiss officials. The Contraloría General de la República was created to oversee the legality of public administration. Most important, autonomous institutions, with complete independence in their operations and management, were entrusted with multiple new public functions.

The junta decreed significant institutional reforms. Most prominent was the nationalization of the banking system. The Instituto de Defensa del Café, created in the 1930s to regulate the relationships between the participants in the coffee pact, was nationalized and was transformed into the Oficina del Café. Its most important function has been to determine the price that the processor (*beneficio*) must pay the small producer. In addition, the *beneficio* has been required to devote a proportion of the credit received from the nationalized banks to finance the small producers, under terms and conditions regulated by law.

The Consejo Nacional de Producción, created by the Calderón Guardia administration as a department of the Banco Nacional, was transformed in 1948 into a semiautonomous institution that was to promote crops for domestic consumption. It became an autonomous institution in 1956. The Instituto Costarricense de Electricidad, created in 1949, was entrusted with power generation and telecommunications. The Central Bank was created in 1950 during the Ulate administration. Also in 1950, the Civil Service law, the Municipal Autonomy Law, the Organic Law of the National Banking System, and the Organic Law of the Central Bank were enacted. The Instituto Nacional de Vivienda y Urbanismo was established as an autonomous institution in 1954 to expand the low-income housing programs initiated a decade before. The Instituto Costarricense de Turismo was created in 1955. The Ferrocarril Eléctrico al Pacífico, a public enterprise since the construction of the railroad at the end of the nineteenth century, was transformed into another autonomous institution, and the Junta de Defensa del Tabaco (Tobacco Board) was established in 1956. The Instituto de Tierras y Colonización (1961), the last major institution created during this period, was entrusted with land tenure and colonization issues.

Note

1. Raúl Prebisch (1901–86), at the time executive secretary of the Economic Commission for Latin America and later director-general of the United Nations Conference on Trade and Development (UNCTAD), argued that the terms of trade tend to shift to the disadvantage of agriculture and that it was in the interests of developing countries to industrialize behind protective tariffs.

6 Protectionism and the Regional Common Market: 1963–73

In 1963 Costa Rica was still a small, rural, open economy. Exports, however, had been significantly diversified, and Costa Rica finally joined the Central American Common Market (CACM) that year. Substantial structural transformations were taking place, and the public sector continued to grow rapidly. Political stability remained the country's most outstanding achievement. Social and economic indicators improved even beyond the relatively high levels attained by 1950. In many respects Costa Rica no longer resembled the simple country of the first half of the twentieth century. During the following decade the country enjoyed rapid economic growth and stability, until the first oil shock.

Initial Conditions for 1963–73

By 1963 Costa Rica's population had increased to 1,379,800. The population growth rate, although still high, had declined to 3.7 percent a year from a peak of 4.0 percent a year in 1961. The population was even younger than it had been a decade before; the median age was 16 years. GDP amounted to CR$3,404 million (about US$514 million), and GDP per capita was CR$2,467 (US$373), about 1.5 times the 1950 nominal figure. In constant 1966 colones, GDP had almost doubled, from 1,773 million to 3,476 million, and GDP per capita had increased from 2,066 to 2,519.

About two-thirds of the population was classified as rural, and 63 percent of the labor force was employed in rural areas. Despite the slow change in the urban-rural breakdown, structural transformation was rapid, and it modified the character of both urban and rural areas. The share of agriculture in employment declined to 50 percent. The share of agriculture in GDP, in current prices, declined 16 points, from 41 percent in 1950 to 25 percent in 1963. In real terms, however, this share did not change at all. Thus, the nominal reduction merely reflected a price effect, as the domestic terms of trade of agriculture deteriorated from 124 in 1957 to 99 in 1963. The sharp decline of the share of agriculture in employment and the stability of its share in real GDP reflected substantial improvements in the productivity of labor in agriculture.

The importance of manufacturing did not change much between 1950 and 1963. Its share in GDP reached 14 percent, while its share in employment remained at 12 percent. Rapid growth took place in the activities that reflected the expansion of the public sector. The share of general government in nominal GDP increased to 11 percent.

In 1963 exports amounted to US$95 million, having increased 1.7 times since 1950. Imports amounted to US$124 million, about 2.7 times more than in 1950. The consequence was a trade deficit of about 6 percent of GDP, which contrasted with a surplus of about 6 percent of GDP in 1950. Bananas, which represented 65 percent of exports in 1950, accounted for only 23 percent in 1963. Coffee contributed 32 percent in 1950 but 48 percent in 1963. Both crops together accounted for 72 percent of exports, as against 97 percent in 1950. Beef and sugar had grown to 11 percent of the total. These figures reflected the significant process of agricultural diversification that took place in the late 1950s and early 1960s. An important stimulus was the reallocation—in part to Costa Rica—of the U.S. sugar quota after the Cuban revolution. Other exports had also grown, to 18 percent of the total.

Government was much larger than in 1950. Central government revenues were about 3.4 times more than in 1950 and represented 13 percent of GDP, and central government expenditures were 5.2 times more than in 1950 and amounted to 14 percent of GDP. The consequence was a central government deficit of about 1.1 percent of GDP. Several autonomous institutions, with separate budgets, had been created. Thus, the most important structural transformation was the substantial increase in the public sector, as employer and as a claimant of available resources.

The labor force increased 1.4 times between 1950 and 1963, to 408,100; employment stood at 379,900 by 1963. Whereas employment in the private sector increased less than 1.3 times, employment in the public sector trebled, and the share of the public sector in employment grew from 6 to 13 percent. The proportion of the labor force covered by social security increased to 29 percent.

Life expectancy gained 7.6 years, reaching 63.3 years. Infant mortality declined from 90 to 80 per 1,000 live births. The rate of illiteracy fell to 14 percent of the population 10 years old and older. The greatest gains took place in rural areas, where illiteracy dropped 8.8 points, to 20 percent; in urban areas illiteracy declined to a low 5 percent. The proportion of women 20 to 24 years old who were in school increased from 1.5 to 5.2 percent.

Development Strategy and Protectionism

Two characteristics of the Costa Rican economy are its small size, with the limitations imposed by an insignificant domestic market, and a high degree of openness. In view of its specialized resource endowment and small domestic market, the country always understood that trade must serve as the economy's engine of growth. When Costa Rica joined the CACM at the end of 1963, it consolidated its choice of a protectionist strategy of industrialization through import substitution. This decision implied free trade among the customs union partners and a common, highly protective external tariff barrier for imports from all other countries. Thus, Costa Rica chose simultaneously to increase its openness to Central America and reduce its openness to the rest of the world. In the early days, the consequent increased trade promoted growth, but eventually the protectionist framework of the CACM contributed to stagnation. The customs union, therefore, had a mixed effect.

Given the experience with declining coffee prices just before the formation of the CACM, import substitution was justified mainly as a measure for reducing dependence on international markets and avoiding the fluctuations and uncertainty associated with concentration of exports on a few primary products. It was believed that the regional market offered a greater growth potential and was safer and more predictable than the international market. Manufactured goods, which represented only 4 percent of exports in 1963, grew to 29 percent by 1979. About four-fifths of these exports went, however, to the protected markets of the CACM partners.

Industrialization was a key dimension of the PLN agenda of diversification of the country's productive structure as a means of widening the opportunities available to the emerging professional and small entrepreneurial classes. Thus, blaming traditional exports for the country's instability and stagnation in the late 1950s had the side effect of weakening the political power of the coffee growers and other exporting groups.

Unfortunately, even the whole of Central America was never a sufficiently large market. Market size is a crucial determinant of the costs of industrialization; it determines the degree of viable specialization, the extent of competition, and the opportunities for exploiting economies of scale. Given the small size of the regional market, import substitution led to the establishment of many high-cost industries, substantial monopoly power in domestic markets, and limited competitiveness abroad.

In the earlier stages of the CACM, GDP growth rates were relatively high. In particular, the dramatic increase in Central American trade after entry into the customs union in 1963 led to high growth rates for manufacturing. Manufacturing output grew more rapidly than domestic consumption, which, in turn, was fueled by a renewed successful performance of the main agricultural exports. These rates of growth were not sustained into the 1970s, however. Eventually the easy stages of import substitution were exhausted, and the constraints imposed by the slow growth of domestic demand became binding. The distortions and inefficiencies brought about by protectionism became apparent in the structure of production and in the limited capacity of the manufacturing sector to compete outside the CACM.

High levels of effective protection were adopted for the production of final consumer goods, with low or negative rates of effective protection for raw materials, intermediate inputs, and capital goods. The degree of variation across rates of protection was very large. This reflected a permissive attitude toward the granting of rents and provided ample opportunities for arbitrariness in their distribution. Moreover, in several activities, the value added in the economy has been negative—a phenomenon of extreme waste. Protection was accentuated by favorable tax treatment, fiscal concessions, and other incentives for investment in the industrial sector, as well as by credit and foreign exchange policies that implicitly subsidized these activities. When all the determinants of effective protection were taken into account, "Costa Rica had been the most highly protected country in the region" (Rapoport 1978, p. 705).

The outcome of this structure of effective protection was a very import-intensive manufacturing sector and increasing dependence on imports of raw materials, fuels, intermediate inputs, and capital goods and on the foreign financing that made these imports possible. As a consequence, the share of final consumer goods in total imports steadily declined, to less than 20 percent in the late 1970s. Import constraints in these circumstances thus implied a reduction of activity and employment in the manufacturing sector. This caused major political-economy problems and created strong incentives to borrow abroad in order to postpone balance of payments adjustments.

The protectionist strategy distorted relative commodity prices, turning the domestic terms of trade against agriculture, except during periods of extraordinarily high international commodity prices such as the coffee boom of 1976–77. It also distorted relative factor prices, underpricing capital for privileged sectors and overpricing labor in the modern sectors. Substantial payroll taxes, introduced to finance social programs, raised the effective cost of labor, while several policies—including the tax treatment of investments, a fixed exchange rate that overvalued the domestic currency, tariff exemptions for imports of capital goods, and credit-rationing policies produced by underequilibrium interest rates— underpriced capital for preferred activities and accentuated the capital intensiveness of manufacturing. The reduced capacity of the private sector to absorb labor caused the public sector to become an active residual employer in order to avoid high open unemployment rates. The concentration of qualified workers in large public institutions then facilitated their unionization. These strong unions managed to negotiate high public sector wages and opposed efforts to reduce the size of the government when the fiscal deficit became unmanageable.

Trade Policies

Until 1984 trade policies were closely related to the import-substituting strategy that was adopted and to Costa Rica's adherence to the General Treaty of Economic Integration. The CACM consisted of a free trade zone for the five members, with a common external tariff. Several policy instruments were utilized.

- A common external tariff designed to provide, in all the Central American countries, the same degree of nominal protection against extraregional imports. With few exceptions, it covered all imports from outside the region.
- The San José Protocol, adopted in 1970 at a time of a balance of payments crisis. It allowed a tariff surcharge of 30 percent.
- The Central American Agreement on Fiscal Incentives for Industrial Protection (REIFALDI), which provided new firms with incentives, including tariff exemptions on imports of inputs from outside the region and income tax exemptions for certain types of capital expenditures. These incentives were supposed to be valid for a limited period, but in practice they were always extended.
- Other restrictions on extraregional imports that members were allowed to establish unilaterally in addition to the CACM instruments. Costa Rica utilized exchange rate surcharges to tax certain imports, as well as selective consumption taxes, with higher rates for products imported from outside the region.
- Several export taxes, particularly on traditional commodities.
- An exchange rate policy that lowered the import cost of industrial inputs and penalized exports. According to a World Bank estimate, from 1974 through the onset of the crisis in 1981 Costa Rica maintained an exchange rate that overvalued the colón by about 18 percent, even before correcting for the effect of protection.

This arbitrary and complex set of interventions, rather than scarcity and comparative advantages, became the basis for the allocation of resources. Protection, in turn, generated rents for specific activities and firms, which diverted managerial efforts from productive efforts to active lobbying.

With the aim of encouraging exports of nontraditional goods to markets beyond the CACM, the government introduced in the early 1970s the *certificado de abono tributario* (CAT), which consisted of a tax credit of 15 percent on the f.o.b. export value. It also introduced at a later date the CIEX, a tax credit subsidy based on the increment of exports over the previous year, as well as several duty-free provisions, including drawback schemes. As almost no tariffs on these inputs were paid, even when they were used for other activities, the drawback schemes were not an effective instrument for export promotion. The CAT and CIEX systems were not applied uniformly, and they involved cumbersome procedures. These incentives did not overweigh the antiexport bias introduced by the import-substituting protectionist strategy.

Financial Deepening

In addition to being a small and open economy, until the mid-1970s Costa Rica enjoyed remarkable price stability. Between 1950 and 1969 the annual rate of change of the consumer price index was less than 2 percent a year. The country did not experience double-digit inflation until 1973. Minimal inflation reflected the openness of the economy and an exchange rate that was fixed for long periods. The domestic price level was thus determined by international price movements, during a period when international inflation was also minimal.

The fixed exchange rate reflected, in turn, a revealed preference for monetary stability. The country was willing to adopt the monetary and fiscal discipline that was necessary to sustain the exchange rate, a major objective of Central Bank policy. The official exchange rate remained at CR$5.60 per U.S. dollar from 1950 until 1961, when the colón was devalued to CR$6.62 per dollar. The next devaluation did not take place until 1974, when the exchange rate increased to CR$8.54 per U.S. dollar.

During the 1950s and 1960s the rate of monetary expansion was moderate. Between 1961 and 1971 the nominal money supply, narrowly defined (M1), increased 12 percent a year. Since the rate of growth of real income, although high, was still slower than the growth of money balances, the absence of inflation was a result of the rapid increase in the demand for money.

As a consequence of exchange rate stability, low inflation, and the relatively high rate of growth of real income during the 1960s and most of the 1970s, Costa Rica experienced a significant degree of financial deepening. The ratio of the money supply, in the broad sense of currency and demand, savings, and time deposits (M2), with respect to GDP rose from 19 percent in 1960 to 43 percent in 1978. These ratios reflected a comparatively high degree of money deepening in comparison with other developing countries—particularly those of Latin America, where high and erratic rates of inflation had been a main instrument of financial repression. Most of the monetization of the economy and the provision of a means of payment took place before the 1960s, since by then the ratio of the money supply narrowly defined (M1) had reached contemporary levels. Subsistence and nonmonetary transactions have been a minuscule proportion of the Costa Rican economy since the early 1950s, and banking habits were rapidly adopted. The largest portion of the financial deepening of the 1960s and 1970s was thus associated with nonmonetary deposits. The ratio of quasi-money to GDP increased from 4 percent in 1961 to 19 percent in 1978 as preferences for risk and return led to more diversified portfolios.

This increasing mobilization of funds through the banking system made possible the rapid expansion of domestic credit. Nevertheless, Costa Rica continued to rely heavily on foreign savings to finance domestic investment. In addition, numerous regulations and the administrative allocation of credit fragmented financial markets and increased transaction costs for all market participants. These deficiencies were exacerbated in the late 1970s, as the crisis set in.

CODESA: **The State as Producer**

During the 1960s many Costa Ricans, particularly key leaders of the PLN, adopted ideas about protectionism, nationalism, and planning from the UN Economic Commission for Latin America (ECLA). According to Daniel Oduber,

> In March 1963 we [Costa Rican President Francisco Orlich, U.S. President John F. Kennedy, U.S. Secretary of State Dean Rusk, and Alliance for Progress experts] met in order to discuss the Alliance's program for Costa Rica. The American representatives insisted on the need to abandon classical economic models in order to modernize the country's productive structure, with emphasis on social justice and increasing independence of the national development process. It was necessary to promote larger firms and overcome the reluctance of Costa Rican capitalists toward investing in large enterprises. It was necessary to replace the foreign firms which were exploiting our resources. Foreign investment had to be rationalized and subjected to the same legal framework as domestic firms. All of this required planning, in order to start large projects that, once established, could then be sold and turned over to the domestic savers of the region. (*La Nación*, July 25 and 29, 1982.)

Although a much larger public sector was one of the PLN's objectives, its original leaders had attempted to prevent the concentration of power by creating the autonomous institutions. The independence of the decentralized agencies was, however, no longer compatible with the PLN's desire to increase the role of planning. By 1966 PLN leaders were already complaining that the Costa Rican state was not unitary and coordinated; it was more like a collection of islands in which each institution did what it wanted, while the central government became weaker and weaker (Vargas 1987, p. 10).

The 1949 Constitution gave the autonomous institutions independence with respect to both policy and management. The PLN leaders believed that the agencies' independence in policymaking had to be taken away. The PLN used its majority in the Legislative Assembly to pass a constitutional amendment that would restrict the independence of the autonomous institutions to matters of management. Thus, not only was the public sector growing rapidly, but power had become more centralized.

During the 1960s the political ideology of the PLN underwent several transformations. From the concept of state intervention, it rapidly moved to emphasis on nationalism. According to Oduber, "while not opposing foreign investment, because it is necessary to promote our development, we believed that strategic industries must be entirely Costa Rican." Moreover, in his view, their evolution had to be planned. This was the ideological background for the creation, in November 1972, of the Costa Rican Development Corporation (CODESA), after a decade of debate on its merits.

The establishment of CODESA reflected the desire to promote not only infrastructure but also state productive activities. It was claimed that CODESA was a necessary complement to the nationalized banking system. There was a need for an agency willing to take the risks involved in large undertakings—risks which in the early stages could be very high. Once these risks were reduced and the firm was established in the market, it could be sold to private owners.

During discussion in the Legislative Assembly in 1969, PLN leaders insisted that the new agency must be responsive to the economic policies of the executive and that it had to be a corporation, able to raise funds without legislative authorization. The project was finally approved in 1972, with thirty-seven votes in favor and only eight against. The new institution, a corporation (*sociedad anónima*) with mixed capital, was to promote economic development by strengthening Costa Rican private enterprises within the mixed economy model. It was expected to modernize, rationalize, and expand existing productive efforts and to develop new productive activities.

CODESA's equity was divided into 33 percent from the private sector and 67 percent from the public sector. The private sector, however, never subscribed its share, and CODESA has operated as a public institution managed by a board of directors of whom four represent the public sector and three the private sector. The private sector directors became, in practice, representatives of the chambers, chosen by the executive. CODESA's activities came to typify the marriage of government intervention and rent seeking that was at the root of the fiscal crisis of the early 1980s, as described in chapter 7.

Universal Social Security

Even after the wage ceiling for compulsory participation in the social security system was raised in 1958, services expanded only slowly, despite an increasing demand fueled by rapid population growth. Moreover, the system was not reaching the weakest groups; rather, it covered many who had the means to pay for medical attention and did not need or want the services of the Caja Costarricense de Seguro Social (CCSS). An important reason for this lack of dynamism was the accumulating government debt, which came about because the state did not pay its share with respect to every worker or its contribution as an employer.

Rosenberg describes the struggle to solve the problem of the government's inability to pay that took place between 1959 and 1961. In 1959 Enrique Obregón, a PLN *diputado,* proposed a constitutional reform to force the government to devote 10 percent of the national budget to the CCSS. This proposal was attacked by the Central Bank on fiscal grounds and was rejected in committee. The finance minister, Alfredo Hernández, proposed instead to allocate to the CCSS the revenue from the cigarette tax. This, however, amounted to only CR$11 million, whereas the annual contribution was CR$15 million. The issue was a difficult one because of the severe fiscal disequilibrium, and the debate reflected political-economy conflicts—the struggle for funds among various agencies within a rapidly growing public sector in the presence of fiscal constraints and questions about the role of social security and its effect on economic growth. For the first time the CCSS did not make proposals for its own expansion (Rosenberg 1983, p. 133).

PLN politicians in the Legislative Assembly began to promote more ambitious plans to extend coverage to wide segments of the population, while the CCSS had a cautious and modest program. Whereas the bureaucrats took a narrow view concerning the set of beneficiaries that the institution should serve, the politicians wanted the support of the large segments of the population not yet covered. The PLN also wanted to get credit for the financial consolidation of the CCSS. The tension between the aspirations of the politicians and financial reality grew. The more the CCSS needed to rely on the Legislative Assembly for its financing, the more political rather than technical criteria guided the expansion of its services. Increasingly, the desires of the politicians dominated the caution of the bureaucrats.

In 1961 a constitutional amendment was proposed that would require the CCSS to achieve universal coverage within ten years. The CCSS protested, claiming that as an autonomous institution it had the right to define the size and scope of its services and that it lacked the infrastructure to make this goal feasible. The legislators were surprised by the bureaucratic resistance to a program that would justify a vigorous expansion and transform the institution into one of the most powerful agencies in the country. Moreover, such a constitutional mandate would facilitate the financial independence that the CCSS desired (Rosenberg 1983, p. 144).

At the time, this crucial reform was ignored by most other groups, which considered it merely a formal, legalistic statement that could not be implemented. Moreover, the innovation stemmed from the initiative of individual politicians, not from popular pressure. In May 1961 two constitutional amendments mandated universalization of coverage within ten years and guaranteed that the state would pay its contributions. All forty-five *diputados* were in favor of the reforms, which promised everything but actually gave nothing. Since the mandate had no immediate practical consequences, its redistributive nature was not clearly understood by all. Furthermore, it represented an alternative to costly approaches that would require employers to pay the contributions so far covered by the state. Even the conservative newspaper *La Nación* applauded the reforms, and most Costa Ricans, with their strong orientation toward equity, felt happy that social security had become universal with no apparent immediate cost to anyone.

Neither the executive nor the Legislative Assembly, however, ever included the allocations required by the reforms in their annual budgets. The cigarette tax became a protected source of funds for the CCSS, but by 1961 it covered only 63 percent of the contribution owed that year, and the share kept declining, to 19 percent by 1973. Whereas the state's contribution had grown eight times, the tax revenue only doubled. Moreover, the constitutional amendment on universal coverage generated high expectations. A few months after the reforms, therefore, the managers of the CCSS were back at the Legislative Assembly looking for help; unfortunately, funds were scarce (Rosenberg 1983, p. 147).

In response to the constitutional mandate, social security services expanded substantially during the 1960s. The number of workers insured increased from 92,215 in 1959 to 194,942 in 1969, and the number of beneficiaries, including family members, grew from 148,480 to 779,768. Coverage increased from 26 to 38 percent of the labor force and from 15 to 46 percent of the total population. The most important change was the expansion of health and maternity services to family members, particularly in rural areas. The political decisions were complemented by a massive construction program. In 1968 the CCSS inaugurated the Hospital México, the largest in Central America. The main obstacle to further expansion became, once more, the wage ceiling, which was set at CR$1,000.

Intense political debate on these issues took place between 1969 and 1971. As the end of the ten-year period set by the 1961 reforms for achieving universalization approached, the CCSS was criticized for not facing the issue until the last minute. An early attempt in 1965 to eliminate the ceiling had been successfully blocked by the physicians, and more active debate had been prevented by the state's inability to pay its contributions. The CCSS had been using resources from its pension funds to finance health services (although the two systems were supposed to be independent), and this threatened the financial health of the pension system.

In 1969 a bill to eliminate the wage ceiling was introduced in the Legislative Assembly. It argued that the ceiling was unfair, since universalization by 1971 would imply that those who earned more would pay proportionately less. Already, 70 percent of those with salaries above CR$1,000 were beneficiaries but were paying a contribution that was computed on the basis of the ceiling only. The redistributive gain from elimination of the ceiling would reflect the reluctance of high-income families to use the social security facilities, and the new revenues would allow services to be extended to poorer groups. (Expansion had been delayed by the CR$223 million debt owed by the state.) High-wage bank officials and other employees from autonomous institutions immediately began to lobby against the elimination of the ceiling.

The CCSS argued before the Legislative Assembly that unless the ceiling were eliminated, universalization would be impossible. A key issue in the debate was whether the mandate applied to salaried workers only or to self-employed and unemployed people as well. The commission asked the advice of the physicians, who insisted that priority be given to coverage of the most needy and who feared that elimination of the ceiling would expand services at the top rather than at the bottom of the distribution. Also, the physicians complained that the CCSS did not have the infrastructure to expand its services and that universalization would degrade the quality of treatment. Minister of Labor Danilo Jiménez Veiga defended universalization:

> The great changes that have occurred in Costa Rica in the areas of education, health, and social security have not waited for the optimum circumstances. Social transformations have never been carried out on the basis of feasibility studies guaranteeing that all the necessary elements are in place. They have been the result of a political decision to designate an objective, which has then forced governments to achieve it.

It was a question of principle, not of implementation (Rosenberg 1983, p. 156).

The Asociación Nacional de Fomento Económico (ANFE) opposed both universalization and the elimination of the ceiling, asserting that the emphasis should be on reaching the poorest first and asking who was actually going to pay for the reforms. It argued that the new tax would have a negative incidence on wages and would put upward pressure on prices. In general, the labor unions did not openly support the changes. The Chamber of Commerce claimed that elimination of the ceiling would hurt the economy by levying an additional CR$200 million annually in wage taxes. This tax on labor and the transfer of funds from the private to the public sector, it said, would reduce the country's competitiveness in international markets. The Chamber of Commerce recommended that the ceiling be raised to CR$2,000. The Chamber of Industry warned about the "inflationary" impact of the reform. A compromise was reached that would have provided for the elimination of the ceiling, but by gradual stages. This proposal was defeated in the Legislative Assembly. After much debate, however, the CCSS announced that it would increase the ceiling gradually on its own initiative, and this quieted the opposition from the Chamber of Commerce.

The reforms were approved by a large congressional majority in March 1971. As a consequence, about 40,000 more workers and 134,700 family members were brought under the system in July. By October the physicians were requesting salary increases of 85 percent and better working conditions. These wage demands represented CR$27 million, or about 31 percent of the new revenues generated by the elimination of the ceilings. The doctors went on strike for eleven days—the first time since the 1948 civil war that public servants had paralyzed the provision of vital services as a means of having their demands heard. This not only revealed the vulnerability of the CCSS but also became a precedent for actions by the middle class employed by the government.

7 External Shocks and Fiscal Crisis: 1973–85

By 1973, as a result of rapid economic growth and modernization, Costa Rica had a more diversified economy and a more complex society than in 1950. Agriculture was no longer the most important sector of economic activity, manufactures had become an important share of total exports, and a multitude of new occupations that required higher skills had arisen. Higher labor productivity accompanied a more egalitarian distribution of household income, and poverty had been substantially reduced. The enlarged public sector would continue to grow rapidly during the remainder of the decade as social programs reached every corner of the country. Between 1970 and 1982 the country's economic difficulties grew inexorably and finally reached crisis proportions. Macroeconomic mismanagement, in response to major external shocks, and lack of fiscal control were at the root of the crisis, which was accompanied by the accumulation of a huge foreign debt.

Initial Conditions for 1973–85

The population grew 2.2 times between 1950 and 1973, to 1,871,800. The rate of population growth declined, however, from 4.0 percent in 1961 to 2.5 percent a year in 1973, as a result of a drastic drop in fertility. The population was no longer as young as in 1963. The proportion of those twelve years old and older increased from 60 percent in 1963 to 65 percent in 1973, and the median age was eighteen years.

GDP was CR$10,162 million (about US$1,500 million, between six and seven times its 1950 value in nominal dollars). In constant 1966 colones GDP was 6,934 million, almost two times the 1963 level and almost four times the 1950 level. GDP per capita was CR$5,429 (about US$820, 3.3 times its nominal dollar value in 1950). In real terms GDP per capita was 3,705 constant 1966 colones, almost 1.5 times the 1963 level and almost 1.8 times the 1950 level. In summary, by 1973 the Costa Rican economy had more than twice the population it had in 1950, almost twice the income per capita, and at least four times the GDP.

Rapid urbanization had significantly changed the rural character of the country. Between 1963 and 1973 the proportion of the population living in rural areas declined from 67 to 59 percent. Given the country's small size and the development of an extensive road network, the "rurality" of those remaining in the countryside had been substantially reduced, and a large proportion of the rural population enjoyed relatively easy access to most urban services. Almost 58 percent of the population lived in the Central Valley, where density was particularly high, and 27 percent of the country's population, a larger share than in the past, resided in the San José Metropolitan Area.

The structural transformation that began in the 1950s had continued. The share of agriculture in GDP, at current prices, declined to 19.3 percent, slightly higher than the share of manufacturing, 18.7 percent. The share of general government grew to 12 percent. In real terms this process was slower. By 1973 the share of agriculture in real GDP had declined to 22.6 percent, as against 24.4 percent in 1957, and the share of industry had increased to 19.7 percent, from 14.3 percent in 1963. During the first decade of participation in the CACM the easy stages of import substitution had contributed the most to the growth of manufacturing. In real terms general government's share had declined from 10.9 percent in 1963 to 9.8 percent in 1973.

The domestic terms of trade of agriculture had deteriorated as a consequence of the protectionist strategy of industrialization. Whereas agricultural prices were 11.3 percent lower in 1970 than in 1957, the prices of manufactures were 37.7 percent higher.

The labor force was increasing at more than 3.7 percent a year, and pressures for job creation accompanied this more rapid growth. During 1950–63 agriculture had generated 35 percent of new jobs, but in 1963–73 the figure was only 11 percent. This was in part a response to the reduced availability of uncultivated land and the increasing urban-rural wage differentials.

The proportion of the labor force employed in agriculture had declined by 11.5 points since 1963, to 38 percent—evidence of a substantial improvement in the productivity of labor in agriculture. Employment in manufacturing had gained only 1.2 points, and its share, 13 percent of the total, reflected the limited capacity of the protected sector to generate employment. The remaining sectors absorbed the labor displaced from agricultural occupations; their share increased 10.3 points, to 49 percent of total employment.

In 1973 Costa Rica was a more open economy than earlier as a result of increased trade with its CACM partners and the strong performance of traditional agricultural exports. Exports had been diversified beyond the traditional agricultural commodities (coffee, bananas, sugar, and beef) into manufactured goods for the CACM. The combined share of coffee (27 percent) and bananas (26 percent) was just over one-half of the total, as against 97 percent in 1950 and almost 75 percent in the early 1960s. The share of beef and sugar had increased to 15 percent, and the share of new manufactured and agricultural exports had risen to 32 percent of the total. Total exports amounted to 26 percent of GDP, up from 19 percent in 1963. Total imports had grown more rapidly and amounted to 35 percent of GDP, as against 24 percent in 1963.

The central government's revenues had increased to 20 percent of GDP, as against 13 percent in 1963, and its expenditures represented 18 percent of GDP (14 percent in 1963). The autonomous institutions and other decentralized agencies had become at least as large as the central government.

The labor force had doubled, to 584,900, and total employment had also doubled, to 542,200, since 1950. Whereas employment in the private sector had increased 1.8 times since 1950, in the public sector it had increased 4.9 times. Thus, public sector employees made up 15 percent of the total.

Income distribution had become more egalitarian. The Gini coefficient for the distribution of household income declined from 0.52 in 1961 to 0.44 in 1971. A substantial reduction in poverty had also taken place. Life expectancy had increased by five years since 1963; a Costa Rican born in 1973 could expect to live 68 years. The illiteracy rate had declined to 10 percent of the population 10 years old and older, a gain of 4.1 points since 1963. The greatest gain took place in rural areas, where illiteracy was reduced to 15 percent, while urban illiteracy dropped to 4 percent. The social security system covered 50 percent of the labor force and 60 percent of the population.

External Shocks and Crisis

Like most small, open economies, Costa Rica has always been vulnerable to the influence of external forces. After 1973 it experienced several sizable external shocks that in a relatively short time substantially increased the instability of the economy and magnified its problems of adjustment. These shocks included the two international oil crises; the sharp increase in the international prices of its major exports at the time of the coffee boom and their decline during the world recession of the early 1980s; easy terms for external financing and then loss of access to international financial markets; and war, insurrection, and political instability in Central America.

Between 1954 and 1960 Costa Rica's terms of trade declined sharply and then remained fairly stable (figure 7-1). The first oil crisis brought about a sudden and significant worsening of the terms of trade in 1974. Soon thereafter, however, the country's terms of trade improved greatly, and the value of its exports grew substantially. The 1975 freeze in Brazil's coffee-producing areas led to large increases in international coffee prices, and the prices of other traditional export crops increased as well. The end of the coffee boom and the second oil shock combined, in 1978, to worsen Costa Rica's terms of trade again. Since the index for the terms

Figure 7-1. Costa Rica: Export Prices, Import Prices, and International Terms of Trade, 1950–86

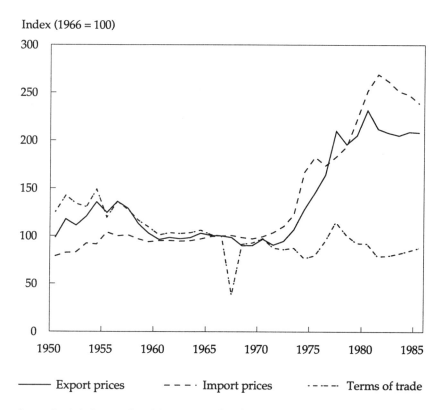

Index (1966 = 100)

——— Export prices   – – – · Import prices   · – ·· – ·· Terms of trade

Source: Statistical appendix table A-19, based on Central Bank figures.

of trade at the end of the 1980s was not particularly low by historical standards, Costa Rica's problems seem to have been related more to the magnitude of the fluctuation in terms of trade in a short period of time than to their secular deterioration.

This sharp fluctuation in relative prices required a major macroeconomic adjustment, at a time when the country's economic structure had become more rigid and when strong political-economy forces discouraged the required policy changes. These external shocks led to the fiscal crisis of 1980–82, but the deeper roots of the difficulties have to be sought elsewhere.

Determinants of the Crisis

In addition to these large external shocks, the crisis reflected the structural consequences of the evolution of Costa Rica's political economy. Given the nature of these long-term trends, sooner or later the country would inevitably have faced difficulties similar to those experienced in the early 1980s. The external shocks therefore determined mostly the timing and the magnitude of the required adjustments; they were not the deepest cause of the crisis. This chapter explores some determinants of the difficulties and attempts to establish their relationship with the same circumstances that help explain Costa Rica's favorable growth-with-equity outcomes.

Although political stability and democratic participation contributed to economic growth and social equity, they also allowed the consolidation of a multitude of interest groups and led to an increasingly rigid deadlock of power shares in a highly contestable political system. Education and social mobility fueled expectations of rising incomes and growing demands for publicly provided goods and services. In combination with the strong concern for equity, these demands led to the institutionalization of numerous growth-reducing fiscal entitlements and transfer payments. These "property rights" contributed to social peace and political stability, but they became a source of fiscal problems when circumstances changed and the implicit transfers were no longer sustainable.

Over time, the nature of government intervention changed. Instead of infrastructural development and formation of human capital, direct redistribution was emphasized during the Figueres (1970–74) and Oduber (1974–78) administrations, through programs such as the Instituto Mixto de Ayuda Social and *asignaciones familiares* (family allowances). The bureaucracy required to manage these programs grew rapidly and demanded, through strong labor unions, privileges for the staffs of these public agencies. When the available resources became scarce, the bureaucracy was protected, at the expense of the beneficiaries of the programs. In addition, the transfers of income implicit in the subsidy and price control schemes (discussed below) created increasing distortions in the country's productive structure and encouraged directly unproductive rent-seeking activities. The political parties responded to these pressures by granting additional entitlements and creating new government agencies.

The expansion of export earnings during the period of extraordinarily high coffee prices and increased foreign borrowing created new opportunities for capturing rents and led to the rapid expansion of all categories of expenditures, particularly in the public sector. The government, already an interventionist welfare state, became a major entrepreneur through the state-owned firms of the Costa Rican Development Corporation (CODESA), and imports grew to constitute almost one-half of the country's aggregate supply of goods and services. When coffee prices dropped, the international terms of trade deteriorated, and the demand for exports declined with the world recession, import capacity fell. As the political and economic climate in Central America worsened, both domestic and foreign investment contracted. The growing fiscal inconsistencies became a crisis.

The administration of Rodrigo Carazo (1978–82) encountered serious difficulty in adjusting to the decline in real income. The powerful manufacturing sector was extremely dependent on imported inputs, and the political constraints on reducing public expenditures were severe. The authorities chose to postpone the adjustment by means of additional borrowing abroad. When foreign inflows dried up, the authorities expanded domestic credit, and when this was not sufficient, they crowded the private sector out of domestic loan portfolios. Increasing inflationary pressures led to the loss of the country's international monetary reserves (after foreign borrowing ceased to replenish them), to devaluation, and to three-digit inflation.

The speed with which the economy deteriorated and the magnitude of the exchange rate and monetary collapse were dramatic. The Carazo administration's refusal to devalue and to achieve fiscal equilibrium in the late 1970s provided a good example of the political-economy forces at work. By then it was evident that the overvaluation of the colón was responsible for declining export volumes and was subsidizing capital flight. Because everyone was convinced that devaluation was inevitable, speculation against the colón was riskless and increasingly profitable. By choosing to defend the exchange rate through borrowing abroad beyond reasonable limits, the Carazo administration imposed heavy burdens on the country's future growth. Speculation increased the market-clearing exchange rate above equilibrium levels, augmenting instability and the magnitude of the adjustment. Controls, rationing schemes, and increasing interventions created new rents to be added to the gains from subsidized capital movements and led to sizable redistributions of income.

Factor Market Interventions

Government policies significantly affected factor utilization through their effect on the country's productive structure. The protectionist strategy of import substitution channeled investment toward the most capital-intensive sectors of the economy and toward the most capital-intensive activities within each sector. Factor price policies accentuated the inducements implicit in the trade interventions. The substantial payroll taxes that were imposed to finance welfare and social security programs meant that the effective cost of labor to employers was considerably higher than the cash wages actually received by workers.

In effect, by the early 1980s social security and other charges levied at least a 26 percent surcharge on wages and salaries. These taxes had increased steadily since the 1950s. To the extent that the revenues collected went to provide direct subsidies or funded social services, they lessened the pressure for increased wages, but their net effect was to dampen the demand for labor. Payroll taxes were both contributed directly by the employer (18.5 percent of wages) and deducted from workers' salaries (7.5 percent).

At the same time, several policies worked to underprice capital for the modern sector. High tariffs on final consumer goods, coupled with low or no tariffs on imports of capital goods, gave incentives for the use of foreign equipment and inputs. Tax incentives for investment in physical capital, as well as reliance on indirect taxation to finance government expenditures, also made capital artificially cheap. An exchange rate that overvalued the colón subsidized imports of capital equipment. Expectations of devaluation, low interest rates on financial savings in colones, and the much higher interest rates on dollar deposits in Panama, Miami, and elsewhere encouraged the export of financial capital. Low interest rates were charged on long-term loans. Domestic capital formation was discouraged, while the use of capital in the modern sector was subsidized. At the same time, the country incurred a huge private and public sector foreign debt.

These interventions, which overpriced labor and underpriced capital, increased the investment required to create a job, reduced the opportunities for generating new employment, and allocated resources away from the country's comparative advantages. The public sector was forced to become a residual employer to avoid open unemployment of a highly skilled labor force. The rapid expansion of the public sector and the income inelasticity of the tax system were among the main causes of the significant fiscal deficit that was at the root of the crisis.

Wage Policies

Legal minimum wages were first mandated in 1933. The Labor Code (1943) established in every province a mixed committee of employers and workers that set minimum wages. In 1949 the Consejo Nacional de Salarios (National Wage Council) was created to determine minimum wages nationwide. The legal minimum wages are binding for private firms only; salaries of public employees are determined through negotiations within each institution (Lom 1975).

Before 1974 legal minimum wages were adjusted every two years; after that, as inflation accelerated, they were revised each year, and since 1980 they have been revised more than once a year. In earlier years the determinations were highly disaggregated; minimum wages were set for 1,143 different activities and occupational categories.

Between 1950 and 1972 the mandated increments did not exceed 10 percent for each two-year period, except in 1958–60. Annual increments were, at most, 5 percent a year. On three different occasions the Consejo did not authorize any increase at all. Minimum wages were frozen from 1954 to 1957, from 1958 to 1962, and from 1964 to 1968—periods when inflation rates were very low. The annual increments became larger after 1972. The range among occupations was particularly wide in 1974, when the mandated changes varied between 10 and 41 percent.

The available information about the actual evolution of wages for different occupations indicates that whereas for low-wage workers the adjustment of the legal minimum wage may have been one of the main determinants of actual wage increases, for the middle- and high-wage occupations actual wages increased beyond the established levels. This reflected the rapid growth of labor productivity. Since firms that paid wages above the legal minimum were not required to change them at the time of the adjustment, actual increases were more gradual than the discrete mandated changes. This lack of correlation between adjustments of the legal minimum wage and actual wage increases was evident during the 1960s and the first half of the 1970s.

Between 1964 and 1976 average wage levels in the manufacturing sector increased rapidly, even in years in which no adjustments were made in the legal minimum wage. During the economic expansion of the 1960s and early 1970s excess demands for specific labor skills (middle- and high-wage occupations) exerted an upward pressure on market wages. Another determinant of these wage increases might have been upward mobility toward higher-productivity occupations, induced by the modernization of the country's productive structure. These rapid wage increases in the modern sector were consistent with rapid economic growth and with the improvement in income distribution experienced during the 1960s. They cannot be attributed to increased unionization and collective bargaining power because unions were weak during the 1960s and early 1970s.

That average wages did not change substantially during the months immediately after the adjustments suggests that only a small proportion of the labor force was being paid just the legal minimum and that the rest, particularly in urban areas, were receiving higher salaries. Evasion of the minimum wage regulations was easier in agricultural occupations. Modern sector firms used the legal minimum only for unqualified new entrants.

Before 1973 Costa Rica lacked a clearly defined or specific wage policy. Adjustments in legal minimum wages passively followed rapid economic growth, while average wages increased in real terms. Wage policies became more active in 1974, at the time of the first oil crisis, when specific distributional goals were adopted. Although in April 1974 the legal minimum wages increased by a weighted average of 28 percent, that average included a wide range of percentage adjustments that were inversely related to the existing wage levels for the different occupations. Whereas the lowest wages increased by 41 percent, the highest wages increased by only 10 percent.

These discriminatory adjustments reflected the a priori adoption of an explicit government policy that, proceeding from the perception that the lowest-income groups had been most heavily affected by the acceleration of inflation, attempted to narrow the existing gaps in earnings. Similar objectives were reflected in the equal absolute increases for all wage levels in the public sector. This discriminatory policy was continued, although to a lesser extent, in the following years. There is evidence of important reductions in wage differentials, as a consequence.

Some have claimed, however, that these wage policies had a limited distributional impact (Trejos 1983). A large proportion of the lowest-income households was concentrated in rural areas, where legal minimum wages were less effectively enforced, and wage policies were irrelevant for the significant portion of the poorest who were not wage earners. Artificial attempts to increase the lowest salaries may have induced replacement of unskilled labor by capital and caused unemployment. In the long run the groups with the greatest bargaining power, such as public sector workers, managed to use wage policies in their favor, but the poorest were not likely to be among these groups.

Credit Allocation Policies

Credit affects income distribution in several ways. Access to credit is an important determinant of the rates of growth of the wealth of different producers. The wealth of those who have access to loans increases in comparison with the assets of those without access. In addition, if credit is subsidized, the implicit transfer directly affects distribution, and if loans are not repaid, a transfer accrues to the defaulters.

Basing access to credit on assets owned perpetuates differences in wealth; if access to credit discriminates in favor of the rich and against the poor, it accentuates existing wealth and income differences. If, in addition, the interest rates charged are less than the social opportunity cost of the claims on resources lent, the implicit subsidy has a regressive impact on distribution because it is necessary to become a borrower to be a beneficiary and because the amount of the grant transferred is directly proportional to the size of the loan.

During the 1960s the interest rates charged on loans by the state-owned banks were positive in real terms and implied only a moderate subsidy. In the 1970s, however, the implicit subsidy was substantial, even under conservative assumptions about the opportunity cost of credit. Interest rates were negative during the mid-1970s and early 1980s. The amount of the subsidy transferred was particularly substantial in 1973, 1974, 1979, 1981, and 1982, when savers received significantly negative rates, in real terms, on their deposits, and the inflation tax on all holders of financial assets was high. Under the conservative assumption that the social opportunity cost of the loans was 10 percent a year in real terms, the rate effectively charged on loans during 1974 was a negative 20 percent. Thus, the implicit rate of subsidy was 30 percent; of every colón loaned, 30 cents was a free transfer to the borrower.

Agricultural credit represented almost 60 percent of the value of gross agricultural output and more than one-half of the loan portfolios of the banks. This meant that in the important case of agriculture the grant transferred through subsidized credit represented the equivalent of 20 to 25 percent of the value of gross agricultural output.

Only between 30 and 40 percent of all agricultural producers had access to bank credit, while the remaining 60 to 70 percent were excluded from the subsidy. There was a high degree of portfolio concentration. In the case of the Banco Nacional de Costa Rica, which granted more than one-half of all agricultural credit in the country, less than 2 percent of all loans accounted for more than 60 percent of the amounts loaned for agriculture, and about 10 percent of all loans accounted for more than 83 percent of the amount of credit granted. This meant that about 1 percent of all agricultural producers in Costa Rica were receiving more than 65 percent of the agricultural credit granted by the banks and more than 65 percent of a substantial subsidy, equivalent to almost 25 percent of the value of agricultural output in 1974.

As inflation rates declined during the second half of the 1970s and nominal interest rates increased, the subsidy declined in magnitude, but it remained important. It increased significantly again during the early 1980s, while the loan portfolio became even more concentrated. By the end of the decade, it was estimated, about 50 percent of the banks' loan portfolios represented defaulted loans. This meant a significant transfer to the few privileged, very large borrowers who did not repay their loans.

Although specific information is not available, industrial credit appears to have been equally concentrated. Despite the large number of small and medium-size establishments, Costa Rica's industrial structure has been highly concentrated, with a few firms generating the largest share of employment, output, and profits and receiving the largest share of industrial credit. For instance, in 1975 firms that employed 200 persons or more, which represented less than 2 percent of all manufacturing enterprises, employed about 33 percent of the labor force in manufacturing and generated about 44 percent of the sector's value added. At the other end of the distribution, firms that employed fewer than twenty persons, which accounted for more than 80 percent of all establishments, employed 20 percent of the labor force and produced only 10 percent of manufacturing value added. Moreover, the industrial subsectors that generated the largest share of value added were dominated by the activities of one or two firms. Most of these firms were family enterprises or were owned by a small group of closely linked shareholders. Financial repression policies therefore had negative effects on both growth and equity.

Price Stabilization Policies

The most important government intervention in direct price determination in Costa Rica has been in the market for staples (*granos básicos*)—rice, corn, beans, and sorghum. In recent years these crops have represented almost 10 percent of value added in agriculture. Rice and sorghum are produced by large farmers and corn and beans by small farmers. Large rice producers, who represent 10 percent of the total, produce 70 percent of rice output; small corn and beans producers (90 percent of the total) produce 80 percent of the output of those crops. Rice and sorghum are highly mechanized; beans and corn are highly labor intensive. Labor input per hectare is about six times greater in corn and beans than in rice and sorghum. On the small farms about two-thirds of the labor is supplied by the household. Self-consumption is important in corn and beans (Céspedes and others 1984b).

Policy regarding these staples can be divided into three stages: a simultaneous attempt to promote production and stabilize prices (1950–74); an emphasis on stimulating production and exporting at a loss (1974–82); and attempts to achieve self-sufficiency without generating an exportable surplus (1982–85).

Policies to encourage production included the establishment of a minimum price and the guaranteed purchase by the Consejo Nacional de Producción (CNP) of any quantity of output at that price. Stabilization policies attempted to smooth the domestic impact of variations in international prices and to avoid increases in consumer prices. The two policies were contradictory, and the CNP did not succeed in preventing fluctuations. Setting a comparatively high minimum price for producers and a relatively low maximum price for consumers generated deficits that were financed with the profits from the state monopoly on liquor production and, in particular, with Central Bank credit.

Self-sufficiency was a major objective of the Oduber administration (1974–78), in part as a reaction to the rise in international oil prices. According to the 1975–78 National Basic Grains Program, no problems were expected in achieving self-sufficiency in rice. In the case of beans, exceptional yield increases were required, and self-sufficiency in corn was to be achieved by 1978. Increased sorghum production was expected to reduce corn imports. By 1976 several problems with these objectives became clear. That year the country produced a surplus of 60,000 tons of rice, at a domestic price well above the international price, and the minimum price for the next crop had to be reduced. Since self-sufficiency in corn and sorghum had already been achieved, price reductions were recommended for these crops as well. The Rural Development Program for 1977–79 insisted on the goal of self-sufficiency and predicted exportable surpluses. High prices, which induced exportable surpluses of rice, were kept through 1982, but increasing losses by the CNP led the authorities to revise this policy.

After the crisis the Central Bank became an important lobbyist against protectionism, particularly in the case of rice. It stated that the "present price support and marketing systems eliminate economic rationality (minimum cost) at the producer level. This has to be changed, so that exports are undertaken by the producers themselves and not the CNP" (Lizano Fait and Sagot 1984). The CNP did not establish a support price for the 1985–86 rice crop and did not promise to buy the grain. Instead, it facilitated futures contracts between private producers and processors. This substantial change in policy was a response to the accumulated losses of the CNP and the monetary consequences of Central Bank financing of those losses.

According to experts, differences in support price policies have helped bring about major crop substitutions by making corn less profitable than rice. By 1983, however, the country was producing exportable surpluses of white corn at prices well above international prices, with the same implied losses. Cultivation of yellow rice and sorghum, which compete for the same land used for white corn, has become marginal, and imports of these crops have been required. Bean production has encountered severe difficulties. Most of the output has been produced with traditional low-yield techniques on the most marginal land.

Rice and corn were sometimes sold domestically for less than the support price. The resulting losses, along with losses on exports, were financed by the Central Bank, which was legally required to do so until 1989, and by the profits from wheat sales by the CNP (Corrales 1985, p. 19). The CNP has a monopoly on imports and exports of these staples. To avoid the arbitrage that may result when the state sets both a minimum price for producers and a maximum price for consumers that is below the producer price, the CNP sells only through its own stores. In the 1980s, for example, the producer support price for beans was above the international price, and the consumer maximum price was below the international price. To prevent arbitrage, the CNP marketed imported beans (of different quality and characteristics) through private stores and sold the domestic beans only through its own stores. Consumers of sorghum and yellow corn have paid more than the international price.

Discouragement of production has been clearer in the cases of sugar and coffee for domestic consumption, eggs, milk, and, at times, beef for domestic consumption. The domestic consumer has sometimes paid more than the international price for these products. Maximum domestic prices for sugar have been set below the international price to subsidize consumption. As a result, Costa Rica has one of the world's highest levels of per capita consumption of sugar, and illegal exports of sugar are significant. Increasing domestic demand and slow production have shifted sugar away from the international to the domestic market. Egg production has been similarly penalized, leading to the disappearance of the less efficient small producers. Large producers have not requested price increases, in hopes of further monopolizing the market. A maximum domestic coffee price is set by law, but the input (coffee from the *beneficios*) has been sold at auction. The amounts available for the auction are the residuals from exports, which are managed by the Oficina del Café. Since there is no relation between the controlled domestic consumer price and the auction prices, which reflect the international price, processors of coffee for domestic consumption have a difficult time.

The price set for milk declined in real terms in the 1980s because the nominal price changed only slowly in a highly inflationary environment. Milk production did not decline as much, thanks to technological change; as the price of beef fell, dual-purpose cattle were diverted to milk production in new areas. Average yields, however, declined substantially. Since the price of live cattle is freely set in the *plaza* (exchange), the producer receives a good price, but the butcher has to be inventive to bypass the restrictions on the prices of certain cuts.

CODESA and the Politician-Entrepreneur

More than any other public sector institution, CODESA represented the new approach to state interventionism that characterized the Oduber administration (1974–78). Its purposes went beyond the modernization of the public sector that had been prominent in the agenda of the young politicians of the Centro para el Estudio de los Problemas Nacionales who joined Figueres in the junta after the 1948 civil war and in his first administration. With increasing impetus, the state promoted productive activity through the expansion of infrastructure, access to credit, and protectionist subsidies. Large investments in human capital formation were complemented by specific programs to train the labor force. In the late 1970s the role of the state expanded beyond its traditional functions into productive enterprises that competed directly with the private sector.

The Refinadora Costarricense de Petróleo (RECOPE) was established in 1963, with 15 percent state participation, to refine gasoline. In 1973 the state acquired control of 65 percent of the stock and by the end of 1974 was the sole owner. Although RECOPE was the object of much criticism, the purchase of its stock from a multinational corporation was not in itself perceived as a threat to the private sector, given the nature of the activity and the uncertainties brought about by the oil crisis. Major political-economy debates took place, however, regarding the use of RECOPE's "profits," which reflected a substantial gasoline tax. In 1976 RECOPE financed TRANSMESA, a subsidiary of CODESA that provided public transport in San José, and in 1978 it purchased 50 percent of the stock of FERTICA, a private fertilizer plant.

CODESA, created in 1972, began to grow rapidly after 1975. Its subsidiaries engaged in all kinds of productive activities—in railroads, fertilizer, cement, aluminum smelting, sugar, cotton, agribusiness, forestry, aquaculture, ferries, maritime and urban transport, and drawback export firms. In some cases CODESA took over bankrupt firms or participated in mixed capital firms. It also initiated projects that failed. It cosigned numerous loans for private firms and provided financing for a few. Most of its energies and resources were devoted, however, to the establishment and promotion of fully owned subsidiaries (Vega 1982, p. 62).

The productive activities developed by CODESA have not been profitable. For all the years recently evaluated by Arthur D. Little, Inc., CODESA's losses were always more than 25 percent of sales. The accumulated losses for 1976–83 represented 35 percent of the 1983 value of all the assets of its subsidiaries. Not one of the twelve principal subsidiaries made a profit in any year of the period, and all had losses every year.

These losses were not a coincidence; an examination of the feasibility studies for the projects showed serious deficiencies. Moreover,

A detailed analysis of the evolution of the main macroeconomic variables has made it evident that, unfortunately, CODESA did not significantly contribute to the rapid economic growth experienced by Costa Rica during earlier periods, and that it clearly had a substantial weight in worsening the recent crisis. CODESA's unrestricted access to Central Bank credit, which in 1983 represented one-half of all domestic credit for the public sector and 18 percent of all credit from the banking system, and which was used to pay for operational expenses and to service CODESA's huge external debt, acquired in connection with the creation of the corporation's largest subsidiaries, has been a major force in the deterioration of public sector finances and in the crowding out of credit for the private sector. (Cited in Vargas 1987, p. 16.)

An evaluation by the Chamber of Industry claimed that in 1983 CODESA's enterprises contributed 1.8 percent of GDP, employed between 0.3 and 0.9 percent of the labor force, used 18 percent of all domestic credit, and had losses equivalent to 57 percent of their assets. Total sales in 1984 amounted to CR$2,283 million, but total losses were CR$1,487 million. All of CODESA's subsidiaries were technically bankrupt. The corporation's debt to the Central Bank amounted to more than CR$10,000 million (Vargas 1987, p. 16).

This sad story is not surprising. Since CODESA is a state enterprise, its losses, rather than hurting its shareholders, have been socialized. This hybrid (a state agency constituted as a private corporation and engaging in activities previously in private hands) seems to have created the worst of both worlds. CODESA was not restricted by the traditional political controls on government agencies, and it lacked the profit discipline that constrains private firms. Projects were evaluated on the basis of the size of the initial disbursement—the larger and more visible the initial invest-ment, the happier the politician who announced it. In private business the initial investment is frequently the most painful moment in the evolution of the enterprise, and concern for profitability leads the owners to minimize the investment required to obtain a given flow of future net returns. This was not the case for CODESA. Its worst feature seems to have been its almost unrestricted access to financing; the Central Bank directly provided the funds required for any given investment. As a result, there was no limit on the size of the enterprises financed (Vargas 1987, p. 20).

Productive activities in direct competition with the private sector created tension in the cordial and symbiotic relations that had developed between the state and the industrial groups. CODESA's privileged access to loans and the resulting crowding out of the private sector in credit portfolios were also a reason for concern. The confrontation between the state and the industrial community reflected the increasing power within the Partido Liberación Nacional (PLN) of politician-entrepreneurs. The origin of this group may be linked to the centralization of political power and the changes in economic policies that took place during the 1970s. Whereas in the 1950s the autonomous institutions had provided a means for new groups of professionals and technocrats closely linked to the PLN to gain access to the direct exercise of power, after 1969 party leaders promoted the centralization of power in the executive.

The politician-entrepreneurs associated with the PLN derived their power from their control of the state. From their high positions as heads of the most important autonomous institutions and government enterprises and in the executive, they accumulated an immense influence over economic policies. The increasing complexity of the state and of the tasks to be performed translated into high salaries and social status, which these technocrats and politicians used to venture into private business. They developed their skills in the political arena and then became entrepreneurs mostly through their privileged access to credit and other implicit subsidies. When not in power, they ran highly protected enterprises. The direct control of the state has been essential for their accumulation of economic and political power (Sojo 1985).

CODESA represented the confluence between the interests of the politician-entrepreneurs and of those who promoted greater state interventionism. The corporation was created with the support of the Chamber of Industry, which perceived the new activities as complementary to the private sector. The traditional industrialists, however, could not prevent the development of activities in direct competition with the private sector and could not attract CODESA's funds toward private firms (Achío and Escalante 1985).

Toward the end of 1978 some members of CODESA's board of directors studied the possibility of selling some of the subsidiaries. The Legislative Assembly enacted the Ley de Regulación de la Venta de Acciones de Empresas de Propiedad Pública (law for the regulation of the sales of stock of public enterprises). This law prohibited the sale of stock to foreigners and limited to 2.5 percent the maximum share that one individual could acquire. It was later modified to allow the sale of up to 40 percent of a given enterprise to foreigners. In March 1984 the Ley de Equilibrio Financiero del Sector Público (law of financial equilibrium for the public sector) authorized the sale of CODESA's subsidiaries at the price set by the Contraloría General de la República. In March 1985 the U.S. Agency for International Development gave Costa Rica US$140 million to pay the corporation's debt and so facilitate the sale of the subsidiaries.

The Crisis and the Financial System

During the 1960s and most of the 1970s Costa Rica experienced a significant process of financial deepening, the result of vigorous economic growth and relative price stability. The ratios of the monetary aggregates to GDP, the proportion of private savings channeled through the banking system, and the number of bank branches increased rapidly.

Costa Rica's financial system suffered significantly in the crisis, however—probably more than any other sector. There was a clear fiscal reason for this. The deterioration of the country's international terms of trade, other external shocks, and inappropriate policy responses to those shocks caused real incomes to decline after 1977. The recession sharply reduced the rate of growth of government revenues, but public sector expenditures continued to grow rapidly. It was difficult, moreover, to increase taxes in the face of the economic recession, pessimistic expectations, and strong motives for capital flight.

The authorities attempted to cushion the effects on aggregate spending of the decline in income by increasing public sector deficits and, in the beginning, financing them by borrowing abroad. The stock of accumulated public sector deficits financed abroad eventually reached the limit that foreign lenders were willing to accept. Since programmed expenditures were not reduced, the continuing deficits had to be financed with domestic credit.

The expansion of domestic credit at a rate too high to maintain domestic price stability made it impossible to sustain the fixed exchange rate regime. The crowding out of the private sector in bank loan portfolios contributed to the stagnation of output and to the crisis.

Inflationary pressures led rapidly to the loss of the country's large stock of international monetary reserves (accumulated when the price of coffee was high), to additional borrowing abroad in order to replenish those reserves, and to accelerating domestic inflation, once reserves were exhausted and access to foreign borrowing ceased. The wholesale price index increased 65 percent in 1981 and 108 percent in 1982; the consumer price index increased 65 percent in 1981 and 90 percent in 1982. Exchange controls, multiple rates, devaluation, and floating exchange rates followed.

The financial repression that accompanied this attempt to postpone the adjustment to the fall in real income led to a dramatic contraction of the domestic financial system in real terms. The money supply (M2) dropped from 12,105 million constant colones (excluding dollar denominated deposits) in 1978 to 8,322 million colones (excluding dollar denominated deposits) in 1982, only 69 percent of its 1978 real value (figure 7-2). M1 fell from 5,438 million colones in 1978 to 3,032 million in 1982, which was only 56 percent of the 1978 real value and was comparable to the 1970 level.

Between 1970 and 1975 real domestic credit increased at an average annual rate of 7.1 percent. This rate of increase more than doubled between 1975 and 1978. Although mobilization of domestic resources declined from 1978 on, domestic credit, aided by the inflow of foreign funds, increased through 1980, when it reached 14,097 million constant 1978 colones. During 1981 and 1982, however, domestic credit dropped dramatically. By 1982 it had declined to 5,875 million constant 1978 colones—only 41.7 percent of the 1980 level. Even after some recuperation in 1983, real domestic credit was still at its pre-1975 level.

The contraction was particularly acute in the case of domestic credit for the private sector, which declined in real terms from 8,544 million colones in 1978 to 3,060 million in 1982, only 35.8 percent of the former value. In a few years the banking system's supply of real loanable funds to the private sector had been reduced to one-third of its original (1978) value. Costa Rican firms experienced a painful loss of access to bank credit for investment and working capital, in part because inflation eroded the purchasing power of the loan portfolios, in part because of the crowding out of the private sector in those portfolios. To make matters worse, inflation and devaluation had reduced the real value of

Figure 7-2.   Costa Rica: Total Domestic and Private Sector Credit and Total Liquidity, 1950–86
(outstanding balances at end of year)

Billions of 1978 colones

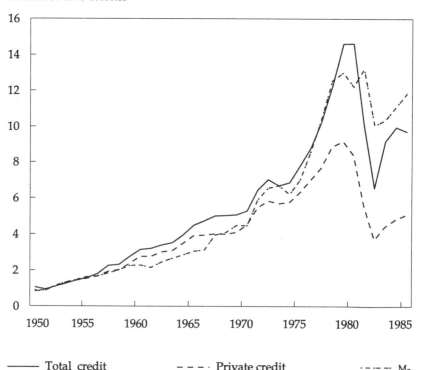

Source: Banco Central de Costa Rica, Crédito y Cuentas Monetarias.

the firms' own funds, and the firms, for all practical purposes, had lost their access to foreign borrowing because of the moratorium on the public external debt and the generalized turmoil in Central America.

Domestic credit for the public sector continued to increase through 1980, when it reached 6,247 million constant 1978 colones. In the following two years, however, it too declined dramatically. By 1982 it amounted to only 2,852 million, or 45.6 percent of the 1980 level. In the race between the expansion of credit for the public sector and inflation, inflation was the easy winner. The strategy was self-defeating. Once the country's international monetary reserves were exhausted, the accelerated expansion of credit contributed to the decline of its real value.

The crowding out of the private sector in loan portfolios was pronounced. Whereas between 1961 and 1975 the share of the private sector in domestic credit declined only from 87.1 to 79.5 percent, by 1981 its share had dropped to 55.7 percent. Moreover, before 1974 the private sector received at least three-quarters of the annual net increment in domestic credit, but by 1980 this share had declined to one-third.

The Determinants of Economic Stagnation and the Crisis

A slow but steady loss of dynamism of production was among the long-term trends of the Costa Rican economy that explained the crisis of the early 1980s. The causes of this gradual stagnation included changes in the relative availability of resources and their productivity. Distortionary economic policies and the accumulation of directly unproductive activities also contributed.

Rapid population growth and the exhaustion of the agricultural frontier reduced the amount of available land per person. Agricultural output could no longer grow simply by expanding the cultivated area, and distorted relative prices that penalized investment in many agricultural activities hindered increases in yields. Factor price policies did not promote labor-intensive activities, and the modern private sector failed to generate enough jobs to absorb the growing labor force. Public sector jobs grew less rapidly after the crisis.

In the early 1980s the ratio of gross domestic investment to GDP was below its historical levels. This reflected macroeconomic instability and the higher risks of economic activity. Inflation rates were higher and less predictable than in the past, and, in combination with price controls, they sharply increased uncertainty about relative profitability. Perceptions of political risks also increased because of the circumstances in Central America. Low investment levels were accompanied by a massive crowding out of the private sector as a result of the continued overexpansion of the public sector. Public investment increased from one-fourth of the total in the early 1970s to two-fifths in the 1980s.

The ratio of public expenditure to GDP increased from less than 10 percent in the early 1950s to almost 70 percent toward the end of the

1970s. The number of government agencies grew from 65 in the early 1950s to 185 in 1980, and public employment increased from 6 to 20 percent of the labor force. The growth of the public sector was particularly excessive in the 1970s, when the coffee boom made possible its expansion beyond sustainable levels. To finance this expansion, the tax burden increased from 18 percent of GDP in the early 1970s to 24 percent a decade later. The public sector received 60 percent of the increments in domestic credit in the late 1970s, as against 20 percent early in the decade.

The loss of dynamism of the economy also reflected the decreasing opportunities for import substitution within the CACM, the distortions introduced by protectionism in both agriculture and manufacturing, and the spread of rent-seeking behavior. In summary, the Costa Rican economy accumulated many features that worked to reduce growth. These included changes in relative factor endowments, the increasing distortions in relative prices, protectionism, and an excessively large public sector. When the country had to face the adjustments imposed by the unusual external shocks, these long-term trends contributed significantly to the crisis.

8 *From Coffee Exports to State Enterprises*

Costa Rica has differed from other developing countries that are similar to it in size, resource endowment, and geopolitical circumstances. The country's unusual combination of growth and equity outcomes has been explained here as the product of long historical processes of interaction between political and economic factors.

The evolution of the country's socioeconomic and political system has been complex. The outcomes have been the result of a combination of several fortunate, mutually dependent circumstances that have usually complemented one another. They have reflected, moreover, a sustained social effort over time, with improvements in one dimension reinforcing progress in others, frequently after long gestation periods and experimental preparatory efforts. In this sense, Costa Rica's "technology" for socioeconomic and political progress has shown important economies of scope.

The following sections summarize the main conclusions of this part of the book and present plausible hypotheses about the political-economy story behind the outcomes in growth, distribution, and the alleviation of poverty. The main thesis—that the same circumstances explain both the successful outcomes and the recent crisis—is further discussed.

The Growth-with-Equity Outcomes

During 1950–85 Costa Rica enjoyed rapid economic growth. It was, however, vulnerable to external events, as indicated by the wide fluctuations in the annual rate of growth of real income, particularly after adjustment for changes in the country's international terms of trade. Although growth and instability were compatible in the long run, adjustment to external shocks presented a major challenge for macroeconomic management in the short run. The growth-stability tradeoff was at the root of crucial policy decisions in this open economy.

The main social indicators reflected a better quality of life in Costa Rica than would be predicted for countries with the same per capita output. That many of these indicators were already exceptional by 1950 suggests that it is necessary to take a very long perspective in explaining the outcomes. These outcomes were the result not of specific interventions but of policy clusters and cumulative processes. Most indicators continued to improve after 1950 as the infrastructure was expanded and institutions were strengthened. The consequences of the conflicts arising in a more complex society, of the weaknesses introduced by the protectionist strategy of development, and of the limits to the sustainability of welfare and other entitlements once access to foreign savings declined were felt only with a long lag. This made it difficult for voters (and researchers) to assess the performance of different administrations.

Income inequality has been moderate, and a substantial reduction in poverty was observed during most of the 1950–85 period. Alleviation of poverty was complemented by effective assistance programs for the indigent and other critical groups. Thus, Costa Rica has been an example of growth-with-equity. In effect, there has been a strong positive correlation between rapid economic growth, increasing equality, and the alleviation of poverty, not only as a long-term trend but also for specific periods. The slower growth of the late 1950s coincided with a less egalitarian distribution of income; the very rapid growth of the 1960s was associated with a substantial decline in the concentration of the distribution of income and with major reductions in poverty; the mixed growth record of the 1970s was accompanied by minor changes in income distribution; and the negative growth of the early 1980s coincided with a deterioration of the distribution of income and with increased poverty. In Costa Rica's institutional and political framework, when growth led, equity followed.

Determinants of Growth-with-Equity

Economic growth was the result of both increased factor supplies and higher factor productivities. Changes in factor supplies included a comparatively high rate of physical investment, made possible by substantial inflows of foreign savings; a significant investment in human capital through emphasis on nutrition, health, and education; and an expanding agricultural frontier, as the rapid development of the country's infrastructure made available for cultivation previously inaccessible land. Factor productivity increased in response to technological innovations, particularly in agriculture. There was more integration of factor and product markets, and labor was particularly mobile. The country's productive structure became more diversified. The modern sectors expanded, as did the domestic market, the population, and output.

Although the protectionist strategy of development introduced distortions and induced unproductive behavior, which reduced factor productivity, the economy maintained a substantial openness toward international markets, which allowed exploitation of pronounced comparative advantages given buoyant world demand. On balance, therefore, despite less than optimal policies, the positive influences on growth predominated for most of the period. The negative impact of protectionism, however, steadily undermined efficiency and eventually weakened growth.

Political stability promoted economic growth because it favored investment and the strengthening of institutions. The absence of political unrest attracted substantial flows of foreign savings, and the stable legal framework permitted a reliable definition of property rights and efficient enforcement of contracts. A peaceful environment of law and order reduced risks and lowered transaction costs. Political stability thus served as an effective counterbalance to economic instability in promoting investment and growth.

Political stability also contributed, however, to the consolidation of interest groups, to an increasingly rigid deadlock of power shares, to complacency and overconsumption, and to the accumulation of growth-reducing fiscal entitlements. Over time, the demands on available resources and the waste associated with directly unproductive activities had an increasingly negative effect on growth.[1]

Because there was no army, defense expenditures were very low, freeing resources for health, education, and the building of infrastructure. The emphasis on equity reinforced the formation of human capital and, after a long period of gestation, further contributed to long-term growth. Education and social mobility, however, fueled rising expectations and growing demands for public sector services. This, combined with a strong concern for equity, led to the institutionalization of numerous entitlements and transfer payments, to the overexpansion of the public sector, and, eventually, to a major fiscal crisis.

High rates of economic growth, in turn, made the pursuit of equity objectives feasible. Income growth, supplemented by a substantial use of foreign savings, financed progress in education, health, communications, and transport and the provision of electricity, water, and other basic services. The growth of household income fueled demand for these services and made it possible to cover the opportunity costs (time) and the complementary expenses (for example, transport and food) associated with the demand. Economic growth and improvements in the standard of living for wide segments of the population went hand in hand.

Whereas earlier the main beneficiaries of public sector services had been the swelling middle-income groups, now the poor increasingly shared in the fruits of growth. The equity-oriented system was expensive, however, and a large bureaucracy evolved to administer it. The growing financial burden contributed to the fiscal crisis, and an increasing proportion of the shrinking available resources went to pay employees, at the expense of the target populations.

Given Costa Rica's unusual initial conditions, for most of the period economic growth and improvements in the labor market were themselves responsible for increased equality in income distribution and for alleviation of poverty. Only after the mid-1970s were explicit redistributive policies important to equity outcomes. The effect of these policies was mixed, however, because of the constraints imposed by the fiscal crisis of the early 1980s.

In general, improvements in distributional equality, growth, and political stability reinforced each other. In the short run growth was determined by external trade conditions, and equity followed. As long as the actual rates of growth coincided with the expected rates of growth, conflicts were kept to a minimum and equity was promoted. But when external events reduced the country's purchasing power, excessive entitlements and less than optimal policies tended to retard growth, and the dynamic interactions were not always positive.

The Formation and Role of Deeply Rooted Initial Conditions

The country's initial conditions in 1950 are important for understanding the 1950–85 outcomes. These conditions included several deep-seated sociopolitical features that distinguished Costa Rica from its neighbors: political stability, democratic institutions, mechanisms for reducing the concentration of power, an efficient legal system, and a generalized concern with equity. The low transaction costs and reduced risks offered by a well-functioning political and legal system promoted growth, while the widespread distribution of the fruits of growth helped to prevent political unrest.

Costa Rica's exceptional circumstances in 1950 were the result of long historical processes. The small population, limited trade, and crushing poverty of colonial Costa Rica fostered minimal social divisions, self-sufficient and independent farm-household homesteads, and rural democracy. There was no market for land, which was viewed as essentially in limitless supply. Taxation discouraged large landholdings, and possession was denied to none.

The introduction of coffee accelerated the privatization of land, prompted an early definition of individual property rights as distinguished from communal rights, and encouraged the consolidation of small landholdings. The timing was critical. In 1821 Costa Rica became independent, escaping colonial taxation and mercantilist regulations. It could therefore devote all the coffee profits to building the infrastructure needed to export the new crop. Ecological conditions were favorable for coffee cultivation, and coffee became the economy's engine of growth. It was the key factor in the development of Costa Rica's infrastructure, institutional organization, and productive structure, and it lifted the country out of the backwardness of colonial poverty. Coffee's technological features facilitated the preservation of Costa Rica's unique social structure of equality and its land tenure pattern of small farms. The interest in coffee shared by most Costa Ricans also contributed to the formation of a common ideology.

The introduction of coffee into a system of small property holdings created a delicate equilibrium that imposed mutual interdependencies and norms of reciprocity among social groups and facilitated the consolidation of an implicit contract. The actors in this balancing act were the complex farming-processing-exporting enterprises (the *beneficios*), the small and medium producers who used family labor, and the landless workers. The implicit pact was a social mechanism for dealing with the risks of the new long-term investment and overcoming the shortcomings of small size. It made possible the exploitation of economies of scale and scope in production and marketing, more efficient use of information, easier access to credit, and the reduction of transaction costs. Land was relatively abundant, reservation wages were high, and mechanizing coffee production was impossible. All this created critical demands for labor inputs, so that even landless workers participated in the implicit contract. The interlinked market organization not only reflected a dominant optimizing economic arrangement; it also guaranteed a politically stable distribution of the new rents.

The politically dominant coffee exporters became increasingly vulnerable to the demands of the other partners in the coffee pact and were forced to open the political arena to widespread participation. These relationships gradually led to the emergence of a national ideology of equality and participation and to the local version of the liberal state. Government was transferred to an enlightened elite that specialized in educational and political affairs and exercised power with a large degree of class neutrality and formal rationality. The resulting legal framework promoted the growth of both economic activity and a democratic society.

By the turn of the century most of the process of infrastructural adaptation and institutional organization for the exploitation of comparative advantages was well advanced. The Costa Rican state had managed to guarantee a high degree of domestic security. It had created a legal system to protect property rights and market freedoms and to manage the basic social relationships implicit in the coffee pact. The interlinked credit, output, and labor markets made possible efficient production and marketing transactions and a widespread distribution of the rents from the vent-for-surplus activities. Thus, the success of coffee reflected an organization capable of realizing the potential of the country's resource endowment while at the same time creating an advantageous political system. This was facilitated by the country's small size and the concentration of a homogeneous population in the Central Valley.

Banana exports also succeeded in exploiting the country's comparative advantages, although through an entirely different arrangement that adapted organizational forms prevailing in other countries.

Whereas coffee was fully integrated into the domestic economy, banana cultivation developed as an isolated enclave. Coffee was owned completely by Costa Ricans; the banana enterprise was owned by a foreign corporation. Coffee was produced on small family-owned plots; bananas were cultivated on large plantations with hired (and frequently foreign) labor. Rather than a social compact, the banana plantations spawned the most serious labor conflicts in the country's history. Because the plantations were isolated from the rest of the country, however, this conflict did not have spillover effects. Capital intensity, sophisticated technology, and critical marketing links for exports of the perishable bananas created explicit or implicit barriers to entry, but the fruit companies undertook the development of the required infrastructure, organization, and technology. Foreign ownership prevented these factor intensities and the large scale of operations from influencing the domestic distribution of income and also facilitated the eventual taxation of the fruit companies. The timing of the introduction of bananas was critical; the powerful banana companies entered the stage only at the end of the nineteenth century, when the Costa Rican state, legal institutions, and democratic traditions were already consolidated. Costa Rica was thus in a good position to exercise control over the banana sector.

Institutional innovation and policymaking in Costa Rica have been characterized by pragmatism, experimentation, and consensus building. The country's revealed preference for stability and attachment to legal ways have led to the increasing institutionalization of compromise and the resolution of economic conflicts in the political arena. Thus, during the Great Depression the relationships among the participants in the coffee economy began to be formally regulated by the state. This model of institutionalization of the political solution of economic conflicts, with the state as arbiter, was frequently replicated. Political solutions, however, have been less responsive than the market to changes in resource scarcities and comparative advantages and have shown a tendency to break down during periods of rapid structural transformation. Institutionalization of the solutions has led to rigidity and to reduced efficiency.

The preference for stability was a response to the risks and vulnerability of a small, open economy. Risk management required the development of mechanisms of voluntary solidarism and the recognition of interdependencies, as reflected in the coffee pact. Feelings of solidarism were intensified by the ethnic, economic, and social homogeneity of Costa Rican society and by the country's small size. The ideology of solidarism and equality provided a springboard for launching the social security system in the 1940s, and successive administrations of different persuasions have preserved and intensified this strong concern with equity.

Growth and structural transformation during 1950–85 led to a more complex society, to less personal contact, and to a less commonly held ideology. Costa Ricans found it difficult to reproduce the voluntary social contract of the coffee sector in other sectors, and legislated replicas have been less efficient. Solidarism was replaced by an increasingly unsustainable system of legislated entitlements and forced transfers.

The Legacy of the 1940s and the Change in Ideology

For more than three decades Costa Rica experienced major transformations that slowly modified the exceptional conditions of 1950. During this time the country's political and economic institutions evolved from the liberalism, softened by a strong voluntary solidarism, that had characterized the earlier development toward an interventionist, protectionist welfare state. The main turning point was in 1948, when the proponents of a new social-democratic view gained power and began to replace the local version of a liberal ideology. The events of the 1940s, including the 1948 civil war, greatly influenced the situation in 1950. The political arena has since been dominated by the actors of the 1940s.

The Calderón Guardia administration (1940–44) recorded significant achievements (the founding of the University of Costa Rica, the social security system, the Labor Code, and the New Industries law) but also made political mistakes that led to the 1948 civil war. Young professionals, intellectuals, and small entrepreneurs, grouped in the Centro para el Estudio de los Problemas Nacionales, opposed the administration and began to develop a new, "scientific and pragmatic" social-democratic ideology that gradually replaced the liberal legacy of the previous century. This group was particularly worried about monoculture and foreign investment and strongly promoted industrialization.

When the Picado administration did not recognize the results of the 1948 presidential election, the young social democrats had an opportunity to seize power. Ruling by decree, the junta, led by Figueres, introduced major economic and political reforms. The army was abolished, the banking system was nationalized, the United Fruit Company was required to pay a 15 percent income tax, and several autonomous agencies were created, while the social reforms of the 1940s were retained. A new constitution, representing a compromise between the two struggling ideologies, was enacted in 1949. During the 1950–85 period new groups of small rural and urban entrepreneurs, professionals, and public sector employees used the power of the state to reduce the economic and political supremacy of the old coffee exporters and to try to capture the rents derived from a protectionist strategy of industrialization and the transfers available from the expanded social security system.

Before the 1950s income and wealth were associated with Ricardian land rents and exports of a vent-for-surplus. The successful exploitation of the comparative advantage in coffee increased the earnings of small-scale units of production, of landless workers, and of small noncoffee sectors that were allowed to share in the coffee pact as a preventive measure. The successful exploitation of the comparative advantage in bananas meant increased earnings by a foreign investor and increased tax revenues that were used to provide public goods such as infrastructure and education. Rents, therefore, were widely distributed among the population, for the most part through market forces, in response to technological considerations and factor scarcities.

During 1950–85 the old coffee alliance was gradually replaced by a new coalition of state-dependent groups located in public agencies, state-owned enterprises, and highly protected private sector enclaves whose income and wealth derived from their rent-seeking and revenue-seeking activities, through the manipulation of protectionist and interventionist policies. The distribution of the newly created quasi-rents increasingly took place in the political arena, through the legislation of explicit and implicit taxes and subsidies, instead of through the market, and reflected relative political power rather than economic competitiveness. The resulting entitlements exceeded available resources, eventually leading to a fiscal crisis.

Costa Rica in the 1950s: A Larger Government

The rural character of Costa Rican society in 1950 reflected a comparatively low productivity of labor in agriculture. Although 55 percent of the labor force was employed in agriculture, the sector contributed only 41 percent of GDP. Coffee and bananas accounted for 97 percent of total exports, for about 66 percent of value added in agriculture, and for 25 percent of GDP. Subsistence production was already diminishing in importance. Manufacturing was small and primitive. Despite increasing demands for services by a rapidly growing population, the government was small; only 6 percent of employed persons worked in the public sector. Comparatively favorable social indicators reflected the availability of a skilled, literate labor force and a substantial investment in human capital.

The structure of society corresponded to the simple organization of the economy and the dominance of coffee. It included the participants in the coffee pact—the prominent exporters as well as the small producers and landless laborers—and the associated bankers and importing merchants. It also included the isolated banana plantation workers, small groups of artisans, and a relatively influential rural middle class. The labor unions in the banana plantations had been banned because of their affiliation with the Communist party, and those in urban areas were inactive. The Chambers of Commerce, of Agriculture, and of Industry were not active, either. An urban middle class of small merchants and entrepreneurs, professionals, graduates from the recently created University of Costa Rica, teachers, technicians, managers, and white-collar employees had been actively participating in the political arena, but, because of the small domestic market, they lacked economic opportunities outside the traditional exporting activities. It was these groups that fortuitously gained access to power with the 1948 civil war and expressed their aspirations through the Partido Liberación Nacional (PLN).

The ostensible justification for the civil war was to protect the electoral process, but the war also gave the new social democrats an opportunity to gain power and to govern under exceptional circumstances. They dramatically reoriented the country's economic and social policies. Costa Rica's simple, narrow economy offered few opportunities for new entrepreneurial ventures. The groups were eager to use the power of the state to diversify the country's productive structure and to generate opportunities for entrepreneurship and rent seeking. Nationalization of the banks was the most important step.

Although the political agenda of the new social democrats was to take power from the traditional exporters, importers, and bankers, they wanted not to destroy the economy but to create new economic opportunities for themselves. Most members of the emerging groups lacked financial resources and resented their limited access to bank credit (a consequence of World War II and of fiscal mismanagement during the 1940s). The nationalization of the banks provided an opportunity to create a new set of entrepreneurs. For similar reasons they urged the diversification of productive structures to allow greater participation by new social forces, encouraged cooperatives as instruments for the survival of small property, and supported the idea of the state as a scientific promoter and organizer of economic activity. They used government to develop infrastructure (roads, electricity, and the like) and to create numerous autonomous institutions intended to promote economic development while avoiding the concentration of power. Although they preserved the social security reforms of the 1940s, they did not expand them. Structural transformation, growth, and the modernization of the state, rather than equity, were their main concerns in the 1950s. They redistributed wealth, but in the form of new opportunities for the middle classes.

The dramatic reforms of the junta were followed by the conservative Ulate administration (1949–53). Economic growth, fueled by the rapidly expanding international economy and high coffee prices, was brisk, despite occasional setbacks caused by floods and drought. Rovira Mas (1987, p. 23) called this period "a brief oligarchic restoration." For Ulate, coming to power after a decade of fiscal mismanagement, the main objectives were to sustain budgetary and balance of payments surpluses and to maintain the external value of the colón—easy goals, in view of the buoyant world market conditions. In addition, the public debt was substantially reduced, and price stability was restored. No new reforms were introduced, except for the creation of the Central Bank, but neither were any of the earlier institutional innovations revised. In the movement toward a new version of the state, there was already no turning back.

The election of Figueres (1953–58) accelerated these institutional changes, as numerous new autonomous agencies were created. Despite their desire to take power away from the coffee exporters, the social democrats nevertheless understood the key role that coffee played in the economy, and coffee exports were promoted in innovative ways. Additional considerations were the opportunities presented by the extraordinarily high price of coffee on world markets—the price increased from US$0.67 a pound in 1949 to US$1.49 a pound in 1954—and the desire to strengthen the country's importing capacity, domestic demand, and tax base to facilitate the introduction of new activities.

At the international level the Figueres administration actively campaigned for the cartelization of the coffee-producing countries. Domestically, it promoted the use of fertilizers, new varieties, and modern technologies to increase yields. Most of the rapidly expanding agricultural credit from the nationalized banking system was targeted toward investment in coffee. Yields increased sharply to become the highest in the world. At the same time, the Figueres administration increased the income tax on the banana companies from 15 to 30 percent and negotiated higher wages for plantation workers.

The ultimate objective of the social-democratic economic policies of the 1950s was the diversification of the country's economic output and the creation of new entrepreneurial groups. Among the new crops and activities promoted were basic grains for domestic consumption, beef and dairy cattle, sugarcane, cotton, and fishing. Construction of infrastructure—highways and feeder roads, bridges, ports, airstrips, electricity-generating plants, and industrial water supplies—and technological improvement through research and extension were emphasized. Redistributive initiatives sought to serve both equity objectives and the enlargement of the domestic market. The expansion of employment in the public sector was also expected to increase domestic demand. But nationalistic fears about foreign investment, and the absence of industrialists among the main PLN leaders, prevented the group from openly supporting the industrialization bills debated during those earlier years.

The debate about incentives for industrialization went on for more than six years and led to the Industrial Promotion Law of 1959. The Chamber of Industry, already influential and 100 members strong, launched a massive campaign on behalf of manufacturing interests to promote passage of this bill. Opposition came from the Chamber of Commerce, the oldest private sector association in the country. The conservative Echandi administration (1958–62), fearful that the PLN would claim another victory in Congress, sponsored the bill.

The opposing forces were the emerging class of small manufacturers, on the one hand, and the established coffee growers and importers of consumer goods, on the other. Given the strength of the latter, it is doubtful that the Chamber of Industry could have won, had it not been for two external factors: the drastic decline in coffee prices and the growing momentum of the Central American integration movement, sponsored by the UN Economic Commission for Latin America (ECLA). (This followed the clear historical pattern of important policy shifts always being triggered by major external shocks.) The industrialization bill, which was mainly a response to those immediate pressures, was soon superseded by the protectionism of the Central American Common Market (CACM). The conflict between the new industrialists and the old exporters deepened, however, when the Echandi administration showed reluctance to sign the 1960 integration treaties.

The rapid growth of the early 1950s, fueled by the postwar expansion of traditional exports, was interrupted toward the end of the decade, when coffee prices declined. During 1950–63 growth was accompanied by substantial structural transformation. While the share of agriculture in GDP fell from 41 to 26 percent and the share of manufacturing hardly increased, the share of general government and other public sector–related activities, such as banking, transport, and public utilities, rose from 21 to 30 percent. The proportion of the labor force employed in agriculture declined from 55 to 50 percent, and the share of manufacturing did not change at all, but the share of the personal services sector increased from 18 to 24 percent. Public sector employment grew at 8.8 percent a year, as against 1.9 percent in the private sector. The decline in the relative importance of agriculture thus reflected the expansion not of manufacturing but of government and related services.

Growth resulted essentially from the exploitation of pronounced comparative advantages in and expanding world demand for coffee and bananas and from major productivity gains in the cultivation of several crops. Because of the wide ownership of factors of production in coffee, large segments of the population benefited. The new crops and products that were promoted—sugar, dairy products, beef, and cotton—were more capital-intensive than coffee and were usually cultivated by larger landowners. Sharply increased taxation of the banana companies, in addition to high coffee and import taxes, financed heavy investments in infrastructure and the expansion of public sector employment. The great net winners of the fruits of economic growth in the 1950s, therefore, were the public sector and the growing bureaucracy. In 1953, for example, on the basis of the fiscal surplus accumulated by the Ulate administration, the PLN legislated an additional thirteenth month of salary (*aguinaldo*) for all public employees, which they still receive. Specific groups within the private sector were especially advantaged, such as new firms engaged in constructing infrastructure and government-sponsored housing. It appears that the distribution of household income deteriorated during the 1950s, as most gains accrued to an expanding, but still small, middle class.

Costa Rica in the 1960s: Protectionism

In the mid-1960s Costa Rica was a small, rural, open economy with an unexploited agricultural frontier still available. Between 1950 and 1963 policies to promote diversification had reduced the share of coffee and bananas from 97 to 72 percent of total exports. Beef and sugar grew to account for 11 percent, reflecting in part the reallocation of the U.S. sugar quota after the Cuban revolution. The public sector had grown significantly: central government expenditures had increased 5.2 times since 1950; numerous autonomous institutions with separate budgets had been created; and public sector employment had doubled. Life expectancy had climbed to 63 years of age, and illiteracy had declined to 14 percent of the population. The structure of society had not changed much, however, except for the steady expansion of the middle classes.

Increasingly, industrialization and participation in the CACM had become key components of the PLN agenda to diversify the economy. The Echandi administration, in contrast, heavily emphasized agriculture, which had been badly hurt by the drop in world coffee prices and the decline in banana export revenues. Exporters, represented by Jorge Borbón, the chairman of the Coffee Office and minister of agriculture and industry, lobbied for and obtained subsidized targeted credit and other advantages for agriculture. For the first time, funds borrowed abroad were used for production credit rather than for infrastructure. The Chamber of Industry was unsuccessful in lobbying for a reallocation of a portion of those funds to manufacturing. Borbón, with the support of his brother-in-law Manuel Jiménez, chairman of the Chamber of Sugar Producers, also opposed participation in the CACM. They claimed that Costa Rica was essentially a country of farmers, that the industrial incentives were nothing more than tax evasion schemes, and that little was to be gained, since the Central American economies were competitive rather than complementary. They were able to block the signing of the treaties—probably the last time that the agricultural interests, as a whole, defeated the industrial interests. After the victory of the PLN and the advent of the Orlich administration (1962–66), Costa Rica formally joined the customs union, in 1963.

By joining the CACM, Costa Rica consolidated its choice of a protectionist strategy of import-substituting industrialization. This step, which followed an interlude during which an attempt was made to promote manufacturing on the basis of the minuscule domestic market, represented the adoption of an intermediate trade policy. Costa Rica chose to look outward with respect to the rest of Central America and inward with respect to the rest of the world. Fields (1988) called this "export-led growth within a regionally protected framework." It may just as well be termed "import substitution at the regional level," since the overall pattern was one of extremely high protection, with many triple-digit effective tariff rates. The Central American market was never sufficiently large to avoid high costs and substantial monopoly rents. The dispersion of the rates of effective protection was very high. There was a permissive attitude toward granting protection and ample opportunities for rent seeking. Politically influential sectors managed to obtain especially favorable incentives, while other sectors lagged substantially behind. Given the strength of pressure groups in Costa Rica, it is not surprising that "when all the determinants of effective protection were taken into account, Costa Rica was the most highly protective country in the region" (Rapoport 1978). The implicit subsidies increased the economic and political power of the industrialists, leading to further privileges.

"Economic planning" was introduced in Costa Rica in 1963 as a precondition for the disbursement of funds from the Alliance for Progress. It was clearly a task for which the Costa Rican government lacked organizational talent; the required information, human resources, and administrative channels were not in place. As one of the pioneers recalled, when the government was faced with the insistence that a plan be completed before funds could be used, numbers were invented. The neoliberal Trejos administration (1966–70) abandoned the idea of drafting a national plan but moved successfully to a more formal analysis of the operation of the economy. In addition, during both administrations specific projects to promote particular crops were a by-product of planning.

The Orlich administration encouraged the further improvement of coffee yields and Costa Rica's participation in the International Coffee Agreement. To compensate for the resulting strengthening of the coffee classes, the administration also promoted the formation of cooperatives of small coffee producers. The establishment of the highly successful Federation of Coffee Cooperatives was a serious challenge to the old exporting *beneficios*.

Until 1956 the United Fruit Company (United Brands) had exercised absolute control over Costa Rica's banana production. In that year it was joined by the Standard Fruit Company (Castle and Cook) and in 1965 by the Banana Development Corporation (Del Monte) and COBAL. Substantial increases in production were made by domestic entrepreneurs, who signed long-term contracts with the multinationals for sales at a fixed price. By 1975 these independent producers were growing 41 percent of the bananas exported, on plantations that were large by Costa Rican standards but small when compared with those run by the fruit companies. Among these new producers were numerous professionals and politicians, many without any previous experience in the banana trade, who received abundant subsidized credit from the nationalized banks for up to 90 percent of their total investment. The banana program was financed by the Costa Rican government against the opposition of the World Bank, which refused to fund it. Organized in the powerful ASBANA (Association of Banana Producers), the new entrepreneurs represented an emerging class of politicians turned businessmen, with massive support from the state. The foreign companies began to replace bananas with African oil palm and other crops and eventually abandoned the production of bananas to avoid increasingly costly labor strikes. Other sectors similarly promoted by the PLN were sugar, beef, and cotton. Conflicts between the sugarcane growers and the sugar refineries were solved by the creation of LAICA, a tripartite institutional arrangement similar to that for coffee, and a conflict between beef producers and exporters was settled through the creation of a state-owned meat-processing firm, which later became a cooperative (Montecillos).

The highest rates of sustained economic growth in recent times were experienced in the late 1960s. Between 1963 and 1973 GDP grew at 7.2 percent a year. Before Costa Rica joined the CACM, the rates of growth of agriculture and of manufacturing were similar, but thereafter industry grew twice as rapidly (10.8 percent a year, compared with 5.5 percent), particularly in the early years of expansion of trade within the customs union. The share of manufacturing in GDP increased from 14 to 20 percent in real terms, while the share of agriculture declined in nominal terms but remained fairly constant in real terms. This reflected a significant deterioration of the domestic terms of trade of agriculture. The proportion of the labor force employed in agriculture declined to 38 percent, whereas a decade after Costa Rica had joined the CACM the share of manufacturing in employment had not changed much. Employment increased more rapidly in the public than in the private sector.

Exports continued to be Costa Rica's engine of growth. The volume of exports increased 17.4 percent a year during 1965–69. The high rates of GDP growth reflected the dramatic increase of exports to Central America. The share of manufactures in total exports climbed from 4 percent in 1963 to 29 percent in 1979. The same period saw a substantial expansion of traditional agricultural exports. For 1965–69 export volumes increased 9.4 percent a year for coffee, 22.2 percent for bananas, 12.0 percent for beef, 13.4 percent for sugar, and 25.2 percent for all other exports (Céspedes, Di Mare, and Jiménez 1986, p. 175).

Given the high import intensity of manufacturing, import substitution was successful as long as exports of primary commodities were growing rapidly. Under the protectionist policies, however, the rents extracted from natural resources on the basis of comparative advantages began to be used to support the more capital-intensive manufacturing sector. The consequences of this reallocation of resources did not become evident until a decade later. Growth in the 1960s reflected, in addition to expanding exports, significant increases in agricultural productivity (the consequence of augmented land yields, greater skills, and a better utilization of labor in the economy).

A substantial improvement in the distribution of income and a major alleviation of poverty also took place during the 1960s. High rates of output growth, combined with great occupational mobility, led to higher incomes for large segments of the population and a more egalitarian distribution. The shares of households with intermediate incomes increased, mostly at the expense of those with the highest incomes. Furthermore, the proportion of the poor declined from about 50 percent of the total population in the early 1960s to about 20 percent in the mid-1970s. Among Latin American countries, Costa Rica had the highest rate of growth of employment in modern nonagricultural activities and the quickest reduction of underemployment and of subutilization of the labor force. It was also the country with the highest rate of absorption of the labor force.

All this reflected considerable enlargement of the modern sectors. Dualism was rapidly eliminated. At least 75 percent of the labor force became salaried. Differences in the distribution of skills within the labor force were the main determinants of inequality. The share of labor in total factor payments increased from 57 to 63 percent during 1960–71. These improvements were not the result of government policies or redistributive measures; rather, they reflected the high rate of growth, the modernization of the economy, the process of structural transformation, the integration of the labor market, and the high level of education and skill acquisition of the labor force. Improvements in distribution and poverty alleviation were the fruits of growth acting on favorable initial conditions.

Until the mid-1970s average wages actually increased faster than the legal minimum wage, reflecting a growing demand for labor in the modern sectors of the economy. These wage increases could not be attributed to unionization. Factor-price policies (high payroll taxes and subsidies for capital utilization) actually favored capital over labor. Moreover, major administrative and organizational constraints slowed the universalization of social security. The system had been set up on the basis of contributions by the workers, the employers, and the state, and eligibility required a permanent salaried job. This excluded the self-employed, who were mostly in agriculture, and the unemployed. Because of the weak organizational framework, health services were offered first in the large urban centers, and the ceiling on the contribution implied that the poorest paid the highest proportion of their wage to the system.

Costa Rica in the 1970s: Redistribution

By the early 1970s, as a result of substantial economic growth and significant modernization, Costa Rica had a considerably more diversified and complex economy than in 1950. The population had doubled, and so had income per capita. Agriculture was no longer the most important sector, and new, more skilled occupations attracted the labor force. Rapid urbanization had significantly reduced the rural character of society. As the labor force grew, the favorable land-to-labor ratio shrank, modifying comparative advantages and generating strong pressures for job creation. Employment in the public sector had reached 15 percent of the total. Despite protectionism, the economy was even more open than before as a result of increased trade with Central America, a growing demand for imported inputs and capital goods, and the continued strong performance of traditional exports. Coffee and bananas represented just over one-half of total exports. Total imports amounted to 35 percent of GDP, and the country had begun to use substantial amounts of foreign savings for domestic investment. Life expectancy had increased to 68 years of age, and illiteracy had dropped to less than 10 percent of the population.

The state-promoted accumulation of human capital, through education, training, and health care, even for the children of the poor, and the natural rise in wages through the working of the labor market were the most effective mechanisms for improving the distribution of income and for alleviating poverty. Rapid economic growth had made possible the steady incorporation of new groups into a modern, more affluent society. Participation by new groups in the process of development was limited, however, by serious organizational problems. Reaching the scattered population beyond the Central Valley, particularly on the Atlantic coast, was a great challenge because of the high per capita cost of the infrastructure required. This process was begun by the Trejos administration, which built the first road from the Central Valley to Port Limón. Additional problems were presented by marginal sectors, which did not participate in the labor market, the main mechanism for income improvement.

The Figueres (1970–74) and Oduber (1974–78) administrations, going beyond the traditional emphasis on growth, highlighted equity issues and adopted the first major redistributive policies. The ceiling on social security contributions was eliminated in 1971, and the movement toward universal coverage was accelerated. Social security services were offered to the self-employed and to the indigent. Health clinics reached into the countryside. The Instituto Mixto de Ayuda Social was created to provide assistance to the poorest. After a lively debate, the family allowances program (*asignaciones familiares*) was adopted in 1974, to be financed with additional payroll taxes. Among its goals was the redistribution of 2 percent of national income to the poorest 20 percent by 1978. It included components for health, food, nutrition, housing, land, training, and pensions. The program suffered from organizational deficiencies that limited its success. A large portion of the funds was spent on logistics and staffing and did not reach the targeted beneficiaries, while less-poor nontargeted beneficiaries also shared in the distribution of food and other services.

Specific distributive goals were also incorporated in wage policies after the first oil crisis, in 1974. Adjustments to the legal minimum wage included a wide range of increases that were inversely related to existing wage levels. Whereas in 1974 the lowest wages increased 41 percent, the highest rose only 10 percent. This policy may have had a limited distributive impact, since most low-income households were in rural areas, where minimum wages were less effectively enforced, or were not wage earners. Growth itself had earlier promoted equity; the explicit shift of emphasis toward equity, at a time when growth was beginning to decline, turned out to be less successful. The expanded welfare system created an excess demand for the available resources, which made macroeconomic management more difficult, particularly in view of the acute external shocks of the late 1970s. The 1976 coffee boom had provided an opportunity to expand the welfare system beyond sustainable levels, and the attempt to incorporate everybody into a system of forced transfers and other entitlements led to a major fiscal crisis when additional foreign savings were not available to continue financing the outlays.

The promotion of manufacturing, in the context of the CACM, initially accelerated growth, as a result of increased trade. These high rates of growth were not entirely sustained in the 1970s; the early, easy stages of import substitution were exhausted, the inefficiencies brought about by protectionism limited competitiveness in markets outside the CACM, and exports were discouraged. The artificial incentives became less and less powerful, and the constraints imposed by the size of the regional market became binding. Productivity growth slowed. Increasingly powerful groups devoted more and more resources to directly unproductive activities, and their success added new distortions to the system. The high degree of political participation typical of Costa Rica led to the proliferation of pressure groups that pursued their own interests. As additional groups were formally incorporated into the distribution of entitlements, privileges had to be granted to almost every sector. The public sector became larger and larger, introducing additional bureaucratic controls and regulations. Autonomous institutions and state-owned firms became important pressure groups in their own right. The nationalized banks, which had behaved as a private banking system at first, became increasingly politicized. Financial repression and nationalization constrained institutional growth and left Costa Rica with an obsolete financial system.

The net result was an unsystematic pattern of protection. Within the byzantine mosaic of implicit taxes and subsidies, it became difficult to identify the net winners and the net losers. Protectionism was not an orderly strategy but the haphazard result of historical events and relative political strengths.

The multiplicity of entitlements reflected participation in policymaking by wide segments of the population. In the end, Costa Rica was undecided between promoting manufacturing and promoting agriculture. Whereas the production of most final consumer goods was heavily protected, the production of raw materials and intermediate goods was discouraged. High levels of effective protection also developed within agriculture. Some specific activities—such as rice production, which was pursued capital-intensively on large landholdings—received excessive incentives, while other activities were penalized. All this brought about a slow deceleration of growth (interrupted only by the coffee boom) and the end of the continued improvement in income distribution that had characterized the previous decade. In addition, the voluntary reciprocity that had prevailed earlier was steadily replaced by compulsory transfers that were made to prevent political disaffection. These problems were accentuated by the major external shocks of the 1970s.

Nationalistic feelings were not important in policy decisions until 1970, when the Costa Rican student movement prevented an agreement with ALCOA for aluminum exploitation. Increasingly, however, key PLN leaders adopted ECLA's ideas about protectionism, nationalism, and planning. These ideas provided the ideological background for the creation of the Costa Rican Development Corporation (CODESA), the instrument for the state's direct intervention in production activities, and represented the new approach of PLN leaders close to Oduber. CODESA's purposes went beyond the modernization of the public sector and the promotion of new private entrepreneurs espoused by the young social democrats of the 1940s. The role of the state was now extended into productive activities that competed directly with the private sector. These activities never became profitable, but CODESA's unrestricted access to Central Bank credit contributed significantly to the deterioration of public finances and the crowding out of the private sector from credit portfolios. Its enterprises used 18 percent of all domestic credit but contributed only 1.8 percent of GDP and 0.3 percent of total employment. CODESA, unrestricted by the political controls typical of government agencies or by the market discipline of private firms, became a major factory of new quasi-rents. The larger the project, irrespective of profitability, the larger the rents created. Productive activities that competed directly with the private sector created tensions in the symbiotic relationship that had developed between the state, in the hands of the PLN, and the industrialists.

The confrontation reflected the increasing power within the PLN of the politician-entrepreneurs, whose strength derived from their control of the state. From their prominent positions as heads of the autonomous institutions and state-owned enterprises, as well as in the executive branch, they accumulated immense influence over economic policies. In view of the complexity of the state and of the tasks performed, these technocrats earned high salaries and enjoyed a prominent social status. These advantages allowed them to venture into private business, where they made use of their privileged access to credit and to other implicit subsidies. During PLN administrations they were close to the highest levels of government; when not in power, they ran their highly protected enterprises. CODESA represented the confluence of the interests of this group and of those who favored greater state intervention.

The extension of state economic activity coincided with the strengthening of the middle classes and the proliferation of organizations created by and for them. The expansion of the middle classes was closely associated with the growth of the public sector and, in particular, of the autonomous institutions. The largest number of lobbying associations represented two groups: professionals and government employees, and (mostly) large agricultural, manufacturing, and commercial entrepreneurs. Small and medium-size producers had fewer organizations of their own, except for the coffee cooperatives. Lizano Fait (1975) noted that whereas the productive middle classes (those involved in directly productive activities) were interested in profitability and innovation and were subject to risk, the bureaucratic middle classes were more interested in the stability of their jobs than in entrepreneurship and more interested in the level of their wages than in profits. The productive middle classes had a high propensity to save, but the bureaucratic middle classes attempted to copy the consumption patterns of the upper classes. Their main demands were redistributive and attempted to prevent the operation of market forces. Protectionism and the too rapid expansion of the public sector led to the rapid growth and strengthening of the bureaucratic middle classes and the relative stagnation of the productive middle classes. Because they were in charge of important public services, the bureaucrats managed to extract important privileges by threatening strikes. The PLN cultivated these middle classes through wage increases and income transfers and promoted a certain mobility of the lower classes into the bureaucracy to reduce popular pressures and allow the middle classes to absorb the most talented members of the lower classes. Increasing government intervention was the mechanism used to favor the upper classes and the bureaucracy simultaneously. The former were granted opportunities for rent seeking, and the latter were allowed artificially high levels of consumption. As long as there was rapid economic growth and an ample supply of foreign savings, the system was stable.

Costa Rica in the 1980s: Crisis

The extraordinary expansion of export earnings during the coffee boom and increased foreign borrowing provided new opportunities for creating rents and rapidly expanding aggregate spending. When the boom was over, it was difficult to adjust to the decline in real income. The influential manufacturing sector was dependent on imported inputs (because of the high import-intensity of protected activities), and the powerful public sector unions prevented any reductions in government expenditures. The authorities chose to postpone adjustment by increasingly borrowing abroad until foreign funds were no longer available. Then domestic credit expanded, the private sector was crowded out of credit portfolios, and inflation and devaluation ensued. Inflation and devaluation reflected income entitlements that added up to a total well above the available income from productive activities and the country's importing capacity. As a result, the exchange rate and the financial system collapsed.

The crisis exhibited a clear ratchet effect. During each boom, entitlements expanded. Powerful groups took advantage of the new income levels to incorporate the claims of new groups and so expand their political base. When the economy contracted, it was politically impossible to eliminate already established entitlements outright, and exclusions became implicit, through inflation and crowding out. For decades, abundant foreign savings helped to carry this cycle to ever higher levels. When almost every segment of society had been incorporated into the entitlements and foreign savings stopped flowing in, a severe crisis was unavoidable.

By the late 1970s, even before the crisis exploded, there were signs that inequality in income distribution was no longer declining. When the crisis struck, income distribution became more unequal. During the worst three years output per capita declined 17 percent, unemployment rates doubled, and inflation reached three digits. Between 1980 and 1982 real wages declined 40 percent and consumption per capita dropped 27 percent. Poverty increased, to encompass 30 percent of the population. Between 1971 and 1983 real income in rural areas declined only for the poorest 10 percent of the households, but in urban areas it declined for all but the 10 percent richest households. The crisis produced a generalized impoverishment of the urban population and a significant concentration of income. The growth-reducing accumulation of redistributive entitlements eventually hampered equity.

Note

1. Directly unproductive activities are described in Bhagwati 1982.

Statistical Appendix A
Costa Rica

Table A-1. Costa Rica: Land Use, 1963, 1973, and 1976
(thousands of hectares)

Use	1963	1973	1976
Cropland	610.0	490.6	527.2
Annual crops	143.1	141.0	187.6
Commercial horticulture	1.4	3.3	4.0
Fallow	180.0	124.8	124.8
Other cropland	85.0	14.3	14.3
Subtotal	409.5	283.4	330.7
Tree crops	200.5	207.2	196.5
Livestock	935.7	1,558.1	1,738.0
Natural pasture	535.7	825.6	921.1
Improved pasture	400.0	732.5	816.9
Forest	1,097.1	1,000.1	1,000.0
Woodland	819.3	716.5	716.5
Shrubland	227.8	283.6	283.5
Cities and roads	25.3	73.9	101.9
Not identified	2,468.8	2,013.2	1,768.8
Total	5,135.9	5,135.9	5,135.9

Source: Costa Rica, Dirección General de Estadística y Censos, 1963, 1973; Costa Rica, Ministerio de Agricultura, Oficina de Planificación Sectorial Agropecuaria, 1979.

Table A-2. Costa Rica: Population Growth, 1950–85

Year	Population (thousands)	Growth rate (annual percentage change)
1950	858	n.a.
1951	887	3.4
1952	918	3.5
1953	951	3.6
1954	986	3.7
1955	1,024	3.8
1956	1,067	4.2
1957	1,109	3.9
1958	1,150	3.7
1959	1,192	3.7
1960	1,235	3.7
1961	1,286	4.0
1962	1,330	3.4
1963	1,380	3.7
1964	1,431	3.7
1965	1,482	3.6
1966	1,534	3.5
1967	1,585	3.3
1968	1,635	3.2
1969	1,684	3.0
1970	1,735	3.0
1971	1,779	2.5
1972	1,826	2.6
1973	1,872	2.5
1974	1,919	2.5
1975	1,968	2.5
1976	2,018	2.5
1977	2,070	2.6
1978	2,126	2.7
1979	2,184	2.7
1980	2,245	2.8
1981	2,306	2.8
1982	2,370	2.7
1983	2,433	2.7
1984	2,497	2.6
1985	2,562	2.6

n.a. Not applicable.

Source: Costa Rica, Dirección General de Estadística y Censos, and Centro Latinoamericano de Demografía, 1976, 1983.

Table A-3. Costa Rica: Birth, Death, and Population Growth Rates, Selected Years, 1910–82

Year	Per thousand population		Growth rate (percent)
	Birthrate	Death rate	
Period averages[a]			
1910–20	46.3	29.8	1.7
1920–30	45.7	27.1	1.9
1930–40	45.3	23.2	2.2
1940–50	44.5	18.2	2.6
1950–55	47.6	12.4	3.5
1955–60	48.3	10.8	3.8
1960–65	45.3	9.1	3.6
1965–70	38.3	7.9	3.0
1970	33.3	7.3	2.6
1971	31.7	6.5	2.5
1972	31.5	6.5	2.5
1973	29.9	5.6	2.4
1974	29.6	5.4	2.4
1975	29.6	5.2	2.4
1976	29.8	5.0	2.5
1977	31.1	4.6	2.7
1978	32.1	4.3	2.8
1979	32.0	4.0	2.8
1980	31.0	4.0	2.7
1981	30.0	4.0	2.6
1982	30.0	4.0	2.6

Note: Figures differ from those in table A-2 because different methodologies were used to estimate population figures for noncensus years.

a. Average annual rates for the corresponding period.

Source: Academia de Centroamérica 1981; Rosero Bixby 1980.

Table A-4. Costa Rica: Population, by Age and Sex, Selected Years, 1950–85
(thousands)

Category	1950	1960	1970	1980	1985
Total population	858.2	1,236.1	1,735.1	2,245.4	2,562.0
0–14 years old	373.2	586.5	799.8	863.9	937.5
15–64 years old	455.8	612.2	879.8	1,301.6	1,526.6
65 years and older	29.3	37.3	55.5	79.9	97.8
Men	431.3	622.7	875.0	1,134.5	1,293.5
0–14 years old	189.3	298.0	406.5	440.9	478.5
15–64 years old	228.0	307.0	442.3	656.5	770.2
65 years and older	13.9	17.7	26.2	37.0	44.8
Women	426.9	613.4	860.1	1,111.0	1,268.5
0–14 years old	183.9	288.5	393.3	423.0	459.0
15–64 years old	227.7	305.2	437.5	645.0	756.4
65 years and older	15.3	19.7	29.3	42.9	53.1

Source: See table A-2.

*Table A-5. Costa Rica: Economically Active Population, by Age and Sex,
Selected Years, 1950–85*
(thousands)

Category	1950	1960	1970	1980	1985
Total labor force	286.5	364.5	519.2	768.1	899.7
12–14 years old	16.1	14.5	18.5	23.4	16.9
15–64 years old	259.3	339.1	484.7	726.4	863.2
65 years and older	11.1	11.0	16.0	18.3	19.6
Men	245.0	308.0	422.5	588.5	677.1
12–14 years old	14.6	12.7	15.4	19.0	14.1
15–64 years old	220.1	285.1	392.3	552.9	645.4
65 years and older	10.3	10.2	14.8	16.6	17.6
Women	41.5	56.6	96.5	179.5	222.7
12–14 years old	1.5	1.8	3.0	4.3	2.9
15–64 years old	39.2	54.0	92.4	173.5	217.8
65 years and older	0.8	0.8	1.1	1.7	2.0

Source: Computed from tables A-4 and A-8.

Table A-6. Costa Rica: Employed Labor Force, by Age and Sex, Selected Years, 1950–85
(thousands)

Category	1950	1960	1970	1980	1985
Total employed labor force	274.8	339.1	481.9	722.7	838.1
12–14 years old	13.4	10.1	11.4	18.8	14.4
15–64 years old	250.9	318.8	456.1	686.0	804.5
65 years and older	10.5	11.0	14.4	17.9	19.2
Men	233.4	283.6	389.4	557.3	633.1
12–14 years old	11.9	8.5	9.3	15.4	12.0
15–64 years old	211.8	265.6	366.8	525.8	603.9
65 years and older	9.7	10.2	13.4	16.1	17.2
Women	41.4	55.4	92.4	165.5	205.1
12–14 years old	1.5	1.5	2.1	3.3	2.5
15–64 years old	39.1	53.1	89.4	160.5	200.6
65 years and older	0.8	0.8	1.0	1.7	2.0

Source: Computed from tables A-5 and A-9.

Table A-7. Costa Rica: Unemployed Labor Force, by Age and Sex, Selected Years, 1950–85
(thousands)

Category	1950	1960	1970	1980	1985
Total unemployed labor force	11.7	25.4	37.3	45.4	61.6
12–14 years old	2.7	4.4	7.1	4.6	2.5
15–64 years old	8.4	20.3	28.6	40.4	58.7
65 years and older	0.6	0.0	1.6	0.4	0.4
Men	11.6	24.4	33.1	31.2	44.0
12–14 years old	2.7	4.2	6.1	3.6	2.1
15–64 years old	8.3	19.5	25.5	27.1	41.5
65 years and older	0.6	0.0	1.4	0.5	0.4
Women	0.1	1.2	4.1	14.0	17.6
12–14 years old	0.0	0.3	0.9	1.0	0.4
15–64 years old	0.1	0.9	3.0	13.0	17.2
65 years and older	0.0	0.0	0.1	0.0	0.0

Source: Computed from tables A-5 and A-9.

Table A-8. Costa Rica: Labor Force Participation Rates, by Age and Sex, Selected Years, 1950–85
(percent)

Category	1950	1963	1973	1980[a]	1985[a]
Total population	52.8	49.7	48.4	49.5	50.5
12–14 years old	27.8	17.2	13.4	13.8	10.6
15–64 years old	56.8	55.4	55.1	55.8	56.5
65 years and older	37.8	29.5	28.8	22.9	20.2
Men					
12–14 years old	50.0	29.7	22.0	21.9	17.5
15–64 years old	96.5	92.9	88.7	84.2	83.8
65 years and older	74.1	57.6	59.5	44.9	39.5
Women					
12–14 years old	5.2	4.4	4.4	5.2	3.8
15–64 years old	17.3	17.7	21.1	26.7	28.8
65 years and older	5.6	4.1	3.9	4.0	3.8

a. As of July.

Source: Costa Rica, Dirección General de Estadística y Censos, 1950, 1963, 1973; Costa Rica, Dirección General de Estadística y Censos, and Ministerio de Trabajo y Seguridad Social, various years.

*Table A-9. Costa Rica: Open Unemployment Rates, by Age and Sex,
Selected Years, 1950–85*
(percent)

Category	1950	1963	1973	1980[a]	1985[a]
Total labor force	4.1	6.9	7.3	5.9	6.8
12–14 years old	16.5	30.5	37.5	19.8	16.0
15–64 years old	3.2	6.0	5.9	5.6	6.8
65 years and older	5.3	0.0	9.2	2.4	2.7
Men	4.8	7.9	8.1	5.3	6.5
12–14 years old	18.2	32.9	39.3	19.0	15.4
15–64 years old	3.7	6.8	6.5	4.9	6.5
65 years and older	3.7	0.0	9.3	2.7	2.3
Women	0.2	2.1	4.3	7.8	7.9
12–14 years old	0.6	14.4	28.6	22.6	18.5
15–64 years old	0.2	1.7	3.3	7.5	7.9
65 years and older	0.0	..	8.4	0.0	0.0

.. Negligible.
a. As of July 1.
Source: Costa Rica, Dirección General de Estadística y Censos, 1950, 1963, 1973; Costa Rica, Dirección General de Estadística y Censos, and Ministerio de Trabajo y Seguridad Social, various years.

Table A-10. *Costa Rica: Open Unemployment and Visible and Invisible Underemployment Rates, 1976–83*
(percent)

Area and unemployment category	1976	1977	1978	1979	1980	1981	1982	1983
National								
Open unemployment[a]	6.2	4.6	4.5	4.9	5.9	8.7	9.4	9.0
Visible underemployment[b]	2.8	2.9	3.1	4.7	4.6	5.8	7.0	6.2
Open unemployment + visible underemployment	9.0	7.5	7.6	9.6	10.5	14.6	16.4	15.2
Invisible underemployment[c]	4.1	3.7	3.2	2.9	3.0	2.9	7.4	4.7
Total	13.1	11.2	10.8	12.5	13.5	17.4	23.8	19.9
Rural								
Open unemployment	5.8	4.1	3.6	4.2	5.9	8.4	8.3	8.7
Visible underemployment	3.3	3.2	3.2	5.2	4.8	7.2	7.8	7.2
Open unemployment + visible underemployment	9.1	7.3	6.8	9.4	10.7	15.6	16.1	15.9
Invisible underemployment	—	4.3	3.9	3.5	3.6	3.6	9.0	5.3
Total	—	11.6	10.7	12.9	14.3	19.2	25.1	21.2
Urban								
Open unemployment	6.8	5.2	5.6	5.7	5.9	9.1	10.5	9.3
Visible underemployment	2.2	2.5	3.1	4.1	4.3	4.3	6.1	5.1

Open unemployment + visible underemployment	9.0	7.7	8.7	9.8	10.2	13.4	16.6	14.4
Invisible underemployment	—	2.9	2.6	2.2	2.4	2.1	5.6	4.0
Total	—	10.6	11.3	12.0	12.6	15.5	22.2	18.4
San José Metropolitan Area								
Open unemployment	6.1	5.5	5.4	5.2	5.0	8.3	11.3	8.5
Visible underemployment	1.4	2.4	2.6	3.7	3.6	3.2	5.3	4.3
Open unemployment + visible underemployment	7.5	7.9	8.0	8.9	8.6	11.5	16.6	13.2
Invisible underemployment	—	2.9	2.4	2.1	2.1	2.0	5.6	3.6
Total	—	10.8	10.4	11.0	10.7	13.5	22.2	16.8

— Not available.

a. People actively looking for a job who could not find one, as of July 1.

b. People who could find only part-time jobs despite their wish to work more, as of July 1. The rate is the unemployment equivalent of the difference between 47 hours a week and the number of hours actually worked.

c. People who could only find work for less than the legal minimum wage, as of July 1.

Source: Céspedes and others 1983a; Costa Rica, Dirección General de Estadística y Censos, and Ministerio de Trabajo y Seguridad Social, various years.

Table A-11. Costa Rica: GDP, in Current and Constant 1966 Prices, 1950–85

Year	GDP, current prices		GDP, 1966 prices	
	Millions of colones	Growth rate (percent)	Millions of colones	Growth rate (percent)
1950	1,446.3	n.a.	1,772.9	n.a.
1951	1,563.5	8.1	1,863.3	5.1
1952	1,708.9	9.3	2,131.8	14.4
1953	1,886.6	10.4	2,190.0	2.7
1954	2,039.4	8.1	2,490.0	13.7
1955	2,225.0	9.1	2,405.1	−3.4
1956	2,291.7	3.0	2,403.1	−0.1
1957	2,500.4	9.1	2,674.6	11.3
1958	2,609.0	4.3	2,798.7	4.7
1959	2,678.5	2.7	2,919.8	4.3
1960	2,860.5	6.8	3,096.5	6.1
1961	2,929.3	2.4	3,066.9	−1.0
1962	3,186.6	8.8	3,316.8	8.1
1963	3,404.2	6.8	3,475.5	4.8
1964	3,608.2	6.0	3,619.7	4.1
1965	3,928.5	8.9	3,975.5	9.8
1966	3,186.6	9.2	4,288.4	7.9
1967	3,404.2	8.1	4,530.7	5.7
1968	3,608.2	10.6	4,914.6	8.5
1969	3,928.5	10.3	5,184.5	5.5
1970	6,524.5	15.4	5,573.5	7.5
1971	7,137.0	9.4	5,951.3	6.8
1972	8,215.8	15.1	6,438.0	8.2
1973	10,162.4	23.7	6,934.3	7.7
1974	13,215.7	30.0	7,318.8	5.5
1975	16,804.6	27.2	7,472.5	2.1
1976	20,675.6	23.0	7,884.8	5.5
1977	26,330.7	27.4	8,586.9	8.9
1978	30,193.9	14.7	9,125.1	6.3
1979	34,484.4	14.2	9,575.8	4.9
1980	41,405.5	20.0	9,647.8	0.8
1981	57,102.7	37.9	9,429.6	−2.3
1982	97,505.1	70.8	8,742.6	−7.3
1983	129,314.0	32.6	8,992.9	2.9
1984	163,010.9	26.1	9,714.5	8.0
1985	197,919.8	21.4	9,784.6	0.7

n.a. Not applicable.

Source: Banco Central de Costa Rica, *Cuentas Nacionales de Costa Rica*, various issues.

Table A-12.   Costa Rica: GDP *per Capita, in Current and Constant 1966 Prices, 1950–85*

Year	GDP per capita, current prices		GDP per capita, 1966 prices	
	Millions of colones	Growth rate (percent)	Millions of colones	Growth rate (percent)
1950	1,685	n.a.	2,066	n.a.
1951	1,762	4.6	2,100	1.6
1952	1,861	5.6	2,321	10.5
1953	1,983	6.6	2,302	–0.8
1954	2,068	4.3	2,525	9.7
1955	2,173	5.1	2,349	–7.0
1956	2,148	–1.2	2,252	–4.1
1957	2,255	5.0	2,413	7.1
1958	2,269	0.6	2,434	0.9
1959	2,247	–1.0	2,449	4.5
1960	2,314	3.0	2,505	2.3
1961	2,278	–1.6	2,385	–4.8
1962	2,396	5.2	2,494	4.6
1963	2,467	3.0	2,519	1.0
1964	2,522	2.2	2,530	0.4
1965	2,650	5.1	2,682	6.0
1966	2,796	5.5	2,796	4.3
1967	2,924	4.6	2,868	2.2
1968	3,135	7.2	3,006	5.2
1969	3,358	7.1	3,078	2.4
1970	3,760	12.0	3,212	4.4
1971	4,012	6.7	3,345	4.1
1972	4,500	12.2	3,527	5.4
1973	5,429	20.6	3,705	5.0
1974	6,886	26.8	3,813	2.9
1975	8,539	24.0	3,797	–0.4
1976	10,246	20.0	3,907	2.9
1977	12,716	24.1	4,147	6.1
1978	14,205	11.7	4,293	3.5
1979	15,792	11.2	4,385	2.1
1980	18,440	16.8	4,297	–2.0
1981	24,759	34.3	4,089	–4.8
1982	41,148	66.2	3,689	–9.8
1983	53,152	29.2	3,696	0.2
1984	65,280	22.8	3,890	5.2
1985	77,252	18.3	3,820	–1.8

n.a. Not applicable.
Source: Banco Central de Costa Rica, *Cuentas Nacionales de Costa Rica*, various issues.

Table A-13. Costa Rica: GNP and Gross National Income (GNI), GNP per Capita, and GNI per Capita, in Constant 1966 Prices, 1966–84

Year	GNP		GNI		GNP per capita		GNI per capita	
	Millions of colones	Growth rate (percent)	Millions of colones	Growth rate (percent)	Millions of colones	Growth rate (percent)	Millions of colones	Growth rate (percent)
1966	4,195.1	n.a.	4,195.1	n.a.	2,735	n.a.	2,735	n.a.
1967	4,425.6	5.5	4,399.8	4.9	2,792	2.1	2,738	0.1
1968	4,797.2	8.4	4,666.4	6.1	2,934	5.1	2,854	4.2
1969	5,080.8	5.9	4,935.9	5.8	3,017	2.8	2,931	2.7
1970	5,485.4	8.0	5,433.7	10.1	3,161	4.8	3,132	6.9
1971	5,873.4	7.1	5,620.4	3.4	3,301	4.4	3,159	0.9
1972	6,247.7	6.4	5,911.9	5.2	3,422	3.7	3,238	2.5
1973	6,728.8	7.7	6,409.4	8.4	3,595	5.1	3,424	5.7
1974	7,172.3	6.6	6,525.6	1.8	3,737	3.9	3,400	-0.7
1975	7,251.6	1.1	6,700.0	2.7	3,685	-1.4	3,405	0.1
1976	7,618.3	5.1	7,464.4	11.4	3,775	2.4	3,699	8.6
1977	8,322.3	9.2	8,762.4	17.4	4,019	6.5	4,232	14.4
1978	8,774.2	5.4	8,811.7	0.6	4,128	2.7	4,146	-2.0
1979	9,131.3	4.1	8,862.8	0.6	4,182	1.3	4,059	-2.1
1980	9,082.5	-0.5	8,805.3	-0.6	4,045	-3.3	3,921	-3.4
1981	8,682.3	-4.4	7,903.3	-10.2	3,765	-6.9	3,427	-12.6
1982	7,723.4	-11.0	6,988.8	-11.6	3,259	-13.4	2,949	-13.9
1983	8,125.4	5.2	7,458.1	6.7	3,340	2.5	3,066	4.0
1984	8,794.3	8.2	8,234.5	10.4	3,522	5.4	3,298	7.6

n.a. Not applicable.
Source: Banco Central de Costa Rica, Cuentas Nacionales de Costa Rica, various issues.

Table A-14. Costa Rica: GDP, by Sector, in Constant 1966 Prices, 1957–85

Year	Agriculture Millions of colones	Agriculture Growth rate (percent)	Manufacturing Millions of colones	Manufacturing Growth rate (percent)	Construction Millions of colones	Construction Growth rate (percent)
1957	652.0	n.a.	377.0	n.a.	122.3	n.a.
1958	687.0	5.4	397.9	5.5	149.7	22.4
1959	696.1	1.3	410.1	3.1	160.1	6.9
1960	780.6	12.1	428.3	4.4	140.3	-12.4
1961	809.3	3.7	406.0	-5.2	156.7	11.7
1962	858.9	6.1	437.2	7.7	176.4	12.6
1963	856.4	-0.3	495.7	13.4	176.9	0.3
1964	893.8	4.4	552.1	11.4	159.1	-10.1
1965	912.1	2.0	664.0	20.3	185.7	16.7
1966	994.1	9.0	730.9	10.1	184.9	-0.4
1967	1,072.3	7.9	778.9	6.6	199.3	7.8
1968	1,169.1	9.0	888.4	14.1	217.7	9.2
1969	1,290.6	10.4	947.0	6.6	219.5	0.8
1970	1,343.6	4.1	1,036.3	9.4	229.1	4.4
1971	1,405.6	4.6	1,120.3	8.1	268.6	17.2
1972	1,481.8	5.4	1,238.3	10.5	327.6	22.0
1973	1,565.5	5.6	1,364.8	10.2	337.7	3.1
1974	1,539.0	-1.7	1,538.4	12.7	364.0	7.8
1975	1,585.7	3.0	1,587.1	3.2	384.7	5.7
1976	1,593.6	0.5	1,679.2	5.8	464.7	20.8
1977	1,628.7	2.2	1,893.0	12.7	482.8	3.9
1978	1,736.2	6.6	2,048.2	8.2	510.8	5.8
1979	1,744.8	0.5	2,102.8	2.7	609.4	19.3
1980	1,736.1	-0.5	2,119.6	0.8	602.7	-1.1
1981	1,824.6	5.1	2,109.0	-0.5	471.9	-21.7
1982	1,738.8	-4.7	1,868.6	-11.4	321.4	-31.9
1983	1,808.3	4.0	1,902.2	1.8	336.5	4.7
1984	1,990.3	10.1	2,100.0	10.4	415.9	23.6
1985	1,880.4	-5.5	2,142.2	2.0	439.2	5.6

Year	Commerce Millions of colones	Commerce Growth rate (percent)	General government Millions of colones	General government Growth rate (percent)	Electricity and water Millions of colones	Electricity and water Growth rate (percent)
1957	552.8	n.a.	323.4	n.a.	29.2	n.a.
1958	560.6	1.4	328.4	1.5	28.6	-2.1
1959	592.3	5.7	337.6	2.8	35.4	23.8
1960	629.8	6.3	348.2	3.1	39.3	11.0
1961	585.4	-7.0	340.0	-2.4	38.8	-1.3
1962	664.0	13.4	356.7	4.9	38.7	-0.3
1963	694.0	4.5	379.6	6.4	42.5	9.8
1964	713.2	2.8	395.7	4.2	48.4	13.9
1965	802.3	12.5	430.3	8.7	58.7	21.3

(Table continues on the following page.)

Table A-14 (continued)

Year	Commerce Millions of colones	Growth rate (percent)	General government Millions of colones	Growth rate (percent)	Electricity and water Millions of colones	Growth rate (percent)
1966	879.4	9.6	454.8	5.7	64.4	9.7
1967	896.9	2.0	459.4	1.0	71.1	10.4
1968	964.9	7.6	466.0	1.4	84.2	18.4
1969	977.7	1.3	503.6	8.1	93.2	10.7
1970	1,109.5	13.5	549.2	9.1	106.4	14.2
1971	1,159.3	4.6	594.4	8.2	120.3	13.1
1972	1,248.0	7.7	642.6	8.1	131.6	9.4
1973	1,354.8	8.6	678.5	5.6	139.6	6.1
1974	1,345.0	−0.7	746.1	10.0	152.6	9.3
1975	1,288.0	−4.2	769.8	3.2	156.1	2.3
1976	1,402.0	8.9	799.1	3.8	169.8	8.8
1977	1,653.2	17.9	839.1	5.0	181.6	6.9
1978	1,722.6	4.2	881.1	5.0	191.4	5.4
1979	1,794.0	4.1	932.7	5.9	201.2	5.1
1980	1,740.8	−3.0	966.7	3.6	224.9	11.8
1981	1,556.3	−10.6	984.3	1.8	242.4	7.8
1982	1,374.2	−11.7	955.8	−2.9	252.6	4.2
1983	1,418.2	3.2	940.5	−1.6	303.6	20.2
1984	1,579.9	11.4	954.6	1.5	313.3	3.2
1985	1,652.6	4.6	959.4	0.5	290.1	−7.4

Year	Transport Millions of colones	Growth rate (percent)	Finance Millions of colones	Growth rate (percent)	Real estate Millions of colones	Growth rate (percent)	Other services Millions of colones	Growth rate (percent)
1957	115.5	n.a.	85.5	n.a.	282.3	n.a.	134.6	n.a.
1958	121.6	5.3	91.5	7.0	290.3	2.8	143.1	6.6
1959	135.4	11.3	98.2	7.3	302.5	4.2	152.1	6.3
1960	143.0	5.6	105.7	7.6	316.1	4.5	165.2	8.6
1961	138.9	−2.9	107.8	2.0	320.6	1.4	163.4	−1.1
1962	144.0	3.7	118.0	9.5	339.5	5.9	183.4	12.2
1963	147.4	2.4	127.5	8.1	360.6	6.2	194.9	6.3
1964	155.1	5.2	135.5	6.3	361.6	0.3	205.2	5.3
1965	167.7	8.1	154.7	14.2	373.6	3.3	226.4	10.3
1966	179.7	7.2	165.9	7.2	391.7	4.8	242.6	7.2
1967	198.9	10.7	178.8	7.8	424.1	8.3	251.0	3.5
1968	221.3	11.3	194.3	8.7	445.4	5.0	263.3	4.9
1969	239.8	8.4	196.3	1.0	441.6	−0.9	275.2	4.5
1970	247.7	3.3	216.1	10.1	447.7	1.4	287.9	4.6
1971	275.6	11.3	235.7	9.1	470.1	5.0	301.4	4.7
1972	307.5	11.6	257.1	9.1	485.0	3.2	318.5	5.7
1973	356.7	16.0	203.3	10.2	519.9	7.2	333.5	4.7
1974	407.0	14.1	329.2	16.2	546.4	5.1	351.1	5.3
1975	432.2	6.2	359.5	9.2	564.8	3.4	344.6	1.9

Year	Transport Millions of colones	Transport Growth rate (percent)	Finance Millions of colones	Finance Growth rate (percent)	Real estate Millions of colones	Real estate Growth rate (percent)	Other services Millions of colones	Other services Growth rate (percent)
1976	457.3	5.8	380.4	5.8	582.7	3.2	356.0	3.3
1977	512.2	12.0	410.1	7.8	603.1	3.5	383.1	7.6
1978	572.1	11.7	444.1	8.3	623.6	3.4	395.0	3.1
1979	643.0	12.4	486.3	9.5	649.2	4.1	412.4	4.4
1980	676.4	5.2	500.4	2.9	664.7	2.4	415.5	0.8
1981	671.7	−0.7	490.4	−2.0	676.0	1.7	403.0	−3.0
1982	666.3	−0.8	494.3	0.8	682.1	0.9	388.5	−3.6
1983	673.6	1.1	522.0	5.6	689.0	1.0	396.3	2.0
1984	700.6	4.0	551.7	5.7	700.0	1.6	408.2	3.0
1985	716.7	2.3	573.2	3.9	711.2	1.6	419.6	2.8

n.a. Not applicable.
Source: Banco Central de Costa Rica, *Cuentas Nacionales de Costa Rica*, various issues.

Table A-15. Costa Rica: Structure of GDP, *in Current Prices, 1950–80*
(percent)

Year	Agri-culture	Manufac-turing	Construc-tion	Commerce	General government	Other
1950	40.9	13.4	—	19.1	5.4	21.2
1951	40.9	13.4	—	19.0	5.8	21.2
1952	41.0	13.1	—	18.3	6.3	21.3
1953	40.3	13.3	—	19.0	6.7	20.7
1954	38.8	13.4	—	19.7	7.4	20.7
1955	38.3	13.3	—	19.5	7.7	21.2
1956	33.5	13.9	—	20.2	8.7	23.7
1957	30.2	12.9	4.9	21.1	7.5	23.4
1958	28.3	13.5	5.7	20.7	8.1	23.7
1959	25.7	13.6	6.1	21.2	8.9	24.5
1960	26.0	14.2	4.9	21.0	9.0	24.9
1961	25.7	14.0	5.5	20.1	9.5	25.2
1962	25.8	14.0	5.8	20.5	9.3	24.6
1963	24.5	15.0	5.6	20.4	9.5	25.0
1964	24.6	16.0	4.8	20.4	9.5	24.7
1965	23.5	16.8	5.2	20.2	9.7	24.6
1966	23.2	17.0	4.8	20.5	10.6	23.9
1967	23.0	16.9	4.9	19.8	10.7	24.7
1968	23.0	17.5	4.9	19.7	10.6	24.3
1969	23.0	17.8	4.8	19.7	10.9	23.8
1970	22.5	18.3	4.7	21.0	10.6	22.9
1971	20.2	18.6	4.8	21.0	11.4	24.0
1972	19.5	18.4	5.2	20.1	12.1	24.7
1973	19.3	18.7	5.0	20.2	11.8	25.0
1974	19.4	20.8	5.2	21.1	11.9	21.6
1975	20.3	20.4	5.2	19.1	12.4	22.6
1976	20.4	19.7	5.8	18.5	13.0	22.6
1977	21.9	19.0	5.2	19.5	12.9	21.5
1978	20.4	18.7	5.5	19.7	14.0	21.7
1979	18.5	18.3	6.4	20.4	15.0	21.4
1980	17.8	18.6	6.2	20.1	15.2	22.1

— Included under Other.
Source: Banco Central de Costa Rica, *Cuentas Nacionales de Costa Rica*, various issues.

Table A-16. Costa Rica: Structure of GDP, *in Constant 1966 Prices, 1957–85*
(percent)

Year	Agriculture	Manufac-turing	Construc-tion	Commerce	General government	Other
1957	24.4	14.1	4.6	20.7	12.1	24.1
1958	24.6	14.2	5.4	20.0	11.7	24.1
1959	23.8	14.0	5.5	20.3	11.6	24.8
1960	25.2	13.8	4.5	20.4	11.3	24.8
1961	26.4	13.2	5.1	19.1	11.1	25.1
1962	25.9	13.2	5.3	20.0	10.8	24.8
1963	24.6	14.3	5.1	20.0	10.9	25.1
1964	24.7	15.3	4.4	19.7	10.9	25.0
1965	22.9	16.7	4.7	20.2	10.8	24.7
1966	23.2	17.0	4.3	20.5	10.6	24.4
1967	23.7	17.2	4.4	19.8	10.1	24.8
1968	23.8	18.1	4.4	19.6	9.5	24.6
1969	24.9	18.3	4.2	18.9	9.7	24.0
1970	24.1	18.6	4.1	19.9	9.9	23.4
1971	23.6	18.8	4.5	19.5	10.0	23.6
1972	23.0	19.2	5.1	19.4	10.0	23.3
1973	22.6	19.7	4.9	19.5	9.8	23.5
1974	21.0	21.0	5.0	18.4	10.2	24.4
1975	21.2	21.2	5.2	17.2	10.3	24.9
1976	20.2	21.3	5.9	17.8	10.1	24.7
1977	19.0	22.0	5.6	19.2	9.8	24.4
1978	19.0	22.4	5.6	18.9	9.7	24.4
1979	18.2	22.0	6.4	18.7	9.7	25.0
1980	18.0	22.0	6.2	18.0	10.0	25.8
1981	19.4	22.4	5.0	16.5	10.4	26.3
1982	19.9	21.4	3.7	15.7	10.9	28.4
1983	20.1	21.2	3.7	15.9	10.5	28.6
1984	20.5	21.6	4.3	16.3	9.8	27.5
1985	19.2	21.9	4.5	16.4	9.8	28.2

Source: Banco Central de Costa Rica, *Cuentas Nacionales de Costa Rica,* various issues.

Table A-17. Costa Rica: Domestic Terms of Trade Index, by Sector, 1957–85
(1966 = 100)

Year	Agriculture/ GDP	Manufac- turing/GDP	General govern- ment/GDP	Agriculture/ manufacturing
1957	123.7	91.9	62.0	134.7
1958	115.1	95.0	69.2	121.1
1959	108.0	96.8	77.0	111.6
1960	103.3	102.3	79.8	100.9
1961	97.6	105.8	85.4	92.3
1962	99.7	106.1	86.2	94.0
1963	99.3	105.5	86.7	99.3
1964	99.5	105.1	87.1	94.7
1965	102.5	100.5	90.0	102.0
1966	100.0	100.0	100.0	100.0
1967	97.2	98.1	106.0	99.1
1968	96.8	96.8	111.5	99.8
1969	92.5	97.2	111.9	95.2
1970	93.4	98.3	107.8	95.1
1971	85.6	98.6	114.1	86.8
1972	84.7	95.4	121.7	88.8
1973	85.6	95.2	120.3	89.9
1974	90.8	96.4	117.0	94.2
1975	95.8	96.0	120.4	99.8
1976	100.8	92.5	128.0	109.0
1977	115.4	86.2	132.2	134.0
1978	107.3	83.5	144.8	128.5
1979	101.5	83.4	154.4	121.8
1980	98.9	84.6	151.6	116.9
1981	119.0	84.7	127.9	140.5
1982	140.7	95.1	106.2	129.5
1983	115.0	108.6	122.8	105.9
1984	118.8	119.4	147.1	99.5
1985	n.a.	n.a.	n.a.	97.3

n.a. Not available.

Note: The first three indexes were computed by dividing the index of the implicit deflator in the particular sector by the implicit GDP deflator. The last index was obtained by dividing the implicit deflator for the agricultural sector by the index of the implicit deflator for the manufacturing sector.

Source: Banco Central de Costa Rica, *Cuentas Nacionales de Costa Rica,* various issues.

Table A-18. *Costa Rica: Components of Aggregate Supply and Demand, in Constant 1966 Prices, 1966–85*

Year	GDP Millions of colones	GDP Growth rate (percent)	Imports Millions of colones	Imports Growth rate (percent)	Aggregate supply Millions of colones	Aggregate supply Growth rate (percent)	Private consumption Millions of colones	Private consumption Growth rate (percent)	Government consumption Millions of colones	Government consumption Growth rate (percent)	Investment Millions of colones	Investment Growth rate (percent)	Exports Millions of colones	Exports Growth rate (percent)
1966	4,288.4	7.9	1,319.7	n.a.	5,608.1	n.a.	3,191.2	n.a.	536.5	n.a.	817.3	n.a.	1,062.7	n.a.
1967	4,530.7	5.7	1,401.8	6.2	5,932.5	5.8	3,369.7	5.6	547.3	1.9	872.8	6.8	1,142.7	7.5
1968	4,914.6	8.5	1,595.3	13.8	6,509.9	9.7	3,596.7	6.7	557.3	1.8	812.2	-1.2	1,493.7	30.7
1969	5,184.5	5.5	1,828.9	14.6	7,013.4	7.7	3,792.5	5.4	590.2	5.9	990.5	14.9	1,640.2	9.8
1970	5,573.5	7.5	2,269.7	24.1	7,843.2	11.8	4,176.9	10.1	659.6	11.8	1,128.6	13.9	1,878.1	14.5
1971	5,951.3	6.8	2,452.0	8.0	8,403.3	7.1	4,241.0	1.5	738.8	12.0	1,399.9	24.0	2,023.6	7.7
1972	6,438.0	8.2	2,471.2	0.8	8,909.2	6.0	4,444.6	4.8	790.8	7.0	1,297.4	-7.3	2,376.0	17.4
1973	6,934.3	7.7	2,676.6	8.3	9,619.9	7.9	4,676.8	5.2	838.7	6.1	1,539.5	18.7	2,555.1	7.5
1974	7,318.8	5.5	2,771.1	3.5	10,089.9	5.0	4,734.6	1.2	909.5	8.4	1,671.6	8.6	2,774.2	8.6
1975	7,472.5	2.1	2,568.1	-7.3	10,040.6	-0.5	4,837.4	2.2	961.0	5.7	1,522.7	-8.9	2,719.5	-2.0
1976	7,884.8	5.5	2,983.6	16.2	10,868.4	8.2	5,039.0	4.2	1,036.0	7.8	1,926.5	26.5	2,866.9	5.4
1977	8,586.9	8.9	3,731.7	25.1	12,318.6	13.3	5,726.2	13.6	1,126.7	8.8	2,365.0	22.8	3,100.7	8.2
1978	9,125.1	6.3	4,011.7	7.5	13,136.8	6.6	6,204.7	8.4	1,168.0	3.7	2,355.2	-0.4	3,408.9	9.9
1979	9,575.8	4.9	4,128.7	2.9	13,704.5	4.3	6,353.3	2.4	1,258.1	7.7	2,573.1	9.3	3,520.0	3.3
1980	9,647.8	0.8	3,987.0	-3.4	13,634.8	-0.5	6,238.0	-1.8	1,276.4	1.4	2,753.3	7.0	3,367.1	-4.3
1981	9,429.6	-2.3	2,936.9	-26.3	12,366.5	-9.3	5,705.7	-8.5	1,204.8	-5.6	1,714.5	-37.7	3,741.5	11.1
1982	8,742.6	-7.3	2,404.9	-18.1	11,147.5	-9.9	5,158.0	-9.6	1,174.1	-2.5	1,278.1	-25.4	3,537.3	-5.5
1983	8,992.9	2.9	2,785.1	15.8	11,778.0	5.7	5,446.8	5.6	1,139.6	-2.9	1,700.7	33.1	3,490.9	-1.3
1984	9,714.5	8.0	3,082.3	10.7	12,796.8	8.7	5,841.6	7.2	1,183.9	3.9	1,886.8	10.9	3,884.5	11.3
1985	9,784.6	0.7	3,266.9	6.0	13,051.5	2.0	6,092.6	4.3	1,196.4	1.1	2,032.8	7.7	3,729.4	-4.0

n.a. Not applicable.
Source: Banco Central de Costa Rica, *Cuentas Nacionales de Costa Rica,* various issues.

Table A-19. Costa Rica: Export Prices, Import Prices, and International Terms of Trade, 1950–85

Year	Export prices Index (1966 = 100)	Export prices Growth rate (percent)	Import prices Index (1966 = 100)	Import prices Growth rate (percent)	Terms of trade Index (1966 = 100)	Terms of trade Growth rate (percent)
1950	98.4	n.a.	78.8	n.a.	124.9	n.a.
1951	117.5	19.4	82.5	4.7	142.4	14.0
1952	111.0	−5.5	83.0	0.6	133.7	−6.1
1953	120.5	8.6	92.4	11.3	130.4	−2.5
1954	135.6	12.5	91.4	−1.1	148.4	13.8
1955	124.2	−8.4	104.1	13.9	119.3	−19.6
1956	136.0	9.5	100.0	−3.9	136.0	14.0
1957	128.7	−5.4	101.0	1.1	127.3	−6.4
1958	112.8	−12.4	96.9	−4.2	116.4	−8.6
1959	102.8	−8.9	93.9	−3.1	109.4	−6.0
1960	96.2	−6.4	95.1	1.3	101.1	−7.6
1961	98.3	2.2	95.2	0.1	103.3	2.2
1962	97.0	−1.3	94.6	−0.6	102.5	−0.8
1963	98.2	1.2	95.0	0.4	103.4	0.9
1964	102.8	4.7	96.9	2.0	106.1	3.5
1965	100.5	−2.2	99.3	2.5	101.3	−4.5
1966	100.0	−0.5	100.0	0.7	100.0	−0.3
1967	98.3	−1.7	100.5	0.5	97.9	−2.1
1968	89.8	−8.6	98.3	−2.2	91.4	−6.6
1969	90.0	0.2	97.0	−1.3	92.7	1.4
1970	96.7	7.4	99.4	2.5	97.3	4.9
1971	90.6	−6.3	103.6	4.2	87.4	−10.2
1972	94.5	4.3	110.1	6.3	85.8	−1.8
1973	106.5	12.7	121.9	10.7	87.4	1.9
1974	127.7	19.9	167.1	37.1	76.5	−12.5
1975	145.2	13.7	182.9	9.3	79.5	3.9
1976	164.2	13.1	173.7	−4.9	94.5	18.9
1977	209.8	27.8	182.9	5.3	114.7	21.4
1978	195.8	−6.7	193.6	5.9	101.1	−11.9
1979	205.2	4.7	222.1	14.7	92.4	−8.6
1980	231.6	12.9	252.1	13.5	91.9	−0.5
1981	211.9	−8.5	269.2	6.8	78.7	−14.4
1982	207.8	−1.7	261.7	−2.8	79.2	0.6
1983	205.1	−1.0	251.2	−4.0	81.6	3.0
1984	208.8	1.8	247.5	−1.5	84.4	3.4
1985	208.2	−0.3	238.5	−3.6	87.3	3.4

n.a. Not applicable.
Source: Banco Central de Costa Rica 1986.

Table A-20. Costa Rica: Value of Exports and Imports and Trade Balance, 1950–85

Year	Exports Millions of U.S. dollars	Exports Growth rate (percent)	Imports Millions of U.S. dollars	Imports Growth rate (percent)	Trade balance (millions of U.S. dollars)
1950	54.1	n.a.	45.7	n.a.	8.4
1951	62.2	14.8	55.3	21.0	6.9
1952	72.7	17.1	67.2	21.5	5.6
1953	79.9	9.9	72.8	8.3	7.1
1954	84.4	5.6	80.1	10.0	4.3
1955	81.0	−4.0	87.0	8.6	−6.0
1956	68.4	−15.6	91.1	4.7	−22.8
1957	84.7	23.8	102.3	12.3	−17.6
1958	92.7	9.4	99.0	−3.2	−6.2
1959	77.3	−16.6	102.3	3.3	−24.9
1960	84.3	9.1	110.4	7.9	−26.1
1961	84.2	−0.1	107.2	−2.9	−23.0
1962	93.0	10.5	113.3	5.7	−20.4
1963	95.0	2.2	123.8	9.3	−28.8
1964	113.9	19.9	138.6	12.0	−24.7
1965	111.8	−1.8	178.2	28.6	−66.4
1966	135.5	21.2	178.5	0.2	−42.9
1967	143.8	6.1	190.7	6.8	−46.9
1968	170.8	18.8	213.9	12.2	−43.1
1969	189.7	11.1	245.1	14.6	−55.4
1970	231.2	21.9	316.7	29.2	−85.5
1971	225.4	−2.5	349.7	10.4	−124.4
1972	280.9	24.6	372.8	6.6	−91.9
1973	344.5	22.6	455.3	22.1	−110.9
1974	440.3	27.8	719.7	58.1	−279.3
1975	493.3	12.0	694.0	−3.6	−200.7
1976	592.9	20.0	770.4	11.0	−177.5
1977	828.2	39.7	1,021.4	32.6	−193.3
1978	864.9	4.4	1,165.7	14.1	−300.8
1979	934.4	8.0	1,396.8	19.8	−462.4
1980	1,001.7	7.2	1,523.8	9.1	−522.1
1981	1,008.1	0.6	1,208.5	−20.7	−200.4
1982	870.4	−13.7	893.2	−26.1	−22.8
1983	872.6	0.3	987.8	10.6	−115.3
1984	975.6	11.8	1,094.1	10.8	−118.5
1985	933.2	−4.3	1,109.0	1.4	−175.8

n.a. Not applicable.
Source: Banco Central de Costa Rica 1986.

Table A-21. Costa Rica: Exports and Imports as a Share of GDP, in Current and Constant Prices, 1950–85
(percent)

Year	Exports/GDP		Imports/GDP	
	Current prices	1966 prices	Current prices	1966 prices
1950	27.6	—	23.4	—
1951	26.9	—	24.4	—
1952	28.2	—	26.5	—
1953	28.3	—	26.2	—
1954	28.1	—	26.1	—
1955	25.0	—	26.0	—
1956	21.7	—	26.7	—
1957	23.8	—	27.5	—
1958	24.8	—	25.8	—
1959	20.7	—	25.9	—
1960	21.4	—	26.2	—
1961	21.1	—	25.1	—
1962	22.9	—	26.1	—
1963	22.2	—	27.2	—
1964	24.6	—	28.6	—
1965	22.8	—	33.3	—
1966	25.0	25.0	30.9	30.0
1967	25.2	25.5	31.5	31.0
1968	28.2	30.8	32.8	32.2
1969	26.9	32.0	32.2	34.2
1970	28.2	34.2	35.0	39.6
1971	27.3	34.6	37.6	39.9
1972	30.2	37.4	36.6	37.0
1973	30.8	37.3	36.9	36.5
1974	33.1	37.9	48.0	37.9
1975	30.1	36.4	38.5	34.4
1976	28.9	36.4	34.9	37.8
1977	30.9	36.1	36.3	43.5
1978	28.2	37.4	36.0	44.0
1979	26.9	36.8	37.2	43.1
1980	26.5	34.9	36.8	41.3
1981	43.3	39.7	48.2	31.1
1982	45.1	40.5	42.2	27.5
1983	36.0	38.8	36.8	31.0
1984	34.4	40.0	34.0	31.7
1985	30.7	38.1	32.5	33.4

— Not available.
Source: Banco Central de Costa Rica, Cuentas Nacionales de Costa Rica, various issues.

Table A-22. Costa Rica: Value of Selected Exports as a Share of Total
Exports, 1957–80
(percent)

Year	Coffee	Bananas	Beef	Sugar	Other primary commodities	Manufac- tures
1957	48.7	38.6	2.6	0.1	—	10.0
1963	47.6	27.1	6.0	5.4	—	13.9
1964	42.0	24.8	7.0	4.5	—	21.7
1965	41.6	25.3	4.6	4.2	—	26.7
1966	38.8	21.5	5.2	6.4	—	28.1
1967	38.4	21.7	6.7	5.9	—	28.0
1968	32.3	25.0	7.3	5.1	—	30.3
1969	29.4	27.1	7.0	4.8	—	30.7
1970	31.6	28.9	7.8	4.4	—	27.7
1971	26.3	28.4	9.2	5.7	—	30.0
1972	27.8	30.0	10.9	4.3	—	27.4
1973	27.2	26.3	9.6	6.2	—	30.6
1974	28.3	22.3	7.8	5.5	—	36.0
1975	19.6	29.2	7.7	9.8	6.0	27.7
1976	26.0	25.1	7.7	4.2	6.1	31.1
1977	38.5	18.2	6.2	1.9	7.5	27.8
1978	36.3	19.6	7.1	1.8	9.2	25.9
1979	33.8	20.4	8.8	1.9	7.1	28.0
1980	24.2	19.8	7.0	4.0	8.2	36.8

— Not available.

Source: Banco Central de Costa Rica, Principales Estadísticas sobre las Transacciones de Costa Rica en el Extranjero, various issues.

Table A-23. Costa Rica: Consumer Price Index , 1950–85
(1975 = 100)

Year	December CPI		Annual average CPI	
	Index	Rate of change (percent)	Index	Rate of change (percent)
1950	33.81	n.a.	32.61	n.a.
1951	34.50	2.0	34.83	6.8
1952	34.15	–1.0	33.86	–2.8
1953	33.90	–0.8	34.10	0.7
1954	36.66	8.1	35.14	3.0
1955	37.33	1.8	36.60	4.2
1956	37.05	–0.8	36.98	1.0
1957	38.32	3.4	37.72	2.0
1958	39.05	1.9	38.72	2.7
1959	38.92	–0.3	38.83	0.3
1960	40.15	3.2	39.14	0.8
1961	40.21	0.1	40.08	2.4
1962	42.28	5.1	43.16	2.7
1963	43.03	1.8	42.40	3.0
1964	43.26	0.5	43.44	2.5
1965	42.89	–0.9	43.16	–0.6
1966	43.71	1.9	43.23	0.2
1967	44.86	2.6	43.76	1.2
1968	46.42	3.5	45.51	4.0
1969	48.01	3.4	46.74	2.7
1970	50.07	4.3	48.92	4.7
1971	51.05	2.0	50.43	3.1
1972	54.56	6.9	52.75	4.6
1973	63.23	15.9	58.93	11.7
1974	82.55	30.6	74.43	26.3
1975	99.44	20.5	92.78	24.7
1976	104.36	4.9	103.49	11.5
1977	109.84	5.3	107.81	4.2
1978	118.75	8.1	114.29	6.0
1979	134.37	13.2	124.79	9.2
1980	158.27	17.8	147.43	18.1
1981	261.29	65.1	202.03	37.0
1982	474.90	81.8	384.10	90.1
1983	525.72	10.7	509.41	32.6
1984	616.93	17.3	570.28	11.9
1985	684.33	10.9	656.11	15.1

n.a. Not applicable.
Source: Banco Central de Costa Rica 1986.

Table A-24. Costa Rica: Wholesale Price Index, 1950–85
(1966 = 100)

Year	December WPI		Annual average WPI	
	Index	Rate of change (percent)	Index	Rate of change (percent)
1950	109.9	n.a.	99.5	n.a.
1951	95.8	–6.9	102.5	3.2
1952	89.6	–6.5	92.2	–10.2
1953	87.4	–1.9	87.9	–4.7
1954	94.6	8.2	91.9	4.6
1955	95.9	1.4	93.7	2.0
1956	94.6	–1.3	94.7	1.1
1957	93.1	–1.7	94.2	–0.5
1958	94.6	1.7	94.9	0.7
1959	92.2	–2.5	94.0	–0.9
1960	97.6	5.8	93.7	–0.3
1961	96.6	–1.0	96.2	2.7
1962	98.3	1.8	95.8	–0.4
1963	99.0	0.7	98.3	2.6
1964	100.9	1.9	99.9	1.6
1965	99.2	–1.7	99.1	–0.8
1966	100.8	1.6	100.0	0.9
1967	106.2	5.3	103.3	3.3
1968	109.8	3.5	108.4	4.9
1969	115.9	5.5	113.0	4.2
1970	125.3	8.2	120.3	6.5
1971	130.3	4.0	128.0	6.4
1972	140.4	7.8	135.0	5.5
1973	177.6	26.4	157.0	16.3
1974	245.3	38.2	219.5	39.8
1975	279.7	14.0	266.9	21.6
1976	299.9	7.2	291.6	9.3
1977	322.1	7.4	313.6	7.5
1978	352.3	9.4	337.9	7.8
1979	437.1	24.1	392.4	16.1
1980	521.5	19.3	485.3	23.7
1981	1,132.6	117.2	802.3	65.3
1982	2,028.5	79.1	1,670.3	108.2
1983	2,148.2	5.9	2,108.0	26.2
1984	2,410.3	12.2	2,270.3	7.7
1985	2,594.5	7.6	2,506.3	10.4

n.a. Not applicable.
Source: Banco Central de Costa Rica 1986.

Table A-25. Costa Rica: GDP *Deflator, 1950–85*

Year	Index (1966 = 100)	Rate of change (percent)
1950	81.6	n.a.
1951	83.9	2.8
1952	80.2	−4.4
1953	86.1	7.4
1954	81.9	−4.9
1955	92.5	12.9
1956	95.4	3.1
1957	93.5	−2.0
1958	93.2	−0.3
1959	91.7	−1.6
1960	92.4	0.8
1961	95.5	3.4
1962	96.1	0.6
1963	97.9	2.5
1964	99.7	1.8
1965	98.8	−0.9
1966	100.0	1.2
1967	102.3	2.3
1968	104.3	2.0
1969	109.1	4.6
1970	117.1	7.3
1971	119.9	2.4
1972	127.6	6.4
1973	146.5	14.8
1974	180.6	23.3
1975	224.9	24.5
1976	262.2	16.6
1977	306.6	16.9
1978	327.8	6.9
1979	361.2	10.2
1980	429.2	18.8
1981	605.6	41.1
1982	1,115.3	84.2
1983	1,438.0	28.9
1984	1,641.8	14.2
1985	1,884.8	14.8

n.a. Not applicable.
Source: Banco Central de Costa Rica 1986.

Table A-26. Costa Rica: Official and Free-Market Exchange Rates, Annual Averages, 1950–79
(colones/U.S. dollar)

Year	Official rate	Free-market rate
1950	n.a.	8.50
1951	n.a.	7.65
1952	n.a.	6.75
1953	5.60	6.63
1954	5.60	6.63
1955	5.60	6.63
1956	5.60	6.63
1957	5.60	6.63
1958	5.60	6.63
1959	5.60	6.63
1960	5.60	6.63
1961	5.60	6.62
1962	6.62	n.a.
1963	6.62	n.a.
1964	6.62	n.a.
1965	6.62	n.a.
1966	6.62	n.a.
1967	6.62	7.77
1968	6.62	7.32
1969	6.62	n.a.
1970	6.62	n.a.
1971	6.62	8.57
1972	6.62	8.57
1973	6.62	8.57
1974	6.62/8.57	n.a.
1975	8.57	n.a.
1976	8.57	n.a.
1977	8.57	n.a.
1978	8.57	n.a.
1979	8.57	n.a.

n.a. Not applicable.
Source: Banco Central de Costa Rica 1986.

Table A-27. Costa Rica: Monthly Exchange Rate, 1980–85
(colones/U.S. dollar)

Year and month	Official rate	Bank rate	Free-market rate	Central Bank free rate
1980				
April	8.60	8.54	8.74	n.a.
May	8.60	8.54	8.71	n.a.
June	8.60	8.54	8.76	n.a.
July	8.60	8.54	9.01	n.a.
August	8.60	8.54	9.71	n.a.
September	8.60	8.54	9.80	n.a.
October	8.60	11.30	11.46	n.a.
November	8.60	11.86	12.09	n.a.
December	8.60	14.25	14.36	n.a.
1981				
January	8.60	13.17	13.28	n.a.
February	8.60	14.17	14.04	n.a.
March	8.60	15.51	17.29	n.a.
April	8.60	16.56	18.83	n.a.
May	8.60	17.00	18.92	n.a.
June	8.60	18.40	19.30	n.a.
July	8.60	18.86	20.84	n.a.
August	8.60	18.84	22.99	n.a.
September	8.60	18.84	26.33	n.a.
October	8.60	30.39	36.66	n.a.
November	8.60	36.74	37.40	n.a.
December	8.60	35.80	38.00	n.a.
1982				
January	20.00	36.05	39.75	n.a.
February	20.00	37.05	42.12	n.a.
March	20.00	37.49	44.15	n.a.
April	20.00	38.00	48.39	n.a.
May	20.00	38.00	48.50	n.a.
June	20.00	38.00	53.66	52.37
July	20.00	38.00	62.40	55.00
August	20.00	38.19	59.60	57.16
September	20.00	40.00	n.a.	53.58
October	20.00	40.00	n.a.	51.28
November	20.00	40.00	n.a.	47.00
December	20.00	40.00	n.a.	45.17
1983				
January	20.00	40.00	n.a.	44.86
February	20.00	40.00	n.a.	44.66
March	20.00	40.00	n.a.	44.43
April	20.00	40.00	n.a.	44.17
May	20.00	40.00	n.a.	44.10
June	20.00	40.14	n.a.	43.96
July	20.00	41.00	n.a.	43.10

Table A-21 (continued)

Year and month	Official rate	Bank rate	Free-market rate	Central Bank free rate
August	20.00	41.00	n.a.	42.81
September	20.00	41.07	n.a.	42.10
October	20.00	41.25	n.a.	42.77
November	20.00	42.46	n.a.	n.a.
December	20.00	43.15	n.a.	n.a.
1984				
January	20.00	43.15	n.a.	n.a.
February	20.00	43.15	n.a.	n.a.
March	20.00	43.15	n.a.	n.a.
April	20.00	43.15	n.a.	n.a.
May	20.00	43.16	n.a.	n.a.
June	20.00	43.50	n.a.	n.a.
July	20.00	43.75	n.a.	n.a.
August	20.00	43.75	n.a.	n.a.
September	20.00	44.50	n.a.	n.a.
October	20.00	44.90	n.a.	n.a.
November	20.00	47.50	n.a.	n.a.
December	20.00	47.50	n.a.	n.a.
1985				
January	20.00	47.52	n.a.	n.a.
February	20.00	48.09	n.a.	n.a.
March	20.00	48.53	n.a.	n.a.
April	20.00	48.84	n.a.	n.a.
May	20.00	49.08	n.a.	n.a.
June	20.00	49.84	n.a.	n.a.
July	20.00	50.46	n.a.	n.a.
August	20.00	51.10	n.a.	n.a.
September	20.00	51.62	n.a.	n.a.
October	20.00	52.12	n.a.	n.a.
November	20.00	52.64	n.a.	n.a.
December	20.00	53.12	n.a.	n.a.

n.a. Not applicable.
Source: Banco Central de Costa Rica 1986.

Table A-28. Costa Rica: Average Monthly Wage, in Constant 1975 Colones, by Sector, 1972–85

Period	All workers	Agriculture	Manufacturing	Services
1972				
July	1,490	727	1,371	—
1973				
March	1,532	777	1,406	2,103
July	1,443	731	1,332	1,944
November	1,420	736	1,310	1,853
1974				
March	1,314	674	1,219	1,727
July	1,379	713	1,306	1,817
November	1,371	709	1,241	1,818
1975				
March	1,300	709	1,202	1,705
July	1,344	718	1,243	1,816
November	1,306	698	1,191	1,723
1976				
March	1,330	725	1,235	1,744
July	1,418	727	1,235	1,970
November	1,461	754	1,276	2,014
1977				
March	1,458	860	1,358	1,915
July	1,590	879	1,321	2,060
November	1,555	916	1,394	2,059
1978				
March	1,635	991	1,446	2,168
July	1,618	951	1,394	2,223
November	1,715	1,012	1,513	2,320
1979				
March	1,724	1,061	1,502	2,314
July	1,714	1,030	1,482	2,331
November	1,700	1,083	1,532	2,155
1980				
March	1,656	1,030	1,477	2,220
July	1,847	1,019	1,550	2,723
November	1,731	1,075	1,507	2,332
1981				
March	1,632	1,002	1,463	2,136
July	1,562	940	1,469	1,982
November	1,381	901	1,224	1,770
1982				
March	1,286	875	1,253	1,612
July	1,099	736	1,057	1,352
November	1,182	846	1,151	1,399

Table A-28 (continued)

Period	All workers	Agriculture	Manufacturing	Services
1983				
March	1,263	858	1,290	1,448
July	1,330	926	1,220	1,644
November	1,571	1,018	1,642	1,857
1984				
March	1,499	1,019	1,202	1,785
July	1,414	1,018	1,208	1,627
November	1,483	1,005	1,236	1,648
1985				
March	1,534	1,009	1,362	1,853
July	1,599	1,045	1,381	1,883
November	1,647	1,120	1,415	1,935

— Not available.

Note: Wage figures have been deflated by the consumer price index for low- and middle-income groups in the San José Metropolitan Area.

Source: Unpublished data from the Caja Costarricense de Seguro Social.

Table A-29. Costa Rica: Average Monthly Wage, in Constant 1975 Colones, by Institutional Sector, 1972–85

Period[a]	Private sector	Public sector	Central government	Autonomous institutions
1972				
July	1,178	2,198	2,106	2,284
1973				
March	1,177	2,323	2,222	2,416
July	1,096	2,203	2,162	2,239
November	1,096	2,153	2,116	2,189
1974				
March	1,020	2,003	1,983	1,992
July	1,062	2,106	2,046	2,155
November	1,048	2,107	2,100	2,114
1975				
March	1,022	1,934	1,937	1,932
July	1,006	2,082	2,030	2,122
November	987	1,979	1,956	1,996
1976				
March	1,022	1,993	1,975	2,005
July	1,027	2,236	2,452	2,068
November	1,115	2,273	2,211	2,321
1977				
March	1,132	2,158	2,237	2,101
July	1,120	2,316	2,407	2,252
November	1,290	2,325	2,418	2,253
1978				
March	1,261	2,463	2,466	2,460
July	1,210	2,491	2,636	2,385
November	1,290	2,325	2,765	2,446
1979				
March	1,316	2,587	2,678	2,524
July	1,276	2,589	2,522	2,638
November	1,307	2,427	2,265	2,556
1980				
March	1,267	2,454	2,453	2,455
July	1,285	2,945	3,647	2,455
November	1,280	2,603	2,676	2,555
1981				
March	1,250	2,372	2,365	2,376
July	1,177	2,295	2,195	2,363
November	1,079	1,999	1,953	2,031

Table A-29 (continued)

Period[a]	Private sector	Public sector	Central government	Autonomous institutions
1982				
March	1,007	1,854	1,812	1,881
July	884	1,535	1,492	1,563
November	992	1,558	1,485	1,608
1983				
March	1,044	1,711	1,457	1,888
July	1,075	1,854	1,718	1,946
November	1,229	2,245	1,955	2,462
1984				
March	1,187	2,145	1,877	2,326
July	1,197	1,804	1,841	1,783
November	1,226	1,947	1,796	2,032
1985				
March	1,258	2,097	1,821	2,279
July	1,288	2,247	1,907	2,487
November	1,356	2,241	1,955	2,440

Note: Wage figures have been deflated by the consumer price index for low- and middle-income groups in the San José Metropolitan Area.

Source: Unpublished data from the Caja Costarricense de Seguro Social.

Table A-30. Costa Rica: Annual Growth Rates of Average Monthly Wage, in Constant 1975 Prices, by Sector, 1972–85
(percent)

Period [a]	All workers	Agriculture	Manufacturing	Services
1972–73				
July	–3.2	0.6	–2.8	—
1973–74				
March	–14.2	–13.3	–13.4	–7.5
July	–4.4	–2.5	–2.0	–6.5
November	–3.5	–3.7	–5.3	–1.9
1974–75				
March	–1.1	5.2	–1.4	–1.3
July	–2.5	0.7	–4.8	–0.1
November	–4.7	–1.6	–4.0	–5.2
1975–76				
March	2.3	2.3	2.7	2.3
July	5.5	1.3	–0.6	8.5
November	11.9	8.0	7.1	16.9
1976–77				
March	9.6	18.6	10.0	9.8
July	6.4	20.9	7.0	4.6
November	6.4	21.5	9.2	2.2
1977–78				
March	12.1	15.2	6.5	13.2
July	7.2	8.2	5.5	7.9
November	10.3	10.5	9.9	12.7
1978–79				
March	12.1	7.1	3.9	6.7
July	7.2	8.3	6.5	4.9
November	10.3	7.0	1.3	–7.1
1979–80				
March	–3.9	–2.9	–1.7	–4.1
July	7.8	–1.1	4.4	22.5
November	1.8	–0.7	–1.6	8.2
1980–81				
March	–1.4	–2.7	–0.9	–3.8
July	–15.4	–7.8	–5.2	–27.2
November	–20.2	–16.2	–18.8	–24.1
1981–82				
March	–21.2	–12.6	–14.4	–24.5
July	–24.9	–33.1	–32.0	–33.9
November	–8.1	–22.1	–24.0	–20.8

Table A-30 (continued)

Period [a]	All workers	Agriculture	Manufacturing	Services
1982–83				
March	−1.8	−1.9	3.0	−10.2
July	21.0	25.8	15.4	21.6
November	32.9	20.3	42.7	32.7
1983–84				
March	18.7	18.8	−6.8	23.3
July	6.3	9.9	−1.0	1.0
November	−5.6	−1.3	−24.8	−11.3
1984–85				
March	2.3	−1.0	13.3	3.9
July	13.1	2.7	14.3	15.7
November	11.1	11.4	14.5	17.4

— Not available.

a. Annual rates of growth are computed from March to March, July to July, and November to November.

Source: Unpublished data from the Caja Costarricense de Seguro Social.

Table A-31. Costa Rica: Annual Growth Rates of Average Monthly Wage, in Constant 1975 Prices, by Institutional Sector, 1972–85
(percent)

Period[a]	Private sector	Public sector	Central government	Autonomous institutions
1972–73				
July	–7.0	–0.2	2.7	–2.0
1973–74				
March	–13.3	–13.8	–10.8	–17.5
July	–3.1	–4.4	–5.4	–3.8
November	–4.4	–2.1	–0.8	–3.4
1974–75				
March	0.2	–3.4	–2.3	–3.0
July	–5.3	–1.1	–0.8	–1.5
November	–5.8	–6.1	–6.9	–5.6
1975–76				
March	0.0	8.1	2.0	3.8
July	2.1	7.4	10.8	–2.5
November	13.0	14.9	13.0	16.3
1976–77				
March	10.8	8.3	13.3	4.8
July	9.1	3.6	–1.8	8.9
November	15.7	2.3	9.4	–2.9
1977–78				
March	11.4	14.1	10.2	17.1
July	13.8	7.6	9.5	23.0
November	0.0	11.0	14.4	8.6
1978–79				
March	4.4	5.0	8.6	2.6
July	5.4	3.9	6.7	10.6
November	1.3	–5.9	–18.1	4.5
1979–80				
March	–3.7	–5.1	–8.4	–2.7
July	0.8	13.8	44.6	–6.9
November	–2.1	7.3	18.1	–0.1
1980–81				
March	–1.3	–3.3	–3.6	–3.2
July	–8.4	–22.1	–39.8	–3.7
November	–15.7	–23.2	–27.0	–20.5
1981–82				
March	–19.4	–21.8	–23.4	–20.8
July	–24.9	–33.1	–32.0	–33.9
November	–8.1	–22.1	–24.0	–20.8

Table A-31 (continued)

Period [a]	Private sector	Public sector	Central government	Autonomous institutions
1982–83				
March	3.7	–7.7	–19.6	0.4
July	21.6	20.8	15.1	24.5
November	23.9	44.1	31.6	53.1
1983–84				
March	13.7	25.4	28.8	23.2
July	11.3	–2.7	7.2	–8.4
November	–0.2	–13.3	–8.1	–17.5
1984–85				
March	6.0	–2.2	–3.0	–2.0
July	7.6	24.6	3.6	39.5
November	10.6	15.1	8.9	20.1

a. Annual rates of growth are computed from March to March, July to July, and November to November.

Source: Unpublished data from the Caja Costarricense de Seguro Social.

Edgardo Favaro
Alberto Bensión

II Uruguay

Introduction

Uruguay is a small country of about 3 million people nestled between Argentina and Brazil at the mouth of the Río de la Plata. This river, one of the most important navigable streams in South America, provides a deep-water port with a large capacity for transoceanic shipping traffic. The country was part of the Spanish viceroyship of the Río de la Plata. In the wave of independence movements that swept over Latin America in the early nineteenth century, Uruguay became a separate nation on the diplomatic initiative of Great Britain, which wanted to create a buffer between Argentina and Brazil to reduce the potential for territorial conflict.

The land that became Uruguay was first settled by Europeans in the sixteenth century. The early immigrants came from Spain, but in the nineteenth century and early twentieth century a large number of immigrants arrived from other European countries, especially Italy. Today, Uruguay's population has approximately equal proportions of descendants of Spaniards and Italians and important smaller segments of descendants of immigrants from other countries of Europe and South America.

Uruguay's territory—177,000 square kilometers, flat and level, with temperate climate and abundant rain—is especially suitable for raising livestock. For many generations, grazing cattle and sheep on natural pasture has been the country's most important economic activity. The cattle were raised first for their hides and later for meat and meat products, and the sheep for their wool. The livestock economy is characterized by relatively large ranches that employ land-intensive methods of production.

Until the early 1970s Europe was the main export market for Uruguay's livestock products. The industry then began to feel the adverse effects of measures taken by the consumer countries to protect their domestic producers of livestock and livestock products from the competition of more efficient producers—including Uruguay.

Uruguay is heavily urbanized; about one-half of the population lives in the Montevideo metropolitan region. This urban concentration is consistent with the light labor intensity of ranching, which accounts for most of the country's agricultural land.

For much of the nineteenth century after independence, Uruguay experienced violent struggles for power that sometimes reached the proportions of civil war. For many years, however, Uruguay has been regarded as a model country that has followed democratic traditions. With minor lapses, there have been regular and periodic elections, competing political parties, and free and open debate in political campaigns. The electorate is literate and informed and participates heavily in the electoral process. The counting of ballots is honest, and the winners take office.

For many decades, except during the late 1960s, social relations within the community have been calm and nonviolent. The population is relatively homogeneous. On average, the material condition of life in Uruguay is high in comparison with that of most other developing countries. Policies adopted years ago have brought about a more equal distribution of income than would be produced by market forces.

Economic growth has been meager during the past five decades. Except for a short period of import-substitution-led growth in the immediate postwar period and during 1979–81 and a period of export-oriented expansion between 1974 and 1978, growth performance since the Great Depression contrasts dramatically with the dynamic behavior of the economy in the first century after independence.

Both the stubborn stagnation that lasted from 1957 to 1973 and the significant expansion achieved between 1974 and 1981 are remarkable episodes in the context of the contrasting behavior of the world economy. Uruguay's economy stagnated when the world economy was expanding enormously, and it performed well while the rest of the world was reeling from the 1973 oil crisis. These contrasts suggest that domestic variables, rather than external circumstances, may be the most plausible candidates for explaining patterns of GDP growth and income distribution in Uruguay. This study gives particular attention to how external events and economic policies combined after World War II to encourage the adoption of new technologies and the expansion of the country's endowment of human and physical resources and to how they affected income distribution. It examines and interprets the factors behind the adoption and maintenance of different economic policies during the period.

Chapter 9 surveys economic growth and income distribution between 1955 and 1985. Chapter 10 discusses the reasons for the dynamic behavior of the economy and the high standard of living prevailing in 1930 and the transition to economic stagnation and price instability during 1930–55. The degree of openness of the economy, monetary instability, and the role of the state are identified as the main explanations for economic performance. Chapter 11 analyzes growth and income distribution between 1955 and 1973 and discusses the rationale for the maintenance of economic policies that have had a high cost in that they slowed the rate of growth of the economy. Chapter 12 looks at the role of external factors and domestic policies in modifying the patterns of growth and income distribution during the past decade. Chapter 13 summarizes the main conclusions of the study.

9 Economic Growth and Income Distribution

FOR A BRIEF PERIOD after World War II, Uruguay enjoyed sustained economic growth led by the manufacturing industry and, in particular, by the production of substitutes for imports. But in the mid-1950s the economy entered a period of stagnation. Between 1955 and 1973 GDP grew less than 1 percent a year, and in 1975 real income per capita was barely above its 1956 level. The immediate reason for this poor economic performance was the low level of investment during the period. Between 1955 and 1973 investment was less than depreciation allowances; thus, capital stock grew until the late 1950s and contracted thereafter (table 9-1). The population grew at a very low 0.6 percent a year between 1963 and 1975 (table 9-2); 170,000 out of a population of 2.8 million emigrated.[1] The outward population movement closely paralleled the destruction or stagnation of the capital stock.

Table 9-1. Uruguay: Economic Indicators, Selected Periods

Period	g	I/GDP	P	E	O
1956–59	–0.9	12.2	19.6	1,806[a]	22.6
1960–61	3.2	15.5	30.4	—	22.3
1962–68	0.3	12.0	55.7	3,550[b]	19.6
1969–70	5.4	11.1	18.6	12,600	18.4
1971–73	–0.6	10.0	62.6	19,700	19.0
1974–78	4.1	13.6[c]	40.8	—	36.4[c]
1979–81	4.7	17.7	46.2	—	41.4
1982–85	–4.3	11.2	46.8	—	40.3

— Not available.

Note: g = average annual rate of growth of GDP; I/GDP = average investment/GDP ratio; P = average rate of inflation; E = average number of emigrants; O = degree of openness of the economy (exports plus imports divided by GDP).

a. 1955–59.

b. 1963–68.

c. 1975–78.

Source: Banco Central del Uruguay; Banco de la República Oriental del Uruguay (BROU); Uruguay, Dirección General de Estadística y Censos.

Table 9-2. *Uruguay: Population, Selected Years*

Item	1963	1975	1985
Age group			
0–14 years	725,209	752,588	—
15–64 years	1,673,972	1,763,025	—
64 years and over	196,329	272,816	—
Urban or rural			
Urban (Montevideo)[a]	1,202,757	1,237,227	1,303,942
Rural	1,392,753	1,551,202	1,626,622
Total	2,595,510	2,788,429	2,930,564

— Not available.

a. Montevideo is the only large city in Uruguay.

Source: Uruguay, Dirección General de Estadística y Censos, *Censo Nacional de Población y Vivienda*, various years.

High emigration suggests low job opportunities[2] and low real wages, particularly for skilled workers. Real wages fell behind those in Argentina and Brazil. Low investment suggests either a low expected return on investment or a resource constraint. Estimates of the average return of the capital stock during the period point to low productivity of capital (Harberger and Wisecarver 1978). The absolute level of investment was also constrained by the size of the budget deficit and by the low level of domestic savings (table 9-3), but although savings were low, international capital inflows should have provided resources for investment. Another possibility is that growth was hampered by the scarcity of foreign exchange, which is a significant element in gross capital formation. The experience of the Uruguayan economy after 1974 suggests that

Table 9-3. *Uruguay: Net Savings, Net External Resources, and Net Investment, Selected Periods*
(percentage of GDP)

Period	Net savings [a]	Net receipt of external resources [b]	Net investment
1956–59	–2.1	6.7	4.6
1960–61	1.6	4.2	5.8
1962–68	1.5	–0.9	0.6
1969–70	1.1	2.1	3.2
1971–73	3.0	0.5	3.5
1974–79	3.4	4.2	7.6

a. Net investment minus net external resources.

b. Imports minus exports.

Source: Díaz 1984. The depreciation charges used to calculate net investment are from Harberger and Wisecarver 1978.

this constraint was built into the policy regime rather than imposed by structural constraints on exports or imports.

There are three economic explanations for the low expected return on capital, low investment, and, ultimately, poor economic performance during this period.

- Since its early stages, import substitution in Uruguay has involved direct and indirect taxation of agricultural exports. The result has been a structure of relative prices that discouraged domestic production of exportable goods and investment in agriculture. In addition, external shocks posed new obstacles to the traditional export sector. The fall in the price of wool after the end of the Korean war induced domestic producers to reduce output, and the protectionist agricultural policies adopted by the European Communities (EC) in the late 1960s narrowed the external market for agricultural exports.
- In the mid-1950s the expansion of import-substituting industry began to be restricted by the size of the domestic market. The establishment of the Latin American Free Trade Agreement in the 1960s was an unsuccessful attempt to overcome this constraint.
- Uruguay faced increasing price instability during the period. In the late 1940s and early 1950s the relaxation of credit limits and the expansion of the Central Bank's discounting of private short-term bills sparked monetary instability. Double-digit inflation, coupled with interest rate ceilings and a fixed exchange rate, led to the distortion of relative prices and the misallocation of resources. In the 1960s a new source of credit expansion emerged as the public sector began to run significant deficits. Monetary expansion under a fixed exchange rate regime led to frequent balance of payment crises, step devaluations, and increasing instability that fostered capital flight and discouraged investment.

Although the closure of the economy, the consequent discouragement of investment in the agricultural sector, and price instability were recognized as having high social costs, protectionism and monetary mismanagement prevailed, except for two short episodes during the 1960s.

There were political reasons for the persistence of these damaging policies during those years. A reduction in tariffs and export taxes would mean increased land prices, lower wages, and higher prices for beef (which accounts for a significant share of consumer expenditure, particularly for low-income people). Although the higher beef prices would encourage producers to raise more cattle, the increased supply of beef would not come on the market for three or four years. Thus, a change in agricultural price policy might well generate consumer discontent and the consequent short-run political costs without offering significant immediate political benefits—a combination presumably not very attractive for a government with a short and finite horizon (Sapelli 1985).

Political Developments and Economic Outcomes

All the monetary and fiscal variables associated with inflation follow a regular cycle in Uruguay. Inflation almost always peaks in the year following an election, whereas government expenditure, the rediscounting of commercial bills, and the fiscal deficit peak in election years (Díaz 1984). The implication is that in election years the party in office resorts to expansionary policies to obtain voter support. Because the administration is reluctant to devalue, it restricts foreign exchange transactions and represses inflation until after the election. This electoral cycle produced significant departures of the real exchange rate from its equilibrium level during 1955–73. The most interesting attempts to reverse both stagnation and inflation followed a pattern consistent with the election cycle hypothesis.

There are two main political parties in Uruguay, the Colorados and the Blancos. In 1959 the Blanco party took office after almost a century of Colorado party rule. During its first year in office the Blanco administration introduced significant reforms in commercial and exchange rate policies. It eliminated import quotas and multiple exchange rates and implemented a floating exchange rate regime. The public sector, however, ran significant deficits, and exchange rate pressures developed in late 1961 and continued into 1962, an election year. The authorities' reluctance to devalue induced a significant loss of foreign reserves and an upsurge of inflation in 1963.

The second stabilization attempt came in 1968, one year after a Colorado party administration took office. The authorities sought to reduce the inflation rate of 180 percent a year by means of a shock strategy, including a wage and price freeze. After some encouraging results during 1969 and 1970, when the inflation rate fell to 20 percent, fiscal discipline was relaxed in 1971—an election year—and unremitting exchange rate pressures developed. Once again, the authorities' reluctance to devalue the peso in an election year led them to impose severe restrictions on foreign currency transactions and to repress inflation until the next administration.

Crises and Reforms

Economic stagnation and high inflation rates gradually engendered social and political instability in the 1960s and led to a systematic erosion of democratic institutions. There were major strikes in such key sectors as the slaughter industry and banking and continuous clashes between the government and labor unions. The appearance of an urban guerrilla movement in the late 1960s was followed by an increasing involvement of the military in political affairs and finally by a coup in 1973. Between 1971 and 1973 the rate of economic growth was negative. Although the fiscal deficit declined from 5.9 to 1.5 percent of GDP, the inflation rate accelerated, and the country experienced a significant outflow of capital.

The energy crisis of 1973 had a dramatic impact on the Uruguayan economy. A threefold increase in the price of oil, coupled with EC restrictions on beef imports, led to a terms of trade loss equivalent to 2.1 percent of GDP and to a severe external crisis in 1974. The balance of payments went from a current account surplus of US$37.1 million and a net reserve gain of US$6.4 million in 1973 to a current account deficit of US$118.0 million and a net reserve loss of US$79.8 million in 1974. A fiscal deficit equivalent to 30 percent of government expenditure and 4.4 percent of GDP developed as the government increased subsidies in an attempt to sustain real income levels for the working classes while real national income was declining. Wage and price policies and an accommodating monetary policy contributed to an inflation rate that exceeded 100 percent.

There were no significant changes in economic policy during the first year of the military government that took over in June 1973. The oil shock and the inability of existing policies to cope with the altered international circumstances, however, led the authorities to appoint a new economic team in July 1974. This team introduced a significant twist in economic policy: a program of price stabilization and economic reforms that gradually freed domestic prices from administrative controls and liberalized the tight restrictions that had been imposed on foreign trade and payments. The basic objectives of the program were to improve economic efficiency and to promote and diversify nontraditional exports— those other than animal products and their derivatives.

Between 1974 and 1977 the authorities abolished import licensing and quotas, reduced the average level and dispersion of nominal tariffs, introduced subsidies for exports of nontraditional products, and lowered taxes on exports of agricultural goods. They deregulated the foreign exchange and capital markets, eliminated interest rate ceilings, and allowed unrestricted inflows and outflows of capital. They tightened controls on public sector expenditure, improved the economic performance of public utilities, eliminated the personal income tax and widened the application of the value added tax, decontrolled many consumer prices, reduced social security taxes on labor, and kept the exchange rate in line with domestic and foreign prices.

A second wave of reforms, including important changes in agricultural policies, began in 1978. Price controls and export restrictions had significantly hampered the growth of the agricultural sector. In 1978 controls on domestic prices for agricultural goods were abolished, beef and wool exports were liberalized, export taxes were eliminated (as were import taxes for some agricultural inputs and capital goods), and imports of agricultural goods were authorized subject to a 35 percent tariff on the FOB price. In addition, tax exemptions that had benefited export-oriented activities were eliminated, social security taxes were reduced, and the application of the value added tax was extended. A stabilization program was adopted; the exchange rates were set in advance, to be valid for specified periods. Other measures were a gradual, predetermined tariff reduction program, a further reduction in social security taxes, a reduction in subsidies for nontraditional exports, the elimination of subsidized credit for exporters, and a program of deregulation in the agricultural sector.

Following these reforms, growth and investment improved remarkably, but there was no significant progress regarding price stabilization. GDP growth, investment, and emigration exhibited differences from the patterns of the previous decade. Emigration peaked during 1974 and fell steadily thereafter, suggesting that job opportunities had improved. (Even with the downward trend, the number of emigrants remained high until 1978.) The increase in gross capital formation, which became significant after 1976, reflected a higher expected return on capital.

The reallocation of resources within the economy, the elimination of high-cost regulations such as import licenses and quotas, the management of the exchange rate in relation to domestic prices, and the decline in social confrontation appear to be the key explanatory factors behind economic growth before 1977. Since Uruguay experienced adverse terms of trade during the period, it cannot be argued that economic recovery originated in external circumstances. Rather, the change in major economic variables seems to be associated with the opening of the economy to trade and capital flows and with the elimination of the significant distortions caused by the import license and price control regimes that were in force before 1975.

The pattern of growth between 1974 and 1978 was led by export-oriented industrial activities—clothing, leather, shoes, and fishing. The increased significance of these activities was associated with the trajectory of the real effective exchange rate faced by each economic sector. Thus, nontraditional exports, which accounted for less than 50 percent of total exports in 1976, rose to more than twice the level of traditional exports in the late 1970s. In contrast, during 1978–81, the sectors that had led recovery in the previous period contracted as the real exchange rate appreciated, and growth was led mainly by domestically oriented activities (Favaro and Spiller 1990).

Depression and Debt Problems

Several economic variables explain the changes in GDP during 1979–81 and the contraction of the economy at the end of the period. The investment of Argentine capital in land and real estate assets led to a rise in prices and a boom in the construction sector during 1979–80. The announced devaluation of the peso was low in the context of domestic and foreign interest rates, and this induced a significant inflow of capital. The inflow of capital caused a real appreciation of the peso and a contraction of export-oriented and import-competing activities.

It is difficult to isolate this economic situation from political conditions. Since 1977 the military government had made clear its intention to move the country back to a democratic regime, but in 1980 the government failed to gain an electoral majority for a constitutional reform that was supposed to accelerate the transition. In 1982 the government moved toward an agreement with the political parties for a rapid transition to civilian government. The political uncertainty during the period seems to have intensified the deep economic depression that began in the second half of 1981 and continued for the next three years. GDP decreased by 15 percent between 1981 and 1984.

Several external factors contributed to the acute economic contraction.

- The appreciation of the U.S. dollar against European currencies and the yen after 1981 aggravated the overvaluation of the Uruguayan peso, which was pegged to the dollar.
- A series of devaluations by Argentina in 1981—the result of increasing exchange rate pressures—fostered capital flight, spread uncertainty in the region, and displaced Uruguayan exports from the Argentine market.
- A significant increase in interest rates during 1981 led the world into economic recession. Already in early 1981 Uruguay's exchange rate policy and the induced capital inflows had led to an overvalued exchange rate. As the U.S. dollar appreciated and the Argentine and Brazilian currencies depreciated abruptly, the Uruguayan peso moved increasingly out of equilibrium. Between February and November 1982 the authorities tried to restore equilibrium between domestic prices and wages by accelerating the rate of devaluation and freezing wages. But, faced with rising unemployment, they also maintained an expansionary fiscal policy, particularly with respect to state-financed housing construction programs and social security expenditures.

Increasing government expenditure and falling fiscal revenues led to an enormous fiscal deficit (more than 18 percent of GDP in 1982), an increasing external debt, and the exhaustion of international reserves. In November 1982 the authorities abandoned the announced exchange rate regime and allowed the peso to float. During the next three months the peso fell in value by more than 150 percent, and the banking sector suffered a severe run. In 1982 and 1983 the authorities absorbed bad loans from financial institutions and stimulated mergers and acquisitions to prevent bankruptcies. Simultaneously, they were trying to reduce the fiscal deficit and were facing difficulties associated with higher external debt service.

Household Income Distribution

Before 1982 the quality of statistics on personal income was poor, and estimates of the degree of income concentration depended on surveys that used different methodologies. Thus, care has to be exercised when comparing results based on different sources.

A rough comparison of the indicators of household income concentration reveals a trend toward a greater inequality that developed in the 1960s and accelerated in the 1970s. Beginning in the 1980s the distribution of income moved toward greater equality. Data on personal income (restricted to labor earnings) also show a tendency toward higher concentration in the 1970s.

Urban figures for total household income show an increase in inequality between 1980 and 1984, whereas rural income figures exhibit the opposite tendency (tables 9-4 and 9-5). The poorest 40 percent of households received about 16 percent of total income in 1984. Unequal distribution of income is moderate in Uruguay by international standards.

A steady decrease in the share of wages in total income started in 1972 and became acute in the late 1970s (figure 9-1). The increase in employment in the 1970s apparently did not compensate for the drop in nominal wages in relation to the GDP deflator.[3] These observations suggest that the prohibition of labor union activities after 1974 had a significant effect on the level of real wages. But even during the period when unions were active, the share of labor in total income and the average level of real wages were very low in comparison with other countries.

The increased demand for labor during 1974–81 differed among categories of workers. Educational level seems to have significant power in explaining wage differentials during the period, which suggests that highly educated workers were scarce in the short run (table 9-6). Low-skill labor—the type used predominantly in export-oriented activities—increased as a share of total employment, but because of high elasticity, wages for these workers did not rise significantly until the late 1970s.

The authorities' determination to maintain a high real exchange rate during the 1974–78 period, together with the introduction of export subsidies and the reduction of taxes on agricultural exports, brought about an increase in the relative prices of several food items and, initially, a decline in the purchasing power of nominal wages. The net effect on real wages is, however, not clear because this policy also increased the demand for labor. The deregulation of price controls, the increase in the price of public services, the indexation of controlled housing rents, and the liberalization of international capital flows may also have had an initial depressive effect on real wages.

During 1979–81 exchange rate policy induced a significant inflow of capital and an economic boom in the nontradable goods sector. There was an unambiguous increase in real wages and employment and hence in the share of wages in GDP. Since 1982 the decrease in GDP and the

Table 9-4. *Uruguay: Household Income Distribution, Urban (Montevideo), Selected Years, 1961–84*
(cumulative percentage of income)

Percentage of households	1961–62		1963		1967		1976		1980		1982		1984	
	Percentage of income	Cumulative	Percentage of income	Cumulative	Percentage of income	Cumulative	Percentage of income	Cumulative	Percentage of income	Cumulative	Percentage of income	Cumulative	Percentage of income	Cumulative
10	2.5	2.5	2.4	2.4	1.3	1.3	1.3	1.3	2.0	2.0	2.1	2.1	2.2	2.2
20	4.0	4.5	3.9	6.3	3.0	4.3	3.0	4.3	3.6	5.6	3.6	5.6	3.5	5.7
30	5.0	11.4	5.0	11.3	4.4	8.7	4.2	8.1	4.4	9.0	4.4	10.0	4.4	10.1
40	5.9	17.1	6.0	17.6	5.6	14.3	5.3	13.7	5.2	15.2	5.4	15.4	5.5	15.6
50	7.0	24.1	7.2	26.6	6.8	21.1	6.5	21.8	6.6	21.8	6.6	22.0	6.7	22.3
60	8.2	32.4	8.6	33.2	8.0	29.1	7.9	26.2	7.9	29.7	8.0	29.9	8.3	30.6
70	9.7	42.3	10.3	43.5	10.2	29.6	9.7	37.7	9.7	39.4	9.5	39.5	10.1	40.7
80	11.8	54.1	12.0	56.2	13.0	52.6	12.1	49.0	12.1	51.5	12.6	52.1	12.9	53.6
90	15.2	89.3	16.0	72.5	16.9	69.5	16.2	66.0	16.0	67.5	16.6	68.7	17.3	70.9
95	10.0	79.3	10.0	23.2			11.0	77.0	10.9	78.4	11.3	80.0	11.7	83.6
100	10.7	100.0	16.6	100.0	30.5	100.0	23.0	100.0	21.7	100.0	20.0	100.0	17.4	100.0
Gini index	0.3661		0.3706		0.4181		0.4500		0.4237		0.4152		0.4837	

Source: For 1961–62, 1963, 1967, and 1976, Melgar 1982; for 1980 and 1982, Rossi 1982; for 1984, authors' calculations. All results were obtained using methodology described in Kakwani 1980.

Table 9-5. Uruguay: Household Income Distribution, Rural, 1963, 1982, and 1984

Percentage of households	1963		1982		1984	
	Percentage of income	Cumulative	Percentage of income	Cumulative	Percentage of income	Cumulative
10	1.20	1.20	2.05	2.05	2.40	2.40
20	2.85	4.05	3.63	6.68	3.60	6.00
30	3.98	8.03	4.72	11.40	4.60	10.60
40	5.13	13.16	5.79	17.19	5.60	16.20
50	6.41	19.57	6.96	24.15	6.70	22.90
60	7.95	27.52	8.37	32.52	8.10	31.00
70	9.94	37.44	10.16	42.68	9.80	40.80
80	12.71	50.71	14.56	57.24	12.20	53.00
90	17.27	67.46	16.44	73.68	16.30	69.30
95	11.90	79.34	10.88	84.56	11.00	80.30
100	20.66	100.00	18.44	100.00	19.70	100.00
Gini index	0.4236		0.3978		0.4055	

Source: For 1963, Melgar 1982; for 1982, Rossi 1982; for 1984, authors' calculations.

transfers associated with increased external debt service have worked to reduce earnings from both labor and capital. Capital earnings appear to have fallen more abruptly than real wages—a result that explains the leveling of income distribution during the period.

Figure 9-1. Uruguay: Wages as a Share of GDP, 1954–82

Percent

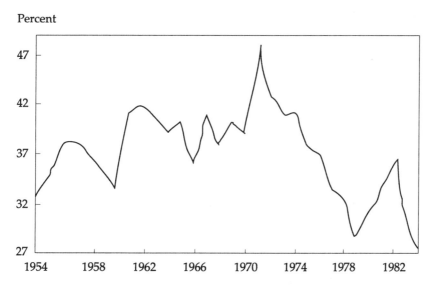

Source: Based on Banco Central del Uruguay, *Cuentas Nacionales*, and Uruguay, Dirección General de Estadísticas y Censos. *Anuario Estadístico*, various years.

Table 9-6. Uruguay: Educational Level and Workers' Income, Montevideo, 1972 and 1979
(income of workers who did not complete primary school = 100)

Educational level	1972	1979
Did not complete primary school	100.0	100.0
Completed primary school	108.9	115.5
Completed primary school but did not complete secondary school, first level	108.7	118.0
Completed secondary school, first level	132.7	170.5
Completed secondary school, first level, but did not complete secondary school, second level	117.3	144.2
Completed secondary school, second level	137.4	198.0
Completed secondary school, second level, but did not complete university	148.5	229.7
Completed university	211.3	563.0

Note: Primary education is six years. Secondary education includes a first stage (four years) and a second stage (two years of pre-university training).
Source: Indart 1981.

Poverty

The sustained process of economic growth experienced up to 1930 and again in the immediate postwar period combined with extremely favorable terms of trade to give Uruguay a high standard of living in the early 1950s, compared with other Latin American countries. There is only ambiguous evidence about the effect that the period of stagnation between 1955 and 1972 had on poverty.

The proportion of poor households—those with incomes less than one-half the national average—has been stable. It was 30 percent in 1967, 35 percent in 1976, and 30 percent in 1982 and again in 1984 (Instituto de Economía 1971; Uruguay, Dirección General de Estadística y Censos, *Encuesta de Hogares* 1976, 1982, 1984).

Social Indicators

Table 9-7 shows public expenditures on health, education, and social security. The trend for the first two indicators has been ambiguous since the 1960s. The share in GDP of public expenditure on education and health decreased steadily, but since public expenditure basically consists of labor earnings and real wages declined during the period, the level of services may not have declined. The share in GDP of social security expenditures remained constant throughout the period.

Although the share of education in the overall government budget declined during the period, evidence from census figures points toward an improvement in quality. The number of primary school pupils per

Table 9-7. Public Expenditure in the Social Sectors, Selected Years, 1961–83
(percentage of GDP)

Year	Education	Health	Social security
1961	4.3	1.3	9.4
1972	2.3	0.4	12.8
1980	1.9	1.1	10.6
1983	1.6	0.8	12.9

Source: For 1961, authors' estimates; for 1972, 1980, and 1983, International Monetary Fund 1985, table 5.7.

teacher and the number of secondary school students per building decreased.

Pupils per teacher	1959	1972	1981
National	32	25	21
Montevideo	35	27	25
Rural	31	24	19

Students per building	1970	1981
National	966	642
Montevideo	1,641	1,310
Rural	684	433

The educational level of the urban labor force has improved (table 9-8), and the already high literacy rate has increased. (In the table below, the 1963 figures are for the population eight years of age and older; the 1975 figures are for ten years and older.)

Literacy rate	1963	1975
Montevideo	94.6	96.9
Uruguay	91.0	94.3

The number of hospital beds in public health facilities (a proxy for the quality of public health services) fell, according to figures from the Ministerio de Salud Pública.

Number of hospital beds	1962	1970	1975	1980	1984
Montevideo	6,380	5,551	4,402	4,094	5,068
Rural	7,609	7,042	6,810	6,446	3,779
Total	13,989	12,593	11,212	10,540	8,847

This trend, however, is explained by the lower incidence of tuberculosis and by changes in the treatment of psychiatric cases that reduced hospitalization. More direct measures of the health of the population

Table 9-8. Uruguay: Educational Level of the Labor Force, Montevideo, 1972 and 1979
(percent)

Educational level	1972	1979
Did not complete primary school	25.8	15.6
Completed primary school	39.6	38.1
Completed primary school but did not complete secondary school, first level	10.3	11.2
Completed secondary school, first level	11.1	14.7
Completed secondary school, first level, but did not complete secondary school, second level	2.3	3.3
Completed secondary school, second level	4.0	6.8
Completed secondary school, second level, but did not complete university	4.3	6.6
Completed university	2.5	3.7
Total	100.0	100.0

Source: Indart 1981.

indicate a general improvement. Life expectancy at birth has increased, as shown by census data.

Life expectancy	Total	Male	Female
1963–64	68.46	65.51	71.56
1974–76	68.89	65.66	72.41
1980–85	70.34	67.11	73.74

Figures from the Ministerio de Salud Pública indicate a considerable decline in the infant mortality rate over the study period.

Year	Deaths per 1,000 live births
1950	64.0
1955	53.2
1960	54.3
1965	55.2
1970	50.2
1975	48.6
1985	29.3

Available housing has increased, according to census figures.

Number of houses	1963	1975	1985
Montevideo	348,997	374,541	419,579
Rural	416,328	505,124	565,315
Total	765,325	879,665	984,894

Public expenditure has played a significant part in this expansion of housing. During the second half of the 1970s the Banco Hipotecario (the

Table 9-9. Uruguay: Number of Houses Constructed, 1977–84

Year	Total	Financed by BHU	Other
1977	13,196	2,447	10,749
1978	16,450	3,605	12,845
1979	20,413	7,121	13,292
1980	26,418	15,006	11,412
1981	26,956	12,632	14,324
1982	19,394	8,730	10,664
1983	17,390	7,473	9,917
1984	13,852	3,405	10,447

Note: BHU, Banco Hipotecario del Uruguay.
Source: Based on unpublished data from Cámara de la Construcción and Banco Hipotecario del Uruguay.

public mortgage bank) developed an ambitious plan for subsidizing construction of new houses for low-income families. This program financed 80 percent of housing constructed between 1975 and 1985 (table 9-9).

To summarize, although the public expenditure indicators are contradictory, the available evidence indicates that the standard of living in Uruguay has risen during the past three decades.

Notes

1. Emigrants were concentrated in the 15–34 age group and were mainly males with a higher level of education than the average for Montevideo (Aguiar 1982).

2. The annual rate of growth of employment between 1963 and 1975 was 1.4 percent, whereas the economically active population grew at a rate of 0.7 percent. Of 160,000 new jobs created between 1963 and 1975 at least 45,300—28.3 percent—were in the public sector.

3. Official wage indexes have serious shortcomings and must be treated with caution. The use of 1968 as a base period for comparisons is questionable because the general freeze in wages and prices imposed by the government during that year caused serious distortions in relative prices. In addition, the official index does not incorporate true wage increments during part of the 1970s. There is evidence for a steady decline in real wages since the early 1960s; this trend is consistent with an observed contraction in the stock of capital and growing inefficiency in the economy.

10 Historical Background to 1955

During Spain's colonial rule, what is now Uruguay was part of the viceroyship of the Río de la Plata. Although these lands were discovered in 1516, they did not attract Spanish attention because they lacked mineral resources, human resources—the indigenous inhabitants were too fierce to be used as laborers on plantations—and agricultural land useful for marketable crops such as sugar or cotton.

In 1611 Hernandarias, a Spanish colonial officeholder, introduced cattle, which grazed on the Uruguayan prairies and reproduced rapidly in the following decades. This was the start of an industry that is still the main source of the country's wealth.

Until the late 1700s cattle were raised for their hides. Bandits from Brazil, profiting from the low level of control in the country, preyed on the cattle industry. Large parcels of land were given to the first settlers and, later on, to recipients of favors from the authorities. At the beginning of the nineteenth century, however, a significant share of land remained in public hands. Much of Uruguay was virtually a commons. Landed property rights, let alone the real capacity to exploit them, were little developed during this period.

Montevideo, founded in 1724, had the best natural harbor in the area. In the late 1700s it began its development as the main port in the region, attracting most of the trade destined for the present territory of Argentina. This led to an early conflict of interest with Buenos Aires.

Independence and Early Political Development

In the 1810s the inhabitants of the right bank of the Uruguay River joined a movement against the restrictive Spanish commercial regime that had been imposed in neighboring Buenos Aires. Although the initial goal was a change in colonial commercial practices, the movement eventually culminated in independence. The first constitution was adopted in 1830, but for several decades thereafter the new presidential regime was unable to control the country. Only three of the twenty-five governments in office between 1830 and 1903 finished their terms without facing serious revolutions. Continuous civil war between the constitutional government and local rural leaders, or *caudillos*, diminished the government's authority.]

The 1830 Constitution called for a Parliament composed of a House of Representatives and a Senate. Representatives were elected by direct vote; senators were elected indirectly through departmental electoral colleges. (The country was initially divided into nine departments, or political districts, and later into nineteen departments.) Since majority rule prevailed in both cases, the minority was not represented at the department level. Uruguayan democracy was hardly more than a formal label during the nineteenth century. Fraud was rampant, and the number of voters in the overall population was negligible. In 1905 the voting population amounted to less than 5 percent of the total population.]

[The Blanco and Colorado parties, founded in 1836, were primarily military bands rather than groups distinguished by ideological differences. Between 1838 and 1851 there was continuous war between the Blancos, who controlled the rural areas, and the Colorados, whose stronghold was Montevideo.] Argentina, Brazil, and several European countries intervened in the struggle. By the end of the "Guerra Grande," in 1851, the country was a shambles. The cost of the unrest was enormous. Both sides frequently expropriated ranchers' horses without proper compensation. Ranchers of British or French origin were privileged in that they could call on the power of their embassies to secure adequate compensation for damages.

In 1853 a national army was created. It was not a professional army with a stable officer corps, and it was no match for the forces that could be assembled against it by the *caudillos* (Moore 1978). The foundation for a genuine professional army was laid in 1865, when Uruguay (under Venancio Flores), Argentina, and Brazil declared war on Paraguay. Uruguay suffered heavy casualties in this war of the Triple Alliance; of 2,000 troops who went to war, only 250 survived.

In 1868 Flores was assassinated, and Lorenzo Batlle, his former war minister and a general in the army, took office. Thus began a period of almost two decades when all presidents were either former war ministers or were eventually ousted by the military, which dominated politics through its powerful Montevideo garrison. Batlle modernized the army, which was unabashedly Colorado, and used its power to keep his enemies in check.

In the era of military ascendancy the army evolved from guaranteeing the political survival of civil administrations (1868–75) to implementing military control over the political system for "the good of the nation" (under Lorenzo Latorre, a former army colonel who dismissed Parliament) and finally to exercising military domination for the advantage of military elites (under Máximo Santos). After 1886 its role shifted from permanent intervention in political affairs to compliant rectitude. President Máximo Tajes, the last of the active military rulers, reduced the size of the Montevideo garrison by sending units out into the countryside and developed a national police force that could serve as a countervailing force against the army. His successor, Julio Herrera y Obes, who had been Tajes's minister of the interior, expanded the police force, created a complex, bureaucratized chain of command, and appointed loyal officers to key positions. The process of subordination was completed during the first José Batlle administration (1903–07).

In 1872 a peace agreement between the warring parties gave the Blancos control over four of the existing twelve departments of Uruguay. Thus began the practice of rule by "coparticipation." In 1897 war broke out between the national government and a large rebel army assembled by the Blanco party. After six months of fighting, peace was made under an agreement that increased from four to six the number of departments controlled by the Blancos while leaving their military capacity intact.

In 1903 José Batlle, the son of Lorenzo Batlle, was elected president, although he was the Colorado party candidate least acceptable to the Blancos. His nomination created unrest among the Blancos, who were suspected of commanding an army larger than that of the national government. To counter the Blancos, Batlle, who openly disavowed the 1897 coparticipation agreement, increased the size of the national army by nine or ten times. In 1904 he went to war with the Blancos and defeated them, thus closing a period of war and unrest, opening a road for peaceful political competition, and consolidating the authority of the state.

After the war Batlle took steps to limit the military's ability to intervene in political affairs. He reduced the army from roughly 35,000 to 10,000 men, increased the number of military units, divided the territory among three military commands, and integrated Blanco officers into the regular army. Most important, he introduced measures that increased the prestige of the political system and eliminated the battlefield as a legitimate arena for achieving political goals.

Demographic Changes

The Uruguayan population remained stable for some time after independence. Between 1852 and 1872, however, it grew at an annual rate of 6.0 percent with the arrival of large numbers of European immigrants, predominantly from Italy and Spain.

Immigration brought about a rapid growth of the country's population in the last three decades of the nineteenth century. In 1889, 46.8 percent of Montevideo's population was foreign born. Whereas two-thirds of the foreigners were economically active, the proportion was barely one-fourth among native Uruguayans. The differing ratios are explained by differences in the age composition of the two groups.

In 1908 the country's population was a little more than 1 million, of which 17.4 percent were foreigners and 29.7 percent lived in Montevideo. (Already at the time of independence approximately one-fourth of the population lived in Montevideo.) Between 1908 and 1929, while the country's population and labor force grew at 2.3 and 2.5 percent a year, respectively, Montevideo's population and labor force expanded at 3.5 and 4 percent a year.

Immigration was interrupted by World War I but proceeded rapidly in its aftermath. Between 1919 and 1930 almost 200,000 people immigrated to Uruguay. After 1932 a number of policy measures were introduced to curb immigration. These culminated in a restrictive immigration law, passed in 1936.

Economic Developments to 1890

In the late 1700s a hung beef industry developed, and by 1860 half a million animals were being slaughtered each year. This industry increased the market value of cattle, which until then had been valued only for their hides. Two plants that produced concentrated beef and corned beef were founded in the 1860s.

Sheep breeding, introduced in the 1860s (see table 10-1), was more labor-intensive than cattle raising, since sheep require continuous supervision, and it attracted skilled European labor. The new industry also required the enclosure of fields. The development of sheep raising and the rise in the market value of cattle increased the value of land (table 10-2) and gave further impetus to the demand for an adequate definition of property rights.

Table 10-1. Uruguay: Livestock, Selected Years, 1852–1908
(thousands)

Year	Cattle	Sheep
1852	1,888	796
1860	5,218	2,594
1874	4,745	9,753
1886	6,254	17,246
1890	5,282	13,757
1894	5,205	12,821
1898	4,827	15,537
1902	7,029	17,927
1908	8,193	26,287

Source: Finch 1980; Favaro 1990.

Table 10-2. Uruguay: Land Prices, 1852–1939
(pesos per hectare)

Period	Current price[a]
1852–56	0.60
1857–61	2.09
1862–66	3.47
1867–71	4.81
1872–76	6.17
1877–81	6.38
1882–85	8.94
1886–90	16.06
1891–95	14.93
1896–1900	15.74
1901–05	21.94
1906–10	39.45
1911–13	67.01
1918–22	66.49
1923–27	65.90
1928–32	62.23
1933–39	50.53

a. Average price per hectare.
Source: For 1852–1913, Barrán and Nahum 1967–78; for 1918–39, Finch 1980.

In the late 1860s the absence of well-defined property rights impeded the introduction of wire fencing. This, in turn, discouraged attempts to improve the quality of the herd and fostered a floating population of wanderers who provided the manpower used by the *caudillos* in their periodic uprisings. During this period a group of cattle producers established the Asociación Rural del Uruguay (ARU), a ranchers' organization that advocated the modernization of the country and articulated the interests of the leading rural entrepreneurs. The founders of the ARU were aware of the possibilities for improving technology in the livestock sector and of the opportunities offered by the enlarged world market. They lobbied strongly for the establishment of the institutional basis necessary for modernizing the country. For example, they were in favor of measures that would define property rights, improve rural communications and security, and upgrade the educational level of the population. The ARU emphasized the virtues of thrift and effort, the leading role of agriculture in the country, and the need to reduce discretionary state power. It was highly critical of the political elite of the time and provided expert advice and ideological support to the military governments that ruled the country beginning in 1874.

Latorre's administration laid the groundwork for Uruguay's economic growth in the twentieth century. Mandatory field enclosure, the buildup of an operational police force, and the definition of rights to use public lands under precarious tenancy created an institutional environment appropriate for the introduction of new technology. Latorre also established a national public school system that helped to adapt the skills of a rapidly growing population to the demands of a period transitional to modernization. This period was also the starting point for protectionism in Uruguay.

The political instability of the 1830–90 period may not have provided the most appropriate environment for economic growth, but the economy nevertheless seems to have grown rapidly. By 1890 Uruguay had achieved a privileged position in comparison with other countries in the region and with Europe. An estimate of the country's 1866 GDP put output at 48 million pesos—approximately US$350 million at 1978 prices. This puts income per capita at US$875 (at 1978 prices). Although high, the estimate is consistent with the observed flow of immigration to Uruguay during those years. It has been estimated that GDP grew at 5.3 percent a year during 1830–80. This appears reasonable when compared with the rates of growth of tariff revenue (5.3 percent for 1828–88) and of exports and imports (4.3 percent for 1830–90), as shown in tables 10-3 and 10-4.

Economic growth during the period is explained by more efficient land use and by significant flows of immigration and foreign investment. Three characteristics of land use are noteworthy: new production techniques were introduced and altered, over time, when appropriate; land

Table 10-3. Uruguay: Fiscal Revenue, Selected Years, 1829–1924
(for ranges, period averages)

Year	Customs (U.S. dollars)	Total (U.S. dollars)	Customs revenue/total revenue (percent)
1829	582,234	751,040	77.6
1839	1,728,621	2,619,762	66.0
1854	1,380,000	3,715,586	37.2
1862	1,489,300	2,863,324	52.1
1872	7,207,907	8,099,554	89.0
1880	4,409,946	7,015,558	62.9
1888	9,000,000	13,793,796	65.3
1898	9,872,977	15,101,948	65.4
1904	9,162,211	18,018,791	50.9
1907–08	13,194,681	26,517,723	49.8
1911–12	16,904,546	37,556,760	45.1
1915–16	11,811,075	35,173,942	33.6
1919–20	16,593,560	44,936,537	37.0
1923–24	17,788,027	50,692,744	35.1

Source: Acevedo 1933.

Table 10-4. Uruguay: Growth Rates of Exports and Imports, 1830–1930
(average annual percentage change)

Period	Exports	Imports
1830–60	2.8	3.9
1860–80	6.6	4.4
1880–90	4.0	5.2
1890–1900	0.1	–3.0
1900–10	3.4	5.5
1910–14	9.2	–2.3
1915–25	2.4	8.9
1830–90	4.3	4.3
1890–1914	2.9	0.6
1915–30	1.7	5.7

Source: Uruguay, Dirección General de Estadística y Censos, *Anuario Estadístico*, various years.

use followed the signals provided by world market prices and benefited from increased international trade; and, even though the introduction of sheep raising increased the use of labor, land exploitation was low in labor intensity. Even at this early stage, the country was already highly urbanized. One reason for early urbanization was the role played by Montevideo as the main port of the region.

There was no domestic currency before the 1850s. In 1857 two commercial banks were founded and were allowed to print bank notes convertible to gold or silver. In 1862 a gold-peso parity was established that remained unchanged until 1935. Thus, the government did not resort to inflation to finance fiscal deficits, and the country benefited from remarkable price stability. The absence of unified state power during these decades considerably limited the influence that the government and its policies had on the allocation of resources and the distribution of income.

Economic Developments to 1930

Between 1890 and 1930 Uruguay experienced a moderate rate of economic growth, consolidated a modern polity, and shaped the basis for a welfare state. GDP grew at an annual rate of 2.8 percent between 1880 and 1930 (Díaz 1979). Exports grew at 2.9 percent a year between 1890 and 1914 and 1.7 percent a year between 1915 and 1930; imports grew at 0.6 and 5.7 percent a year during those periods. Other indicators suggest that the growth rate slowed during these years. For example, according to Acevedo (1933), the amount of freight that passed through the port of Montevideo increased from about 960 tons in 1880 to almost 1,700 tons in 1910 but was only about 1,625 tons in 1920. (By 1930 the figure had risen to about 2,300 tons.) Population growth also slowed during the period (table 10-5) as a result of both a lower birthrate and reduced immigration.

The Livestock Sector

Land prices, which had increased at 8.5 percent a year between 1858 and 1888, rose only 3.3 percent a year between 1888 and 1930. From 1912 on, the price of land diminished. The evolution of the price of land was the mirror image of the changes in the value of the output of the rural sector that had been made possible by technological improvements and by the definition of property rights.

Technological innovations introduced during the last quarter of the nineteenth century permitted the shipment overseas of frozen beef and paved the way for the development of the slaughter industry during 1900–20. The first slaughterhouse was established in 1902. Originally a Uruguayan capital venture, it was later bought by Argentine investors. Two U.S. firms, Swift (in 1912) and Armour (in 1917), began exporting Uruguayan beef to the United Kingdom; they came to handle 8 percent of total slaughtered cattle. The availability of refrigeration overcame the constraint of low international demand for hung beef and meat concentrates and expanded the demand for cattle. The consequent increase in prices provided further incentives for introducing technical innovations to improve the quality of the herd.

The drop in international meat prices after the end of World War I caused the domestic price of cattle to decline. After reaching a peak price of US$68.40 in 1920, the average price of steers fell to US$45.70 and US$31.80 in the next two years. Domestic producers viewed this downward trend as a consequence of collusion among slaughterhouses.

Table 10-5. Uruguay: Population Growth, 1895–1934

Period	Natural rate of increase	Migration rate	Total rate of increase
1895–99	28.6	0.1	28.7
1900–04	25.2	0.9	26.1
1905–09	23.6	2.2	25.8
1910–14	23.0	1.3	24.3
1915–19	17.8	0.2	18.0
1920–24	17.5	2.6	20.1
1925–29	16.7	3.9	20.6
1930–34	14.3	1.2	15.5

Note: The natural rate of increase is the average annual birthrate per thousand minus the average annual death rate per thousand. The migration rate is the average annual number of migrants per thousand base population.

Source: Finch 1980.

In 1928 the authorities established the Frigorífico Nacional, a public slaughterhouse. The logic behind this move was that the new slaughter-house would reduce the meat-packing companies' market power and set a floor for the domestic price of cattle. This argument reflected enormous confusion regarding the determinants of the domestic price of beef and the origins of the slaughter companies' supposed market power. Any such power (if it existed) was located in the international market. Unless Uruguay was able to affect world market prices, the government's strategy was bound to be unsuccessful—as turned out to be the case. The founding of the Frigorífico Nacional was a landmark in a series of misguided political decisions that severely distorted the domestic beef market, created disincentives to invest in the sector, and finally caused foreign investment to abandon the activity in the late 1950s.

Tariffs

Before 1874 Uruguay had a uniform 20 percent tariff on imports. Taxa-tion on imports was not protectionist in intent; rather, it was the country's main source of fiscal revenue. The first protectionist law, enacted in 1875 during the Latorre administration, implied a general increase in tariffs as well as a differentiated treatment of inputs and final goods. The rise in protectionism was interrupted in 1879 by a general reduction of tariff levels—by as much as 50 percent for certain items—but in 1881, 1886, and 1888 further steps were taken toward the closure of the economy. Table 10-6 shows the change in imports of consumer goods during this period.

The introduction of higher tariffs appears to have been an attempt to redistribute part of the earnings of the rural sector among other social groups, particularly the urban population. Interestingly enough, the first protectionist law was passed by a government strongly influenced by the rural entrepreneurs who had led the process of modernization of the country.

Table 10-6. Uruguay: Imports of Consumer Goods, Selected Periods, 1872–1900
(thousands of U.S. dollars)

Imports	1872–74	1888–90	1890–1900
Beverages	8,897	13,408	7,379
Food	455	333	99
Clothing	5,038	2,091	1,396
Other	2,606	2,002	685
Total	16,996	17,834	9,559

Source: Anichini, Caumont, and Sjaastad 1978.

Public Enterprises

Another significant development of the period was the replacement of private investment, usually of foreign origin, with public firms. In most cases these firms were granted legal monopolies.

In 1911 the Banco de la República Oriental del Uruguay (BROU), originally a commercial mixed-capital bank, was nationalized. In addition, a public insurance company was funded and was given a legal monopoly in most insurance lines. In 1912 the government nationalized the mortgage bank and established another monopoly, a national power-generating firm. In 1916 the national port services administration was founded; in 1928 a mixed-capital company was allowed to construct and operate, under a legal monopoly, a new telephone system that displaced two private suppliers; and in 1931 a public oil-refining and alcohol-producing monopoly (ANCAP) was established.

Although explanations of the expansion of the public sector during the first decades of the century have emphasized the role of ideas, it is difficult to account for the course of events in terms of ideology. In general, the original investment in areas such as railroads, water supply, and power generation was made on the initiative of the private sector. An agreement with the state laid down the basis for public regulation, usually through a rate-of-return control. During this period the political system appears to have been extremely vulnerable to pressures from the private sector to intervene in economic affairs. Once intervention had taken place, there was a tendency to create rents by establishing a legal monopoly.

In the 1910s public sector activities were expanded mainly to prevent bankruptcies. (The exceptions were in port services and insurance.) Thus, the nationalization of the BROU in 1911 was the last step in a series of events that began with the collapse in 1893 of the National Bank, a predecessor of the BROU. The failure of the National Bank, which owned the company that supplied electricity to Montevideo, also led to the development of a public power company. The new company, operating with municipal support, was granted a monopoly right to supply electricity to Montevideo in 1905 and a national monopoly in 1912. Similarly, the nationalization of the mortgage bank had its origin in a state initiative in 1912 to prevent the bankruptcy of a private mortgage bank. Public sector involvement in railroads can be traced back to 1915, when action was taken to prevent the failure of a private railroad company.

This process of public sector expansion reduced competition because in most cases the public companies were given legal monopoly rights. Legal monopolies were not always put into force immediately, but they eventually became binding. The second wave of public sector expansion, in the late 1920s and 1930s, also involved grants of monopolies. (The mixed-capital slaughterhouse established in 1928 benefited from a monopoly right to supply beef to Montevideo.)

Electoral Politics and Social Policies

In the 1890s the Blanco and Colorado parties began a gradual process of transformation into political organizations able to spread ideas and attract votes and adherents. A new breed of professional politicians who came mainly from the middle classes and were able to run a complex organization displaced the traditional elites in the parties' leadership.

José Batlle was one of the architects of this transformation from elite to mass politics. He was a member of a generation that expressed dissent with the military governments of the previous decade and had confidence in the modernization of the country and the consolidation of democracy. Although Batlle's policies were based on deeply rooted beliefs, they also suited the objectives of the Colorado party under his rule. Batlle pursued the unification of the country under a single authority and the consolidation of a modern democracy. This implied, in 1903, the disavowal of the Pact of 1897 and the elimination of war and revolt as legitimate means of achieving political goals. Changes in the political system were required, including a higher degree of mass participation and honest electoral practices that encouraged the opposition to compete under democratic rules.

To counter the Blanco party, Batlle had to enlist the support of urban groups. One means for doing this was through income redistribution policies that favored the urban population. Batlle's protectionist policies redistributed part of the value of agricultural output to urban groups, in addition to increasing the government's revenues to meet the financial needs implied by the enlargement of the national army.

During 1900–20 Uruguay developed, under José Batlle's leadership, a vast program of social reforms that transformed the country into one of the world's first welfare states. Working conditions were improved, and in 1904 a social security system was established that provided coverage to public employees who were more than 60 years of age and had worked for thirty years. In 1919 coverage was extended to the private sector and in the 1920s to women with children who had been employed at least ten years.

Batlle's reforms have often been explained as the triumph of his socialist ideas. Although the influence of ideology cannot be denied, the social reforms enacted by the Colorado governments seem to have been more intended to obtain the support of the growing and politically active urban population.

It is likely that Batlle's policies toward the British-owned public utilities and the Catholic Church during this period were strongly influenced by his desire to develop a unified authority and a modern state. Thus, a divorce law was enacted, religious education in primary schools was eliminated, and the state and the Church were definitely separated. In this context, Batlle's stand against British firms appears to be motivated less by a deep ideological opposition to foreign investment than by fear of the companies' power, compared with the weakness of the Uruguayan state, or by the desire to put pressure on the companies to keep prices in check.

During this period both parties pursued similar social policies. The 1921 Colorado party program favored old age pensions, social security benefits, minimum wages, free medical assistance, and protectionism. It opposed an income tax, which it considered a tax on labor. The Blanco party in 1906 advocated social security benefits, the mandatory eight-hour day, and state mediation in conflicts between unions and firms.

The similarities in the social policies pursued by the parties reflected their competition for the support of the growing urban population. Although the Blanco party was still considered the party that represented the interests of agriculture and the Colorado party was seen as the political representative of urban groups, their ideological differences were minor and were associated with their particular current interests. The Blanco party's concern about the enlargement of the state appeared to stem more from its inability to share part of the power to appoint public employees than from deeply rooted ideas. Thus, this issue was given low priority in the party agenda once the political system managed to co-opt the minority party.

The political reforms enacted during the first two decades of the twentieth century established basic rights and procedures that created incentives for the parties to compete according to democratic rules. And, as the menace of civil war and revolt receded, so did the prospects of military interference in political affairs.

The 1919 Constitution introduced proportional representation, the direct vote for all candidates, and the secret ballot, and it significantly reduced the grounds for suspending the right to vote. A public bureau was given the responsibility for registering all citizens able to vote and for creating a directory that allowed electoral control and severely limited fraud. The 1910 electoral law established the simultaneous vote for party and candidate. Under this system votes for different candidates on a particular party list were added up. The party with the largest number of votes won the elections, and the group with the largest number of votes within the party captured executive power. The law established proportional representation for the election of senators and representatives (although each department had a minimum number of representatives), a unique political district for the election of senators, and a unique list for candidates for the executive, the Senate, and the House of Representatives. This peculiar electoral regime enabled the political parties to face internal disputes and factions without experiencing formal divisions, but it often fostered a low degree of agreement and a level of ideological heterogeneity that posed difficulties for the party in office. Voters had little control over their representatives because of the rigidity imposed by lists that tied together the elections for Parliament and the executive.

To sum up, the development of the modern Uruguayan state was accompanied by increased public sector intervention in the economy through a general trend toward protectionism, the establishment of public enterprises (most of them endowed with legal monopolies), and the development of a welfare state. These changes in the pattern of regulation signaled a trend in public policy toward income distribution objectives that favored urban areas. This tendency was a response to the growth in the numbers and proportion of the urban population and to changes in the political system that consolidated democratic processes and initiated an era of mass politics. Heavy taxation of agriculture allowed the state to capture and redistribute a significant share of the enormous rents created by the definition of property rights and the introduction of modern technology during the last decades of the nineteenth century. Although initially this did not have a significant detrimental effect on technological innovation, after the 1910s the burden of taxation led to a decrease in the price of land and, ultimately, to the stagnation of the livestock sector, which had no incentive to introduce technological improvements at the prevailing relative prices.

Initial Conditions, 1930–55

The political system developed in the 1920s and 1930s implied a higher degree of professionalism in the political parties and an increasing demand for funds to support party politics. The expansion of the public sector was an invaluable source of employment for party adherents and militants. Uruguayan democracy included features that favored collusion and power sharing between the Blancos and Colorados. Two examples were the constitutional reform of 1919 and the Pacto del Chinchulin.

The 1919 Constitution was the result of a pact between the *batllista* government of Feliciano Viera, which supported a collegiate executive, and the majority of the Constitutional Assembly elected in 1916, which opposed such a collegium. The pact established an executive consisting of a president, elected for a four-year period by direct popular vote, and a National Administration Council of nine members representing both the majority and the minority parties. Its members served for six years, and one-third of the membership was elected every two years. Within the new organization some ministries reported directly to the president and others reported to the National Administration Council. The reform institutionalized power sharing and fragmented decisionmaking at the executive level.

The Pacto del Chinchulin—literally, pork barrel—was an agreement between groups within the Blanco and Colorado parties. It provided that the participation of representatives of the majority and the minority parties in the direction of public enterprises would be determined by the proportions each had in the National Administration Council. The pact led to the establishment of ANCAP, the national oil-refining and alcohol-producing monopoly.

This organization of the political system, coupled with fragmentation within the political parties, gave rise to multiple centers of decisionmaking that were largely unchecked and that disregarded the consequences of their decisions for society as a whole. Thus, the political system combined collusion with an incapacity to recognize the costs of various public services for society as a whole. These properties of the Uruguayan political regime were to impose a very large cost when the country began experiencing the consequences of the Great Depression.

Political Developments

In 1930 Gabriel Terra, the leader of a group within the Colorado party that opposed the collegial executive established under the 1919 Constitution, was elected president. Terra's administration coincided with the beginning of the Great Depression. The value of the country's exports contracted, its real income declined, and unemployment increased (table 10-7).

From the beginning of his term, in 1930, Terra campaigned against the executive organization established by the constitutional reform of 1919. He argued that the structure of state power defined by that reform was not appropriate to the demands imposed on the government by the crisis. Terra argued forcefully for the elimination of the collegium, but he faced strong opposition both inside the Colorado party, where he was opposed by the *batllistas*, and from the Blanco party. In 1933 Terra dissolved Parliament.

Terra managed to get support for a new constitutional reform that returned the country to a presidential regime and established a Senate of thirty members, fifteen of whom belonged to the majority faction of the winning party and fifteen to the majority faction of the minority party. This peculiar structure meant a de facto veto of any law that was not supported by the ruling majorities of both parties. Terra's coup

Table 10-7. Uruguay: Effects of the Great Depression on the Uruguayan Economy, 1930–35

Year	Unemployment[a] (thousands)	Net ranchers' income (millions of dollars)	GDP (1930 = 100)
1930	30.0	67.4	100.0
1931	—	53.0	79.8
1932	38.8	31.8	53.2
1933	40.8	40.8	39.2
1934	28.0	50.1	45.1
1935	26.6	66.0	38.9

— Not available.

a. Number of individuals.

Source: Millot, Silva, and Silva 1972.

appears to have been a response to the incapacity of a fragmented and collusive political system to confront a severe external shock. This interpretation is consistent with the steps taken by his administration to centralize the different social security regimes under a single authority and with the design of a Senate structure that drastically limited the power of small political factions.

Terra imposed severe restrictions on the expansion of government expenditures. In fact, during his period in office, wages and salaries in the public sector were reduced in nominal terms, and social security expenditures were held down. Ironically, the incentives created by the protectionist policies implemented during this period were to contribute to the enlargement of public employment in the next two decades.

Alfredo Baldomir, who had been chief of the Montevideo Police Department under Terra, was elected president in 1938. He maintained the same political alliances as his predecessor until 1942, when he dismissed Parliament and called on the *batllistas* and the minority of the Blanco party to participate in the government. Under the prosperity associated with the war period the country returned to a mixed executive power organization with the constitutional reform of 1942. In 1951 a new constitution was adopted. It provided for a collegiate executive, and it institutionalized power sharing by specifying that the executive boards of public enterprises would contain three members from the majority party and two from the minority party. The return to power sharing and the fragmentation of power were facilitated by the improvement in the terms of trade during World War II and the Korean war.

Uruguay and the Great Depression

The protectionist policies followed in most countries during the Depression, coupled with rising unemployment and falling real income, confronted the Uruguayan government with two alternatives for reestablishing external equilibrium: maintaining an open economy and accepting deflation, or introducing policy measures that would isolate the economy from foreign competition. In addition, since government revenue depended heavily on tariff collection, the contraction in international trade flows meant that the government faced an incipient fiscal deficit.

Terra's reaction toward both external and domestic disequilibria was a mix of orthodox policy and interventionism. The links between the Uruguayan economy and the rest of the world were severed by restrictions on trade and immigration, and an inward-looking growth strategy was substituted for the open economy model that had provided favorable conditions for rapid growth in the hundred years after 1830. The size and scope of public sector activities grew steadily. Interventionism replaced the liberal state of the 1800s. Monetary restraint, a distinctive attribute of the economic policy of the 1800s, was gradually loosened, and the country was lured from the path of price stability. Exchange controls (introduced in 1931), higher tariffs, and quantitative restrictions on imports led to repressed inflation, which distorted relative prices and misdirected investment, imposing an additional toll on economic growth. Protectionist measures created incentives to invest in import-substituting activities. These tendencies had been seen in previous crises, but the 1930s were unique in the degree to which the economy was isolated from the rest of the world.

Isolation led to the development of an import-substituting industry and the creation of powerful vested interests in favor of protectionism. Meanwhile, the growth of agriculture slowed, and the beef sector stagnated. The establishment of multiple exchange rates and quotas increased the power of the state to influence the allocation of resources and created rents by restricting access to foreign currency. The closure of the economy concealed the long-run costs of an increase in the government bureaucracy and thus favored its expansion.

Livestock and Agriculture

The technical improvements in the livestock herd that had occurred with the development of the beef industry and the export of chilled and frozen beef did not continue past the 1920s. Beef production reached the limits imposed by the carrying capacity of the land and then stagnated; the amount of meat produced per animal remained unchanged. The decline in the profitability of marginal investments in the sector can be attributed to changes in the external market and to the domestic policies followed after the 1930s.

The decline in world trade caused by the Great Depression hit Uruguayan beef exports, which had depended almost exclusively on the British market. In 1932 the Ottawa agreements gave preference to British producers over competitors in the beef market and set quantitative restrictions on Uruguayan exports to Britain. Prices recovered in the late 1930s, but domestic producers were unable to capture this increase in earnings because of domestic policies. These included, in addition to specific and relatively unfavorable exchange rates for beef exports, a complicated system that regulated beef exports and the supply of beef to the Montevideo market.

During the late 1930s and 1940s Uruguay signed agreements with the United Kingdom specifying the quantities and prices of meat exports. Because these agreements meant a very low price for cattle in some years, the authorities paid slaughterhouses a subsidy to maintain higher prices. After World War II Uruguay was able to expand its markets and obtain better prices for its exports, but it still had to comply with the agreements. The administration of these subsidies and transfers led to acrid public disputes between the slaughterhouses and the authorities in the 1950s. The slaughterhouses' complaints concerned discriminatory practices that restricted their access to domestic cattle, rising costs, and the increasingly overvalued domestic currency. Finally, at the end of the decade, foreign investors abandoned the sector.

Although the livestock sector as a whole stagnated in the 1930s, during the next two decades the composition of its output changed as the share of wool and dairy products in total production rose. The increased significance of wool in total agricultural output was in part the result of the introduction of new breeds of sheep that were specialized to produce wool rather than mutton. The yield of wool per animal rose. The size of the sheep herd increased, and since the carrying capacity of the land remained unchanged, beef production contracted.

In general, the variations in the composition of the constant output of the livestock sector were attributable to changes in the relative prices of beef and wool in the world market that induced replacement of cattle by sheep. The increased importance of dairy products in total output was a result of the establishment of milk-processing plants, which provided a stable demand for milk and created incentives for expanding total production.

The stagnation of the livestock sector did not attract the attention of the community at large until the 1950s, probably because it was over-shadowed by the dynamic growth of manufacturing and some pro-tected agricultural crops during the 1940s and early 1950s. Only one isolated voice—that of Julio Martínez Lamas—warned of the perverse effects on agriculture of the pro-urban income distribution policies and called for a drastic change in economic policy (Martínez Lamas 1930).

The number of hectares devoted to crops had been increasing since the beginning of the century, although the amount of land allotted to this purpose was still relatively small. In the 1930s and 1940s the land area planted in such crops as sunflower, wheat, and sugar increased significantly. The development of these crops was encouraged by spe-cific protectionist policies that prevented competition from imports and were designed to make the country self-sufficient in these products. During the 1940s price support policies and subsidized credit led to a significant rise in the number of hectares planted in wheat.

Manufacturing and Trade

The protectionist policies of the 1930s brought about remarkable changes in the structure of the economy. In 1930 manufacturing ac-counted for 12.5 percent of GDP and the livestock sector for 14.9 percent. In 1955 the livestock sector had shrunk to 10.7 percent of GDP, while the industrial sector had swollen to 22 percent.[1] Manufacturing replaced livestock as the leading growth activity. Between 1930 and 1955 total GDP grew 2.5 percent a year, but the average growth was 4.9 percent for manufacturing and barely 1.2 percent for the livestock sector (tables 10-8 and 10-9 and figure 10-1).

Table 10-8. Uruguay: GDP at Constant Factor Cost, 1930–55
(millions of 1961 pesos)

Year	Agriculture	Manufacturing	GDP
1930	1,600	1,010	8,063
1935	1,556	1,133	7,647
1940	1,763	1,563	8,834
1945	1,694	1,823	9,641
1950	2,144	2,505	12,358
1955	2,496	3,303	15,039

Source: Banco Central del Uruguay, *Cuentas Nacionales*, various years.

The share of consumer goods in total imports contracted steadily. This trend, which began in the 1920s, was reinforced in the 1930s and 1940s by protectionist policies that favored the importation of raw materials and capital goods over that of consumer goods (table 10-10). The share of exports in total GDP fell from 12.5 percent in 1930 to 8 percent in 1955. Thus, as the country pursued an inward-looking growth strategy, the domestic market replaced export expansion as the main source of economic growth.

The structure of manufacturing GDP changed significantly between 1936 and 1954. The most dynamic sectors within manufacturing were those oriented toward the domestic market. Thus, the share in GDP of rubber, chemicals, and oil refining—import-substituting activities—increased, while that of food, an export-oriented sector, declined (table 10-11).

As the price of importable in relation to exportable goods rose sharply, the demand for labor in urban areas increased. This led to higher real wages and higher industrial employment (table 10-12). The rising cost of labor, originally a market phenomenon, was reinforced at the end of

Table 10-9. Uruguay: Manufacturing, Selected Years, 1930–55
(millions of 1961 pesos)

Year	Number of enterprises	Number of employees	Value (millions of 1961 pesos) Production	Machinery	Average number of employees per enterprise
1930	7,116	77,588	—	—	10.9
1936	10,286	65,339	2,251	280	6.4
1948	20,523	111,255	3,815	—	5.4
1955	21,102	161,879	7,511	2,415	7.7

— Not available.
Source: Unpublished data from Uruguay, Ministerio de Industrias y Trabajo, Dirección de Industrias; Acevedo 1933.

Figure 10-1.   Uruguay: The Livestock Herd, 1920–85

Beef cattle (millions)

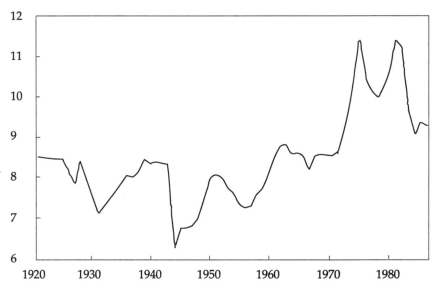

Sheep (millions)

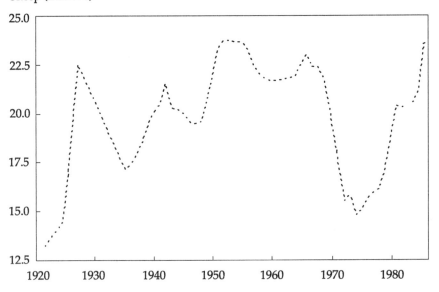

Source: Favaro 1990.

Table 10-10. Uruguay: Composition of Imports, Selected Periods, 1908–56
(percent)

Period	Consumer goods	Raw materials	Capital goods	Total
1908–10	40.7	52.4	6.9	100.0
1924–26	29.5	60.4	10.1	100.0
1939–40	22.6	68.1	9.3	100.0
1948–50	16.6	61.5	21.9	100.0
1954–56	11.1	66.2	22.7	100.0

Source: Finch 1980.

the period by increased public sector employment, the practices of wage boards, and higher social security taxes on labor.

Public Enterprises

Between 1930 and 1955 the number of public firms increased, as did the goods and services they supplied. The firms' monopoly rights, which had been nominally in force since their foundation, were now enforced, as in the cases of the public insurance and power companies.

The history of public intervention in alcohol production illustrates the attitude of the authorities toward the creation and appropriation of rents during the period. The first steps toward the establishment of a monopoly in alcohol production date back to 1912 and to Batlle's desire for public intervention in that supposedly highly profitable industry. Alco-

Table 10-11. Uruguay: Structure of Manufacturing GDP, 1936 and 1954
(percent)

Sector	1936	1954
Food	29.1	14.5
Beverages	13.2	12.0
Tobacco	3.8	3.0
Textiles	7.9	9.5
Shoes and clothing	10.4	5.7
Paper	1.3	1.8
Printing	4.0	3.5
Rubber	0.8	2.5
Chemicals	4.6	6.7
Oil refining	0.1	10.1
Nonmineral metals	4.9	5.7
Metallic products	4.8	3.9
Electric products	0.9	3.5
Other	14.2	17.6
Total	100.0	100.0

Source: Unpublished data from Banco Central de Uruguay.

Table 10-12. Uruguay: Employment in Manufacturing and Real Wages, 1930, 1947, and 1955

Year	Wages (1930 pesos)	Employment (number of workers)
1930	66.3	54,143
1947	107.3	109,918[a]
1955	163.5	141,100[b]

a. 1948.
b. 1952.
Source: Sapelli 1985; Instituto de Economía, Universidad de la República, *Estadísticas Básicas*, 1969.

hol production, which had developed in previous decades under the umbrella of protectionism, was highly concentrated. This characteristic led Batlle to favor expropriation because, as he argued, the real alternatives in that market were either a private or a public monopoly. When the leading firm in the sector opposed expropriation, the government retaliated by lowering tariffs, and the share of domestic production in total consumption fell from about 70 percent of the market to 10 percent. Although it could hardly be said that the market was being monopolized at that time, the authorities gave a legal monopoly in alcohol production and oil refining to ANCAP.

The expansion of state activities during the early 1930s was marked by the displacement of private investment—as in the cases of telephones, oil refining, alcohol, and the beef industry, where the Frigorífico Nacional was given the monopoly on supplying beef to the capital city—and by the establishment of legal monopolies. Until 1931 two private companies provided telephone service. In 1931 the national power company was given a legal monopoly in the sector, displacing private investment in telecommunications.

After World War II a third wave of public sector expansionism reached the railroads, public urban transport, and water supply. The regulation of public utilities, which allowed a "fair" rate of return on capital, biased the optimal capital-labor ratio toward higher capital intensity, as illustrated by the railroad system, with its countrywide network of winding rail lines. The state lacked sufficient information to control effectively the costs reported by the public utilities. Furthermore, the authorities favored investment and price policies that emphasized distributional objectives; they penalized price discrimination and favored cross-subsidization. These sources of conflict led to frequent disputes between state agencies and the public utility firms. The unfavorable atmosphere decreased the incentives to invest in expanding and renewing capital equipment. Ultimately, British enterprises were nationalized, the investors being compensated by the state.

Before the 1930s the administration of public firms was fairly efficient. After the Great Depression, however, the expansion of state activities was accompanied by a steady trend toward political use of the firms. The collusion between the Blanco and Colorado parties under the new type of coparticipation agreed on in the 1930s and the closure of the economy to foreign competition during the period reduced the political costs of using the existing monopoly rents to finance political clientelism and favored management practices that disregarded efficiency and expanded public employment.

Money

Uruguay maintained an orthodox monetary tradition from independence to the Great Depression. During most of the period the peso was freely convertible into gold, and the stock of money was demand-determined under the price-specie flow mechanism. Although the monetary authorities made the Uruguayan peso inconvertible in 1914, until 1939 money issue remained legally constrained by the size of the gold stock.

In 1931 the monetary authorities established exchange controls, and four years later they fixed a new, lower exchange parity. Not until 1939 was the expansion of domestic credit relieved of the legal constraints that tied it to the size of the gold stock, and price stability was maintained until the mid-1940s (table 10-13).

In 1939 the monetary authority was permitted to rediscount commercial bills without a ceiling, provided that the bills were backed by real transactions. This policy found theoretical support in the "real bills

Table 10-13. Uruguay: Rate of Growth of Money, Credit, Income, and Prices, 1930–55

Period	M	L	P	m	l	g
1930–35	1.7	−2.2	−0.7	2.4	−1.5	−1.0
1935–40	7.8	5.1	2.3	5.4	2.7	1.5
1940–45	14.2	7.8	4.9	8.9	2.8	1.6
1945–50	7.8	15.9	5.4	5.1	10.0	5.1
1950–55	7.5	14.8	11.1	−3.2	3.3	4.3
1930–45	7.7	3.4	2.1	5.5	1.3	1.2[a]
1945–55	9.2	15.3	8.2	0.9	6.1	4.5

Note: M = rate of growth of nominal M_2; L = rate of growth of credit to the private sector; P = rate of growth of the Consumer Price Index; m = rate of growth of the stock of real M_2; l = rate of growth of real credit to the private sector; g = rate of growth of GDP.

a. 1935–45.

Source: Unpublished data from Banco Central del Uruguay; Uruguay, Dirección General de Estadística y Censos; and Banco de la República Oriental del Uruguay.

doctrine"; it was argued that since the creation of money was supported by a previous real transaction, expansion of credit was not inflationary. Inflation, which had been nil in the twenty years before this innovation, crept up until by 1950–55 it was running 11.1 percent a year. At least in this initial stage, the inflation originated in subsidized credit expansion that benefited import-substituting manufacturing firms.[2]

Monetary expansion and price instability distorted the working of the capital market—the banking system and the stock exchange. The higher rate of inflation led the public to reduce its holdings of real money and other financial assets after the early 1950s, and savings were channeled toward assets that provided an adequate hedge against inflation, often bypassing the traditional financial intermediaries. Thus, an imperfect arbitrage between savers and investors fragmented the capital market into segments in which the social rate of return was not equalized.

Interest rate ceilings and an exchange rate that failed to keep pace with domestic price changes had significant effects on the distribution of income. Tax revenues provided by inflation were used to subsidize banks and credit recipients, since the government kept a balanced budget during the period. The increased number of financial institutions entering the market in the 1940s and early 1950s suggests the existence of high expected profits in this activity during the period.

Summary

Beginning with the Great Depression, Uruguayan society experienced significant changes that altered the structure of the polity. Urban areas grew rapidly as a result of the incentives created for the development of import-substituting industry, the expansion of public sector employment, and the higher standard of living in urban, in relation to rural, areas. Thus Montevideo grew from 460,000 to 900,000 inhabitants between 1930 and 1943. Secondary school enrollment expanded from 6,000 students in 1930 to 12,000 in 1942 and 65,000 in 1957. The scope of the social security system was considerably enlarged, and retirement benefits were increased; after 1948 the social security system returned to a decentralized administration. The number of public sector employees exploded, from 42,700 in 1929 to 58,000 in 1938 and approximately 168,500 in 1955.

The enlargement of the government bureaucracy and the development of import-substituting industry were financed by heavy implicit taxation of the livestock sector through the prevailing multiple exchange rate regime, the tariff structure, and the direct taxes levied on exports. The burden of taxation brought about a decline in the price of land and induced migration from rural to urban areas, reinforcing the political rationale for pro-urban income distribution policies. The administrations that held office following recovery from the consequences of the Great Depression made increasing use of state power to develop a political clientele by restricting trade and expanding public sector employment. Although the policies followed during the period initially encouraged economic growth in manufacturing, this growth did not last because it was constrained by the size of the domestic market. The livestock sector experienced a contraction that was masked by favorable external circumstances until the end of the Korean war but became dramatically evident in its aftermath.

Notes

1. As a result of significant price incentives in the 1945–55 period, the share of crops in agricultural GDP increased from 25 percent in 1930 to 35.7 percent in 1955.

2. The main source of monetary expansion before the 1960s was credit creation. Before 1967 monetary authority was vested in the Banco de la República Oriental del Uruguay (BROU), a commercial public bank. After the reforms in banking regulations of 1939 and the 1940s, this institution was allowed to print money to finance its own credit expansion and the discounting of commercial bills from other banks. Since credit was associated with subsidized interest rates, it involved real transfers to debtors. Under conventional accounting rules, however, these transfers are not counted as government expenditures.

11 Economic Stagnation and Price Instability: 1955–73

Uruguay in the early 1950s could be considered a country in which most of the aspirations of the population had been fulfilled. Following the 1933–42 dictatorship the country enjoyed a democratic system based on two political parties that were supported by an estimated 90 percent of the voters. Income per capita was the highest in Latin America as a result of the general progress experienced up to the turn of the century, the high rate of economic growth recorded during 1945–55, and the relatively high prices of the country's export commodities during and following World War II. The economic structure had been diversified, but the share in exports of livestock products remained high, and the important livestock sector was stagnant.

The high indices in education and health and a progressive expansion of the social security system (which mainly sought to protect retirees) were the most outstanding features of a welfare state that had evolved early, in comparison with other countries of the region and even of the world. Montevideo was the center of an active academic and cultural life with standards comparable in many respects to those of many developed countries. Until the defeat of the Colorado party in 1958, Uruguay continued implementing an essentially *batllista*-based policy whereby government decisions were designed to favor the urban population.

The Political Situation

In 1951 a constitutional amendment instituted the *colegiado* system (a multiperson executive power that had been advocated by José Batlle) in place of the one-man presidency. The same system was extended to municipalities and public enterprises, with representation for both majority and minority parties.

Until 1958 the Blanco party remained internally divided. This division dated back to 1933, when a majority led by Luis Alberto de Herrera voted with the traditional faction of the party while a minority voted independently, refusing to support Herrera in his party's dispute with the

Colorados. Under Herrera's leadership the Blanco party developed a basically pragmatic policy, distrustful of ideology and based on liberal ideas and strong individualism. The party showed a preference for agriculture and free trade and some indifference—sometimes even hostility—toward industrialization and the increasing interference of the state in economic affairs. But many of Herrera's ideas had to coexist with the electoral needs of the Blanco party, especially in Montevideo. Hence there were contradictions; some of Herrera's followers and other party sectors advocated a welfare state, industrial development, and state action for redistributional purposes.

Despite their differing ideologies, the traditional parties operated under an implicit agreement that allowed the political system to work. Political activity in the twentieth century led to respect for a democratic government and to compromises on the important problems about which the parties traditionally disagreed, such as the size of the state and the form of government. Public sector appointments were distributed proportionately among the voters and partisans of both parties. The progressive increase in the role of the state became a way of offering jobs to voters of both parties, especially in Montevideo, which received many migrants from rural areas. Thus, more electoral "clients" were ensured, and the social unrest that might have arisen from unemployment was curtailed. Political parties became the means for obtaining pensions, free medical assistance, water, and telephones. Even though such services were theoretically available to the whole population, state mismanagement or a lack of installed capacity caused shortages that were rationed by the Blanco and Colorado parties for patronage purposes. These characteristics of the political system reinforced the autonomy of political groups in relation to economic groups—a situation that was already emerging in the early twentieth century. Political work increasingly became a career activity, and political workers were the beneficiaries of a special system that arranged for public financing of electoral campaign expenditures and for special retirement conditions.

Population and Social Classes

By mid-century Uruguay's population growth rate was very low and was similar to that in richer countries during the same period. In particular, the birthrate was low, in part because of the population's high educational level, concentration in urban areas, and lack of strong religious beliefs. The low birthrate brought about a progressive aging of the population, with a strong predominance of those over 60 years of age. This implied that in years to come the costly social security system developed in previous decades would impose an increasing economic burden on the active population.

More than two-thirds of the population lived in urban areas, and about 40 percent of the total population lived in Montevideo. Industrial development and the growth of the public sector after the 1930s encouraged high migration from rural areas to Montevideo. About 50 percent of the country's economically active population worked in the service sector. Employment was higher in manufacturing than in agriculture.

In the 1950s social security beneficiaries numbered almost 30 percent of the active population. Many recipients remained economically active. In addition, many people were employed "under the table," and taxes on their earnings were not remitted to the social security system.

European immigration was important to the formation of the Uruguayan population. In general, the immigrants were craftsmen and workers whose preference for settlement in urban areas, particularly Montevideo, contributed to urbanization and to the growth of the service sector.

Unlike other countries in Latin America, Uruguay exhibited a remarkable degree of social integration and had a dominant middle class, which accounted for between 47 and 66 percent of the total population. The upper class consisted principally of landowners who, although constituting a minority, had strong economic power and dynamic organizations that defended their interests. The basis of upper-class economic power was landed property. Many landowners lived in Montevideo and engaged in industry, commerce, and banking.

There is no accurate information regarding the importance and structure of the rural middle class. A small proportion of this group worked as technicians, managers of small farms, medium-size rural producers, small leaseholders, and even small landowners who also worked temporarily as wage earners. This rural middle class lacked strong organizations to express its interests, and in general terms its interests were promoted by the rural upper class. The rural middle class was represented by political groups within both traditional parties, such as those led by Tomás Berreta in the Colorado party during the 1940s and Benito Nardone in the Blanco party in the 1950s.

The large number of small enterprises devoted to industry, commerce, and other services gave rise to the urban middle class, an extraordinarily heterogeneous conglomerate that included small property owners and a wide range of public and private employees. Public employees were an important part of this group. Among private sector employees, those in the banking sector had the highest salary levels during the 1950s and early 1960s. The heterogeneity of the middle class prevented it from being effectively organized. Existing organizations represented the interests of certain sectors of the class rather than of the whole class. The only power these groups had was derived from their numbers, which had always attracted the interest of traditional parties and, more recently, of the leftist parties.

The urban upper class was made up of a small number of owners in manufacturing, commerce, and banking who represented a large proportion of production in these sectors. As in the case of agriculture, this class had organizations that worked in defense of its interests. A Marxist-oriented study has underlined the strong links between the urban and rural upper classes, identifying owners and families who simultaneously carried out activities in more than one sector (Trías 1970).

The lower class in rural areas had never organized unions, as urban workers had. Legislation, however, ensured rural workers certain benefits, such as a minimum wage level and some forms of health protection. Labor was the most important sector of the urban lower class. Workers in the large industrial enterprises in Montevideo established labor unions of increasing size and power, which may have helped them attain a relatively acceptable standard of living, especially in comparison with other countries in Latin America. The coexistence of various political tendencies, basically anarchistic or communist oriented, within the urban proletariat prevented the formation of a single major organization, thus limiting the strength of the labor movement and its capacity to influence the country's politics until the 1960s.

Ideology and the Economy

With the exception of the period between 1933 and 1942, a democratic ideology dominated the country's political life during the first half of the twentieth century. This ideal manifested itself in several important achievements shared by most Uruguayans, including a welfare state, public enterprises, and import-substituting industries. There was, moreover, a feeling of pride when Uruguayan democracy was compared with the authoritarian regimes that characterized most Latin American nations at that time. Uruguay's special situation within the continent generated rather conservative attitudes, especially in some sectors of the middle class. Economic and social stability and a wish to maintain their salary levels, employment, educational levels, and health and social security benefits became the most important values in the minds of many Uruguayans.

Political nationalism has never been dominant in Uruguay, probably because of the country's weakness in relation to its neighbors, Brazil and Argentina, and because of the absence of important border conflicts. The nationalization of British utilities and the hostility expressed by cattle owners toward foreign-owned slaughterhouses did not represent a deeply rooted attitude.

An aversion to change and risk was a common social attitude that easily evolved into an overly critical spirit and a certain tendency toward pessimism. As these values spread and government intervention in the economy increased, people lost confidence in entrepreneurial activity and even became hostile toward the idea of profit as an index of economic success. The social standing of entrepreneurs was low in

Uruguay during the postwar period once the waves of immigration of previous decades had ended (Graceras 1970).

The rise of various state enterprises during the first half of the century and the promotion of industry after the Great Depression were an expression of certain economic ideas that were contrary to the notion of free trade and were common among the nation's politicians and economists. Only the organizations that represented rural producers and commerce opposed the ideas that dominated the period, and these groups were not successful. Even the agricultural sector was divided between producers of meat and wool, who supported free trade, and wheat producers, who benefited from government price support policies.

During that time the Universidad de la República, a free public institution that had a monopoly in the supply of higher education and no enrollment restrictions, exerted a great influence on the country's ideological structure. Student movements promoted active participation by students in the administration of the university, support of labor union claims, and a strong stand against U.S. foreign policy. As a consequence, the university usually clashed with the government, sometimes violently, over funding and over various economic and foreign policy measures.

Few Uruguayan intellectuals held conservative ideas; most were leftist and confrontational in orientation. In the postwar period Uruguayan intellectuals gradually began to break away from the traditional political parties. This situation led to the political radicalization of those intellectuals and, in general, to their abstention from participation in political parties. Indeed, intellectuals were progressively secluded within the university and were isolated from the country's political and economic life.

Initial Conditions, 1955

By the mid-1950s the performance of the Uruguayan economy was deteriorating, after a decade of sustained economic growth. The average annual growth rate of GDP was 5.4 percent between 1945 and 1950 and 4.2 percent between 1950 and 1955. According to several estimates made at the time, Uruguay's income per capita was the highest in Latin America (Balassa 1986).

The performance of the economy between 1945 and 1955 was uneven. Growth occurred in import-substituting industry and, as a result of price support policies, in the dairy sector and agricultural crops. Between 1945 and 1955 crop production increased at more than 9 percent a year, mostly as a result of the dynamic expansion of wheat production. The beef sector stagnated, but wool production increased under favorable world market conditions.

During 1945–55 the industrial sector grew at an annual rate of 7.7 percent as a consequence of the import-substitution strategy in force after the Great Depression. The share of manufacturing in GDP increased to surpass that of agriculture. The most significant growth occurred in domestically oriented industries—rubber, metals, electricity, chemicals, and paper.

Even though the share of industry in GDP had risen, Uruguay was still an agricultural nation. Agriculture accounted for about 15 percent of overall GDP; of this, livestock accounted for 60 percent and crops for the remainder. Meat and wool made up more than 70 percent of livestock production and dairy production about 20 percent. Meat and wool production supplied the raw materials for a large industrial sector that included slaughterhouses, textiles, and leather manufacturing. Whereas domestic consumption of beef represented a significant part of total beef production, more than 90 percent of wool production was exported. As a whole, livestock production and the meat-, wool-, and leather-processing industries accounted for about 30 percent of GDP. This group of agricultural and industrial activities produced almost 90 percent of the nation's exports.

During the 1940s exports increased continuously; in 1940 they amounted to US$71 million and in 1950 to US$270 million. The expansion of the value of exports was mainly the result of an increase in the international prices of beef and wool during this period. The price of Uruguayan exports peaked in 1951 and declined sharply thereafter. Domestic consumption of beef increased, and the volume exported consequently declined. Imports expanded steadily, and the share of raw materials and capital goods in total imports increased.

Almost all investment and production decisions in agriculture were subject to government interference. The domestic prices of beef and wool were strongly influenced through an implicit form of taxation built into the prevailing multiple exchange rate regime. The supply of beef to Montevideo was assigned to a state-controlled slaughterhouse, while private slaughterhouses were allowed only to export. The beef retail trade was subject to administrative permits that severely restricted entry. Crop production was encouraged through price support policies and the creation of buffer stocks; highly protective tariffs gave substantial incentives for sugar and sunflower production. The supply of milk to Montevideo was assigned to a monopoly, and milk prices were subject to administrative controls.

The extent of protection for manufacturing implied isolation from foreign competition. Domestic competition was also severely limited by the barriers to entry implicit in restricted access to foreign exchange. The management of multiple exchange rates and quotas promoted the importation of raw materials and capital goods and penalized imports of consumer goods and traditional exports. The financial sector was subject to interest rate ceilings and discriminatory credit subsidies.

Expansionary domestic policies led to a significant current account deficit, which induced a decline in international reserves and an increase in the external debt during 1951–55. The inflation rate, which averaged 5.5 percent a year between 1946 and 1950, increased to 11.1 percent between 1951 and 1955.

In general, the policies followed during the period seem to have contributed to a reduction in the degree of inequality and poverty in Uruguayan society. In 1950 Uruguay's social indices compared favorably with those of most developed countries.

The Structure of the Economy and of Society

Of Uruguay's area of 18.7 million hectares, the 16.5 million hectares suitable for agriculture (livestock raising and crops) are fully in use for production. Ninety percent of the land is given over to livestock, mostly in natural pastures, and the remaining 10 percent to crops. In contrast to other countries in Latin America, livestock production in Uruguay has been independent of dairy production. Usually, sheep and beef cattle have coexisted on the same ranches, while milk production has been carried out on small holdings close to urban centers.

In the 1945–55 period livestock was raised on about 50,000 properties totaling about 15 million hectares in area. The dominant productive technique was grazing on natural pasture. The value of land represented more than 60 percent of overall capital in livestock production, and the stock of bovines and sheep accounted for most of the remainder. About two-thirds of the land given over to livestock was exploited by the owners, while the rest was worked by leaseholders.

Landed property was highly concentrated; 2 percent of the producers held 30 percent of the land suitable for livestock in holdings larger than 2,500 hectares. Of 50,900 livestock raisers, 43,600 owned 26 percent of the land. The share of investment in machinery and equipment in the total capital of livestock firms declined in direct proportion to the size of the ranch. The use of seeded pastures in livestock raising was not significantly different for different sizes of holding.

In the manufacturing sector, about 60 percent of production was generated by traditional activities such as food, beverages, tobacco, textiles, garments, wood, and leather. At the beginning of the period the only significant exporting industry was meat processing, but over time the textile industry became increasingly important. More than 50 percent of industrial production was generated in enterprises of more than 100 workers, which constituted a very small proportion of the total number of firms. Enterprises with fewer than nineteen employees were in the majority but accounted for only 16 percent of total production. The industries with a higher capital-labor ratio were rubber, tobacco, paper, and chemicals; the garment and furniture industries were the most labor-intensive activities. Uruguay's small size and easy communications among regions made for national markets and forestalled price or quality differences between goods consumed in Montevideo and in rural areas.

Foreign investment in manufacturing came mainly from the United States following the establishment of the slaughterhouses in the early twentieth century. Foreign investment increased from US$6 million to US$28 million in the 1940s, especially in import-substituting activities such as textiles, chemicals, and electrical appliances and in banking.

INTEREST RATES. Interest rate regulations were imposed on banking activities but were not binding until the end of the period, when inflation became an intractable problem in Uruguayan economic life.

TRADE. The traditional influence of Argentina and Brazil in the border areas brought about an active informal trade in those regions. A decisive factor in determining the intensity of this trade was differences in exchange rate policies, which caused large variations in Uruguay's competitive capacity during some periods. Consumer goods from Brazil and Argentina were smuggled into Uruguay when the latter had an overvalued exchange rate, and Uruguayan cattle, textiles, and even some imported goods were smuggled to neighboring countries when the opposite occurred.

FOREIGN OWNERSHIP. In general, there were no limitations on foreign ownership of domestic assets in spite of various parliamentary proposals, never approved, that would have prohibited the purchase of land by foreigners or restricted their presence in border areas. Generally, foreign investment in agriculture was insignificant except for landownership by Brazilian firms and individuals in border areas. Laws were passed, however, that restricted land leasing to discourage absentee landlordism.

LABOR. The labor market remained relatively free during the 1950s—at least when compared with the rigidity introduced a few years later by unions and by the government's anti-inflationary policies. Since 1943 the executive has participated directly in determining wages in the private sector through its compulsory presence in negotiations between enterprises and unions. It has been pointed out that the government's vote has generally favored workers' aspirations, bringing about a significant increase in wages, especially during 1945–55. In addition, since the public sector accounted for more than 20 percent of the country's economically active population, wages in the public sector indirectly influenced wages in the private sector. (In the early 1960s approximately 21 percent of the country's active population was employed in the public sector—60 percent in the central government, 11 percent in municipalities, and 29 percent in public enterprises.) The degree of distortion introduced by the presence of the state in the labor market seems to have been more important for less-skilled than for highly skilled workers, as indicated by the higher salaries for less-skilled workers in the public sector compared with those in the private sector.

THE GOVERNMENT BUDGET AND SOCIAL SERVICES. As of 1955, more than 50 percent of public sector GDP was generated by the central government; the remainder came from the state's participation in manufacturing, public utilities, and banking. By the mid-1950s the share of the public sector in GDP was about 16.5 percent. Public sector investment accounted for 24 percent of total investment. About 75 percent of that investment consisted of construction; the residual was machinery and equipment.

In the early 1960s government tax revenue (including social security taxes) amounted to 23 percent of GDP. The share of indirect taxation in total revenue was 55 percent, followed by social security taxes (32 percent). Thus, direct taxation was a minor share of revenues. Government expenditure amounted to 25 percent of GDP. More than 50 percent of that expenditure consisted of social security transfers, approximately 33 percent was for government administrative services, and barely 10 percent was for health and education.

By the early 1950s Uruguay had established a highly advanced welfare state, especially where education and retirement benefits under the social security system were concerned. The public education system had expanded considerably since the late nineteenth century. By 1905 public schools accounted for about 75 percent of the total number of students, there were secondary schools in all department capitals, and both enrollment at the university and the scope of instruction had expanded remarkably. The public school system continued to improve throughout the century and contributed greatly to the relatively high educational level of the society in the 1950s.

Free medical assistance was provided to the poor through public hospitals and through private institutions that provided services on the basis of prepayment and closed physician panels. The public health system was used by more than 10 percent of the population in Montevideo and between 15 and 47 percent of the population in other department capitals. The private health system covered 87 percent of the population in Montevideo and between 50 and 85 percent of the population in other department capitals.

The social security system covered work-related accidents, as well as maternity expenses for women employees and wives of employees enrolled in the system. Retirement benefits accounted for about 90 percent of the total expenses of the social security system. In general, employees reaching a certain age—60 years for men and 55 for women—who had worked a minimum number of years (usually thirty) were entitled to retirement benefits equivalent to a certain percentage of their wages. The same benefits covered individuals with working disabilities and the families of those who had suffered work-related accidents.

Beginning in 1958 all private employees were protected against unemployment under a general system that had previously covered only workers in the slaughter and wool storage sectors.

The social security system was financed through wage taxes paid by the worker and by the firm. The system encountered increasing financial difficulties during the 1960s. Although social security tax rates were increased, tax evasion, coupled with economic stagnation, limited the resources available for financing the explosive increase in the system's expenditures. Social security expenditures expanded for several reasons. (a) The ratio of the economically active population to retirees declined continuously after 1964, when it was estimated at 1.96. (b) In past decades retirement benefits were granted with excessive generosity to retirees who had not completed thirty years of work. (c) Most of the financial reserves of the system generated in previous periods were used to purchase public debt instruments that were issued to finance fiscal imbalances. As inflation soared, the social security system suffered a capital loss on these investments at the same time that its financial needs became increasingly acute. During the 1960s the central government began making continuous transfers to the system.

PUBLIC ENTERPRISES. In the 1950s public enterprises, as legal monopolies, refined oil; supplied alcohol, electric power, telephone communications, water, insurance, port services, and rail and air transport; granted mortgage loans for house construction; managed the state casinos; and fished for certain marine species. Other public firms competed with the private sector in urban transport, banking services, cement production, and hotel services. Public enterprises were increasingly a source of patronage. Their management was left to politicians appointed by the majority and minority parties, which were entitled to share appointments of new employees. The existence of legal monopolies in most services excluded competition and led to a gradual deterioration in the quality of the services. Monopoly rents were gradually dissipated by expanded employment and growing inefficiency, and investment was postponed because of lack of concern about the future.

Political Events, 1955–73

The postwar period saw a gradual movement of foreign investment from the export sector and the public utilities toward import-substituting manufacturing. This trend reflected a change in the expected rate of return for different economic activities that had its origin in the protectionist policies developed after the Great Depression.

The decision of foreign meat processors to abandon their investments in Uruguay came at a time when Uruguay was encountering difficulties in the European beef market. These difficulties mounted in 1969, when the British government imposed restrictions on Uruguayan beef imports on sanitary grounds, and became more acute after the entrance of the United Kingdom into the European Community.

In 1961 most South American countries signed the Latin American Free Trade Association (LAFTA) agreement. Tariff concessions by the signatory countries led to an increase in Uruguayan imports from Brazil and Argentina and a decline in imports from the rest of the world, while Uruguayan exports remained largely unaffected by the treaty. The LAFTA agreement was a further step in the long-term process of import substitution rather than a move toward the creation of a common market. Its most significant consequence was trade diversion rather than trade expansion.[1]

The Colorado party won the 1954 elections, and within the party, the *batllista* sector, under the leadership of Luis Batlle Berres, obtained a large majority. In the years that followed, minority groups within the party carried on intense ideological and personal disputes with the winning faction. The Blanco party, in turn, was divided between Herrera's followers, who still represented the majority within the party, and groups opposed to Herrera that had electoral support in Montevideo.

Colorados and Blancos in Power

The 1954 Colorado government followed the main guidelines of postwar *batllismo*: it promoted import-substituting industries and refused to accede to the agricultural sector's demands. The decline in the terms of trade following the Korean war did not modify the government's attitudes regarding strong state intervention. In 1955 and 1956, for instance, exchange and foreign trade controls were tightened to restrict imports and make possible new bilateral trade agreements with other countries. In 1957 the exchange market was closed, and imports were prohibited. The agricultural sector resisted these policies and often succeeded in bypassing them by smuggling cattle across the border and by building up inventories of wool while pressing for a more favorable exchange rate.

In the 1958 elections the Colorado party faced the alliance of the Blanco party with the Liga Federal de Acción Ruralista (LFAR), an organization led by a journalist whose campaign against the Colorado party's pro-urban economic policies had strong support in rural areas. The stagnation of the economy, coupled with renewed inflation and shortages, added to the discontent even in urban areas, a traditional stronghold of the Colorado party. The Blanco party won the elections for the first time in ninety-three years, and by a wide margin. In 1962 the Blanco party won again, but by a narrower margin than in 1958.

The ideological background of the Blanco party and the increasing disillusionment with the economic policy in force during the 1955–58 period ensured that the new administration would favor agriculture and less government intervention in the economy. Its first steps were clearly based on those principles. Over time, however, it abandoned the defense of free-market policies. In 1962 it maintained an overvalued exchange rate, and it incurred an enormous fiscal deficit during 1963–66.

The Blanco administration initially attempted to bring the relative domestic prices of agricultural and manufactured goods close to those prevailing in the world market. These efforts, however, faded as a consequence of the strong opposition of urban sectors and the influence of the Cuban revolution of 1959, the Alliance for Progress, and the Economic Commission for Latin America (ECLA).

With the deaths of the two most outstanding leaders of the traditional parties—Herrera in 1959 and Luis Batlle in 1964—factional disputes flared up, and new leaders arose. A similar evolution took place within the centrist Christian Democrats and the left; groups formed around electoral alliances led by the Socialist and the Communist parties, respectively. The dynamics of the political process and the formation of new groups and electoral alliances reflected a search for adequate responses to the deepening economic and social difficulties of Uruguayan society.

Labor and Politics

The labor movement was becoming increasingly significant in political life. Until the mid-1960s, however, it was divided between an organization led by the Communist party and a coalition of leftist noncommunist unions. The economic stagnation and the inflation that set in after 1955 paved the way for increasing labor unrest, initially among industrial workers but later among employees of banks and public utilities. The 1960s saw many strikes, in both the public and the private sectors, and the armed forces were often brought in to help the police maintain order. In 1964 the labor movement finally achieved unification under the Convención Nacional de Trabajadores (CNT). According to its statutes the CNT's main objective was to obtain a "society without exploitation." Between the mid-1960s and 1973 union activity (which, like manufacturing, is essentially an urban phenomenon) grew far beyond the search for better working conditions and higher salaries and pursued social and economic changes such as agrarian reform and monopolistic public control of banking and external trade. Most union leaders of the period belonged to left-wing political parties. The influence of the Blanco and Colorado parties in the labor unions was almost insignificant.

Between 1956 and 1968 price instability gave rise to labor-management disputes in certain strategic sectors and to the adoption of *medidas prontas de seguridad* (MPS)—measures that were at first transitory but later were adopted permanently. (The MPS procedure, which is similar to a state of siege, permits the confinement of citizens when there is internal turmoil.)

During 1968–73 open confrontation between the government and the unions occurred. Ten general strikes took place in 1968. The government decreed a price and salary freeze in June, imposed the MPS, and subjected public employees in such strategic services as natural gas, water, electricity, oil, and communications to certain military regulations. In 1969 a bank strike led to violence, including terrorist attacks in support of unions, and the executive imposed military regulations on striking employees. In 1970–71 labor-management disputes were increasingly associated with violence.

In 1972, with a new administration in office, the unions declared open war on the executive. A survey of 300 industrial entrepreneurs found that a majority of those interviewed believed that the nation was close to collapse, essentially because of lack of discipline in labor. A third of the people interviewed considered the guerrilla movement and unions to be part of a leftist conspiracy. A significant number considered the CNT, not the guerrilla movement, to be the principal subversive threat in the late 1960s and early 1970s (Rial 1984).

Union and enterprise pressure groups were in constant conflict during this period. Although mutual interest in the maintenance of a status quo should have limited confrontation, common interests failed to act as a restraint, possibly because union leaders believed that the government was implicitly committed to bailing out firms that faced troubles, whatever the source of their problems.

The Gestido Administration

The 1966 elections took place in a dynamic and unstable political climate, and the Colorado party won. The winning faction within the party was led by Oscar Gestido, a retired army general of much personal prestige, somewhat conservative and with relatively successful governmental experience in the management of the public railway. Gestido won by a very narrow margin over a party faction led by Jorge Batlle, the son of Luis Batlle.

In his campaign Batlle had proposed a constitutional amendment that would solve certain important institutional problems faced by the country. This amendment was approved in 1966 with the support of the majority sectors in both traditional parties and was a clear expression by politicians of the time regarding institutional inefficiencies that were hampering governmental functions. The most important change brought about by the amendment was the replacement of the collegium by a presidential regime. The amendment also introduced changes designed to achieve tighter control of public enterprises. To limit parliamentary authority, initiatives in legislation dealing with retirement, tax forgiveness, and price and salary fixing were reserved to the executive. For bills deemed to warrant "urgent consideration," special procedures were set up under which Parliament had to reach a decision within a specific time period. The government's term in office was increased from four to five years to permit longer-term policies.

The new administration adopted a policy of strong state intervention-ism and attempted to conciliate the demands of opposing interest groups. The result was an upsurge of inflation and, in December 1967, a 100 percent devaluation of the currency.

The Pacheco Administration and the 1971 Election

Jorge Pacheco took office in December 1967, on the death of Gestido, and served until 1971. The Pacheco administration inherited an economic situation that was highly unstable, mainly because of monetary misman-agement. In June 1968 the government implemented a price stabilization program based on a temporary price and wage freeze. The unions opposed the plan, and the ensuing labor-management disputes forced the authorities to impose the MPS to restore internal order. Beginning in 1968, intense disputes between the government, opposing political par-ties, and unions created a crisis in Uruguayan politics, which had tradi-tionally been favorable to compromise and opposed to confrontation. Constant conflicts between the executive and Parliament occurred. The executive limited union activity, banned radical leftist political parties, and closed daily and weekly newspapers, temporarily or permanently. The university authorities openly confronted the executive.

After 1967 an urban guerrilla movement inspired by the ideas spread by the Cuban revolution appeared on the Uruguayan political scene. This was the Movimiento de Liberación Nacional (MLN), better known as Tupamaro. Its founders were mostly former members of leftist par-ties who distrusted democratic methods and openly advocated the use of violence as a legitimate means of taking over the government. Up to 1970, however, the Tupamaro guerrillas avoided terrorist actions and direct confrontation with the police.

Despite open disputes between the executive and legislative powers, widespread violence, and continuous labor-management confronta-tions, the 1971 elections were held according to democratic procedures. Both traditional parties participated, taking ideological stands some-what contradictory to those historically assigned to them. The Colorado party seemed to abandon its conventional economic and social *batllista* paradigm for more conservative attitudes. The Blanco party, in turn, seemed to have set aside its conservative rural orientation to seek struc-tural changes, including an agrarian reform.

Another distinctive feature of the 1971 election was the appearance for the first time in the country's political history of a third major political party. Several leftist parties that had rarely obtained more than 5 percent of the vote joined forces with a few dissidents from traditional parties to form a coalition called the Frente Amplio (FA). This new party, with General Liber Seregni as its presidential candidate, obtained about one-fifth of the total vote and became established as the second most power-ful force in Montevideo.

The Colorado party won narrowly. Within the Colorado party the winner, by a relatively large margin, was Juan María Bordaberry, the candidate of the party faction led by the outgoing president, Pacheco. Bordaberry's political program followed the main ideas of the Pacheco administration and included a strong stand against the unions and the guerrilla movement.

The Bordaberry Administration and the Resurgence of Military Influence

The new government inherited many problems. The large fiscal and external deficits made a new stabilization plan necessary; the unions were very active; and the administration faced a strong opposition in Parliament, a growing military presence in national affairs, and open warfare with the guerrillas.[2]

In April 1972 the level of violence in the antiguerrilla confrontation led Parliament to declare a state of siege in which personal rights and guarantees were suspended. The armed forces and the police used force to suppress the guerrillas. Between April and June 1972 accusations in Parliament concerning violations of human rights abounded, as did confrontations between the executive and legislative powers (and even within the executive itself) regarding this issue.

During this period the military and its organizations participated openly in political life. Civilian control of the armed forces deteriorated. Confrontations between the armed forces and the legislative and executive powers revealed a weakening of the military hierarchy; that is, power in the armed forces lay in the hands of officers directly commanding the troops and not with the higher levels of the hierarchy.

During the second half of 1972 the intrusion of the military into politics was evident. The military was participating in the repression of illicit dealings, accusing members of Parliament of being linked to the guerrilla movement, and insisting on having an active role in decisions affecting national development. This intrusion took place during a time of extreme weakness in government caused by lack of parliamentary support, which in turn led to further debilitation.

In February 1973 the military leaders rejected the president's appointment of a retired general as minister of defense and forced his withdrawal. Neither Parliament nor the unions forcefully challenged this rebellious act, which in fact met with apathy and even with the sympathy of the left wing and the unions. These groups saw populist expressions in communiqués written by the military command, and they viewed the ascent of the military as a way of institutionalizing structural economic reforms that they considered desirable.[3]

The isolation of President Bordaberry at that time probably greatly conditioned the subsequent political solution, which provided for the participation of military leaders in the government.[4] The personal ambition of some of the most important military chiefs and the deeply rooted belief that political parties were not able to solve the country's serious problems helped to shape the alliance between the president and the armed forces. The failure of the political system to solve the problems affecting Uruguayan society during the foregoing decades and lack of confidence in the democratic system appear to have been the dominant factors behind the June 1973 military coup.⟩

An Analysis of the Period

The period 1955–73 was one of stagnation in production. After a decade of rapid growth following World War II, deceleration became evident between 1954 and 1957. From the mid-1950s to 1973 the country's GDP did not grow except for a short period in the late 1960s; thus, in 1970 GDP per capita was at the same level as in 1957. Between 1955 and 1960 the primary sector experienced a downward trend. In the 1960s agricultural output fluctuated greatly, mainly because of the performance of crops (since livestock production remained constant). Manufacturing grew continuously until 1957, declined from 1957 to 1963, and recovered slightly in the remainder of the period. After 1955 the ratio of investment to GDP declined sharply.

Accurate information on unemployment during 1955–73 is not available, but stagnation in production must have led to increased unemployment levels, compared with previous years. The number of public employees expanded significantly as clientelism spread.

The period was characterized by a rapid increase in the inflation rate. The rate of increase of domestic prices followed a steady upward trend, from less than 10 percent a year in the mid-1950s to a peak of 168 percent in the first half of 1968. Price and salary freezes in 1968 reduced the inflation rate to less than 20 percent during 1969–70, but the fiscal deficit created in 1971 led to an inflation rate of 95 percent in 1972.

External Influences

Between 1955 and 1973 three external factors brought about important changes in the Uruguayan economy: the decline in terms of trade after the Korean war, the decision of foreign slaughterhouses to abandon their investments in the country, and the founding in 1961 of LAFTA.

After 1940 the volume of Uruguay's exports hardly grew. Export values, however, increased at an average annual rate of 8 percent between 1943–45 and 1953–55 because of the rise in international prices, especially of wool. Once prosperity came to an end following the Korean war, export earnings declined more than 40 percent.

The fall in terms of trade, coupled with expansionary domestic policies, brought about a serious balance of payments disequilibrium during the second half of the 1950s. The persistent external deficit caused a loss of reserves and an increase in the external debt. Instead of adjusting the economy to the new external circumstances by devaluing the currency and drastically reducing expenditures, the authorities severely restricted imports and limited subsidies, particularly during 1957, thus preventing further expansion of manufacturing.

Fiscal and Exchange Rate Policy

The stagnation of production in the late 1950s did not bring about immediate changes in economic policy. Foreign trade policies gave priority to industrial growth based on import substitution. A differential exchange rate policy favored the importation of raw materials and machinery for industry, financed through a lower exchange rate for beef and wool exports.

The contraction in export earnings that followed the Korean war reinforced the overvaluation of the exchange rate, as is shown by differences between the official exchange rate, fixed by the Banco de la República and applied to all imports and exports, and the financial exchange rate, which was determined in a free foreign exchange market and which applied to all other transactions. In 1957 the financial exchange rate was 37 percent higher than the official exchange rate for commercial transactions, and in 1958 it was 144 percent higher. In 1957 the exchange markets were closed and imports were totally prohibited. This adversely affected domestic activity by reducing the supply of imported inputs.

Although public sector financial deficits occurred during the period, they were not the principal causes of monetary expansion during those years. The increase in the money supply was mainly a result of banking credit policy for both the public and the private sectors, which was based on the rediscounting of commercial papers at subsidized rates by the Banco de la República. The inflation rate, which averaged 8 percent a year between 1949 and 1954, jumped to an annual average of 23 percent between 1955 and 1960. At the same time, the interest rate was administratively fixed below the inflation rate, which motivated capital outflows, especially in 1957 and 1958.

In 1959 the Blanco party administration introduced important changes in economic policy. Under the terms of a standby credit from the International Monetary Fund (IMF), the government drew up an economic plan based on widespread reform of the foreign exchange and foreign trade systems, with a large foreign exchange devaluation designed to change domestic price relationships in favor of agricultural production and so foster recovery in that sector. In December 1959 the government submitted a law that eliminated all provisions that fixed (or authorized the executive to fix) exchange rates and promoted free imports of all goods. In addition, there was a significant exchange devaluation, exchange markets were unified, and all controls on capital movements were revoked.

Thus, a complex system of multiple exchange rates and quotas was dismantled. The law, however, empowered the executive to set tariffs of 300 percent over the c.i.f. value on luxury goods, dispensable goods, and goods that competed with domestic industry; to prohibit for up to six months imports of such goods; to introduce advance deposits on imports; and temporarily to exempt some imports from taxes. Certain exports, such as greasy wool, were taxed between 25 and 50 percent, and other traditional exports were taxed between 5 and 50 percent.

This law was implemented by several executive decrees, starting in 1960. After a transition period, in September 1960 an import system was introduced that set three tariff rates—10 percent for inputs, 40 percent for noncompetitive goods, and 150 percent for luxury goods. The latter two categories were subject to an advance deposit of 100 percent over their c.i.f. import values. All import prohibitions were lifted. The export tax on greasy wool was set at about 35 percent over the f.o.b. price and the export tax on beef at 5 percent over the f.o.b. price.

A new personal income tax was also approved, replacing a tax that had been imposed only on the net income of enterprises. This law provided for several tax exemptions that favored new industries and exports, thus giving incentives for reinvesting profits and bringing in capital. Enforcement of this change in the tax system was delayed, and the new tax did not change the structure of revenues significantly, since the income tax was less than 5 percent of the total.

Between 1959 and 1961 the decline in the fiscal deficit contributed to better control of the sources of money creation (table 11-1). The country, however, experienced continuous imbalances in the external sector, and increasing inflation reinforced economic stagnation during the 1960s. In 1962 fiscal and exchange policies brought about a massive capital flight from the private sector, giving rise to a loss in international reserves and an increase in the external debt.

In 1963 a dual exchange market was reestablished. Use of the official exchange rate, fixed by the Banco de la República, was compulsory for exports, imports, and public debt service. All other transactions were carried out under free fluctuating rates, without government intervention. Tariffs and advance deposits on imports were increased. The management of public finances was less strict than in previous years. This was especially the case in 1965, when a deficit of 5 percent of GDP was recorded.

In 1964 and 1965 the external deficit led to exchange market pressures. Instead of devaluing the peso, the authorities further restricted imports at a time when the ratio of exchange rates in the two markets was 3 to 1. At the end of 1965, as part of an agreement with the IMF, a new devaluation took place (from 24 pesos/dollar to 65 pesos/dollar), both markets

Table 11-1. Uruguay: Macroeconomic Indicators, 1955–72

Indicator	1955–59	1960–62	1963–67	1968–72
1. Real exchange rate (1961 = 100)	61.2	104.4	102.6	94.9
2. Public expenditure/GDP (percent)	12.0	16.4	15.6	15.4
3. Public income/GDP (percent)	10.8	14.6	12.5	13.3
4. Fiscal balance/GDP (percent)	−1.2	−1.8	−3.1	−2.1
5. Real wages (1961 = 100)				
Manufacturing	91.7	96.8	97.7	92.4
Public sector	91.7	87.1	102.2	91.1
6. M1 (growth; percent)	17.0	17.0	60.0	47.0
7. Real interest rate on deposits	−10.0	−15.0	−32.0	−20.0
8. GDP (variation; percent)				
Total	−0.9	1.4	−0.2	2.2
Agriculture	−3.9	−0.2	0.3	0.4
Manufacturing	0.2	−1.2	−0.1	3.4
9. Unemployment rate	—	—	8.4	8.0
10. Change in consumer prices (percent)	17.0	24.0	55.0	47.0
11. Investment/GDP (percent)				
Total	12.9	15.3	11.5	10.8
Public investment	2.6	2.8	2.5	2.6
Private investment	10.3	12.5	9.0	8.2
12. Exports (millions of U.S. dollars)	160	153	176	206
13. Imports (millions of U.S. dollars)	204	220	172	206
14. Public sector external debt (millions of U.S. dollars)	156	253	297	400

— Not available.

Source: Banco Central del Uruguay, *Boletín Estadístico*, various issues; Instituto de Economía, Universidad de la República, 1969.

were unified, and certain imports were prohibited. In 1967 import quotas were introduced, tariffs on imports were increased to a maximum of 300 percent, and several advance deposit systems were set up. Export taxes were eliminated in 1969.

CIDE and the Ten-Year Plan

In 1960 the Blanco government created the Comisión de Inversiones y Desarrollo Económico (CIDE) to coordinate public sector investment, analyze Uruguay's economic situation, and prepare an economic development plan. In 1963 the commission published an analysis of the economy and in 1965 it issued a ten-year plan. CIDE's activities were part of a regional trend toward preparing national development plans in order to secure external aid from the Alliance for Progress, which relied on ideas developed by ECLA during the previous decade.

CIDE attributed economic stagnation to the exhaustion of the import-substitution model for industry and the structural incapacity of agriculture to apply the technology needed to increase production. The commission regarded inflation as a consequence of economic stagnation and of subsequent social conflicts.

The ten-year plan sought to increase and rationalize public sector investments and selectively promoted certain investment projects in the private sector. It advocated major economic reforms: an agrarian reform designed to overcome the limits imposed by the structure of landed property and land tenancy; the modernization of the state through administrative and institutional reforms and changes in the fiscal system; the implementation of a short-term program combining an adequate exchange rate policy with both monetary and fiscal mechanisms; and an agreement between the government, the private sector, and the unions with respect to price and wage policies.

With the exception of the change proposed in agricultural tenancy, all the changes suggested by CIDE were implemented in the following years. Thus, after 1966 a Central Bank, an Office of Planning and Budget, a Public Sector Labor Bureau (Oficina de Servicio Civil), and a Foreign Trade Bureau (Dirección General de Comercio Exterior) were created. Some new import-substitution sectors were promoted in agriculture (sugar beet and sugarcane) and industry (car assembly), and changes were made in taxation and in the adjustment for inflation in the tax scheme.

The Left considered the proposed structural changes insufficient and believed they would not lead to significant changes in production and income distribution. Furthermore, the rejection of changes in the structure of property in the agricultural sector was considered a clear expression of the opposition of members of the dominant class to any changes, even changes that would affect their personal interests only slightly.

At the other ideological extreme, the plan was criticized for not giving prime importance to inflation and to the role of fiscal and monetary disequilibria as causes of inflation. The plan's structuralist interpretations concerning agricultural stagnation were much criticized because of the low importance given to the distortion of relative prices and to the adverse effects of distortion on agricultural earnings.

In addition to the plan's own failings, the political situation worked against initiatives designed to overcome economic difficulties. The unprecedented fiscal deficit of 1965 came in the same year that CIDE demanded relatively cautious management of public finances in order to solve the problem of inflation. Similarly, a social agreement between government, entrepreneurs, and employees was readily spoiled by continuous conflicts between the government and the unions.

The Colorado government elected in 1966 started its term by oscillating between two opposing economic views. A group inside the party adhered to ECLA ideas and to CIDE's proposals for structural changes and for a social agreement between the groups that best represented entrepreneurs and workers. Another group advocated drawing up a stabilization program that would give priority to the struggle against inflation within the framework of fiscal and balance of payments adjustments.

The Stabilization Plan

During his first year in office Gestido favored an ECLA (*desarrollista*) approach, especially in late 1967, when outstanding leaders of the Colorado party's left wing were appointed to ministerial posts. A large fiscal imbalance—the result of measures adopted by the Blanco government in 1966—and weather conditions that adversely affected the food supply led to the abandonment of the *desarrollista* orientation and the implementation of a stabilization plan in December 1967.

The plan started with a devaluation (from 100 pesos/dollar to 200 pesos/dollar) and an agreement with the IMF. The MPS was invoked to counter union reaction. In April 1968 a new devaluation occurred. At the same time, monetary mismanagement led to a 14 percent increase in domestic prices during June 1968. Starting in July, this increase was to be incorporated into wage and salary increases under the terms of previous agreements between most enterprises and unions. Under these circumstances the government imposed a price and wage freeze and took a strong stand against the unions that opposed the price stabilization plan and against entrepreneurs who attempted to avoid price controls. The shock imposed by the stabilization plan had an unambiguous effect on expectations of inflation and explains in part the initial success of the plan. The maintenance of a fixed exchange rate at 250 pesos a dollar also contributed to a rapid decline in the rate of price increase, since the domestic prices of all tradable goods were kept unchanged.

In addition, because the interest rate was not modified, the sharp decline in the inflation rate gave rise to high real interest rates, which contributed to a decline in expenditure and to lower pressures on domestic prices. Tax measures adopted in late 1967 and early 1968 to deal with a public finance deficit were complemented by the effects of the price and wage freeze in June 1968. This freeze restricted wages and other expenditures while increasing the real value of the government's tax revenues. The results of the freeze were favorable. The fiscal deficit decreased from 3.2 percent of GDP in 1967 to 0.2 percent in 1968, and inflation during the second half of 1968 was 2 percent, in contrast to 64 percent in the first half of the year.

Prices rose 14.5 percent in 1969 and 20.9 in 1970, and GDP grew 6.1 and 4.7 percent in those years. During 1968 and 1969 the monetary authority's international reserves increased substantially. The average wage index, for both public and private employees, increased 10 percent in real terms between 1968 and 1970.

Economic Policy under Bordaberry

By mid-1970 the maintenance of a fixed exchange rate had led to an overvalued currency, an external deficit, and a loss in international reserves. The authorities were divided regarding the strategy required to adjust the external deficit. A proposal for a devaluation was disregarded by the president, who did not want to lose popularity in the year before the national elections. The exchange overvaluation was accompanied by a progressive abandonment of fiscal discipline; in 1971 the central government deficit reached 5.8 percent of GDP.

In October 1971 the authorities ordered a salary increase but postponed price adjustments. Thus, the government's decisions brought about a transitory rise in real wages and significantly repressed inflation. In addition, the overvalued currency caused a wide gap between the official and black-market exchange rates and a loss of international reserves.

The economic policies of the Bordaberry government elected in 1971 were similar to those of the Pacheco administration. The new government secretly sold some of the gold that formed part of the international assets of the Central Bank in order to obtain the liquidity necessary for maintaining a normal supply of imports. At the same time, an exchange devaluation (from 250 pesos a dollar to 500 pesos a dollar) was decreed, and a crawling peg system was put in place. This essential change from the previous system was made to avoid the sharp fluctuations in the real exchange rate that had occurred in the past. A more conservative wage policy and a significant increase in the prices of public firms' services made possible a drastic reduction in the fiscal deficit, from 5.8 percent of GDP in 1971 to 2.6 percent of GDP in 1972.

The Bordaberry government considered the possibility of implementing major changes in economic policy—a step devaluation followed by the unification of the exchange market, liberalization of imports, and decontrol of prices and salaries. Although some of these policy changes were included in the 1972–77 economic development plan, the political situation forced the postponement of their implementation. Most of these policy changes were implemented by the military after the June 1973 coup. The contractionary policies followed during 1972 led to a 3.4 percent decline in GDP, while the rate of inflation increased from 36 percent in 1971 to 95 percent in 1972 and the real wage rate fell 19 percent.

The Political Economy of the Period

The political economy of the period was affected by inflation, stagnation, and the distribution of government expenditure and income.

Stagnation

Stagnation in the livestock sector, which began in the 1930s and was reinforced in the 1950s, was one of the most important problems for the Uruguayan economy. Two basic reasons were given during the 1960s for the lack of investment in land-saving techniques (which were considered the only way to overcome the constraint on growth imposed by a fixed supply of land).

THE STRUCTURAL EXPLANATION. The most widely held explanation stressed the structure of lot size, the pattern of land tenancy, and the alleged absence of a strong capitalist motive among ranchers. With some differences, this basic interpretation was shared by the CIDE development plan. According to this interpretation, the distribution of rural holdings resulted in inefficient exploitation of the country's main natural resource, since both large and small rural holdings were subject to diseconomies of scale.

The fixing of a limit below which a holding is considered *minifundio* (too small) and above which it is considered *latifundio* (too large) depends on such things as soil characteristics, proximity to markets, and the degree of technological development. It has been said that 60 percent of rural enterprises, occupying less than 12 percent of the total land area, might be defined as *minifundio*. Less than 3 percent of rural enterprises had areas considered too large for their adequate use, but they occupied 44 percent of the total area of the country. Thus, more than one-half of the total rural area of the country was in rural enterprises of inappropriate size.

Forms of land tenancy ranged from ownership or self-management to leasing or share tenancy. Since existing legislation did not provide a proper definition of the rights of the landowners and tenants with respect to investments and technological improvements, the structure of land tenancy was seen as a significant deterrent to the introduction of modern capital-intensive technology in agriculture. The combination of size and tenancy problems was thought to affect about 84 percent of rural holdings, or 82 percent of the total land area.

The behavior of the agricultural sector during the last decades of the nineteenth century, however, dramatically refutes the idea that entrepreneurial capacity within the sector was lacking and that ranchers were not responsive to profitable opportunities. Investments in wire fencing and improved breeding, which made it possible for the cattle industry to cater to the tastes of the international market, were a direct and rapid response to the increased profitability of investment in the sector. Furthermore, available estimates of the supply elasticity of agriculture and of the changes in land use as a response to relative price changes consistently suggest a strong response of the sector to price incentives (Cobas and others 1985).

The effect on economic growth of institutional conditions such as the structure of lot size and the pattern of land tenancy has not been subjected to rigorous empirical analysis. Favaro and Spiller (1990), using the "survivor's technique," found evidence consistent with an absence of economies of scale in a wide range of lot sizes—500 to 2,500 hectares. There are, however, no studies of differences in the pattern of adoption of new technologies according to land tenancy or lot size.

THE POLICY EXPLANATION. The second interpretation of stagnation in the beef sector, advanced during the 1960s, emphasized the adverse role of discriminatory policies on relative prices and investment incentives (tables 11-2 and 11-3). The main technological characteristic of beef production in Uruguay is its great reliance on the use of land; thus, availability of land is the most important constraint on the expansion of production in the sector. The high taxes traditionally levied on beef and wool production discouraged the implementation of techniques for making more intensive use of land, such as improving pastures to increase their carrying capacity. Taxes that affect prices in the sector reduce land prices in relation to other inputs, since land is the most

Table 11-2. Relative Prices of Beef and of Selected Agricultural Inputs, Uruguay and Other Beef-Producing Countries
(relative price, in tons of beef on the hoof)

Price and year	Uruguay	Argentina	Brazil	United States	France
Per tractor horsepower *(35–40 HP tractors)*					
1963–66	0.70	0.41	0.63	0.20	0.15
1973–76	1.09	0.47	0.34	0.21	0.10
Per ton phosphoric *anhydride*					
1961	0.68	1.80	0.87	0.40	0.44
Per 1,000 liters gas *and oil*					
1961–64	0.20	0.30	0.33	0.10	0.08
1969–72	0.19	0.18	0.31	0.07	0.07
1975–76	0.85	0.31	0.43	0.10	0.10

Source: Reca and Regunaga 1978.

Table 11-3. Relative Prices of Wool and of Selected Agricultural Inputs, Uruguay and Other Wool-Producing Countries, Various Years, 1961–75

Tons of greasy wool needed to purchase:

One HP of 35–50 HP tractors	1961–64	1967–70	1973–75
Uruguay	0.14	0.38	0.31
Argentina	0.15	0.17	0.13
New Zealand	0.06	0.10	0.13
United States	0.09	0.12	0.12

One ton of phosphoric anhydride	1965	1971	1975
Uruguay	0.20	0.53	0.89
Argentina	0.46	0.46	0.90
New Zealand	0.29	0.55	0.42
United States	0.20	0.58	0.53

Source: Reca and Regunaga 1978.

inelastic factor of production. Most of Uruguay's land is not suitable for alternative uses such as crop production.

The low price of land intensifies the use of land, diminishes investment in livestock production, and reduces the technical efficiency of the industry. Livestock are fed on natural pasture and lose weight in the winter. Because of nutritional deficiencies, cattle take longer to reach slaughter weight, and cows are less fertile. In comparison with other countries, Uruguay produces a small quantity of meat per animal and per unit of land (Sapelli 1985).

Several taxes were levied on the agricultural sector, either explicitly or implicitly through taxes on land and other transactions. The most relevant were export taxes and exchange rate policies; during certain periods overvaluation of the currency affected exports in general and the agricultural sector in particular. Industrial protection constituted another form of tax, as it increased the domestic prices of manufactured goods in relation to export prices and created a less favorable relationship between export prices and prices of inputs.

The percentage of the price received by producers was fixed by the government through exchange rates and export taxes; the highest export tax rates occurred when there was a devaluation. (Before the late 1950s the producer price was completely divorced from the international price, but later the prices were more closely related.) These taxes brought about income transfers among producers of exports, producers of import substitutes, and consumers. The measurement of these transfers depends on different parameters. Even though it is clear that the export sector loses income and the import sector benefits, consumers may either gain or lose income, since they benefit from a lower relative price of export goods but have to pay higher prices for imports and nontradable goods. The available data show that in Uruguay the industrial protection policy produces a large benefit for consumers. (The amount of the consumer's benefit depends heavily on the share of agricultural and livestock products in the consumption basket.)

Sapelli (1985) analyzed the overall effect of export taxes, exchange rate policy, and import tariffs on cattle production. His study concluded that to generate a transfer in favor of the state and of beef consumers that in the long run amounted to 7 percent of GDP, cattle production was maintained at one-third of its potential level, imposing a loss in overall GDP of 12 percent. It is clear that the benefit to the state and to consumers has been one of the most powerful motives for the design of Uruguay's agricultural policy in spite of its damaging effects on production.

PROTECTIONISM. Although protectionism in the Uruguayan economy dates back to 1875, it was not until the two decades following the Depression that protectionist policies brought about significant transformations in the economic structure. The principal changes were the development of import-substituting manufacturing and the loss of dynamism in the agricultural sector.

The thrust in protectionist measures, in both 1875 and 1930, coincided with world crises, trade disruption, and deflationary pressures in the world economy, which may have concealed the potential cost of high tariffs. The introduction of tariffs within a framework of deflationary pressures and fixed exchange rates was presumably an attractive strategy for government officials, since it permitted achievement of a new equilibrium at a lower world price level and reduced the adjustment cost associated with the domestic recession.

Even though ECLA strongly supported Uruguay's growth strategy in the 1950s on ideological grounds, ideas seem to have lagged behind the facts, and ECLA can be held responsible only for defending the status quo in the 1960s rather than for shaping protectionism during previous decades. Ignorance with respect to the general equilibrium effects of tariffs may have delayed the reaction to the ideas that manufacturing was a prime factor in determining growth and that the transfer of resources from agriculture would cause no decline in output in the rural sector.

RURAL-TO-URBAN TRANSFERS. The new policies led to the rise of private interest groups whose survival depended entirely on high tariffs and whose power was associated with the duration of the policy. Although Latorre's government was able to lower tariffs by 50 percent in 1879 despite opposition from industry, confirming the short-run perspective of the macroeconomic policy behind the original increase in tariffs, the rapid growth in manufacturing during the 1940s brought about the development of vested interests that resisted any attempt to liberalize the economy in the 1950s and 1960s. Commercial policy was originally adopted to deal with the critical international situation, but its latent distributive purpose is evident if it is examined within the context of the parallel expansion in the size and scope of the public sector, the increase in the size of bureaucracy, and the creation of new public enterprises. Government administrations following the Depression used state power to gain the support of voters by creating trade restrictions and hence rents, by increasing government bureaucracy and hence public employment, and by extending subsidized credit.

Agriculture provided an ideal source of resources to finance import-competing activities and the growing government bureaucracy, since in the short run it could withstand heavy taxation. The tax burden was felt by landowners, who faced a one-time capital loss as the price of land decreased, making the rate of return sufficiently attractive for people to hold and exploit land. The dynamics of the new policy produced migration from rural to urban areas, which reinforced the structure of taxation by making it less costly in terms of votes.

In the short run, the redistributive aspect of taxing agriculture surpassed in importance the welfare loss that accompanied changes in output. In the long run, the new policy proved extremely costly. Rural entrepreneurs reacted against the expropriatory policy, delaying the adoption of land-saving techniques not only because of the risk of income exaction under the prevailing policies but also because of the low rate of return determined by the new relative prices.

There is no reason to assume that the new policies created dramatic shifts in the personal distribution of income or significant changes in landowners' personal wealth. In fact, the landowners may well have succeeded in capturing the rents created in the urban sector. This plausible result illustrates the paradox that although no significant and sustainable change in the distribution of income occurred, the structure of taxation and of the vested interests associated with it prevented growth along the lines of the country's comparative advantage.

Policies that were damaging to the economy as a whole persisted because they served the personal interests of bureaucrats and politicians. Electoral support was achieved through food subsidies and the support of inefficient industries. A reversal in policy would have imposed costs on urban workers, industrial entrepreneurs, and government employees. Landowners would have benefited, but because of the length of the cattle cycle, supply would have declined in the short run. Furthermore, the benefits attributable to a change in policy would not have been felt until the following administration took office—making the strategy unacceptable to a government that had a high discount rate because of its interest in being reelected.

THE 1959 REFORMS. The only attempt to alter the structure of protectionism came in 1959 when the Blanco party sponsored an exchange and trade act that called for moving from quantity restrictions to ad valorem tariffs and eliminating multiple exchange rates. The elimination of import quotas may have affected vested interests, but it is unlikely that the effect was significant, for two reasons. First, whereas under previous regulations the scarcity of foreign currency had led to sharp cuts in import quotas on consumer goods, under the new act high tariffs on imports made the import of finished goods impossible, and there was little difference in the outcome. Second, importers of raw materials and intermediate goods benefited from the lower tariffs under the new policy.

In the short run agriculture benefited from a more realistic exchange rate, but new regulations introduced direct taxes on exports to moderate the rise in domestic prices. Although this was theoretically conceived as a move toward free trade, in practice it was restricted in scope and short-lived. High tariffs virtually prohibited the importation of finished goods and had no significant effects on the allocation of resources. Tariffs on imports raised the prices of importable goods in relation to those of exportables and nontradable goods, shifting demand toward the latter group. Resources were bid toward the import-competing sector and away from production of exportables and domestic goods.

THE EFFECT OF TARIFFS. Since demand for home goods rose while supply declined, tariffs worked to increase the price of these goods. Although tariffs were paid by importers, the consequent changes in relative prices implied that the burden of the tax fell mainly on exporters.

It is only in such extreme cases that the effect of tariffs falls wholly on exports. For example, when there is a high degree of substitutability between home goods and importables, both in demand and supply, the relative prices of importables and home goods do not change. Clements and Sjaastad (1984) suggest measuring the net effect of protection on one sector by using the percentage change in wages as a proxy for the price of home goods; when wages rise by more than the output price, the sector is adversely affected. Between 1940 and 1975 real wages in manufacturing industry increased 69 percent, whereas the price of meat increased only 30 percent.[5]

Since the price of land is determined by demand, a tax on agricultural exports reduces the market value of land and imposes a one-time capital loss on landowners. An indication of the damage that commercial policy inflicts on agriculture is that in 1976 one hectare of average grassland was worth US$175 in Uruguay, US$213 in Argentina, and US$250 in Brazil (Anichini, Caumont, and Sjaastad 1978).

Although the implicit tax produced by a tariff brings about a transfer from exporters to the import-competing sector, a complete analysis of the effects of tariffs on income distribution also requires that the effects of tariffs on consumers be examined. As the relative price of exportables falls, those who consume exportables benefit (other things being equal), whereas those who consume mainly importables suffer losses. Since in Uruguay two-thirds of meat production is consumed domestically, consumers may actually benefit from protection. The size of the gain is larger for the lowest 10 percent of the income distribution because in that bracket 14 percent of total expenditure goes for meat, whereas for the highest 10 percent the figure is only 3 percent.

Three parameters determine who gains and who loses from protectionism: the fraction of protection that is transformed into an implicit tax on exports; the percentage of exportable goods consumed at home; and the percentage of consumption of importables produced at home. Given the implicit tax on exports, the higher the level of domestic consumption of exportables and the lower the fraction of importables produced domestically, the more consumers will benefit. Sciandra (1979) estimated the transfer from the agricultural sector to the rest of the economy as a result of 1979 commercial policy to be 8.7 percent of GDP under free trade. Sapelli (1985), using a higher estimate of nominal protection, obtained a figure of 9 percent of GDP for 1930 and 19 percent for 1961. According to his methodology 97 percent of the transfer resulted in a consumer subsidy in 1930; in 1961 the figure was 63 percent.

Our estimates indicated that in 1930 the transfer from agriculture was 2.4 percent of GDP, which translated into a gain to import-competing industries of 0.1 percent of GDP and a benefit to consumers of 2.3 percent. In 1961 the transfer was 6.1 percent of GDP, or a benefit to import-competing activities of 2.3 percent and a subsidy to consumers equivalent to 3.8 percent.[6] Although consumers clearly gained immediately from a protection policy that implied a tax on beef exports because it reduced the domestic price of beef, import-competing firms shared the spoils in the dynamics of the process.

Sapelli (1985) estimated the effect of the structure of protection on factor prices. He found that in equilibrium, the tariff in force during the period caused a decline in land rents of 8.2 percent and an increase in wages of 7 percent. Using a 1961 input-output matrix and estimated tariff level, he found that manufacturing wages increased 143 percent as a result of commercial policy and that rents declined 43.7 percent.

Inflation

Between 1830 and the Great Depression prices remained virtually unchanged. But during the 1930s the stage was set for monetary mismanagement and price instability.

In 1929 the Banco de la República Oriental del Uruguay (BROU) abandoned intervention in the foreign exchange market, and the gap between the market exchange rate and the 1862 parity became wider. In 1935 the peso was devalued. The gold content established for the peso in 1862 was reduced, and the authorities, regarding the accounting adjustment of the value of the stock of gold reserves as new resources, proceeded to spend this windfall. Until 1939 monetary expansion by the BROU remained constrained by the gold stock and by a ceiling on the fiduciary issue, but the constraint was later relaxed, and the BROU was allowed to rediscount commercial bills maturing in no more than six months, provided that they were related to the sale of goods without a ceiling.

The 1935 devaluation paved the way for a loosening of monetary discipline. It was, however, the authorization to rediscount commercial bills without limit that was the source of future monetary mismanagement. It has been argued that fiscal deficits were not a significant source of monetary expansion before the 1960s. This is true in form rather than in content; rediscounts were in fact a kind of expenditure that did not need parliamentary approval. The share of rediscounts in total credit swelled in the 1950s and 1960s.

One of the uses of rediscounts within the public sector was to finance subsidies for the public railway, real estate construction, employment in slaughterhouses, and urban passenger transport and to extend credits to farmers who exploited state-owned land. In 1963 rediscounting was used to subsidize bank debtors who faced bankruptcy. In 1965 another rediscount line was used to reimburse depositors in banks that had gone bankrupt.

The use of rediscounts was progressively related to private sector activities, especially for industrial organizations that processed agricultural raw materials. During the late 1960s rediscount lines were available for buying wool, cattle, cotton, oleaginous seeds, and raw materials in general, as well as for payment by enterprises of additional wages at the end of the year. In the following years other purposes were added, such as the purchase by nontraditional export industries of raw materials, hides, and sackcloth. Firms that received these funds clearly benefited; during most of the 1960s, when the average annual inflation rate was 44 percent, the interest rate on these credits was between 10 and 12 percent a year.

In 1965 the increasing importance of the deficit in the finances of the central government became a new factor in the inflationary process. The inflation rate increased from an average 30 percent a year between 1960 and 1965 to 81 percent a year in the two-year period 1966–67. The erratic development of the real exchange rate and the continuously negative level of real interest, in the context of increasing inflation, were two important new factors that contributed to stagnation in production during the period. Instability in the real exchange rate reduced the possibilities of export expansion and economic growth. During those years exports were almost exclusively beef and wool.

There is strong evidence showing that inflation had a negative influence on investment in the Uruguayan economy (Favaro 1987). Moreover, two other factors usually associated with inflation—the gap between the financial and commercial exchange rates and the capital account of the net balance of payments—are also significant in explaining the level of investment.

Other evidence pointing in the same direction lies in the history of the capital market. Although Uruguay had a growing and fluid capital market in the period 1935–50, the market started to decline abruptly during the 1950s, while the share of public debt in total traded securities increased as a result of discriminatory tax treatment. The total volume traded in the stock market in 1970 was 9 percent of the volume traded in 1946. During the same period financial assets in the economy decreased significantly; bank deposits and securities were 23.6 percent of GDP in 1945 but only 5.95 percent in 1970. The absence of a well-developed capital market reduced the possibility for private investors to finance capital accumulation through long-term instruments and caused saving to be channeled into investment in real estate and the holding of inventories or of foreign currency.

Inflationary taxation created rents that were received mainly by the government. Until the 1950s the government benefited from inflation because of the decrease in the value of public debt issued in local currency and not indexed. Nevertheless, inflation during those years progressively limited public demand for public debt instruments and eventually led to the closure of those sources of finance. The inflation tax collected by expanding base money gained in importance.

Inflationary taxation was also a source of direct transfers between private net debtors and creditors. Since real interest rates on loans were negative during most of the period under study, credit was rationed and loan recipients received a net benefit, if only because they had access to the credit market. Although import-substituting industry was again the main beneficiary of the transfers induced by negative real interest rates and access to the credit market, the transfers did not increase the net wealth of these firms. In fact, a rather perverse mechanism developed because firms were taxed on their inflationary gains and were thus subject to a dramatic wealth depletion during the period.

Another undoubtedly important factor that affected inflation in Uruguay was the strength of the labor movement and its constant opposition to changes in relative prices that could lower real wages. Continuous strikes by public and private workers during the 1960s were significant limitations on economic policy. For example, important devaluations in exchange rates were generally neutralized in later months by a rise in wages for the purpose of maintaining purchasing power. In the same way, governmental financial deficits were in many cases the result of increases in public employees' salaries, granted to satisfy the unions' demands.

INFLATION AND ELECTORAL POLITICS. The inflation rate tended to change cyclically in tandem with elections; the average duration of the inflation cycle was almost exactly that of the political cycle (Díaz 1984). Five of the six inflationary peaks between 1950 and 1972 correspond to years immediately following election years. All of the monetary and fiscal variables that economic theory generally associates with inflation closely follow the same pattern.

During the year before an election year, the governing party used its control over the nation's monetary and fiscal systems to improve its chances of victory by increasing expenditures and transferring wealth. This behavior can be attributed to the lack of well-defined limits to discretion in a political administration and to a high discount rate associated with reelection interests. Administrations endowed with the power to promote distributive policies and use inflationary finance did not resist temptation, even though such actions had a high social cost. To take, during an election year, conservative measures that reduced the scope of the government's redistributive initiatives would be to risk the support of powerful interest groups and reduce the chances of reelection. As the probability of reelection diminished, price stability in the next period had a very low discount value for the incumbent administration; administrations not yet in power had no means of paying the government in power for its generosity. The result was a type of political equilibrium that was not Pareto optimal.

THE EFFECTS OF INFLATION. In the short run, inflation does not seem to affect real wages significantly, since workers rapidly incorporate inflation into their bargaining for wage increases. In the long run, inflation reduces investment and the capital stock, and it lowers both the level and the rate of growth of real wages. When inflation is associated with financial restrictions such as interest rate controls and credit rationing, the allocation of resources in the economy is distorted, and inefficiency becomes widespread. As the economy withdraws inside its frontier, the burden of waste falls mainly on the factors with the lowest supply elasticity—land and labor.

Inflation is also a tax on a particular form of wealth: net nominal assets. The incidence of price instability on personal income thus depends on the distribution of nominal assets, the return to nominal assets, and the capacity of different individuals to acquire through indebtedness a hedge against this form of taxation. Although there seem to be no economies of scale in holding money, it is likely that the range of assets that provide an adequate hedge against inflation increases with income, particularly when financial repression exists, whereas access to credit lines and the cost of credit are both unequally distributed.

Interest rates that were negative in real terms during the 1960s became a source of additional income for enterprises indebted to the banks. At the same time, interest rates brought about capital depletion of local currency savers. This was, in turn, the main reason for an increasing capital outflow, especially from wealthy savers. An inflation tax also falls heavily on those earning rents from real assets that are fixed in nominal terms. This was the case for landlords in Uruguay, who suffered continuous adverse effects from rent freezes imposed during the 1960s.

Government Expenditures and Income Distribution

The increase in the size and scope of public sector activities became apparent at the beginning of the century and was more pronounced following the Depression. Expansion was part of an ideological scheme that began to be expressed at the beginning of the century through public enterprises and social services. Voters had little control over the actions of government officials, and it was almost impossible for officials to be penalized for promoting political initiatives that involved high costs for society as a whole. Collusion, rather than competition, characterized the political process. The traditional parties reached agreements to increase the number of employees and to bring new activities into the state domain. High political payoffs were associated with increased public expenditures.

In the 1930s the limits on the expansion of government expenditure were loosened as the authorities allowed unlimited monetary expansion through the rediscounting of short-term commercial paper. As a consequence, the increase in the level of government expenditure was unconstrained.

INCOME DISTRIBUTION. In the short run, increased government expenditures have favored a diminution of inequality in Uruguayan society. Since most government expenditure is used for wages, salaries, and social security transfers, expansion appears to redistribute income toward the middle class. Wages and salaries for less skilled labor are higher in the public sector than in the private sector, and government expenditure tends to bid up the price of less skilled labor in the market. The government influences the real wage rate of less skilled labor in the private sector by detaching resources from the rest of the economy and by expanding public employment (mainly by political means).

In the long run, the effect of government intervention on income distribution is far more complicated. The larger the relative size of government expenditure, the more probable it is that a marginal expansion of governmental activity will introduce a distortion rather than a positive externality. Thus, in time an increase in the size of government reduces both the levels of real income and wages and their rate of growth (Favaro, Graziani, and Sapelli 1987). Furthermore, the government creates rents and so gives incentives for rent-seeking activities. When the rate of return on lobbying for privilege is higher than the profitability of introducing new technologies, better quality control systems, or improvements in marketing procedures, firms will invest in lobbying rather than in other activities. In summary, distributionally oriented policies have distorted incentives, inducing investment of both human and physical capital in activities that are highly profitable for agents in the private sector but have a low return for society as a whole.

There is no accurate information on what happened to poverty during the period, but available statistics do reveal progress in such social indicators as the literacy rate, the ratio of teachers to primary school pupils, life expectancy, infant mortality, and housing.

SOCIAL SECURITY. Perhaps one of the most outstanding events during the period was the appearance of certain signs of disequilibrium in the finances of the social security system. The political climate of the time was not favorable for attempts to curb easy access to retirement benefits by, for example, raising the minimum retirement age and abolishing certain grounds for retirement. The increasing difficulties in central government finances restricted the possibilities for substantial additional transfers from the general revenues to the social security system.

Under these circumstances administrative mechanisms were used to defend the finances of the social security system. One was a delay in granting retirement benefits to applicants. Although this was also the consequence of an imperfect system of information on workers' employment backgrounds, it was widely believed that final approval of applications for pensions was subject to the financial possibilities of the system; it was common for a year or more to pass before benefits were granted. No statistics are available to quantify the importance of these delays, although it seems to have been very large.

The second mechanism for defending the finances of the system was the lagged adjustment of pensions in relation to wages. Between 1964 and 1968 pensions grew by 490 percent while salaries increased by 920 percent. It was only in 1969, when this adjustment mechanism was eliminated, that a closer correspondence between wage and pension changes was achieved. This adjustment procedure produced a large deterioration in retirees' incomes. In 1970, for instance, the average pension was only 90 percent of the national minimum wage.

Notes

1. For evidence concerning the effects of trade agreements on trade creation and trade diversion, see Favaro and Sapelli 1989.

2. The armed forces took charge of antiguerrilla warfare in September 1971. The decision implied the creation of a united command of the armed forces and the police to coordinate the fighting. Until then the military had been forbidden to participate in politics, although some military facilities served as detention centers for people arrested under MPS rules between 1968 and 1971.

3. The military command's communiqués 4 and 7, dated February 9 and 10, 1973, were of a nationalist and populist nature.

4. The participation of the armed forces in the administration was institution-alized through the creation of the COSENA, a presidential advisory council consulted in all decisions that affected security and development.

5. The averages for the periods 1936–45 and 1971–78 are used in calculating the increase in the price of meat.

6. The estimates are based on a simplification of Clements's and Sjaastad's (1984) methodology under the extreme assumption that the full burden of the tax falls on exporters. We used as a base for our estimates the share in total value added for 1961 of the beef sector's value added.

12 The Oil Shock and the Resumption of Economic Growth, 1973–84

In June 1973 the executive branch dissolved the parliament that had been elected in November 1971, and a stage of civilian-military government began that would last until February 1985. The intrusion of the military into the political scene, and the coup itself, represented a breach in the political history of the country, which during the twentieth century had enjoyed a high degree of democratic stability. But the democratic system had been deteriorating, as shown by growing social confrontation and by the incapacity of the political system to implement efficient reforms for promoting economic growth. Since the mid-1960s there had been frequent and violent confrontations with the unions, followed by the use—isolated at first and ubiquitous later—of constitutionally exceptional repressive mechanisms (*medidas prontas de seguridad,* or MPS).

Some studies argue that this period saw the loss of one of the attributes usually associated with the *batllista* state—its conciliatory role in the struggle between social groups. It is also true, however, that during those years the government faced direct challenges—long strikes in areas such as public services and banking, and an armed urban guerrilla movement. A more adequate explanation of those years might be that the state was seeking to reestablish authority that had not been exercised in the previous two decades. A distinctive characteristic of the period was the executive's difficulty in obtaining a stable majority in parliament. This promoted the permanent use of the MPS.

The Military in Power

The military intervention in political affairs that began in February 1973 was an unusual phenomenon and a departure from the traditions maintained by the armed forces for almost a century. Over generations the military had been gradually displaced from an active political role through a series of measures adopted by the Tajes and Herrera governments in the 1890s and later consolidated during Batlle's first administration in the early twentieth century.

After the first decade of the twentieth century the national army had developed on a basis of voluntary recruitment and increasingly specialized training. The military education system was organized during Batlle's second administration (1911–15) along lines similar to those of France. This early influence was reinforced by continuous French technical assistance up to World War II; after that, the influence of the U.S. army in military technical assistance was dominant. Although appointments to key commands were influenced by political preferences, military organic laws forbade the use of the armed forces for patronage appointments. Thus the armed forces developed an officer corps of skilled specialists who were almost completely isolated from the country's political life. Most officers came from middle- and low-income families and from rural areas. Family military tradition was a characteristic phenomenon.

Although the military remained neutral in political events up to 1972, they were often used to help the police maintain internal order during periods of labor-management unrest. From the late 1950s to the early 1970s the armed forces were called on with increasing frequency to intervene in labor-management disputes as social unrest spread through the country. Military participation in administration, particularly in the public utilities, gave officers experience and confidence in their capacity to operate public enterprises and consolidated a deep anticommunist perspective among them.

During the 1960s economic stagnation, increasing price instability, social unrest, and political bickering eroded the confidence of the military in the capacity of the political system to solve the country's problems. Political violence was the catalyst for an increasing involvement of the military in civil affairs and for the enlargement of the size of the armed forces shown in the table below. (The data are from Moore 1978.)

Year	Number of military personnel
1945	11,000
1955	6,450
1965	15,400
1970	16,000
1972	21,000
1973	22,000
1977	23,000

The executive's decisions to put the armed forces in charge of the antiguerrilla fight and to unify the security forces under a single command,[1] and the temporary suspension by Parliament of several civil rights to facilitate repressive operations, provided opportunities for sanctioned intervention and gradually lowered the restraints on unsanctioned intervention in civil affairs. In the process, the ambitions of several army leaders, regional circumstances that placed domestic events in a context of international conspiracy, the public image of the rectitude of the military, and the lack of prestige of the political system helped to move the military elite into position as the central policymakers of the nation.

After June 1973 the armed forces established an authoritarian government. Most political and labor union activity was prohibited, rigorous censorship was established, and the opposition was severely repressed. The armed forces' participation in government was institutionalized through the creation of a National Security Council. In addition, the military actively participated in the direction of several public utilities and in the administration of municipal governments.

Demographic Change

In the 1970s some characteristics of the Uruguayan population that had already been observed two or three decades before became more acute—a low birthrate, an aging and increasingly urban population, and an expansion of the number of public employees and of beneficiaries of the social security system. Since the beginning of the 1960s increased emigration had contributed to the low population growth rate. Emigration tended to rise throughout the decade, reaching its peak in 1975. The emigrants were predominantly young males with a higher level of educational achievement than the population as a whole (Aguiar 1982). Net emigration was associated with economic phenomena such as low expectations for future income, compared with expected earnings in the country of destination; with sociological factors such as the existence of an information network that reduced the emigrants' cost of moving and settling; and with political issues—for example, the greater intolerance, the increase in violence, and the rupture of the institutional order in June 1973. Sapelli and Labadie (1987) have studied net emigration from Uruguay to Argentina, the country of destination of more than half the emigrants. Whereas during 1966–72 between 83 and 95 percent of the variance of net emigration could be ascribed to economic variables, between 1973 and 1975 political issues were as significant as economic phenomena in explaining the variance. Emigration appears to have been produced by the lower expected earnings that a stagnant economy offered a worker with higher-than-average education.[2]

Ideology and the Intellectuals

In the 1970s the breach between the intellectuals and the political system that began in the 1950s widened. The intellectuals were much more critical of the political system than of their own stands. The teachings of the university, cultural associations, and intellectual groups were colored by radicalism and seldom extended beyond general propositions that lacked a rigorous evidential and logical grounding (Graceras 1970). The intellectuals' consensus that the political system was incapable of answering society's problems led to the development of a messianic attitude among them rather than to a precise analysis of social problems. In fact, studies in the social sciences did not advance beyond the level of rigor of the essay. The university's organization, based on a rigid structure of faculties and curricula, was oriented toward professional studies rather than scholarly activity, and the social sciences, particularly economics, were not recognized fields of study until the mid-1960s.

In the 1960s the Comisión Interministerial de Desarrollo Económico (Interministerial Commission for Economic Development, or CIDE) was founded. CIDE was strongly influenced by the Economic Commission for Latin America (ECLA) through technical assistance. After 1966 most of the social scientists originally associated with CIDE joined the staff of the recently founded Oficina de Planeamiento y Presupuesto (Office of Planning and Budget, or OPP), became professors at the university's Economic Institute, or served as both researchers and economic advisers. The university had only just created a separate economics curriculum.

Until 1968 no significant ideological differences were noticeable between the economists associated with the OPP and those in the Economic Institute. Both groups had absorbed ECLA's ideas and were influenced by a Marxist interpretation of Uruguayan society. After 1968 the group at the Economic Institute adopted a Marxist view, whereas the OPP economists gradually moved closer to free-market policies. The creation of the OPP as a bureau directly dependent on the president brought the economic advisers associated with it into closer contact with the real world. For example, although many people had predicted that the price and wage freeze of June 1968 would be a certain failure, the economy performed very well during the second half of 1968, and this enhanced the prestige of the defenders of the freeze and their ideas. Also during 1968, economists trained under the neoclassical paradigm by conservative intellectuals, whose teaching would grow in importance in the following years, were appointed to office.[3] The evolution of Cuba after 1959 and Brazil after 1964 coincided to shape a new view of Uruguayan society.

The dominant ideas in the political community at the time were marked by distrust of markets, by the notion that income distribution and growth were competing goals in society, and by the conviction that the state could lead economic development through the design of policies that influenced the decisions of private entrepreneurs.[4]

An Economic Analysis of the Period 1974–82

The energy crisis that began in 1973 had a dramatic impact on the Uruguayan economy. The fourfold increase in the price of oil raised the share of oil in overall imports from 20 to 33 percent, and the world crisis led to an increase in protectionism in the European Communities (EC) that severely disadvantaged Uruguayan beef exports. Both shocks implied a terms of trade loss equivalent to 5 percent of GDP.

The military government faced the dilemma of whether to manage the exchange rate in spite of the external circumstances—maintaining domestic relative prices unchanged and introducing further quantitative restrictions on imports—or to devalue the currency sharply and create incentives for the development of export-oriented activities. Initially, the military administration reacted in much the same way as had the Colorado party after the end of the Korean war. It incurred an enormous fiscal deficit and tightened the already severe restrictions on imports. But in the early 1950s a high level of foreign reserves was on hand to cushion for a while the effects of a drop in the terms of trade, and restrictions on imports were introduced at a time when the level of imports was high. In contrast, the military administration was faced with a shortage of foreign reserves and had already limited total imports to raw materials and intermediate goods, which were needed to maintain economic activity. These circumstances led the military to recognize the dangers associated with the initial strategy and to appoint new economic authorities who introduced sweeping reforms.

The change in policy was led by Alejandro Vegh Villegas, an engineer and economist who had been associated in the previous decade with the implementation of stabilization plans in Argentina and Brazil. Between 1974 and 1977 the government abolished import licenses and quotas, implemented an export promotion program, fully deregulated the foreign exchange market and freed international capital movements, liberalized the domestic capital market, tightened controls on public sector expenditure, improved public utilities' economic performance, reformed the tax system, decontrolled many consumer prices, and reduced social security taxes on labor.

The goals of the strategy implemented by the new economic team were the achievement of fiscal equilibrium and price stability, the financing of the current account deficit, and the resumption of economic growth. The resumption of growth depended on a drastic change in relative prices, which was implemented by sharply devaluing the currency in relation to nominal wages and by introducing export subsidies. Although both transfers to export activities and public investment were increasing, the fiscal deficit was nevertheless reduced by decreasing the level of real wages in the public sector. The current account deficit was financed by liberalizing foreign exchange transactions and international capital flows.

To provide an adequate treatment of the new economic policies, it is convenient to separate macroeconomic developments and short-run policies from long-run targeted economic reforms.

Stabilization

In 1974 Uruguay faced severe domestic and external disequilibrium. Faced with the policy alternatives of a shock treatment or a gradual adjustment, the authorities chose the latter, with respect to both stabilization and the reduction of the external deficit. The rationale for gradualism in domestic stabilization was that a shock treatment for inflation had a low probability of success, given the existence of a fiscal deficit equal to 4.4 percent of GDP. A drastic reduction of the external deficit would have required a dramatic increase in the gap between private savings and investment in order to finance the fiscal deficit, and that would have entailed a further reduction in private consumption (Vegh Villegas 1977).

The aims of the domestic stabilization program were to reduce the size of government expenditure in relation to GDP and to decrease monetary disequilibrium. Both were to be achieved through tighter management of domestic credit and through increasing the incentives to hold money by raising the interest rates paid by banks. The government relied on external savings to finance both the fiscal and external deficits. Beginning in the last quarter of 1974, it enforced a gradual reduction in the level of the fiscal deficit, dismantled subsidies on consumption, expanded credit, and increased the share of public investment in government expenditure.

The main instruments for attracting external savings in the aftermath of the oil crisis were the liberalizations of foreign exchange transactions and of international capital flows that went into effect after September 1974. From 1974 until 1978 the Central Bank maintained a dual exchange rate: a commercial rate that was determined using a crawling peg regime designed to keep a high and stable real parity and a financial exchange rate that was permitted to float in response to market forces.[5]

Between 1974 and 1976 the monetary authorities managed to tighten credit. They eliminated sources of expansion, such as the discounting of commercial banks' credit instruments, and introduced sweeping institutional reforms in the capital market. The Central Bank removed restrictions on commercial banks with respect to their foreign assets positions, authorized all types of currency-denominated contracts, allowed the interest rate on deposits denominated in foreign currency to rise, and eventually eliminated interest rate ceilings.

Between 1974 and 1978 the authorities relied on control of monetary aggregates for price stabilization. The principal monetary policy instrument used during the period was the management of reserve requirements, although open market operations were performed as well. Inflation declined sharply after 1974 but remained high; in 1977 it was 57 percent even though the fiscal deficit had been reduced from 4.4 to 1.2 percent of GDP.

The expansion of monetary aggregates seems to have been the result of a persistent inflow of capital. The unrestricted international capital movements allowed after September 1974 swelled the domestic banking system. Toward the end of the period the monetary authorities were convinced that the openness of the economy left no room for controlling inflation through monetary policy and that monetary aggregates were demand determined. Wage increases lagged behind inflation during the period and could hardly be held responsible for the behavior of domestic prices. Thus, the key to reducing the inflation rate seemed to be to eliminate inflation inertia by changing the public's inflationary expectations and to reduce the rate of devaluation. (This conclusion strongly affected the design of a new exchange rate policy in 1978.) The high level and instability of the inflation rate was probably the result of the real exchange rate rule followed during the period whereby the nominal exchange rate and the money supply were indexed to the price level. (This type of exchange rule ties the actual rate of inflation to whatever it was in the past plus a current-period component that depends on external shocks.)

The Current and Capital Accounts

The current account of the balance of payments deteriorated during 1974 and 1975 as national income and the fiscal deficit fell. The capital account balance, which had traditionally been negative, changed sign in 1975–76 and rose again in 1977–78. During 1975–76 the capital account surplus was a function of the current account imbalance; the inflow of capital financed the excess of expenditure over income. It is not certain whether the surplus in the capital account after 1976 can be interpreted as an accommodation to the existence of a current account imbalance.

It has been argued that opening the capital account in the presence of high protective barriers prejudices the success of a subsequent trade liberalization. According to this view, opening the capital account first generates an inflow of capital that leads, in turn, to a real appreciation of the domestic currency. The Uruguayan experience does not support this hypothesis. Following the opening of the capital account, domestic currency experienced a real depreciation that lasted until 1978. The large inflows of foreign capital did not start until 1977—three years after the capital account was liberalized. Moreover, large capital inflows appear to have been associated with a spread between the domestic interest rate and the yield (measured in domestic currency) of financial investments made in foreign currency.

The inflow of capital, in the context of high expected inflation, brought about a high rate of credit expansion, which, in turn, induced higher expenditures and a deteriorating current account balance. In the absence of a liberalization of international capital flows, the current account deficit would not have been maintained. Hence, to establish external equilibrium, the economy should have experienced a higher real depreciation of the currency and a rise in the real interest rate, which would have had a larger depressive effect on the economy. During 1974 and

1975 the increment in the Central Bank's domestic credit reached 6.8 and 7.0 percent of GDP as a result of the public sector's financial needs. The fiscal deficit remained constant at 4.4 percent of GDP during the period. The increase in domestic credit led to an increase in base money equivalent to 2.9 percent of GDP in 1974 and 3.3 percent in 1975 and a loss in reserves equivalent to 3.9 and 3.7 percent of GDP. Between 1976 and 1978 Central Bank credit to the public sector contracted sharply, paralleling the reduction in the fiscal deficit.

Short-Run Effects

Within the first year of application of the new policy, all monetary aggregates and credit to the public sector contracted in real terms, while the banking system's credit to the private sector increased. Thus, the authorities managed to induce a reduction in the rate of increase of prices and to finance a high public sector financial deficit without detaching resources from the private sector, which could have discouraged private sector activity and delayed recovery.

Within the next three years—September 1975 to September 1978—the rate of growth of money aggregates accelerated. This was particularly true of base money (because of the decrease in reserve requirements) and of M3 (because of the growth in foreign currency–denominated deposits). The rate of growth of credit to the private sector, and of foreign currency–denominated credit in particular, exploded.

In short, the period 1974–78 was characterized by far-reaching changes in the institutional aspects of the financial sector. The authorities liberalized foreign exchange transactions, allowed unrestricted capital inflows, and maintained a high and stable real parity. The exchange rate depreciated sharply with respect to nominal wages, thus encouraging exports. At the same time, the government reduced the fiscal deficit and increased the share of investment in government expenditure. Thus, the structure of total demand changed; exports and investment grew in relation to consumption, and resources were diverted toward these activities.

Long-Run Reforms

The economic authorities appointed in July 1974 tried to strengthen both the role of market forces in the allocation of resources and the links between the Uruguayan economy and the rest of the world. In particular, they were convinced that the economy had to move from an inward-oriented to an outward-oriented, export-led growth strategy. Among the economic reforms implemented between 1974 and 1978, the following deserve close consideration: commercial policy, the export promotion program, tax reform, reduction in the size of the government, and decontrol of most consumer prices.

Between 1974 and 1978 the main commercial policy changes were the elimination of quotas, a reduction in the maximum level of *recargos* (the most important component of import duties), and the simplification of the tariff regime. During the last quarter of 1974 the administration of licenses was relaxed. Among other steps, the cumbersome bureaucratic procedure whereby those interested in importing capital goods had to apply for a permit to a regulatory commission was liberalized. In April 1975 the license regime was discontinued. In addition, a decline in the level of *recargos* brought the maximum rate from 300 percent in 1976 to 90 percent in 1979; all fees charged by the border authorities were consolidated under a single heading, and consular taxes were simplified. As a result of these tariff changes, both the average level and the dispersion of nominal tariffs contracted significantly, and the implicit tariff index (defined as the ratio between the domestic price of importables and exportables divided by the ratio between the foreign price of importables and exportables) declined.

Export promotion was a major area of government concern during 1974–78. It included subsidies for exports, subsidized credit lines for export activities, and fiscal exemptions, as well as administrative devices that simplified the importation of raw materials and intermediate products for the manufacture of export goods. The main export incentive was a subsidy (*reintegro*) that was estimated as a percentage of the f.o.b. price of exports, although it was related in principle to value added. The use of *reintegros* to provide incentives for industrial exports (there were no *reintegros* on traditional exports) began in 1964 but was not significant until a new law authorizing higher subsidy rates and extending the scope of application of this instrument was passed in June 1974. The level of subsidies peaked in 1974 and was then gradually reduced, as shown in the figures below (from Favaro and Spiller 1990, part II).

Year	Percent
1971	13.0
1974	21.5
1977	18.6
1980	12.7
1982	13.2

From 1976 to 1979 industrial exports benefited from subsidized credit lines. According to the terms of the loan, the exporter received in advance a portion of the export revenue, and the exchange rate for repayment was frozen at its level at the time of the operation. Although the loan was formally designated in foreign currency and paid a nominal interest rate in U.S. dollars, in practice the borrower benefited from the exchange rate depreciation during the period before repayment was due. The regime implied, during most of the period of its application, that export activities faced a negative nominal interest rate.

A third export promotion instrument was discriminatory tax treatment for export-oriented activities. Until 1979 firms' net revenue from activities that directly or indirectly involved the manufacture of export goods was tax exempt. Under the 1974 industrial promotion law, investment projects considered to be of high national priority were eligible for fiscal exemptions as well as preferential tax treatment; the main benefit was exemption from all tariffs and port service charges due on imports of capital goods. The tax structure, which relied on a value added tax, allowed taxes paid at different stages of production to be deducted when the final good was exported, thus helping to avoid discrimination against export activities.

Finally, the administration simplified the procedure for the duty-free importation of intermediate goods and raw materials used in the manufacture of export goods. The new regime provided exporters with ready access to intermediate goods at prices comparable to those of their international competitors.

In general, the incentive scheme focused on the nontraditional export sector. The real exchange rate faced by these activities depreciated after 1973 and up to 1978; traditional export goods, although discriminated against, also benefited from the maintenance of a stable parity.

Between 1974 and 1980 the tax regime was completely revised. The main trend was toward simplifying the tax structure, eliminating taxes and exemptions, and trying to cure discrimination against labor use and export activities. The 1974 tax reform reduced taxes on wages, eliminated taxes on the export of Uruguay's two main traditional products, reduced tariffs on imports, and widened the application of the value added tax. Personal income and inheritance taxes were eliminated, and taxes on firms' net earnings were consolidated into one tax (corporations still paid a higher tax rate). Social security wage taxes were reduced, and a tax on estimated agricultural income (IMPROME) was levied. Although the tax reform was significant, both in its scope and in its effect on government revenue, it did not imply a major change with respect to tax pressure, mainly because one source of tax revenue was substituted for another. The share of taxes on foreign trade transactions increased during the period, but its composition changed dramatically; export tax collection diminished while the share of import duties increased. The share of taxes on wages in overall government revenue diminished. The tax reform was related to the export promotion policy through its attempt to reduce the cost of labor, which is used intensively in most nontraditional export activities.

Although the size of the government did not change significantly between 1974 and 1978, the scope of government intervention in economic activity was reduced, and the trend toward expansion of the share of the government sector in GDP was halted. A significant change in the composition of government expenditure was the increase in the share of gross capital formation in overall expenses. In 1978 public sector investment was 4.4 times its 1974 level and represented in absolute terms about 50 percent of total investment (table 12-1).[6]

As of 1974 private firms had to obtain permission from a regulatory agency to increase prices. Similarly, the government determined wage increases for both the private and public sectors. In the second half of 1974 the government established a rigid wage increase regime that implied the prohibition of wage increases that exceeded official guidelines. Later this regime was liberalized, and the government began determining only the minimum rate of wage increase, allowing private firms to negotiate with their workers and employees beyond this floor.

A gradual price liberalization began in 1974, and controls were lifted on most consumer products. In March 1978, however, 46 percent of all items included in the consumer price index basket were still controlled.

Economic Performance, 1974–78

The performance of the economy between 1974 and 1978 shows remarkable differences from that of the previous two decades. The average rate of economic growth for 1974–78 was 4.1 percent, the share of investment in GDP rose from 11.6 to 16.0 percent (table 12-2), nontraditional exports grew at an average annual rate of 32.0 percent, and the share of exports in GDP went from 14.1 to 17.9 percent. Whereas before the reforms traditional exports accounted for more than 75 percent of total exports, by 1978 their share was 36.2 percent. Similarly, the share of final goods in total imports increased from 22.4 to 29.2 percent. Both indicators point to a significant opening of the economy during the period. Employment in manufacturing grew rapidly, and emigration, which had been significant at the beginning of the period, decreased sharply.

The pattern of growth of the economy in the period immediately after the 1974 reforms cannot be reconciled with the behavior in those years of investment, particularly private investment, and of the labor force. Emigration peaked in 1974 and decreased afterward but remained a significant explanatory variable of the demographic behavior of the

Table 12-1. Uruguay: Gross Capital Formation, 1974–78
(millions of new pesos at 1978 prices)

Year	Public sector	Private sector	Total
1974	561	1,677	2,238
1975	1,104	2,037	3,141
1976	1,700	2,331	4,031
1977	1,998	2,323	4,321
1978	2,463	2,480	4,943

Source: Banco Central del Uruguay, *Indicadores de la Actividad Económica Financiera, Producto e Ingreso Nacionales*, 1985, p. 97.

Table 12-2. Uruguay: Economic Indicators, 1974–78

Indicator	1974	1975	1976	1977	1978
Rate of growth of GDP (percent)	1.6	5.9	4.0	1.2	5.3
Gross capital formation as a share of GDP (percent)	11.6	13.5	14.8	15.2	16.0
Traditional exports (millions of U.S. dollars)	238.0	187.1	252.7	261.2	248.6
Nontraditional exports (millions of U.S. dollars)	144.2	174.9	293.8	346.3	437.5
Exports as a share of GDP (percent)	14.1	16.1	18.6	14.0	17.9
Employment in manufacturing (1975 = 100)	—	100.0	104.4	110.9	117.0

— Not available.

Source: Banco Central del Uruguay, *Indicadores de la Actividad Económica Financiera, Producto e Ingreso Nacionales*, various issues; Banco Central del Uruguay, *Formación Bruta de Capital*, various issues.

labor force up to the end of the period. Although investment in the export-oriented sector surged after 1974, overall private investment reacted slowly to the new economic policies. During the early years of the reform economic growth seems to have been the outcome of the reallocation of resources inside the economy, the elimination of numerous distortions implicit in the import license regime in force up to 1975 and in the regime of capital goods imports and price controls, the prohibition of labor union activity, which dampened social conflict, and the reduction in the size of the government.[7]

Economic growth was export-led in the 1974–78 period. Export growth was, in turn, the consequence of the export promotion policy and the relative price changes associated with it. The economy experienced an across-the-board increase in output, employment, exports, and average labor productivity. The largest increase in the average productivity of labor was in export-oriented activities.

The real exchange rate increased substantially. The average increase in the real exchange rate for export-oriented activities was 42.2 percent, but it was 57.1 percent for the import-competing sectors and 72.0 percent for nontradable goods activities. The activities that received the highest percentage subsidies were in the import-competing and nontradable sectors rather than the export-oriented sector.

Time-series and cross-sectional evidence supports the view that the allocation of export subsidies to the import-competing and nontradable goods sectors probably had a negligible effect on economic growth. Sapelli (1985), using time-series data, compared the effects of expanding exports to the region (which depends, in general, on preferential trade agreements or specific subsidies) with those of expanding exports to the rest of the world. He was not able to reject the hypothesis that they differ significantly.[8] Favaro and Spiller (1990), using cross-sectional data on

manufacturing, analyzed the determinants of employment–real exchange rate elasticity and found that industries that made intensive use of capital and of highly skilled workers have a much lower supply elasticity than others. Since export-oriented activities are predominantly labor-intensive and use less-skilled labor (see Bensión and Caumont 1983; Favaro 1987), this finding explains the greater responsiveness of those sectors to changes in relative prices. Export expansion had a positive effect on economic growth—directly because exports are a component of GDP and indirectly through the positive externality im-
·posed by exports on the nonexport sector. In other words, the beneficial effect of export growth spread to the rest of the economy (Favaro and Sapelli 1989b).

In general, although the export promotion program had a remarkable effect on growth, it did not succeed in maximizing exports or value added at international prices per unit of subsidy. There are two reasons for this: the highest percentage subsidies were received by the import-competing and nontradable sectors rather than by export-oriented activities, and Uruguay's export-oriented activities have a higher supply elasticity to relative price changes than do other sectors of the economy.

Income Distribution

Inequality in the distribution of income increased during the 1970s, according to family income surveys, and the real wage rate, as reported in official indexes, fell. The degree of inequality, as measured by the Gini index, went from 0.42 in 1968 to 0.45 in 1976, while the level of average family income increased by 9.2 percent in real terms between 1968 and 1976 and by 6.9 percent between 1976 and 1979. The real wage indexes calculated by the Dirección General de Estadística y Censos (DGEC) and the Banco Central del Uruguay (BCU) show a significant decline in the real wage rate during the 1970s (table 12-3). For 1974–78 the indexes differ in their estimates of the magnitude of the decrease in the real wage rate (Sapelli 1987).[9]

Although the minimum wage remained closer to its level in the base period than did the average real wage rate, it dropped more sharply than the average real wage rate between 1974 and 1978. The fall in the minimum wage rate probably had a significant effect on employment and unemployment during the period.

Functional income data showed a drop in the share of wages and salaries in national income in 1974–78. According to the DGEC, wages and salaries accounted for 40.4 percent of national income in 1974 but for only 31.7 percent in 1978.[10] The magnitude of the recorded fall in real wages contrasts with the evolution of several traditional social welfare indicators, which improved during the period (table 12-4).

The decline in real wages, as measured by official records, also contrasts with the path of consumption of goods that usually have a high

Table 12-3. Uruguay: Real Wage and Minimum Wage Index, 1970–78
(1968 = 100)

Year	Real wage		Minimum wage
	DGEC data	BCU data	
1970	107.1	107.1	108.2
1972	91.8	91.8	123.6
1974	88.4	88.4	129.7
1976	75.8	78.4	114.3
1978	63.2	70.6	98.7

Source: Uruguay, Dirección General de Estadística y Censos; Banco Central del Uruguay, *Boletín Estadístico*, various issues.

income elasticity of demand, such as beverages and tobacco. These goods are mostly nontradables in Uruguay, and their consumption equals domestic production (table 12-5; Sapelli 1987).

Domestic production and imports of electric goods such as refrigerators and radios cannot be reconciled with the dramatic decrease in the real wage rate and in the share of labor in national income shown in the official records.

The policies pursued during 1974–78 led to an increase in inequality. The main reasons were the increase in the openness of the economy, the reduction in the relative size of the government, and the prohibition of labor union activity. These policies pushed ambiguously toward a redistribution of income from unionized to nonunionized workers and, probably, from public workers and employees to nonunionized workers and employees. Although the available indexes suggest immiserization of

Table 12-4. Uruguay: Social Welfare Indicators, 1970–80

Indicator	1970–75	1975–80
Life expectancy at birth (years)	68.8	69.6
Infant mortality (deaths per 1,000 live births)	46.3	41.6
Urban population with access to water supply (percent)	85.9[a]	99.4b
Rural population with access to water supply (percent)	13.3[a]	13.2[b]
Population with access to sewerage (percent)	51.2[a]	57.9[b]

a. 1973.
b. 1977.
Source: Uruguay, Dirección General de Estadística y Censos, *Anuario Estadístico*, various issues.

Table 12-5. *Uruguay: Production and Imports of Consumer Goods, 1974–78*

	Production (1974 = 100)			Imports (thousands of U.S. dollars)		
Year	Beverages	Tobacco	Lottery expenditure	Electrical appliances	Radios	Refrigerators
1974	100.0	100.0	100.0	100.0	—	—
1975	99.0	106.7	109.5	105.9	137.0	—
1976	86.5	112.2	115.5	125.0	200.0	37.0
1977	96.9	110.0	117.9	150.0	904.0	47.0
1978	104.2	111.1	123.8	147.1	514.0	109.0

— Not available.

Source: Uruguay, Dirección General de Estadística y Censos, *Anuario Estadístico*, various issues; Banco de la República Oriental del Uruguay, unpublished data.

the labor force during the period, other indicators hint at an improvement in workers' situation after 1976.

External Influences

In 1976 Alejandro Vegh Villegas, the main author of the economic reforms introduced in 1974, resigned as minister of economy. Vegh remained close to the government, but with his resignation the government lost a strong personality who was both brilliant and independent in judgment.

As of 1978 the economy had experienced four consecutive years of economic growth, for the first time in more than two decades. Employment in manufacturing had increased more than 5 percent a year between 1975 and 1978, and nontraditional exports accounted for more than 60 percent of total exports. The only activity largely unaffected by the new policies was agriculture, which remained stagnant. Although after 1975 the fiscal deficit had contracted sharply, the average rate of inflation remained high, and monetary policy instruments appeared unable to stabilize the economy.

In 1979 the price of oil more than doubled. The second oil shock was accompanied by an expansion of world financial liquidity, an increase in commodity prices, and a depreciation of the U.S. dollar in terms of European currencies and the yen. The appreciation of Argentine currency after 1978 increased the demand for Uruguayan nontradable goods and pushed their price upward, thus inducing an appreciation of the Uruguayan peso. The origin of this influence lay in the close links between the Uruguayan, Argentine, and Brazilian economies through the labor and goods markets that allowed regional trade in a subset of nontradable goods (Favaro and Sapelli 1989a).[11] In 1979, at a time when the country was beginning its stabilization program, these external events brought about a higher imported inflation than had been expected.

In 1980 and 1981 two important external episodes affected Uruguay's economic performance. The appreciation of the U.S. dollar after the last quarter of 1980 implied the automatic revaluation of the peso and a loss of competitive capacity to Uruguayan exports. (Uruguay's exports to the EC had previously benefited from the depreciation of the dollar with respect to EC currencies after 1973.) And the series of devaluations followed by the Argentine currency after February 1981 induced a real depreciation of the Argentine peso. Both circumstances combined to lead to an overvaluation of Uruguayan currency during the period.

Although the economic authorities remained committed to improving the efficiency of the economy by promoting long-run policies such as the trade liberalization program and the liberalization of agricultural prices and price policies, the dominant concern shifted from export expansion toward price stabilization. The behavior of the economy between 1978 and 1982 was strongly affected by the stabilization policies applied in that period and by external events in the region and in the rest of the world.

In October 1978 the Central Bank abandoned active monetary policy, unified the financial and commercial exchange rates, and began to rely exclusively on exchange rate management for stabilization purposes. At the same time the authorities started announcing the future spot exchange rate up to a certain time horizon (which from October 1978 to November 1982 varied from three to nine months) and reduced the pace of depreciation. The logic underlying the new exchange rate regime was that in a small open economy with a fixed exchange rate, the authorities do not have control of monetary aggregates that are demand determined. The difference between the domestic and the international rate of inflation was interpreted as the consequence of the inertia introduced by exchange rate rules and by expectations of inflation. Moreover, in the absence of expansionary forces of net domestic credit such as a fiscal deficit, a passive crawling peg regime tended to perpetuate inflation. Thus, management of the exchange rate within a stabilization plan became crucial not only because the exchange rate directly affected the domestic price of tradable goods but also because the announcement of a lower pace of depreciation would affect the public's expectations of inflation. The authorities believed that in the absence of restrictions on international capital flows, the domestic interest rate would be equal to the international interest rate plus the expected rate of devaluation. Because the new exchange rate regime implied a higher degree of certainty about the path of the rate of devaluation, the difference between domestic and international interest rates was not expected to diverge from the actual rate of devaluation.

The predictions of the authorities regarding the behavior of the price level and the nominal interest rate after the implementation of the stabilization plan differed widely from the actual path of these variables. The stabilization program did not bring about a sharp fall in the rate of inflation until the second half of 1980, even though the public sector ran a surplus and domestic credit to the government fell sharply in real terms. Moreover, the rate of price increase rose during the first year of application of the new exchange rate rule, and the domestic interest rate remained above the sum of the London interbank offered rate (LIBOR) and the rate of devaluation during the period.[12] The acceleration of the inflation rate was the result of the external factors described above and the expansion of domestic aggregate demand induced by the inflow of capital observed during the period.

During the first three years after the implementation of the new exchange rate regime, the real exchange rate appreciated drastically; the exchange rate deflated by the CPI fell at a cumulative annual rate of 21.8 percent during the period. Between 1978 and 1982 the average real exchange rate was lower and the variance of the real exchange rate higher than in 1974–78. Because the appreciation of the currency was led by policies that expanded aggregate demand, it ran parallel with an increase in the level of domestic real activity during 1979 and 1980. This helped to conceal the real effects associated with an overvaluation of the currency.

The fall in the rate of devaluation after September 1978 implied an automatic increase in the yield, measured in foreign currency, of a deposit denominated in domestic currency. Differences between the domestic interest rate and the sum of the international interest rate plus the actual rate of devaluation persisted during the whole period.

Although the acceleration of the rate of inflation during the first year of application of the stabilization plan implied a decrease in the real interest rate—which initially became negative—by the end of 1979 the latter rate was positive, and it remained high to the end of the period. The real interest rate on loans both in domestic and in foreign currency increased steadily during 1980 and remained above 20 percent up to the abandonment of the fixed exchange rate regime in November 1982.

Public concern about the overvaluation of the domestic currency developed during 1981, but the authorities remained committed to the stabilization plan. Uruguay attempted to maintain actual real parity with respect both to the region and to the rest of the world despite adverse circumstances—a severe world recession, accompanied by an increase in the nominal interest rate and a drastic fall in the terms of trade, and a dramatic increase in the real exchange rate in Argentina, which induced deflationary pressure and a recession in the domestic import-competing and nontradable goods sectors. The economy headed into a depression in the second half of 1981.

As of 1981 the authorities were convinced that the exchange rate was sustainable, given the level of the Central Bank reserves, if fiscal equilibrium were maintained. In 1961, however, fiscal discipline was relaxed, and a fiscal deficit appeared for the first time since 1978. The deficit, the equivalent of 2.3 percent of GDP, was the result of two concurring forces:

a significant increase in the government's social security expenditure and, as the economy entered a recession, a sharp decline in real fiscal revenue.

In early 1982 the authorities, faced with an overvalued currency, had a choice between two adjustment strategies.

• They could reestablish equilibrium through a step adjustment in the price of tradable goods—by devaluing the currency, abandoning fixed exchange rules, and floating the domestic currency, or by reducing the level of domestic nominal wages.

• They could achieve equilibrium by gradually increasing the pace of devaluation.

The authorities decided on the latter strategy and initiated contacts with the IMF to discuss a two-year stabilization plan.

As the rate of devaluation was increased, the nominal interest rate rose as well, and the real interest rate achieved record highs, inducing a further recession. The authorities pursued two antagonistic policies: they administered a deflationary adjustment strategy, and they tried to compensate for the fall in real activity associated with the recession by launching an expansionary program of housing construction. The financial needs of the public sector within the context of a fiscal deficit were met through a loss in international reserves and an increase in the level of the external deficit.

In February 1982 the Mexican debt crisis initiated a general debt crisis in the developing countries, and in April 1982 war between the United Kingdom and Argentina led to a drastic reduction in the availability of external financing. The widespread uncertainty regarding the maintenance of the exchange regime led to an increasing move away from domestic money and toward deposits denominated in foreign currency and stimulated an outflow of private capital. The estimated capital outflow during 1982 was US$2 billion.

At the end of 1980 Uruguay's external debt was US$2.1 billion, equivalent to the value of exports for two years. In the following years the debt grew about US$1 billion a year until it reached US$4.2 billion at the end of 1982, equivalent to 4.3 years of export value. A small part of this increment was used to finance public sector investments. One of these investments, the Palmar hydroelectric project, required an incremental debt of more than US$150 million between 1980 and 1982. The Banco Hipotecario incurred additional foreign debt of US$300 million to finance an ambitious plan of housing construction. Lesser amounts of additional foreign indebtedness were incurred to finance investments by the public enterprises in such fields as electric power, telephones, and petroleum. The largest part of the additional foreign debt was incurred, however, by the Banco Central, the Banco de la República, and the central government to cover the loss of reserves induced, especially in 1982, by exchange rate policy.

The private sector also contributed to the enlargement of the foreign debt, but much less than did the public sector. Importers incurred an additional foreign debt of US$100 million to their suppliers, and the private banks' foreign debt increased by US$200 million to permit them to meet the demand for additional credit generated by the increase in domestic economic activity. Deposits by nonresidents in the Uruguayan banking system also increased in the 1980–82 period. In November 1982 the authorities, faced with the scarcity of international reserves and the absence of external sources of credit, abandoned the fixed exchange rule and let the Uruguayan peso float.

The overall management of the 1982 crisis was very poor: the fiscal deficit reached 18 percent of GDP, and the public sector's external debt rose from US$1,464 million to US$2,705 million. The deficit was the result of the combined effect of an expansion in government expenditure, at a time when real income was declining by more than 8 percent, and a recession-induced decline in fiscal revenue. The persistence of high real interest rates after 1980, the drastic changes in relative prices that occurred during the period, and the final devaluation, under circumstances in which 75 percent of the banking system's credit to the private sector was denominated in foreign currency, generated a financial crisis that was the dominant phenomenon during 1983–84.

Trade Policy

The reforms in commercial policy that began in 1974 were followed by a trade liberalization program that attempted to simplify the tariff structure and gradually to reduce the level of protection to a target level of 35 percent. The stages of the program were announced so as to provide the private sector with enough information to minimize adjustment costs, and implementation started by the end of 1979. The first three stages were implemented on schedule and reduced the average level of tariffs; the liberalization plan was, however, stopped in the midst of the 1982 depression.

In 1979, as inflation soared, the government reduced tariffs ahead of the originally planned schedule. These cuts were intended to curb inflation by increasing competition with foreign products in those sectors in which prices were rising faster than was justified by cost increases. The logic underlying the reductions was that only redundant protection and monopoly practices associated with the closure of the economy could explain the behavior of domestic prices. Here, the main concern behind tariff reduction was stabilization policy. Although there was a significant decrease in nominal tariffs, the dispersion of effective protection in several sectors of the economy seems to have increased between 1980 and 1982 (Centro de Investigaciones Económicas 1982).

The authorities tried to use the trade liberalization program begun in 1978 to initiate a change in relative prices that would move resources toward export-oriented activities and away from the import-competing and nontradable sectors. The opposite, however, occurred because the stabilization program was based on an exchange rate rule that implied an appreciation of the real exchange rate, and this appreciation outweighed the tariff reduction effect.

Since GATT rules did not permit the return of direct taxes paid by an export activity, the new regime provided more favorable treatment for export-oriented activities. The benefits obtained by the export-oriented sector from the new regime were, however, dominated by the decrease in the rate and scope of export subsidies.

Agricultural Policy

In August 1978 the government introduced economic reforms that brought sweeping changes to agriculture. It eliminated taxes on the export of beef and wool, which had amounted to as much as 50 percent of the value of exports. In addition, it removed geographic barriers to the marketing of beef, reduced to 10 percent the maximum level of tariffs on farm machinery, liberalized grain prices, and discontinued administrative controls on livestock prices.

These changes coincided with an improvement in the international price of beef that sharply increased the price of livestock and the retail price of beef. Faced with a rise in the domestic price of beef, the authorities reintroduced interventionism by temporarily prohibiting exports, subsidizing the importation of beef, and placing restrictions on livestock credit lines. Thus, although the authorities were committed to providing incentives for growth in agriculture, distributional considerations associated with high food prices frustrated the attempt to change relative prices permanently.

Economic Performance, 1979–82

During the first three years of the 1979–82 period the economy boomed; the average rate of growth of GDP was 4.7 percent. After 1981 the economy entered into a deep recession.

The policies pursued between 1978 and 1982, together with the external favorable influence caused by the overvaluation of the Argentine currency, led to an increase in aggregate demand that induced a rise in both employment and real wages. The second half of 1981, however, saw the beginning of a recession that deepened in 1982, when GDP fell at a rate of 9.4 percent a year (table 12-6). The consequent fall in employment and sharp rise in unemployment made the previous increase in the level of well-being unsustainable.

The ratio of investment to GDP increased from an average of 15.3 in 1976–78 to 18.0 percent in 1979–81. In contrast to the 1974–78 period, private investment was the most dynamic component of overall capital

Table 12-6. *Uruguay: Economic Indicators, 1979–82*

Indicator	1979	1980	1981	1982
Rate of growth of GDP (percent)	6.2	6.0	1.9	−9.4
Gross capital formation as a share of GDP (percent)	18.7	18.6	15.0	10.1
Traditional exports (millions of U.S. dollars)	222.7	415.9	513.0	435.4
Nontraditional exports (millions of U.S. dollars)	565.5	642.7	702.3	587.5
Exports as a share of GDP (percent)	17.9	17.5	18.3	18.1
Employment in manufacturing (1975 = 100)	128.4	127.6	120.0	89.8

Source: Banco Central del Uruguay, *Indicadores de la Actividad Económica Financiera, Producto e Ingreso Nacionales*, various issues; Banco Central del Uruguay, *Formación bruta de Capital*, various issues.

formation; it increased 72 percent between 1978 and 1981, while public investment declined. The share of traditional exports in total exports increased from 36.2 in 1978 to 42.6 percent in 1982. Although the nominal value of nontraditional exports increased 16.9 percent a year between 1978 and 1981, most of the rise was attributable to inflation. Employment in manufacturing increased up to 1979, declined gradually until 1981, and fell abruptly during the 1982 recession.

MANUFACTURING. In 1974–78 growth was led by export-oriented activities; between 1978 and 1982 GDP growth was dominated by the expansion of the import-competing and nontradable sectors. The analysis of sectoral data on manufacturing shows a steady downward trend in employment and output in most export-oriented activities between 1978 and 1982. Employment in the import-competing and nontradable goods sectors increased significantly up to 1979; output in these sectors increased until 1980–81 and contracted thereafter.

Whereas the causality between the real exchange rate faced by the export-oriented activities and the output and employment response is straightforward, the relationship between these variables in the import-competing and nontradable goods sectors is more complex. Even though commercial policy after 1974 considerably reduced the level of tariffs, the degree of protection was still high at the end of the decade. The existence of "water in the tariffs" implied that the domestic price of these goods, and hence the real effective exchange rate, was determined jointly with the level of output and employment. The growth of output and employment in these activities may have been the result of demand or supply factors or both; when demand factors dominated, output and prices moved in line, while the opposite occurred when the impetus came from supply shifts. During 1978–82 the domestic price of these activities moved together. When output and employment declined, the real exchange rate depreciated, suggesting that the expansion of GDP was caused by increased expenditure in the economy.

The increase in aggregate demand observed in the period was attributable to both external factors—such as the increase in Argentine demand for Uruguayan goods, which originated in the overvaluation of the Argentine exchange rate—and domestic sources, such as the inflow of capital induced by the exchange rate regime. In other words, the expansion of aggregate demand and output was caused by temporary circumstances that attracted resources toward the import-competing and nontradable goods sectors. When Argentina devalued its currency, the favorable external shock changed sign, and real activity in the economy declined dramatically.

The composition of nontraditional exports changed over the period, with a steady increase of those activities in which the country had less comparative advantage. The increase in the ratio of imported inputs to nontraditional exports, as shown in table 12-7, suggests that the rise in the share of nontraditional exports originated in the import-competing and nontradable sectors during 1979–81, when Argentine demand was at its peak. Although exports did not decline until 1982, the structure of trade varied, and the impact of exports on growth diminished. The tariff reduction program did not have the expected effect of increasing the price of exportable goods in relation to importable goods inside the economy.

Most of the decline observed in the real exchange rate faced by import-competing activities appears to have been a consequence of exchange rate policy rather than of tariff cuts. Thus, the period 1978–82 saw not trade liberalization—that is, a policy oriented toward narrowing the difference between international and domestic terms of trade—but the opposite. Moreover, the effects of the attempt, implemented in 1978, to reform agricultural policy and promote growth were neutralized by the real appreciation of the domestic currency and by further government intervention. The expansion of the import-competing and home goods sectors, as a consequence of an increase in domestic expenditure,

Table 12-7. Uruguay: Imports under Temporary Admission (ITA) and Nontraditional Exports (NTX), 1978–81
(millions of U.S. dollars)

Year	ITA	NTX	ITA/NTX
1978	75.4	565.5	13.3
1979	109.8	642.7	17.1
1980	113.4	702.5	16.1
1981	98.9	587.5	16.8

Note: Nontraditional exports correspond to one-year forward transactions.
Source: Centro de Investigaciones Económicas 1982.

specific export promotion subsidies, or transitory macroeconomic developments, did not bring about the development of export-oriented activities, and it only temporarily altered the overall rate of growth of the economy.

The trend, begun in 1974, toward reducing the effective cost of labor was continued. Social security taxes on wages were reduced and simplified, and the treatment of wages in different activities was homogenized. The ensuing deficit in the social security system was covered by transfers from the central government. Finally, the fall in public sector revenue as a result of the reduction of taxes on wages was compensated for by increasing the rate and scope of application of the value added tax.

A survey of industrial wages conducted in 1979 showed that the average hourly wage rate paid by import-substituting activities was higher than that prevailing in other sectors of the economy. It also showed that multinational corporations paid higher salaries than the average Uruguayan firm and that the wage level was directly related to firm size (table 12-8). Wages in rural areas were higher than those prevailing in the cities.

The behavior of the labor market during previous decades had been greatly influenced by the state's participation in wage boards and in the determination of wage levels and its role as the employer of a significant share of the labor force. Labor market behavior was also much influenced by union policies. These factors had induced a more uniform wage structure than would have resulted from market forces, and this created disincentives for highly skilled workers and induced emigration by this group. The changes in relative prices observed after 1973 led to an expansion of export-oriented activities, which were relatively more labor-intensive than import-substituting activities and which made more intensive use of unskilled laborers. Export-oriented firms were, on average, newer and smaller than firms oriented toward the domestic market. The power of unions and the role of preexisting wage structures as determinants of absolute and relative wages were therefore less important in these firms. Thus, the rapid expansion of the economy after 1973 produced an uneven increase in wages for different labor categories because of the scarcities of different labor skills and their short-run supply elasticities. Highly educated workers benefited.

The behavior of the labor market between 1979 and 1981 appears to have been dominated by increased demand for labor, which originated in an expansion of aggregate demand in the economy. As the economy prospered, employment, the labor force participation rate, and real wages increased, while unemployment and emigration fell sharply (table 12-9).

INCOME DISTRIBUTION. The tendency toward a more even income distribution observed at the end of the period seems to be related to the increase in the size of the government sector in relation to private sector

Table 12-8. *Uruguay: Average Wage per Hour in Manufacturing, 1979*

Category	Average wage (1979 new pesos)
National	13.59
By sector	
Import substitution	14.29
Export-oriented	10.87
By type of firm	
National	12.78
Multinational	17.49
By size of firm	
More than 200 workers	14.65
50–200 workers	12.46
Fewer than 50 workers	9.50
By location	
Montevideo	13.20
Rural	14.90
By education	
Illiterate	6.64
Primary school	9.90
Secondary school	15.20
University	38.33
By age	
15–19 years	4.90
20–24 years	6.94
25–34 years	11.83
35–44 years	14.53
45–54 years	17.18
55–64 years	20.18
65 and over	32.21
By sex	
Females	7.87
Males	15.21

Source: Instituto de Economía, Universidad de la República, 1982, pp. 55, 65, 70, and 74.

GDP and to the recovery of the import-substituting activities observed in the period.[13]

Recovery Efforts, 1983–84

The 1983–84 period was marked by the effort to manage the domestic financial crisis and the fiscal deficit under severely adverse external circumstances at a time when an internal political transition toward democracy was taking place.

FINANCIAL CRISIS. In the second half of the 1970s credit extended by the banking sector to the private sector grew rapidly. The credits were only

Table 12-9. *Uruguay: Employment, Unemployment, and Emigration,*
1979–84

Year	Unemployment (percent)	Labor force participation (percent)	Employment, Montevideo (thousands)	Emigration (thousands)
1979	9.3	41.2	492	9.0
1980	7.3	42.1	492	5.0
1981	6.7	43.1	510	−0.3
1982	12.3	—	490	—
1983	15.4	—	475	—
1984	14.0	—	492	—

— Not available.
Source: Uruguay, Dirección General de Estadística y Censos, *Anuario Estadístico*, various issues.

short term when they financed investment in fixed assets, and an increasing share of new loans was denominated in foreign currency—matching a trend in banking resources. As the rate of inflation declined after 1979, the real rate of interest increased, beginning a process of transfers from debtors to creditors that eroded the net wealth of indebted firms. The credit market remained liquid, and the financial difficulties faced by indebted firms were disguised by the continuous expansion of the original debt. As soon as the economy entered a recession, however, the flow of banking credit diminished, and a deep crisis became evident.

During 1982 the increasing lack of confidence in the stability of the exchange regime led the public to make deposits in foreign currency rather than in domestic currency. Accordingly, when the banks had to cover their foreign exchange exposure, they accepted only the renewal of credits that were denominated in foreign currencies. In these circumstances, the abandonment of the fixed exchange rate regime in November 1982 and the consequent devaluation of the peso greatly aggravated the domestic debt problem.

At the time of the devaluation the banking system had a considerable percentage of bad loans and a remarkable imbalance between its highly volatile resources and its illiquid portfolio. Faced with a banking crisis, the government acted to bail out banks in trouble, case by case. During 1982–83 the Central Bank intervened to prevent the bankruptcy of four out of twenty-two financial institutions and bought part of the portfolio of the commercial banking system in an attempt to relieve some of the pressure on it. A direct consequence of the Central Bank's efforts to avoid a banking crisis was an increase in government debt outstanding and in debt service. Thus, the expansion of government subsidies to the private sector through the banking system increased the overall fiscal deficit to a record level of 18.2 percent of GDP during 1982.

The 1982–84 period was one of great uncertainty. The sharp depreciation of the peso after the abandonment of the fixed exchange rate was followed by a severe process of adjustment of relative prices. Although the real exchange rate depreciated abruptly after November 1982, export-oriented activities did not respond immediately, and real GDP contracted dramatically, falling 5.9 percent a year between 1981 and 1984. The growing probability that private contracts could not be enforced drastically increased the risk of commercial transactions and added to the depth and persistence of the recession.

POLITICAL CHANGE. Between 1982 and 1984 the military authorities engineered a transition toward a democratic administration. In the national elections of 1982 voters chose the leaders of the political parties, a step that was considered of utmost importance in the transition to a civilian administration. In fact, the elections determined the leverage of the armed forces in bargaining with the politicians over the terms that were to govern the transition and over the role of the military in the new administration. In November 1984 a new government was elected by direct popular vote. The possibility of abrupt changes in economic policy associated with the return to democratic rule added to the uncertainty of the transition period and further delayed a recovery.

It has been argued that the economic strategy followed by the military government after 1974 was extremely unpopular and could only have been implemented under a dictatorship. The response of the military to the fall in the terms of trade was, however, remarkably similar to that of the Blanco party in 1959; if the magnitude of the external shocks is taken into account, only the emphasis on resuming growth was different. Although the administration of the costs associated with the new policy might have been different in a democratic framework, the design of economic policy was certainly severely restricted once the government accepted the achievement of economic growth as a major policy target.

The resumption of growth required the expansion of exports, and that required a permanent change in the price of exportables in relation to goods for domestic consumption. The burden of this change fell on workers and employees in the protected sectors—the public sector and import-substituting activities. Both groups had lost considerable power after the dissolution of the unions and the temporary suspension of periodic elections, a circumstance that reduced the political costs associated with the decline in their real wages.

The financing of economic growth depended on both domestic and external savings. The increase in domestic savings required a rise in interest rates and a reduction in price instability. In addition, since if only domestic savings were available for investment, a further reduction in consumption would have been required, it was necessary to open the capital account to international flows to smooth consumption during a period of rapid capital accumulation. The opening of the capital account made the supply of capital more elastic and further limited the possibility of shifting part of the burden of taxation away from wages and salaries and onto capital.

Except for a short period and in a very partial way, the military administration did not address the problem of developing agriculture. In fact, it seems to have behaved toward this sector in much the same way as had previous administrations.[14]

Commercial policy during the military period was not significantly different from that observed in civilian administrations. The role of ideology in policy seems to have been minor compared with the force of external circumstances. During the first years of the trade liberalization policy the authorities seem to have been willing to incur the costs associated with measures that adversely affected powerful interest groups.

A remarkable change in the government's political sensitivity is evident after 1978, however. In fact, the behavior of the military authorities greatly resembles that of previous administrations in that they postponed the adoption of necessary but unpopular policies, even though the costs of delay were enormous, and permitted the working of external forces that yielded short-run benefits, although the cost proved to be high in the long run. Furthermore, even though the changes in relative prices after 1974 induced the expansion of export-oriented activities, commercial policy reforms did not reach the main export sector—agriculture.

After the military takeover in 1973, the share of government expenditure in GDP initially declined. During this first stage the decrease was the result of a drastic reduction in public employees' wages and salaries and in social security expenses. After 1975 the share of government expenditures in GDP did not vary significantly until the introduction of the stabilization plan of 1978, when it experienced a slight upward trend that coincided with an increase in real wages and social security payments. Government expenditure peaked in 1982 as a result of the expansionary policies followed by the authorities in the midst of the worst domestic recession since the Great Depression.

Several measures adopted by the authorities, particularly those having to do with the social security system, suggest that an unambiguous political motive lay behind the expansion of government expenditure in the early 1980s. In particular, thousands of pensions were increased, transforming what had been a negligible expenditure item into a significant item in the social security budget.

The distribution of the public sector budget during the military administration had three characteristics.

First, the share of the Ministry of Defense in the overall government budget doubled. The increase in the size of the budgets of the armed forces and of the police was related not to an expansion in the number or strength of combat units or to major investments in sophisticated equipment (except for some increments during 1980–81) but rather to an increase in the quality and quantity of health services, social security, and other benefits for present or former members of the armed forces and their families.

The authorities' decisions meant that the share of government investment in overall expenditure increased in relation to the share of consumption. For example, two hydroelectric dams, one of them a joint venture with the Argentine government, were constructed during the period. The decision to commit resources to the expansion of power-generating capacity was no doubt motivated by the energy crisis that began in 1973. The type of project undertaken reveals an intention to demonstrate the incapacity of previous civilian administrations and the military's commitment to the "highest interests of the nation."

Second, the authorities maintained government expenditures for health, education, and social security at close to 14 percent of GDP during most of the period except for 1982. In that year the share increased to 20 percent of GDP, mainly because of the increase in social security expenses. Public expenditure on social programs appears to have contributed to a more equal distribution of income, since the share of the benefits captured by low-income families was, on average, higher than their share in overall income (table 12-10).

Third, the military administration drastically reduced several categories of government expenditure that did not appear explicitly in the public sector budget during the first stage of the period. It eliminated subsidies for beef and other food items, and it insisted on maintaining prices for public utility services that covered their costs. These measures particularly affected the well-being of the middle classes and were consistent with the lack of immediate concern about gaining the support of this group during the first stage of the military administration.

The absence of political opposition to the elimination of several cross-subsidies seems to be attributable to a deeply felt desire to improve efficiency and growth performance during a period of severe external

Table 12-10. *Uruguay: Benefits of Public Sector Expenditure in Social Programs, by Household Income Bracket, 1982*

Household income bracket	Education	Health	Water supply and sewerage	Housing	Social security	Total expenditures	Distribution of income
1st quintile	31.4	34.0	18.0	7.0	10.3	15.6	7.2
2nd quintile	21.0	29.7	18.3	23.9	16.1	18.7	11.8
3rd quintile	17.9	16.1	19.5	17.7	18.8	18.3	14.8
4th quintile	16.3	8.4	23.0	18.6	23.7	20.8	19.9
5th quintile	13.4	11.8	21.2	32.8	31.1	26.6	46.3
Total	100.0	100.0	100.0	100.0	100.0	100.0	100.0
Poorest 50 percent	60.6	73.1	43.9	38.4	34.7	42.8	25.5

Source: Davrieux 1984.

difficulties. This interpretation is supported by the significant cost that expansionary government expenditure policies imposed on growth. Favaro, Graziani, and Sapelli (1987) found that a 10 percent increase in government expenditure causes, at the margin, a 2.3 percent decrease in the output of the private sector. These econometric estimates indicate that although the provision of basic services has a positive effect on the rest of the economy, further government intervention often introduces distortions and inefficiency that reduce total output. This result provides a rationale for the military's concern with reducing the size of the public sector.

The military authorities initially appeared to be committed to carrying out deep reforms in the public sector by, among other steps, eliminating legal monopolies and privatizing several services. Early in the period they dismantled a public urban transport firm that accounted for much of the deficit of the Montevideo municipal government and transformed it into a private company. Later attempts in that direction, however, confronted strong opposition within the armed forces. At the beginning of the military period administration of the public utilities was distributed among the army, navy, and air force, presumably in proportion to their military power. Over time each public firm became a stronghold of a branch of the armed forces, and vested interests developed that strongly opposed any attempt to eliminate legal monopolies or to promote the privatization of nonstrategic sectors.

Government expenditures between 1973 and 1984 exhibited a political cycle similar to that observed during civilian administrations in the postwar period. The initial austerity of the military administrations appears in this context to have been a response to a change in the external circumstances faced by the country in 1974 rather than a consequence of a change in political attitudes. The main differences between the military and the civilian administrations in this respect appear to be a consequence of the institutional changes implemented early in the period, such as the liberalization of foreign exchange transactions and international capital flows, as part of an attempt to promote the country's economic growth.

The first attempt to limit seriously the discretion of the political administrations in the use of inflationary finance and to narrow the costs associated with price instability occurred after the liberalization of foreign exchange transactions and capital flows and the deregulation of financial markets in 1974. The liberalization of foreign exchange transactions introduced the problem of currency substitution and considerably reduced the inflation tax base. The elimination of interest rate ceilings allowed depositors to escape from anticipated inflation, while the disappearance of subsidized credit reduced the role of rationing in the credit market. Under the new circumstances the burden of the inflation tax fell mainly on recipients of credit. The military administration's monetary reforms of 1974 seemed to be intended to attract capital from abroad and so smooth domestic consumption and to create incentives for an increase in the amount of savings channeled toward the domestic capital market.

The stabilization program of 1978 was implemented at a time when the military government had achieved success in several economic areas, even if it had not reduced inflation. An initial expansion of aggregate demand produced growth and an increase in the real wage rate from 1979 to 1981. A successful stabilization program was an attractive achievement for a military government that was beginning a transition toward democracy. Conversely, the failure of the plan turned out to be a major factor in eroding the legitimacy of the authorities.

The attitude of the military government in maintaining the exchange rate policy unchanged, even when it became clear in 1982 that the peso was overvalued, did not differ from that of postwar civilian administrations during election years. The change in policy objectives in the management of the exchange rate after 1978 can be understood when it is kept in mind that price stabilization had popular support, particularly if the policies adopted did not result in short-run output losses (as happened to be the case with the adoption of the announced exchange rate rule). Over time the lack of control of the military authorities by the citizenry resulted in a gradual substitution of "society's goals" for those of narrower special interest groups. This pattern of behavior became evident during 1981 once the existence of an overvaluation in the exchange rate was recognized.

Notes

1. In 1971 the armed forces were invested with the operational control of the 21,000-man national police force; in 1973 they were given legal control of this corps.

2. It is likely that collective bargaining during the period created a disincentive for the most efficient workers within an industry by reducing salary differences across firms and occupational categories.

3. Alejandro Vegh Villegas and Ramón Díaz were the most brilliant personalities associated with the development of a view of the Uruguayan economic crisis that provided an alternative to the dominant ECLA-Marxist interpretation and an analysis of the policies necessary for returning the country to a growth path. During the period Díaz founded *Búsqueda*, a journal that would have enormous influence on the development of a new style of journalism and on the spread of conservative ideas in the society.

4. Such views were also dominant among the military that dismissed Congress in June 1973. In fact, these ideas supported the maintenance of the policies followed by previous civil administrations during the first year of military rule and were displaced only by the force of events associated with the oil crisis and the appointment of Alejandro Vegh as minister of economy in 1974.

5. The commercial rate was used to settle import and export transactions and public sector demands that originated in public debt service. The financial exchange rate was used to settle all other transactions. The gap between the two exchange rates narrowed over the period and was negligible after 1976.

6. The behavior of public sector investment was strongly influenced by the construction of two hydroelectric dams during this period.

7. There is evidence in the Uruguayan case to support the hypothesis that an increase in the size of the government has a negative external effect upon private sector GDP, even without taking into account the possibility of a crowding-out effect on the private sector's endowment of resources. See Favaro, Grazziani, and Sapelli (1987).

8. An increase in exports both to the region and out of the region had a non-export-sector elasticity of 0.64; an increase in exports only to the region had a non-export-sector elasticity of 0.058 (Sapelli 1986).

9. Uruguayan wage indexes exhibit the usual shortcomings associated with Laspeyre-type indexes under circumstances of dramatic changes in relative prices and in the structure of employment. Moreover, the DGEC index for most of the 1970s was constructed by incorporating only the minimum wage increases determined periodically by the government and not the actual increments in both the private and public sector. For subsequent years actual increases are computed, but on an uncorrected basis. The BCU index takes account of actual wage increases after 1978 and adjusts, using a geometric interpolation, the difference between the levels observed in 1978 and the 1975–77 period.

10. ECLA estimated that the share of wages and salaries in national income had decreased from 46.6 percent in 1975 to 45.3 percent in 1978 (Economic Commission for Latin America 1983).

11. This phenomenon implies that the prices of nontradables and of labor in Uruguay are strongly affected by the variables that influence the price of nontradables and the real exchange rate in neighboring countries (Favaro and Sapelli 1989a).

12. Recent econometric tests suggest that the nominal interest rate may be determined by domestic variables in addition to the effect of the international rate of interest and the rate of devaluation. See the estimates obtained within a vector autoregression econometric framework in Favaro and Sapelli (1989a).

13. Functional income data show an increase in the share of wages and salaries in national income for 1979–81. According to ECLA the share of labor in net national income increased from 41.1 to 44.5 percent between 1979 and 1981. Family income surveys show a decrease in the degree of inequality in the distribution of income in urban areas for 1976–82; the Gini index went from 0.45 in 1976 to 0.42 in 1982.

14. In a recent study Sapelli (1985) analyzed the determinants of the share of the international price of beef received by producers and found no significant differences between the Blanco and the Colorado parties and the military administrations. Differences in taxation of the sector appear to be determined more by changes in exogenous factors than by government tastes or preferences.

13 Policy, Institutions, and Economic Performance

This chapter examines how the characteristics and evolution of the Uruguayan polity have interacted with external influences and events to shape economic policy. The analysis focuses on some attributes of the political system that limit the capacity of Uruguayan society to adapt to exogenous shocks such as drastic changes in terms of trade.

The Background of the 1874 Coup

The first stage in Uruguay's political life covers the years from independence to the military coup of 1874. After 1830 the Uruguayan state evolved along the lines of other modern democracies, but the political system did not always work according to formal constitutional rules. Political struggle took the form of continuous civil wars between armed bands grouped around *caudillos*, often supported by foreign countries, rather than democratic competition through fair elections. The period was marked by continuous political turmoil, armed confrontation, and the near-disappearance of a unified state with coercive power over the entire national territory. The country was divided between the Blanco and Colorado parties, each of which controlled parts of the territory according to periodic agreements reached, in general, after military confrontations. The Constitution and the legal state were imposed on a young and immature society by a political elite unable to enforce constitutional rule; thus the legal state did not correspond to the real state and the politics of the time.

After 1865 a new actor, the army, appeared on the political scene. The national army created in the 1850s developed rapidly as a professional institution after the war of the Triple Alliance against Paraguay, and it had a dominant influence in Uruguayan politics from 1868 to 1886. The army's influence was initially exercised through the ministers of war but evolved into direct military rule after the coup of 1874.

The intrusion of the military into politics was prompted by several circumstances. First, the world depression of the late 1860s struck

Uruguay's exports severely, reduced national income, and bred political discontent. Second, the expansion of the livestock sector, through the introduction of sheep breeding, and improvements in the quality of the herd to meet changes in world markets created a rural pressure group that demanded an adequate definition of property rights and an end to civil war. Third, factionalism within the Blanco and Colorado parties and the incapacity of the political system to meet these demands produced a response from an increasingly powerful outsider: the Montevideo military garrison, which dissolved Parliament in 1874.

From Military Rule to Modern Democracy

The second stage in Uruguay's economic and political life runs from the beginning of military rule to the second decade of the twentieth century and corresponds to the formation of the modern Uruguayan state. It is convenient to divide this stage into two periods. In the first period, from 1874 to 1886, the military administrations developed key aspects of a modern state, including the provision of public goods basic for promoting economic growth. The second period, from 1886 to the late 1910s, saw the formation of a modern democracy.

The behavior of the military administrations in the first period came close to the stereotype of a predatory state—that is, a state controlled by a single ruler in which interest groups have almost no influence on government policies (see Lal 1986). Although the army's rule was not contested during Latorre's presidency, military administrations faced strong competition from political parties in the remainder of the period. The military consolidated the state's coercive power, established property rights, enforced internal order, and developed a national education system. It enlarged the size of the army, levied discriminatory tariffs on imports, and occasionally made the currency inconvertible.

Although the consolidation of the state's coercive power increased the rate of economic growth, the measures that permitted the development of a modern democracy should be credited to the civilian administrations that held office from 1886 to the late 1910s. The effort to consolidate a modern democracy at the end of the nineteenth century faced enormous difficulties, beginning with the challenge of neutralizing the army after almost two decades of pervasive military influence. In addition, the country was divided between the Blanco party, which controlled part of the territory and maintained its own army, and the incumbent Colorado party. The elimination of armed confrontation as an acceptable political instrument and the consolidation of a unified state were beneficial because the expansion of the international market for Uruguayan exports at the end of the century had increased the opportunity cost of civil wars. Under these circumstances the Blanco and Colorado parties faced the menace of new military intervention if they continued using violence to resolve their disputes. The elimination of armed conflict and the acceptance of democratic confrontation through periodic elections required the establishment of fair elections that gave legitimacy to elected governments and protected the rights of political minorities. These problems had to be solved in the context of internal party factionalism.

The formation of a modern democracy was an outgrowth of the influence of a new breed of politicians who gradually displaced rural *caudillos* from leading positions within both parties and who were committed to the suppression of armed confrontation as a legitimate political instrument. José Batlle was the most brilliant exponent of this generation of professional politicians and the main architect of the political reforms that made possible the pacification of the country and the development of a modern democracy.

The changes introduced in the political system during the first two decades of the twentieth century included the development of institutions that eliminated electoral fraud and guaranteed fair elections, abolished voting qualifications that had limited the number of eligible voters, and replaced majority rule in parliamentary elections with proportional representation. These changes gave greater legitimacy to the elected authorities and created incentives for using democratic rather than violent procedures to solve political disputes. The introduction of proportional representation and the enlargement of the size of the polity implied an increase in the political power of urban residents at a time when the country was experiencing a significant flow of immigrants, who settled mainly in urban areas. These changes generated demands for pro-urban income redistribution policies, which were met by taxing the rural sector. The characteristics of the rural sector and the expansion of beef exports to the world market combined to provide an ideal source of revenue with which to finance policies designed to obtain the support of urban groups.

Although José Batlle and his followers argued for active intervention in some economic activities, during his administrations state interventionism was not incompatible with foreign investment in new infrastructural services or strategic economic activities. Thus, although ideology was significant, it is likely that the primary motive for the development of a social security system, the defense of labor movement rights, the expansion of public enterprises, and the increase in protectionism was to obtain important urban support for a weak administration. In summary, the importance of Montevideo, the characteristics of the polity consolidated in the period, and the weakness of the political system go far to explain the development of a welfare state during the first two decades of the twentieth century.

The development of a modern political system was also strongly influenced by factionalism within the political parties and the limited democratic traditions in the country. The parties were not ideologically defined, and blocs and factions within each party espoused different visions of appropriate public policies. This tendency was exacerbated by the system of double simultaneous voting and accumulation. Under this system a party could have more than one candidate for the presidency, and the candidate with the largest number of votes on the list of the party that received the largest total number of votes was elected. The arrangement was an ingenious device for maintaining the unity of parties that contained a multiplicity of ideological and personal differences among their members, but it also implied a low degree of control of representatives, both by their constituencies and by the majority faction within the party.

These attributes of the political institutions created incentives for electoral coalitions between candidates of approximately equal strength, who joined forces temporarily to win a parliamentary seat. The candidate who received the largest vote within the coalition took office. This practice led over time to a steady reduction in the number of voters who were truly represented in Parliament and thus distorted voters' preferences (Vernazza 1987).

A consequence of the institutional situation was that the majority faction within each party lacked control over its own representatives. This led to a sort of tyranny of the parliamentary minorities over the executive, which needed minority support that could be obtained only in return for compensation. The results were a severe limitation on the capacity to enact certain laws that might affect powerful interest groups, even if those laws had the support of the majority of the polity, and a systematic bias on the part of Parliament toward increases in expenditures.

Coparticipation, another characteristic of the political institutions that developed in the first decades of the twentieth century, could be interpreted as a mechanism for collusion between the Blanco and Colorado parties. Both parties agreed to expand public sector employment according to a rule of proportional representation of members of the parties. But a more important function of coparticipation seems to have been to overcome party factionalism and its consequences. The participation of the majority of the minority party in the executive under the 1918 amendment to the Constitution and in the administration of public enterprises helped to reduce the costs of reaching the agreements necessary to govern the country.

The political institutions developed during the period penalized voting for parties other than the Blanco and Colorado parties, thus hindering the entry of new competitors. Factionalism continued, however, and hampered the formation of a stable majority in Parliament in support of the executive.

It must be kept in mind that to regard the Uruguayan state of the 1900s as a unity confuses rather than simplifies the interpretation of events. Although economic and social policies and tax policy were consistent with an attempt to exact monopoly rents, this interpretation implicitly assumes more myopia on the part of authorities than is characteristic of a predatory state.

The political institutions diffused responsibility, thus creating perverse incentives among members to adopt a very short time horizon in making decisions. The behavior of politicians under circumstances of diffused responsibility is analogous to the behavior of fishers exploiting an exhaustible species in the absence of well-defined property rights. It is possible that this phenomenon is the main explanatory factor for the development of a cycle of public economic policy.

The Great Depression and Its Aftermath

The growth of government intervention in the economy and the spread of patronage practices in the late 1920s and early 1930s could not be sustained after the decline in terms of trade associated with the Great Depression. The administration had to implement policy changes to adjust the economy to the new external circumstances, but it could not obtain the support of a parliamentary majority for a constitutional amendment and a return to a presidential regime.[1] These circumstances led President Terra to co-opt the majority of the Blanco party and dissolve Parliament. The army acquiesced in the coup, although it did not participate in it. Terra's coup revealed the weakness inherent in Uruguayan political institutions and their inability to make necessary changes in policy when the country was faced with drastic changes in external circumstances.

The new administration succeeded in amending the constitution to establish what was known as the Senate of Fifteen by Fifteen; half of the members were from the majority faction of each party, and there was no representation for the minority factions. Thus, the system discriminated against minorities, which then refrained from voting in some of the elections held during the period.

Under the new arrangement, further intervention in key infrastructural areas, protectionism, and restrictive trade practices continued, signaling an attempt to create new sources of monopoly revenue. At the same time, the authorities adopted a conservative stand with respect to the public sector budget. Public sector wages and salaries and social security transfers were reduced, even in nominal terms. The number of public sector employees, however, increased, from 52,000 in 1931 to 57,500 in 1938.

The development of a vast state machinery that included public enterprises, social security, import quotas and exchange controls, and credit subsidies was a major step in the use of the public sector as a source of monopoly profits. The introduction of quantitative restrictions, such as import quotas, created artificial scarcities that generated rent-seeking activities and provided resources that were important for politicians competing for public support.

The enlargement of government expenditure and employment did not increase provision of public sector goods. On the contrary, government expansion was often associated with the new regulations and the promotion of unproductive activities. Public employment became a locus of disguised unemployment. Hence, public sector wages and salaries represented, at the margin, an income transfer to those who were able to obtain these privileged jobs.

The expansion of government expenditure in the 1940s and 1950s was also associated with an increase in subsidies to the import-substituting sector. These transfers generally took the form of subsidized credit lines and privileged availability of foreign exchange at lower than equilibrium prices. Since the expansion of credit to the private sector was not paralleled by an increase in demand for money, the rate of inflation rose steadily after the late 1940s.

The social system created after the Great Depression and consolidated during 1945–55 favored the development of organizations with redistributive purposes. The greater interference of the state in the economy made it more profitable to invest in developing influence networks than in promoting new sales methods, improving quality, or introducing modern technology for production. The proliferation of regulations created the need for managers whose remuneration was based on the complexity of administrative regimes rather than on the value of marginal product for society as a whole.

The social system, by encouraging lobbying rather than innovation and efficiency in production, had nontrivial consequences for the formation of values and for the development of certain professional skills. In particular, the social prestige of entrepreneurial activity fell drastically when the public came to see that firms' profits were predominantly the result of their ability to obtain privileges rather than a consequence of innovative effort.

Uruguay's experience from the Great Depression to the postwar period exhibits two well-defined stages. The first stage, associated with the Great Depression and the decline in terms of trade, created political tensions that eventually resulted in Terra's coup in 1933. The second stage started with the improvement of the terms of trade in the late 1930s and coincided with the presidency of Baldomir and a transition toward democracy. The restoration of democracy was gradually accompanied by the enlargement of social security benefits; one of the first steps of the new democratic authorities was to undo Terra's decision to centralize all social security regimes under a single authority. The second stage was also marked by the expansion of public sector employment and the introduction of prohibitive tariffs, import quotas, and exchange controls. These examples of clientelism and rent creation appear to be an outgrowth of a political system that rewarded its members for maximizing their current utility without regard for the consequences of their decisions. Thus, politicians followed a strategy of maximization within a short time horizon. The spread of clientelism and rent creation was facilitated when Terra decided (in 1931) to introduce exchange controls that severed the links between the Uruguayan peso and other currencies based on the gold standard and (in 1935) to devalue the peso, interrupting a century-long history of domestic price stability.

Uruguayan society changed remarkably between 1930 and 1942, notably in its urban-rural distribution. (The population of Montevideo almost doubled during the period.) This shift was influenced by policies that favored the development of import-substituting industry. In the next decade, after the restoration of democracy, the larger urban population would place new demands on the political system, leading to an explosion of public sector employment and social security benefits and to pro-urban income distribution policies. Such policies were sustainable while the terms of trade remained favorable and foreign reserves lasted. They collapsed, however, when beef and wool prices dropped at the end of the Korean war and the stock of foreign reserves became exhausted as a result of the continuous current account deficits in the postwar period.

The drive to develop import-substituting industry after the Great Depression appears to be the product of both external events and the erosion of confidence in the private sector. The founding of public enterprises and the development of a social security system in previous decades helped shape ideas that were favorable to increased state intervention in economic affairs and were crucial for the implementation of new protectionist practices in the 1930s.

The decline in the prices of agricultural goods in relation to those of industrial goods reduced the profitability of investment in the livestock sector. This drop in the real rural return was not responsible for the decline in output, which was mainly caused by the technological characteristics of the sector, but it did discourage the improvement of pastures and promoted stagnation. Moreover, although the policies followed in the decades after 1930 increased the profitability of investment in import-substituting industry, thus fostering capital accumulation and growth in these activities, the rate of return on manufacturing investment declined sharply in the mid-1950s (as suggested by changes in investment), and that sector entered a period of stagnation.

The policies followed after the Great Depression and particularly in the postwar period led to an increase in the share of wages in total income and a decline in the share of land rents. Both the level of real wages and the share of wages in total income reached at the time were associated with transitory phenomena, such as very favorable terms of trade and domestic expansionary policies, that were not sustainable in the long run. These policies gave rise to systematic current account deficits. The deficits were disguised as long as the price of the country's exports continued high and foreign reserves lasted, but they became dramatically evident after the terms of trade declined sharply at the end of the Korean war. That external shock drastically reduced the country's national income and the capacity of the rural sector to maintain its level of transfers to the rest of the economy. In addition, it prompted the economy to move toward a new equilibrium through a decline in the rate of capital accumulation, since at the prevailing level of real wages investment became unprofitable.

The adjustment to the change in external conditions required significant changes in domestic policy. These included a contraction in the fiscal deficit and a devaluation of the currency, which in turn implied a drastic fall in real wages and a reduction in the level of implicit taxation on agricultural goods. The reluctance of the authorities to make these policy changes led the country into economic recession and a major external crisis, evoked the opposition of the rural sector, and eventually led to the triumph of the Blanco party in the 1958 elections.

Crisis, Stagnation, and Adjustment

The years between 1955 and 1973 were characterized by economic stagnation, price instability, and a gathering political storm. The import-substituting strategy developed during the two decades ended in a deadlock. Entrepreneurs who had enjoyed favorable credit lines for their initial investments and who expected to capture monopoly rents did not find it profitable to renew equipment when the real return on capital turned out to be low, both because the size of the market implied highly inefficient utilization of capacity and because union activity and public sector policies combined to produce a large increase in the cost of labor. Given the accommodating monetary policies, the result of the systematic fiscal deficits, resistance by pressure groups to relative price changes, and labor-management disputes was spiraling price instability.

The Blanco party administration, which took office in 1959, eliminated multiple exchange rates and import quotas and drastically devalued the currency. The change in relative prices was only transitory, however, as expansionary fiscal policies, coupled with a fixed exchange rate, brought about a gradual appreciation of the peso and an external crisis. The years between 1959 and 1974 saw a recurrent cycle: external crisis was followed by devaluation, a transitory change in relative prices, and a decline in real wages. The process of adjustment met with resistance from unions and pressure groups, which tried to return to the original high real earnings in both the private and public sectors. Accommodating monetary policies fueled the increasing price instability that, under fixed exchange rates, led to frequent external crises.

The period 1955–73 was one of stagnation, price instability, and a gradual erosion of democratic institutions. The inability of successive Blanco and Colorado administrations to meet the crises provoked aggressive behavior by the unions, urban guerrillas, and finally the army.

The role of the unions was heightened by the closure of the economy to foreign competition. Faced with the menace of strikes, firms yielded to labor movement demands for wage increases and passed on the higher costs to their customers. Thus, the dynamics of wage and price increments implied either an accommodating monetary policy or—under the prevailing expectations of inflation—recession. The 1968 stabilization plan attempted to break a mechanism that was driving the economy into increasing price instability. The plan was aborted, however, as a result of the expansionary policies followed during 1971, an election year.

1955–68

The characteristics of the Uruguayan state during 1955–68 fall close to the stereotype of a factional state (see Lal 1986). In general, successive administrations were inclined to yield to demands from pressure groups and often made decisions that conflicted with each other. Economic and social policies became a disorganized mosaic of subsidies and regulations that yielded economic inefficiency and social turmoil.

In reaction, factions of the Blanco and Colorado parties combined to pass the 1966 constitutional amendment, which attempted to increase the authority of the executive. The collegium was eliminated, and a presidential regime was established. The capacity of Parliament to increase government expenditure was restrained by not allowing it to take the initiative in passing laws that would increase the level of expenditure. But this did not substantially alter the course of events.

1968–70

From 1968 to 1970 the Pacheco administration introduced dramatic changes in domestic policies in an attempt to reestablish the authority of the state, which was being contested both by the unions and by urban guerrillas. Pacheco's government shared some characteristics with Terra's. Both administrations took office in the midst of a major internal crisis, engineered measures to avoid a parliamentary blockade, and promoted conservative policies. Terra's administration dissolved Parliament with the support of factions of the Blanco and Colorado parties and adopted a constitutional amendment that displaced from power minority factions within both parties. Pacheco retained Parliament but governed through the use of the *medidas prontas de seguridad*, which allowed the president to bypass parliamentary approval of executive initiatives. Although his policies aroused opposition, Pacheco had at least the acquiescence of the majority of Parliament; the majority of the Colorado party and a conservative faction of the Blanco party supported him. His presidency represented a move toward a predatory state. During the latter part of his term, however, his administration yielded to electoral pressures. Government expenditure rose, and an exchange rate appreciation exactly like those observed in previous administrations opened the road to an economic and political crisis that ended with the coup of 1973.

Oil Shock and Export Problems

The decline in the terms of trade after 1973 forced a significant change in economic policy. The authorities' initial reaction to the rise in the price of oil and the closure of the EC market to Uruguay's beef exports was to restrict imports severely—a strategy similar to that of the Colorado administration after the decline in terms of trade at the end of the Korean war. But the magnitude of the crisis, the low level of foreign reserves, and the pressures to put the economy on a path of sustained growth compelled the government to liberalize exchange transactions and international capital flows and to implement an outward-oriented growth strategy.

The economic and social policies followed between 1974 and 1977 were mainly determined by severe external circumstances. Thus, although the prohibition of labor union activities and the absence of opposition from Parliament probably accelerated policy changes, the military administration's response to the decline in the terms of trade was very similar to that adopted by the Blanco government, which passed the Exchange and Tariff Act of 1959. The differences between the two administrations seem to be more a matter of their attitude toward increasing government expenditure and public sector wages than evidence of a major disagreement in the design of an external adjustment. In fact, although the military reduced public sector employment during the first stage of its period in office, it also redistributed government expenditure, enlarging the size of the armed forces and raising the salaries of military personnel in relation to the salaries prevailing in the rest of the economy. The ability of the military government to reduce the fiscal deficit during those years permitted the maintenance of a high real exchange rate and created incentives for the expansion of export-oriented activities.

In general, the policies of the military administration adversely affected some vested interests, particularly those of unionized workers and public employees, and protected others. The military was reluctant to modify its policies toward agriculture, and it was moderate in reducing the level of effective protection of import-substituting industry. The distribution of export subsidies mainly benefited import-substituting sectors rather than export-oriented activities; the percentage subsidy received by the former was, on average, larger than that obtained by the latter group of industries.

The logic behind the attitude of the administration toward key pressure groups—unionized workers and entrepreneurs in the manufacturing industry and public employees, in particular—during the first stage of the military government can be understood when it is recognized that the prohibition of labor movement activities reduced the ability of both unions and industrial entrepreneurs to lobby for the continuation of transfers from other sectors of the economy. It did, however, strengthen the firms' side in labor-management disputes and may thus have offset the costs of decreasing the level of effective protection for industrial activities. The military did not have to worry about the support of public sector employees except for those of its own constituency.

The second stage of the military government—in particular, the years between 1979 and 1982—was characterized by an increase in the level of effective protection, a real appreciation of the currency, and expansion of government expenditure, especially social security transfers. Thus, the policies followed in this stage differed greatly from those of the 1974–77 period and implied a move away from the export-led growth strategy. Economic events were considerably affected by regional economic circumstances, which implied a strong demand pressure from Argentina and led to an appreciation of the Uruguayan peso.

The military authorities, faced with a large external trade deficit, were reluctant to devalue the peso during an election year until they had exhausted both the stock of foreign reserves and the possibilities of expanding the public sector's external debt.[2] Thus, the management of the exchange rate during 1982 closely resembled that of the preceding civilian administrations. Moreover, such variables as the rate of inflation and government expenditure behaved in a way characteristic of election periods.

In summary, during the first stage of its administration the military made some deep economic policy changes under the pressure of extremely adverse external circumstances. It enjoyed the advantage of insulation from the pressures of some key interest groups. As soon, however, as the armed forces began a transition toward democracy and developed their own political ambitions, their attitudes regarding important economic issues became very similar to those of the Blanco and Colorado administrations in previous periods.

Conclusions

Uruguay managed to grow after the oil shock of 1973 while the rest of the world was in crisis. Conversely, it remained stagnant while world output and trade were increasing rapidly in the mid-1950s and 1960s. Both the domestic economy and the polity have exhibited enormous sensitivity to changes in terms of trade.

The only sound argument for keeping the economy closed to foreign competition is that it allows the country to isolate itself from foreign disturbances. But closure results in a lower rate of growth, and it magnifies the effects of external shocks because it discourages the growth of an export-oriented manufacturing sector and so inhibits the development of a diversified economic structure.

Argentina and Brazil have had a powerful effect on the cyclical behavior of output and other real variables in Uruguay. There is, however, no association between the secular trends followed by real variables in Uruguay and those of its neighbors. Uruguay remained largely unaffected by the dynamic behavior of the Brazilian economy in the 1950s and 1960s. Its periods of growth paralleled stagnation in Argentina, and its periods of stagnation coincided with periods of Argentine economic expansion.

Sustained economic growth in Uruguay has been associated with the expansion of export-oriented activities. The century before the Great Depression and the years between 1974 and 1978 were periods of export-led growth, while the periods 1945–55 and 1979–81 are examples of import substitution–led growth.

Although increased investment and employment are necessary conditions for growth, a high ratio of investment to GDP is not a sufficient condition for sustained economic expansion. The allocation of investment among economic activities is a primary determinant of the overall effect of capital accumulation on real income. The years 1974–77 provide an interesting example of a period when, although private investment did not increase dramatically, the reallocation of investment toward more productive export-oriented activities brought about a remarkable increase in the rate of growth of GDP.

Export-oriented industry is highly sensitive to changes in the real exchange rate. A high and stable real exchange rate, coupled with export subsidies, led to the development of new export activities in the 1970s. Export subsidies compensated in part for the implicit discrimination against export-oriented activities, but these policies had much less effect on economic growth than would have resulted from a uniform tariff reduction. Export subsidies and preferential trade agreements frequently worked to encourage the growth of import-substituting activities rather than the expansion of sectors in which the country had a comparative advantage.

The increase in government expenditure that began in the late 1930s imposed a negative externality on the rest of the economy. Higher government expenditure and employment was not accompanied by an increase in the output of the public sector; on the contrary, it often denoted only the introduction of new regulations and the promotion of directly unproductive activities. The government imposed costs on the private sector.

Domestic price instability affected economic growth. The fixed exchange rates and interest rate ceilings that were in place until the mid-1970s meant that a higher rate of inflation was often accompanied by a loss of welfare as well as by incentives to allocate resources to unproductive activities such as rent seeking. Higher rates of inflation also implied a contraction in the domestic capital market, which constrained capital accumulation.

Exchange controls, interest rate ceilings, and price instability created incentives for capital outflows and limited the size of the domestic capital market, while public sector deficit financing crowded out private sector possibilities for financing investment in the domestic market.

Although the size of domestic saving was a constraint on investment and growth, the limits were endogenously determined by the economic policies followed up to the mid-1970s. The liberalization of foreign exchange transactions and international capital flows eliminated the capital constraint on growth determined by the domestic capital market and considerably enlarged its size. The availability of foreign exchange for financing the importation of capital goods may have hampered economic growth from 1955 to the mid-1970s, but diminished growth was also endogenously determined by economic policies that severely curtailed the expansion of exports and provoked capital outflows.

The level of real wages and the share of wages in national income reached in the mid-1950s were produced by transitory phenomena such as very favorable terms of trade and expansionary government policies that were not sustainable in the long run. The economic reforms of the mid-1970s initially increased the degree of inequality in the distribution of income. There is evidence, however, that growth benefited both less-skilled and highly trained workers. During the second stage of the military period, 1979–82, the degree of equality in the distribution of income increased. Both the extent of openness of the economy and the share of government expenditure in overall GDP had a significant influence on the distribution of income.

Although external circumstances have strongly influenced Uruguay's economic performance in the past four decades, the effect of domestic policies on economic growth and income distribution dominated. The closure of the economy after the Great Depression was the principal determinant of the slow rate of economic growth during the past forty years. The increase in protectionism was the result of both external circumstances, such as the disruption of international trade, and domestic circumstances, such as the relative growth of the urban population and the characteristics of the political system. Demographic changes implied new demands for pro-urban income distribution policies, and the characteristics of the political institutions promoted an anarchic accumulation of regulations. Once adopted, these policies were fiercely defended by vested interests that resisted any change in the status quo. Furthermore, they helped to disguise the perverse effect on economic growth of further government intervention and hence allowed it to occur.

A major finding of this study is the identification of the influence of political institutions on the formation of economic and social policies. The institutions that characterize Uruguayan democracy were developed during a period when party factionalism was common and the menace of military intervention was an important political phenomenon. Although the institutions developed at the beginning of the century were possibly the best conceivable at the time, they proved to be very weak.[3] The executive lacked a stable majority in Parliament. Proportional representation and the accumulation of votes promoted factionalism within the political parties and diminished party discipline. The institutional characteristics of the system also made it difficult for voters to penalize representatives whose policies produced high social costs, a tendency toward systematic expansion of government expenditure, and an incapacity to adjust to changes in external circumstances. These properties of the political system may be the main underlying factors behind the occasional lapses that have characterized Uruguayan democracy during periods of drastic change in world market conditions in this century.

Notes

1. Under the 1918 constitutional amendment the executive had a mixed structure that combined the attributes of a collegium and a presidential regime. Some ministers reported to the National Administration Council, which had a collegial structure with representation of the majority and minority parties.

2. After the defeat of the constitutional amendment proposed by the military in 1980, a new strategy for the transition was devised. The first step was the election of civilian authorities affiliated with political parties through direct popular vote in November 1982. The campaign for candidacies within the parties ended in the nomination of candidates whose political stands were close to those of the armed forces.

3. The relevant issue is the comparison of the actual institutional and economic performance with what would have happened under civil war rather than with what would have happened in a "perfect state."

Statistical Appendix B
Uruguay

Table B-1. Uruguay: Population, 1955–85

Year	Thousands of persons
1955	2,345.6
1956	2,378.4
1957	2,411.7
1958	2,445.5
1959	2,479.7
1960	2,514.4
1961	2,549.6
1962	2,585.3
1963	2,621.5
1964	2,657.6
1965	2,689.3
1966	2,716.2
1967	2,738.4
1968	2,763.3
1969	2,784.9
1970	2,807.6
1971	2,819.5
1972	2,836.6
1973	2,848.6
1974	2,851.1
1975	2,821.8
1976	2,819.1
1977	2,826.9
1978	2,842.1
1979	2,863.3
1980	2,887.7
1981	2,910.0
1982	2,933.7
1983	2,926.6
1984	2,919.4
1985	2,930.6

Source: Méndez 1985.

Table B-2. *Uruguay: Population, by Sex, Age, and Rural or Urban Residence, 1963 and 1975*
(number of persons)

Year and age	Total	Rural			Urban		
		Total	Male	Female	Total	Male	Female
1963							
Total	2,595,510	498,381	281,453	216,928	2,097,129	1,008,933	1,088,196
0–14	725,209	153,227	79,930	73,297	571,982	289,918	284,064
15–64	1,651,139	310,863	181,883	128,980	1,340,276	641,413	698,863
65 and over	196,326	29,419	16,795	12,624	166,907	71,819	95,088
Age not given	22,836	4,872	2,845	2,027	17,964	7,783	10,181
1975							
Total	2,788,429	474,073	269,778	204,286	2,314,356	1,099,634	1,214,722
0–14	752,588	135,017	70,330	64,678	617,571	311,894	305,677
15–64	1,763,025	303,970	179,254	124,716	1,459,055	688,070	770,985
65 and over	272,816	35,086	20,194	14,892	237,730	99,670	138,060

Source: Uruguay, Dirección General de Estadísticas y Censos, *Censo Nacional de Población y Vivienda,* 1963, 1975.

Table B-3. Uruguay: Households, 1963, 1975, and 1985

Location and year	Population in private households (thousands of persons)	Private households (thousands)	Average size of household
Montevideo			
1963	1,174.0	328.0	3.58
1975	1,204.0	370.8	3.25
1985	1,235.0	407.4	3.03
Urban areas of provinces			
1963	923.7	243.0	3.80
1975	1,116.6	317.6	3.52
1985	1,202.0	373.7	3.22
Rural areas of provinces			
1963	447.4	119.0	3.76
1975	386.9	106.1	3.65
1985	376.7	106.1	3.55
Total			
1963	2,545.1	690.0	3.69
1975	2,707.5	794.5	3.41
1985	2,813.7	887.2	3.17

Source: Banco Hipotecario del Uruguay, unpublished data.

*Table B-4. Uruguay: Labor Force and Unemployed Population,
1963 and 1975*

Age and year	Labor force		
	Male	*Female*	*Total*
1963, population age 10 and over			
Total	759,887	252,280	1,012,167
0–14	12,480	4,818	17,298
15–64	721,407	240,414	961,821
65 and over	18,699	3,511	22,210
Age not given	7,301	3,537	10,838
1975, population age 12 and over			
Total	783,584	311,016	1,094,600
0–14	9,889	3,617	13,506
15–64	748,770	301,988	1,050,758
65 and over	24,925	5,411	30,336

Age and year	Unemployed population		
	Male	*Female*	*Total*
1963, population age 10 and over			
Total	275,477	805,375	1,080,852
0–14	100,346	105,074	205,420
15–64	101,889	587,429	689,318
65 and over	69,915	104,201	174,116
Age not given	3,327	8,671	11,998
1975, population age 12 and over			
Total	269,849	797,154	1,067,003
0–14	65,328	69,596	134,924
15–64	110,425	581,689	692,114
65 and over	94,096	145,869	239,965

Source: See table B-2.

Table B-5.   Uruguay: Labor Force, by Sector, 1963 and 1975
(thousands)

Sector	Employed 1963	Employed 1975	Unemployed 1963	Unemployed 1975	No data[a] 1963	No data[a] 1975	Total 1963	Total 1975
All sectors	859.9	1,020.1	98.3	74.5	54.0	—	1,012.2	1,094.6
Agriculture	168.2	167.0	14.7	7.9	0.8	—	183.7	174.9
Industry	197.1	199.0	21.4	9.1	2.2	—	220.7	208.1
Construction	38.3	53.7	16.2	5.7	0.4	—	55.4	59.4
Electricity, water, etc.	4.7	16.0	0.2	0.2	—	—	4.9	16.2
Transport and storage	55.2	52.4	2.8	1.3	0.5	—	58.5	53.7
Commerce	100.9	129.3	8.0	5.2	0.9	—	109.3	134.5
Other services	281.0	368.8	14.6	10.2	2.4	—	298.0	379.0
Seeking work for the first time	—	—	19.9	17.1	—	—	19.9	17.1
No data	14.0	33.9	0.5	17.8	46.8	—	61.3	51.7

— Not available.
a. No figures were available for 1975.
Source: See table B-2.

Table B-6.   Uruguay: Employment, 1964–83
(thousands of persons)

Year	Montevideo	Rural	Total	Public sector	Private sector
1964	430	477	907	224	683
1965	434	487	921	—	—
1966	436	496	932	—	—
1967	434	508	942	—	—
1968	433	506	939	—	—
1969	431	516	947	231	716
1970	439	530	969	—	—
1971	444	537	981	—	—
1972	440	543	983	—	—
1973	436	542	978	—	—
1974	448	552	1,000	—	—
1975	473	563	1,036	—	—
1976	462	535	997	—	—
1977	478	549	1,027	—	—
1978	471	567	1,038	233	804
1979	475	585	1,060	—	—
1980	494	603	1,097	—	—
1981	511	616	1,127	—	—
1982	491	591	1,082	—	—
1983	475	576	1,051	241	810

— Not available.
Source: Vieytes 1984.

Table B-7. Uruguay: Employment and Unemployment, by Sex, 1963 and 1975

Item	1963	1975
Labor force		
Male	719,778	783,584
Female	238,514	311,015
Total	958,292	1,094,599
Employed population		
Male	640,152	730,528
Female	218,837	289,560
Total	858,989	1,020,088
Unemployed population[a]		
Male	79,626	53,056
Female	19,677	21,455
Total	99,303	74,511
Unemployment rate (percent)		
Male	11.06	6.77
Female	8.25	6.90
Total	10.36	6.81

a. Includes persons seeking work for the first time.
Source: See table B-2.

Table B-8. Uruguay: Unemployment Rate, by Activity, 1966, 1971, 1981, and 1984

Sector	1966		1971		1981		1984	
	First half	Second half	First half	Second half	First half	Second half	First half	Second half
Total	7.6	6.9	7.6	7.6	5.8	7.5	14.2	12.6
Manufacturing	6.9	6.2	7.5	8.5	4.7	7.7	12.2	10.7
Construction	16.8	15.8	13.0	9.0	3.9	7.5	18.0	15.4
Commerce	5.6	4.5	4.9	5.3	6.7	5.0	11.0	9.5
Transport and storage	2.1	2.4	3.0	3.4	2.3	4.0	6.5	5.0
Services	3.3	3.5	3.8	3.4	3.2	3.3	8.5	7.2

Source: Uruguay, Dirección General de Estadísticas y Censos, Encuesta de Hogares, Ocupación y Desocupación, various years.

Table B-9. Uruguay: Employment in the Public Sector, 1984

Activity	Number of employed persons
Central government and social security	156,573
Enterprises and banks	56,070
Local government	33,050
Total	245,693

Source: Uruguay, Oficina de Planeamiento y Presupuesto, 1984.

Table B-10. Uruguay: Employment in Public Enterprises, by Activity, 1978

Activity	Number of persons employed
Electric power	10,241
Railroads	9,771
Telephones	8,179
Oil refinery	7,479
Port	5,688
Water	5,139
Commercial bank	3,967
Insurance	1,986
Housing bank	1,159
Fishing	767
Airline	529

Source: Uruguay, Oficina de Planeamiento y Presupuesto, 1978.

Table B-11. *Uruguay: Structure of GDP at 1961 Constant Market Prices, 1955–84*
(millions of new pesos)

Year	Private consumption	Central government consumption	Fixed gross investment	Change in stocks	Exports	Imports	GDP
1955	12,821	1,763	3,135	19	1,914	2,814	16,838
1956	12,596	1,759	2,895	−34	2,470	2,555	17,131
1957	13,698	1,804	2,970	213	1,636	3,017	17,304
1958	12,336	1,794	2,152	44	2,236	1,877	16,685
1959	12,106	1,752	2,261	243	2,028	2,176	16,214
1960	12,933	1,794	2,488	337	2,008	2,758	16,802
1961	12,740	1,828	2,766	126	2,467	2,623	17,304
1962	13,136	1,913	2,828	−88	2,118	2,984	16,923
1963	12,455	1,889	2,324	155	2,212	2,285	16,750
1964	13,559	1,962	2,020	78	2,235	2,498	17,356
1965	12,383	2,113	1,951	41	2,939	1,906	17,521
1966	13,228	2,301	1,919	167	2,606	2,113	18,108
1967	12,747	2,294	2,165	89	2,432	2,362	17,365
1968	12,560	2,485	2,010	−11	2,784	2,186	17,642
1969	13,587	2,488	2,568	−23	2,781	2,688	18,713
1970	14,454	2,783	2,745	−12	2,929	3,304	19,594
1971	14,594	2,595	2,871	176	2,718	3,567	19,387
1972	14,559	2,249	2,341	209	2,526	3,171	18,713
1973	15,084	2,711	1,993	441	2,554	3,448	19,335
1974	14,873	2,892	2,130	206	3,123	3,232	19,992

(Table continues on the following page.)

319

Table B-11 (continued)

Year	Private consumption	Central government consumption	Fixed gross investment	Change in stocks	Exports	Imports	GDP
1975	14,848	2,749	2,982	13	3,842	3,492	20,942
1976	14,001	2,932	3,813	-195	4,888	3,616	21,823
1977	14,188	2,855	4,050	-4	5,148	4,016	22,221
1978	14,920	3,172	4,485	13	5,384	4,371	23,603
1979	16,258	3,588	5,398	211	6,478	5,291	26,642
1980	17,077	3,523	5,675	335	5,945	5,722	26,833
1981	17,482	3,787	5,505	-291	6,312	5,779	27,015
1982	15,791	3,696	4,686	-569	5,648	4,994	24,259
1983	14,348	3,409	3,222	-538	6,511	3,829	23,123
1984	14,089	3,453	2,409	-65	6,489	3,543	22,832

Source: Estimates based on data from Banco Central del Uruguay and Instituto de Economía.

Table B-12. Uruguay: Public and Private Sectors as Shares of GDP,
1955 and 1981
(percent)

	1955			1981		
Activity	*Public sector*	*Private sector*	*Total*	*Public sector*	*Private sector*	*Total*
Agriculture	—	100.0	100	0.3	99.7	100
Fishing	41.6	58.4	100	2.0	98.0	100
Manufacturing	9.6	90.4	100	4.9	95.1	100
Electricity, gas, and water	90.2	9.8	100	98.6	1.4	100
Construction	—	100.0	100	—	100.0	100
Trade	0.5	99.5	100	0.3	99.7	100
Transport and storage	27.4	72.6	100	15.3	84.7	100
Communications	3.1	96.9	100	100.0	—	100
Banking and insurance	34.6	65.4	100	41.0	59.0	100
Housing	—	100.0	100	—	100.0	100
General government	100.0	—	100	100.0	—	100
Other	2.2	97.8	100	1.6	98.4	100
Total	16.5	83.5	100	21.6	78.4	100

— Not available.
Source: Banco Central del Uruguay, *Cuentas Nacionales*, various issues.

Table B-13. Uruguay: Value of Agricultural Production, Selected Years,
1955–80
(percent)

Activity	*1955*	*1960*	*1970*	*1980*
Crops	38	25	36	39
Wheat	15	4	7	15
Other	23	21	29	24
Livestock products	62	75	64	61
Beef	29	36	34	26
Wool	18	25	14	13
Other	15	14	16	22
Total	100	100	100	100

Source: See table B-12.

Table B-14. Uruguay: Industrial GDP, Selected Years, 1955–80
(percent)

Industry	1955	1960	1970	1980
Food	23.3	19.1	22.5	18.9
Beverages	7.7	7.6	11.1	8.3
Tobacco	2.5	3.2	3.6	3.0
Textiles	15.7	12.7	10.3	12.8
Clothing	4.8	5.3	5.0	3.1
Paper	0.9	2.0	2.3	3.3
Rubber	1.0	3.5	1.7	1.9
Chemicals	5.3	6.1	6.6	6.1
Oil	5.1	4.8	4.7	3.4
Capital goods	7.8	7.6	4.2	5.6
Other	25.9	27.1	28.0	33.6
Total	100.0	100.0	100.0	100.0

Source: See table B-12.

Table B-15. Uruguay: Effective Protection in the Industrial Sector, 1975
(percent)

Product	Rate of effective protection
Food	–8.8
Beverages	36.0
Tobacco	225.7
Textiles	88.9
Shoes and clothing	79.7
Wood	—
Furniture	—
Paper products	10.1
Printing	—
Leather products	—
Rubber products	262.0
Chemical products	–18.9
Oil derivatives	71.4
Nonmetallic minerals	–7.1
Basic metals	—
Metal products	282.7
Machinery	—
Electrical apparatus	608.6
Transport equipment	—
Miscellaneous industries	—

— Not available.
Source: Anichini, Caumont, and Sjaastad 1978.

Table B-16. Uruguay: Effective Protection in the Industrial Sector, 1981
(percent)

Product	Rate of effective protection
Consumption goods	46.19
Durables	316.93
Automobiles	378.51
Electrical appliances and communications	262.16
Nondurables	−33.67
Food, beverages, and tobacco	29.33
Shoes and clothing	45.64
Chemical products	59.60
Producer goods	106.78
Intermediate	100.87
Food	−21.30
Textiles	90.69
Tannery	143.21
Paper products	127.03
Chemicals, oil derivatives, and plastics	161.17
Nonmetallic minerals	31.84
Metal products	150.57
Machinery and transport equipment	286.07
Tubes and tires	592.69
Glass	80.68
Industrial machinery	75.37
Automobiles	231.10

Source: Centro de Investigaciones Económicas 1982.

Table B-17. Uruguay: GDP *and* GDP *per Capita, 1955–84*

Year	GDP (millions of new pesos)	GDP (millions of 1961 dollars)	GDP per capita (1961 dollars)
1955	4.6	16,838	7,179
1956	5.2	17,131	7,203
1957	5.1	17,304	7,175
1958	6.6	16,681	6,821
1959	8.9	16,214	6,539
1960	13.6	16,802	6,682
1961	17.3	17,304	6,790
1962	18.8	16,923	6,546
1963	22.4	16,750	6,389
1964	32.6	17,356	6,531
1965	52.5	17,521	6,515
1966	99.6	18,108	6,667
1967	169.8	17,365	6,341
1968	374.5	17,642	6,384
1969	506	18,713	6,720
1970	612	19,595	3,979
1971	722	19,387	6,876
1972	1,242	18,713	6,597
1973	2,561	19,335	6,788
1974	4,546	19,992	7,012
1975	8,166	20,942	7,422
1976	12,638	21,823	7,741
1977	19,915	22,221	7,861
1978	30,930	23,603	8,305
1979	57,625	26,642	9,305
1980	92,204	26,833	9,292
1981	122,453	27,015	9,284
1982	128,696	24,259	8,269
1983	188,437	23,123	7,901
1984	295,546	22,832	7,821

Source: Based on data from Banco Central del Uruguay.

Table B-18. Uruguay: GDP *and Wages, Selected Years, 1955–80*
(millions of new pesos)

Year	GDP	Wages	Wages as percentage of GDP
1955	4.6	1.6	34.8
1960	14	4.7	33.6
1970	612	241	39.4
1980	79,539	24,698	31.1

Source: Based on data from Banco Central del Uruguay.

Table B-19. Uruguay: Industrial GDP, Montevideo and Rural Areas, 1978

Area	Millions of new pesos	As share of total (percent)
Montevideo	7,804	83.7
Rural	1,521	16.3
Total	9,325	100.0

Source: Uruguay, Dirección General de Estadísticas y Censos, 1979.

Table B-20. Uruguay: Labor Productivity, 1963 and 1975

Item	1963	1975
Agriculture		
GDP (thousands of 1961 new pesos)	2,579	2,669
Workers	183,678	174,871
GDP per worker	0.0140	0.0153
Industry		
GDP (thousands of 1961 new pesos)	3,351	4,426
Workers	195,799	205,943
GDP per worker	0.0171	0.0215

Source: Based on data from Banco Central del Uruguay and Uruguay, Dirección General de Estadísticas y Censos.

Table B-21. Uruguay: Exports and Imports, 1950–84
(millions of U.S. dollars)

Year	Current prices		Millions of 1961 dollars	
	Exports	Imports	Exports	Imports
1950	254.2	211.4	204.5	247.8
1951	276.3	316.4	136.4	309.9
1952	208.7	250.9	157.7	238.3
1953	269.5	206.4	207.6	208.7
1954	348.8	273.9	195.0	294.5
1955	183.0	237.6	156.8	234.8
1956	215.7	209.1	196.8	196.5
1957	136.0	252.9	116.8	231.6
1958	155.4	143.1	153.7	132.9
1959	108.3	176.2	110.5	172.1
1960	129.4	217.5	124.4	224.9
1961	174.7	210.9	174.7	210.9
1962	153.7	230.5	153.4	241.9
1963	165.2	176.9	163.1	178.0
1964	178.9	197.9	155.2	200.3
1965	191.2	150.7	173.5	153.5
1966	185.8	164.2	165.4	—
1967	158.7	171.4	151.7	179.1
1968	179.2	159.3	189.6	161.7
1969	200.4	197.3	194.6	200.7
1970	232.7	230.9	218.1	229.8
1971	205.8	228.9	199.3	252.6
1972	214.1	211.6	162.6	238.8
1973	321.5	284.8	173.2	299.8
1974	382.2	486.7	210.6	276.5
1975	383.8	556.5	244.8	294.1
1976	546.5	587.2	327.8	319.0
1977	607.5	729.9	346.2	363.5
1978	686.1	774.3	365.9	377.2
1979	788.1	1,230.8	346.9	489.6
1980	1,058.6	1,602.5	387.9	507.0
1981	1,215.4	1,598.9	446.3	457.0
1982	1,022.9	1,110.0	418.4	339.7
1983	1,045.1	787.5	464.2	255.5
1984	924.6	775.7	403.2	248.7

— Not available.
Source: Banco Central del Uruguay, *Boletín Estadístico*, various issues.

Table B-22. Uruguay: Prices of Exports and Imports, 1955–84
(1961 = 100)

Year	Export price	Import price	Terms of trade
1955	116.70000	101.20000	115.31620
1956	109.60000	106.40000	103.00750
1957	116.40000	109.20000	106.59340
1958	101.10000	107.70000	93.87186
1959	98.00000	102.40000	95.70313
1960	104.00000	96.70000	107.54910
1961	100.00000	100.00000	100.00000
1962	100.20000	95.30000	105.14170
1963	101.30000	99.40000	101.91150
1964	115.30000	98.80000	116.70040
1965	110.20000	98.10000	112.33440
1966	112.30000	96.30000	116.61470
1967	105.80000	95.70000	110.55380
1968	94.50000	98.50000	95.93909
1969	103.00000	98.30000	104.78130
1970	106.70000	105.50000	101.13740
1971	103.20000	90.60000	113.90730
1972	134.40000	100.90000	133.20120
1973	189.30000	108.20000	174.95380
1974	185.20000	200.40000	92.41517
1975	160.00000	215.43000	74.27007
1976	170.10000	209.60000	81.15458
1977	179.10000	228.70000	78.31220
1978	191.20000	233.70000	81.81429
1979	231.80000	286.30000	80.96403
1980	278.40000	359.90000	77.35482
1981	277.80000	398.40000	69.72891
1982	249.50000	366.50000	68.07640
1983	229.80000	345.60000	66.49306
1984	230.90000	345.30000	66.86939

Source: Based on data from Banco Central del Uruguay and Banco de la República Oriental del Uruguay.

*Table B-23. Uruguay: Exports and Imports, Selected Items and Years,
1950–80*
(millions of dollars)

Item	1950	1960	1970	1980
Exports				
Wool	152.7	45.1	47.6	125.6
Meat	43.6	30.6	87.8	170.1
Hides	29.4	15.5	24.3	40.2
Agricultural goods	1.7	0.8	1.0	108.0
Other	26.8	37.4	72.0	614.7
Total	254.2	129.4	232.7	1,058.6
Imports				
Oil	23.8	34.7	33.7	476.5
Machinery	32.4	16.9	26.6	241.4
Vehicles	22.5	21.3	36.1	202.1
Consumption goods	44.8	15.3	14.4	104.7
Other	87.9	129.3	119.9	577.8
Total	211.4	217.5	230.9	1,602.5

Source: Banco Central del Uruguay, *Boletín Estadístico*, various issues.

Table B-24. *Uruguay: Beef Exports, 1961–84*

		f.o.b.	
Year	Thousands of dollars	Tons	Price/ton (dollars)
1961	23,983	51,519	465.5
1962	27,916	—	—
1963	28,887	75,980	380.2
1964	63,422	163,577	387.7
1965	44,200	104,697	422.2
1966	33,768	69,182	488.1
1967	33,673	68,965	488.3
1968	51,851	75,693	685.0
1969	53,922	124,208	434.1
1970	74,118	147,658	502.0
1971	58,878	89,347	659.0
1972	97,883	114,999	851.2
1973	119,607	112,019	1,067.7
1974	134,837	114,079	1,182.0
1975	68,148	106,356	640.8
1976	68,814	185,299	371.4
1977	100,442	127,357	788.7
1978	78,227	114,869	681.0
1979	94,872	77,478	1,224.5
1980	155,445	111,049	1,399.8
1981	213,594	167,958	1,271.7
1982	170,341	160,780	1,059.5
1983	222,862	220,493	1,010.7
1984	129,641	135,426	957.3

— Not available.

Source: Banco Central del Uruguay and Banco de la República Oriental del Uruguay, unpublished data.

Table B-25. Uruguay: Wool Exports, 1961–84

Year	Thousands of dollars	f.o.b. Tons	Price/ton (dollars)
1961	109,832	83,881	1,309.4
1962	81,613	56,370	1,447.8
1963	84,991	53,357	1,592.9
1964	67,476	35,490	1,901.3
1965	90,339	66,387	1,360.8
1966	84,372	66,427	1,270.1
1967	98,903	70,061	1,411.7
1968	77,983	80,159	972.9
1969	67,396	63,824	1,056.0
1970	73,211	70,582	1,037.2
1971	64,648	73,965	874.0
1972	54,477	50,384	1,081.2
1973	97,538	43,040	2,266.2
1974	87,194	40,707	2,142.0
1975	86,567	59,813	1,447.3
1976	100,564	53,358	1,884.7
1977	120,716	55,536	2,173.7
1978	132,014	60,096	2,196.7
1979	101,365	40,014	2,533.2
1980	212,752	74,694	2,848.3
1981	236,107	76,182	3,099.2
1982	295,942	78,204	2,621.9
1983	168,565	71,444	2,359.4
1984	164,517	70,042	2,348.8

Source: See table B-24.

Table B-26. Uruguay: Exports of Frozen Beef, Brazil and Egypt, 1970–84

Year	Brazil	Egypt
1970	2,397	3,887
1971	7,850	3,546
1972	1,002	2,986
1973	—	1,000
1974	48,567	—
1975	23,658	5,416
1976	20,438	29,162
1977	26,380	24,507
1978	52,979	11,416
1979	34,470	3,567
1980	57,004	9,143
1981	62,541	32,971
1982	17,045	28,246
1983	19,543	60,393
1984	23,868	12,064

— Not available.

Source: Banco Central del Uruguay, unpublished data.

Table B-27. Uruguay: Oil Imports, 1961–86
(1961 = 100)

Year	Price	Quantity
1961	100.00	100.0
1962	95.92	121.1
1963	90.71	108.1
1964	92.84	112.9
1965	93.38	103.1
1966	87.21	160.8
1967	86.03	132.3
1968	84.63	119.2
1969	85.99	108.3
1970	85.32	150.9
1971	101.30	146.6
1972	111.18	134.0
1973	142.31	149.5
1974	433.66	153.2
1975	479.12	162.4
1976	491.82	154.6
1977	540.37	163.4
1978	521.69	183.1
1979	767.51	142.5
1980	1,204.27	165.6
1981	1,369.23	155.2
1982	1,331.51	148.1
1983	1,147.56	108.0
1984	1,116.63	110.5
1985	1,119.49	94.7
1986	548.50	118.4

Source: Cámara Nacional de Comercio, Banco Central del Uruguay, and ANCAP, unpublished data.

Table B-28. Uruguay: Balance of Payments, Selected Years, 1950–84
(millions of dollars)

Year	Trade	Other items, current account	Private sector capital movements Registered	Non-registered	Public sector capital movements	Monetary authority
1950	69.7	–23.1	–108.4	19.6	44.1	1.9
1960	–58.5	–15.9	20.6	11.4	14.5	–27.9
1970	21.0	–66.1	32.1	–26.0	12.7	–26.3
1980	–592.3	–99.7	572.9	94.5	178.0	153.4
1984	192.3	–321.5	176.9	–134.2	41.4	–45.1

Source: Banco Central del Uruguay, *Boletín Estadístico*, various issues.

Table B-29. Uruguay: External Debt: Liabilities with Nonresidents,
End of Year, 1955–84
(millions of dollars)

Year	Private	Public	Total
1955	62.1	119.0	181.1
1956	40.9	117.9	158.8
1957	33.6	160.3	193.9
1958	46.8	174.1	220.9
1959	44.2	211.3	255.5
1960	46.5	240.2	286.7
1961	88.7	217.5	306.2
1962	132.0	301.1	433.1
1963	123.6	288.4	412.0
1964	167.9	303.9	471.8
1965	213.5	267.3	480.8
1966	149.8	330.4	480.2
1967	158.8	292.1	450.9
1968	167.2	310.3	477.5
1969	205.9	325.9	531.8
1970	191.5	373.0	564.5
1971	221.7	452.5	674.2
1972	231.3	539.9	771.2
1973	180.4	537.5	717.9
1974	217.6	737.5	955.1
1975	170.7	860.5	1,031.2
1976	173.1	961.8	1,134.9
1977	292.1	1,027.9	1,320.0
1978	329.8	909.7	1,239.5
1979	670.5	1,011.9	1,682.4
1980	973.6	1,179.1	2,152.7
1981	1,664.7	1,464.6	3,129.3
1982	1,550.2	2,705.1	4,255.3
1983	1,391.9	3,197.5	4,589.4
1984	1,507.7	3,180.4	4,688.1

Source: See table B-24.

Table B-30. Uruguay: Consumer Prices, 1950–84

Year	Index (1968 = 100)
1950	0.8
1951	0.9
1952	1.0
1953	1.1
1954	1.2
1955	1.3
1956	1.4
1957	1.6
1958	1.9
1959	2.6
1960	3.7
1961	4.5
1962	5.0
1963	6.1
1964	8.6
1965	13.5
1966	23.4
1967	44.4
1968	100.0
1969	120.9
1970	140.7
1971	174.4
1972	307.8
1973	606.3
1974	1,074.2
1975	1,948.6
1976	2,935.1
1977	4,643.1
1978	6,711.5
1979	11,197.0
1980	18,305.5
1981	24,529.2
1982	29,190.0
1983	43,551.4
1984	67,635.3

Source: Uruguay, Dirección General de Estadísticas y Censos, Indice de los Precios de Consumo, various years.

Table B-31. Uruguay: GDP Deflator, 1955–84

Year	Index (1968 = 100)
1955	1.3
1956	1.4
1957	1.7
1958	2.0
1959	2.8
1960	4.0
1961	4.7
1962	5.4
1963	6.4
1964	9.1
1965	14.8
1966	25.4
1967	46.5
1968	100.0
1969	127.1
1970	144.1
1971	175.8
1972	285.0
1973	618.5
1974	1,091.7
1975	1,813.3
1976	2,667.4
1977	4,163.8
1978	6,053.3
1979	10,802.0
1980	16,278.7
1981	21,259.9
1982	24,810.3
1983	38,158.3
1984	61,053.3

Source: Banco Central del Uruguay, *Cuentas Nacionales*, various issues.

Table B-32. Uruguay: Exchange Rate, 1950–84
(new pesos/dollar, annual average)

Year	Official	Free-market
1950	0.00190	—
1951	0.00190	—
1952	0.00190	—
1953	0.00190	—
1954	0.00190	—
1955	0.00196	0.00343
1956	0.00233	0.00405
1957	0.00303	0.00415
1958	0.00301	0.00735
1959	0.00358	0.01021
1960	0.01130	0.01133
1961	0.01101	0.01104
1962	0.01093	0.01108
1963	0.01430	0.01543
1964	0.01664	0.02135
1965	0.03076	0.05435
1966	0.06449	0.06849
1967	0.10578	0.12837
1968	0.23385	0.23748
1969	0.25000	0.25500
1970	0.25000	—
1971	0.25000	—
1972	0.53600	0.86090
1973	0.86600	0.89600
1974	1.19600	1.62200
1975	2.26000	2.66000
1976	3.34000	3.69000
1977	4.67000	4.73000
1978	6.06000	6.09000
1979	7.86000	7.85000
1980	9.10000	9.09000
1981	10.81000	10.80000
1982	13.93000	13.93000
1983	34.55000	34.55000
1984	56.11000	56.11000

— Not available.
Source: Banco Central del Uruguay, *Boletín Estadístico*, various issues.

Table B-33. Uruguay: Wages, 1957–84
(1968 = 100)

Year	Agricultural sector	Industrial sector	Minimum wage	Government
1957	—	1.7	—	—
1958	—	2.3	—	—
1959	—	3.1	—	—
1960	—	4.1	—	—
1961	—	4.9	—	5.3
1962	—	5.7	—	6.4
1963	—	6.7	—	7.5
1964	—	9.1	—	10.6
1965	11.2	13.6	—	16.7
1966	24.2	26.2	—	24.7
1967	40.9	46.7	—	53.4
1968	100.0	100.0	100.0	100.0
1969	129.1	129.1	128.9	134.9
1970	156.2	152.7	152.2	152.7
1971	206.9	182.4	241.6	200.5
1972	296.8	270.8	380.5	284.2
1973	546.4	515.4	775.6	560.4
1974	1,046.3	906.3	1,393.3	967.5
1975	1,860.5	1,492.1	2,417.8	1,601.0
1976	2,578.9	2,030.6	3,354.3	2,322.5
1977	3,630.2	2,758.5	4,567.7	3,265.2
1978	6,305.0	4,579.3	6,625.4	4,585.2
1979	9,666.3	7,166.1	10,203.7	7,083.3
1980	15,094.9	12,789.8	15,920.2	12,370.6
1981	20,076.8	18,787.3	24,056.0	17,655.6
1982	23,351.3	22,131.7	26,564.5	20,942.8
1983	28,652.0	26,559.3	—	24,492.4
1984	44,814.8	39,177.5	52,858.3	33,146.4

— Not available.

Source: Based on data from Uruguay, Dirección General de Estadísticas y Censos, Banco Central del Uruguay, and Instituto de Economía.

Table B-34. Uruguay: Relative Prices, 1955–84
(1961 = 100)

Year	Real exchange rate[a]	Real wages[b] Industrial sector	Public sector	GDP deflators[c] Agriculture/ industry	Housing/ total
1955	54.6	—	—	105.4	241.0
1956	62.0	—	—	100.8	237.0
1957	72.2	98.6	—	113.8	214.6
1958	63.0	109.7	—	92.2	207.5
1959	54.1	108.0	—	109.0	152.0
1960	121.3	99.9	—	147.8	108.6
1961	100.0	100.0	100.0	100.0	100.0
1962	92.0	103.2	109.2	111.7	100.3
1963	99.5	100.3	105.9	91.9	95.1
1964	82.0	96.5	106.0	109.0	75.2
1965	98.9	91.4	105.7	97.8	61.0
1966	122.9	102.0	90.5	99.5	49.4
1967	109.5	95.7	103.0	76.8	55.2
1968	107.1	91.0	89.6	91.1	58.2
1969	104.3	97.1	105.0	90.8	78.5
1970	90.9	98.7	87.2	87.6	89.5
1971	76.5	95.2	98.5	82.4	97.1
1972	95.9	80.1	79.1	131.9	77.0
1973	83.7	77.3	79.2	125.7	51.2
1974	72.3	76.8	77.1	98.4	50.7
1975	82.3	69.7	70.4	69.3	82.1
1976	85.4	63.0	67.8	64.7	96.3
1977	80.4	54.1	60.2	77.6	104.6
1978	77.7	59.4	58.5	76.6	134.1
1979	67.2	58.2	54.2	79.6	118.5
1980	54.0	63.6	57.9	81.5	146.1
1981	52.9	69.7	61.6	70.7	195.4
1982	60.6	69.0	61.5	69.7	234.4
1983	104.1	55.5	48.2	82.4	186.0
1984	113.6	52.7	41.9	92.4	142.7

— Not available.
a. In terms of consumer prices; inflation in the United States was discounted.
b. In terms of consumer prices.
c. GDP agriculture prices compared with GDP industrial prices and GDP housing prices compared with GDP deflator.

Table B-35. Uruguay: Distribution of Industrial Wages, 1968, 1978, and 1981
(1961 new pesos)

Wages	1968	1978	1981
Blue-collar			
Wages (per hour)	0.0047	0.0029	0.0036
Coefficient of variation	30.59	15.48	20.60
White-collar			
Wages (per month)	1.38	0.75	1.44
Coefficient of variation	36.99	35.30	19.10

Source: Instituto de Economía, Universidad de la República, 1982.

Table B-36. Uruguay: Household Income Distribution: Earned Income, Montevideo, 1968, 1976, and 1979

Percent of households	1968		1976		1979	
	Simple	Acum.	Simple	Acum.	Simple	Acum.
10	2.13	2.13	2.00	2.00	1.61	1.61
20	3.97	6.10	3.52	5.52	2.94	4.55
30	5.10	11.20	4.68	10.20	3.85	8.40
40	6.21	17.41	5.63	15.83	4.75	13.15
50	7.38	24.95	6.83	22.66	5.76	18.91
60	8.74	33.53	8.23	30.89	6.96	25.87
70	10.40	43.93	10.01	40.90	8.49	34.36
80	12.64	56.57	12.48	53.38	10.63	44.99
90	16.08	72.65	16.45	69.83	14.21	59.20
95	10.39	83.04	11.03	80.86	9.74	68.94
100	16.96	100.00	19.24	100.00	31.06	100.00
Gini index		0.3688		0.4054		0.4907
Average income (new pesos of February–June 1973)		115.8		126.5		135.2

Source: Melgar 1982.

Table B-37.   Uruguay: Age and Income, 1972 and 1979
(14–19 years income = 100)

Age group (years)	1972	1979
14–19	100.0	100.0
20–24	158.2	155.2
25–29	195.2	238.2
30–34	208.7	232.5
35–39	249.9	267.0
40–44	251.2	256.8
45–49	224.5	229.4
50–54	218.6	251.0
55–60	253.2	229.9

Source: Indart 1981.

Table B-38.   Uruguay: Industrial Wages Compared with Minimum Wage, 1979
(percent)

Wage earned (minimum wage = 1)	Percentage of workers
Less than 1	2.1
1–2	25.4
2–3	27.0
3–4	16.2
4–5	9.4
5–7.5	9.1
7.5–10	3.7
10–15	3.5
15–20	1.4
20–25	0.9
25–50	1.0
More than 50	0.3

Source: Instituto de Economía, unpublished data.

Table B-39.   Uruguay: Government Wages Compared with Minimum Wage, 1983
(percent)

Wage earned (minimum wage = 1)	Percentage of workers
Less than 1	2.8
1–2	44.4
2.5–3	38.1
3–4	7.0
4–5	3.0
5–7.2	2.9
7.2–10.8	0.1

Source: Contaduría General de la Nación, unpublished data.

Table B-40. Uruguay: Capital Rate of Return, 1967–84

Year	Overall capital	Private capital
1967	4.73	5.90
1968	5.31	6.56
1969	5.74	7.01
1970	6.33	7.62
1971	5.93	7.32
1972	5.60	6.94
1973	6.63	8.20
1974	5.93	7.42
1975	5.92	7.36
1976	6.58	8.00
1977	6.38	7.83
1978	6.82	8.47
1979	7.93	9.99
1980	7.37	9.24
1981	6.96	8.89
1982	5.52	7.20
1983	5.64	7.67
1984	5.76	8.11

Source: Cámara Nacional de Comercio 1986, tables 1 and 2.

Table B-41. Uruguay: Size Distribution of Farms, Selected Years, 1951–80

Hectares	1951		1956		1961		1966		1970		1980	
	Number of farms	Thousands of hectares	Number of farms	Thousands of hectares	Number of farms	Thousands of hectares	Number of farms	Thousands of hectares	Number of farms	Thousands of hectares	Number of farms	Thousands of hectares
1–9	22,070	106	25,037	118	25,797	122	23,453	133	22,982	110	18,176	89
10–49	30,681	728	31,594	742	29,747	693	26,411	607	25,330	580	21,326	497
50–99	10,375	732	10,345	731	9,490	674	8,299	585	7,927	559	7,433	530
100–199	7,814	1,103	7,864	1,104	7,387	1,042	6,880	969	6,603	931	6,958	992
200–499	7,241	2,272	7,157	2,236	6,986	2,174	6,808	2,148	6,734	2,133	6,782	2,166
500–999	3,475	2,444	3,528	2,478	3,712	2,609	3,476	2,459	3,626	2,564	3,792	2,682
1,000–2,499	2,452	3,810	1,332	3,794	2,587	3,994	2,654	4,124	2,784	4,305	2,810	4,332
2,500–4,999	763	2,584	807	2,700	891	3,043	898	3,049	869	2,963	930	2,800
5,000–9,999	316	2,065	287	1,892	280	1,857	260	1,717	253	1,641	217	1,421
10,000 and more	71	1,130	68	965	51	780	54	763	55	732	38	519
Total	85,258	16,974	88,019	16,760	86,928	16,988	79,193	16,534	77,163	16,518	68,362	16,027
Gini index		0.8249		0.8287		0.8326		0.8326		0.8239		0.8073

Source: Instituto de Estadísticas, Censo General Agropecuario del Ministerio de Agricultura y Estadísticas Básicas del Sector Agropecuario.

Table B-42. Uruguay: Land Distribution, by Form of Ownership, Selected Years, 1951–80

Form of ownership	1951		1956		1961		1966		1970		1980	
	Number of farms	Thousands of hectares	Number of farms	Thousands of hectares	Number of farms	Thousands of hectares	Number of farms	Thousands of hectares	Number of farms	Thousands of hectares	Number of farms	Thousands of hectares
Owner	42,840	6,837	43,557	7,044	43,340	7,564	43,656	8,199	45,205	8,700	40,375	8,509
Tenant	30,309	5,692	32,716	5,593	29,303	4,955	22,323	3,910	17,668	3,148	12,077	2,041
Owner/tenant	8,997	4,305	7,315	3,618	7,381	3,925	6,977	3,754	7,395	3,887	7,703	1,735
Other	3,112	140	5,541	505	6,894	544	6,237	671	6,895	782	8,207	3,739
Total	85,258	16,974	89,130	16,760	86,918	16,988	79,193	16,534	77,163	16,517	68,362	16,024

Source: See table B-41.

Table B-43. Uruguay: Industrial Firms, by Number of Workers, 1960, 1968, and 1978

Year and characteristic	Number of workers in firm							Total
	1–4	5–9	10–19	20–49	50–99	100–499	500 and more	
1960								
Firms	21,418	2,501	1,247	755	239	180	26	26,366
Workers	33,569	16,526	16,744	22,370	16,262	34,708	29,040	169,219
1968								
Firms	27,844	—	573	495	210	—	208	29,330
Workers	69,450	—	8,098	15,273	14,594	—	61,208	168,623
Value of production (thousands of new pesos)	43,021	—	10,216	23,831	25,670	—	103,567	206,305
1978								
Firms	6,326	1,867	1,155	741	350	272	39	10,750
Workers	5,331	7,896	11,326	17,555	19,936	44,627	28,728	135,399
Value of production (thousands of new pesos)	778,643	981,246	1,412,495	2,579,603	2,860,550	7,628,940	6,081,641	22,323,118

— Not available.
Source: Uruguay, Dirección General de Estadísticas y Censos, Censo Económico Nacional, 1968, 1979.

345

Table B-44. *Uruguay: Number of Students, by Level of Education, 1967, 1975, and 1984*

Type of school and location	1967		1975		1984	
	Public	Private	Public	Private	Public	Private
Total	430,577	86,519	487,569	99,745	614,303	89,643
Preprimary	—	—	27,477	12,762	41,073	13,381
Montevideo	—	—	12,152	9,346	17,744	8,968
Provinces	—	—	15,325	3,416	23,329	4,413
Primary	280,051	70,283	267,153	55,449	311,580	50,292
Montevideo	94,784	46,821	82,060	37,543	112,343	32,582
Provinces	185,267	23,462	185,093	17,906	199,237	17,710
Specialized and adult	—	—	6,092	—	5,511	—
Montevideo	—	—	1,976	—	—	—
Provinces	—	—	4,116	—	—	—

Secondary	92,593	16,236	112,463	31,389	126,329	2,597
Montevideo	48,984	12,070	48,987	25,429	58,485	2,089
Provinces	43,609	4,166	63,476	5,960	67,843	5,079
Polytechnic	31,415	—	37,553	145	55,608	—
Montevideo	17,452	—	20,133	—	27,246	—
Provinces	13,963	—	17,420	145	28,362	—
Teacher training	7,868	—	4,204	—	10,099	—
Montevideo	2,245	—	1,531	—	4,102	—
Provinces	5,623	—	2,673	—	5,997	—
University	18,650	—	32,627	—	64,104	—
Montevideo	18,650	—	—	—	—	—
Provinces	—	—	—	—	—	—

— Not available.

Source: Uruguay, Dirección General de Estadísticas y Censos, *Anuario Estadístico*, various years, and *Censo Nacional de Población y Vivienda*, various years.

Table B-45. *Uruguay: Number of Schools, by Level of Education, 1967, 1975, and 1984*

Type of school and location	1967		1975		1984	
	Public	Private	Public	Private	Public	Private
Total	2,169	452	2,723	614	3,101	597
Preprimary	—	—	538	231	651	239
Montevideo	—	—	203	136	215	130
Provinces	—	—	335	95	436	109
Primary[a]	1,971	347	2,053	255	2,079	242
Montevideo	197	213	202	146	212	130
Provinces	1,774	134	1,851	109	1,867	112
Specialized and adult	—	—	—	—	104	—
Montevideo	—	—	—	—	—	—
Provinces	—	—	—	—	—	—

Secondary	104	105	132	128	152	116
Montevideo	26	42	43	88	38	77
Provinces	78	63	99	40	114	39
Polytechnic	74	—	—	—	93	—
Montevideo	14	—	—	—	22	—
Provinces	60	—	—	—	71	—
Teacher training	20	—	—	—	22	—
Montevideo	1	—	—	—	1	—
Provinces	19	—	—	—	21	—
University	—	—	—	—	—	—
Montevideo	—	—	—	—	—	—
Provinces	—	—	—	—	—	—

— Not available.

a. For 1967, includes adult and preprimary schools.

Source: Uruguay, Dirección General de Estadísticas y Censos, *Anuario Estadístico,* various years.

Table B-46. Uruguay: Dwellings in Montevideo, by Type of Occupation and Income Level

Income (unidades reajustables)	Number of dwellings	Owners	Tenants and others
0–19	16.7	5.8	10.9
20–29	32.2	11.9	20.3
30–39	40.0	22.0	18.0
40–49	41.2	17.5	23.7
50–74	92.5	53.7	38.8
75–99	62.7	42.9	20.7
100–124	41.6	29.1	20.7
125–250	66.8	41.4	25.4
More than 250	13.7	8.8	4.9

Source: Banco Hipotecario del Uruguay, unpublished data.

Table B-47. Uruguay: Labor Force and Social Security Beneficiaries, Selected Years, 1964–83
(thousands of persons)

Year	Labor force	Labor force covered by benefits		
		Retirees	Illness insurance	Child allowance
1964	977.7	342.2	52.0	284.1
1970	1,047.3	457.8	72.0	334.3
1975	1,110.5	527.7	87.1	335.4
1980	1,182.6	620.4	252.2	484.7
1983	1,242.9	683.4	247.1	454.2

Source: Vieytes 1984, pp. 178, 182, 222, and 228.

Table B-48. Uruguay: Central Government Revenues and Expenditures as a Share of GDP, 1961–84
(percent)

Year	Revenues	Expenditures
1961	15.6	16.6
1962	14.4	18.2
1963	14.4	17.3
1964	14.0	16.1
1965	10.6	15.7
1966	12.5	13.8
1967	10.9	14.1
1968	13.0	13.2
1969	12.2	14.7
1970	13.5	15.2
1971	14.0	18.7
1972	13.6	16.1
1973	14.5	15.9
1974	12.9	17.4
1975	12.1	16.5
1976	13.6	16.2
1977	14.8	26.0
1978	14.1	15.4
1979	14.6	14.4
1980	16.1	16.1
1981	17.4	17.5
1982	15.2	13.0
1983	15.6	19.6
1984	13.5	18.8

Source: Banco Central del Uruguay, *Boletín Estadístico*, various issues.

Table B-49. *Uruguay: Central Government Revenues, by Source, 1955–67*

Source	1955	1956	1957	1958	1959	1960	1961	1962	1963	1964	1965	1966	1967
Direct taxes	12.8	14.6	15.3	17.1	16.2	13.6	11.1	10.1	8.6	8.1	7.6	7.1	8.4
On incomes	3.1	2.9	3.0	3.4	5.3	4.9	4.4	4.0	2.6	2.4	2.6	3.9	3.2
On capital	9.7	11.7	12.3	12.6	10.9	8.7	6.7	6.1	6.0	5.7	5.0	3.2	5.2
Indirect taxes	41.3	38.7	37.1	36.9	36.4	33.0	33.7	29.9	27.1	31.5	37.1	37.9	37.9
Taxes on external trade	14.1	14.5	11.2	5.7	5.5	17.4	17.2	13.1	14.6	13.7	10.8	16.1	13.3
Taxes on wages	31.8	32.2	36.4	40.3	41.9	36.0	38.0	46.9	49.7	46.7	44.5	38.9	40.4
Total	100.0	100.0	100.0	100.0	100.0	100.0	100.0	100.0	100.0	100.0	100.0	100.0	100.0

Source: Based on Banco de la República Oriental del Uruguay and Banco Central del Uruguay, *Cuentas Nacionales*, 1965, 1968, tables 27 and 3.A.2.

Table B-50. *Uruguay: Revenues of the Central Government and Municipalities, by Source, 1968–84*
(percent)

Tax	1968	1969	1970	1971	1972	1973	1974	1975	1976	1977	1978	1979	1980	1981	1982	1983	1984
Direct taxes	6.7	8.1	—	10.6	13.3	13.8	13.5	14.0	15.4	15.9	16.5	16.3	18.6	17.9	17.7	17.6	13.1
On incomes	2.9	3.1	—	4.0	4.9	6.1	6.1	5.9	6.5	6.9	7.5	7.7	10.6	8.4	7.2	7.6	5.2
On capital	3.8	5.0	—	6.6	8.4	7.7	7.4	8.1	8.9	9.0	9.9	8.6	8.0	9.5	10.5	10.1	7.9
Indirect taxes	37.2	39.2	—	42.0	38.8	42.2	46.9	50.3	46.6	47.7	47.1	44.1	46.5	48.7	47.7	44.6	49.6
Taxes on internal trade	19.2	13.6	—	8.0	10.1	12.4	9.0	6.4	8.2	9.5	8.1	13.0	13.6	11.7	9.5	11.1	10.5
Taxes on wages	36.9	39.1	—	39.4	37.8	31.6	30.6	29.3	29.8	27.0	28.3	26.6	21.3	21.7	25.1	26.7	26.8
Total	100.0	100.0	—	100.0	100.0	100.0	100.0	100.0	100.0	100.0	100.0	100.0	100.0	100.0	100.0	100.0	100.0

— Not available.
Source: Uruguay, Oficina de Planeamiento y Presupuesto, various years; for 1968–71, authors' estimates based on the same source.

Table B-51. *Uruguay: Central Government Consumption Expenditure, by Activity, 1955–61*
(percentage of total)

Activity	1955	1956	1957	1958	1959	1960	1961
General services	4.8	46.3	47.8	46.2	45.3	48.4	44.6
General administration		8.0	8.0	8.4	7.1	9.0	9.0
Defense	4.0	15.0	15.8	14.7	15.7	17.7	15.1
Justice		3.9	3.8	3.9	3.6	3.2	3.4
Internal security	1.6	11.3	12.0	12.0	11.9	12.1	10.3
Economic and financial regulation	8.9	8.1	8.2	7.2	7.0	6.4	6.8
Social services	45.3	46.3	45.5	47.3	48.2	45.6	48.2
Education	26.7	27.3	27.4	29.3	29.9	26.6	30.4
Public health	16.6	17.1	16.2	16.3	16.7	17.3	16.3
Social security	1.9	1.8	1.8	1.6	1.5	1.6	1.4
Housing and urbanization	0.1	0.1	0.1	0.1	0.1	0.1	0.1
Economic services	6.6	7.3	6.6	6.4	6.4	5.9	7.0
Agriculture and fishery	2.9	2.9	2.6	2.6	2.6	2.3	2.5
Mining	0.1	0.4	0.2	0.1	0.2	0.5	0.1
Industry	0.7	1.2	0.9	0.9	0.9	0.8	0.8
Transport and storage	2.0	2.0	1.9	1.9	1.9	1.6	2.9
Communications	0.3	0.3	0.3	0.3	0.3	0.3	0.2
Commerce and other services	0.6	0.5	0.7	0.6	0.5	0.4	0.5
Financial services	0.1	0.1	0.1	0.1	0.1	0.1	0.1
Public debt	0.1	0.1	0.1	0.1	0.1	0.1	0.1
Total	100.0	100.0	100.0	100.0	100.0	100.0	100.0

Note: Excludes social security and decentralized offices.
Source: Banco Central del Uruguay, *Cuentas Nacionales,* 1965, p. B157.

Table B-52. Uruguay: Central Government Expenditure, by Function,
as a Percentage of Totals for 1964, 1966, and 1968

| Function | 1964 | | | |
	Consumption	Subsidies	Investment	Total
General services	47.3	15.5	1.6	34.7
General administration	11.6	6.3	—	9.2
Defense	13.0	—	—	8.3
Justice	3.7	—	—	2.3
Internal security	11.7	—	1.1	7.6
Economic regulation	7.3	9.2	0.5	7.3
Social services	46.9	36.1	13.1	41.2
Education	29.0	0.9	7.8	19.4
Public health	15.2	—	3.3	10.0
Environmental hygiene	—	3.6	—	1.0
Social security	2.7	20.9	2.0	7.7
Housing	—	10.7	—	3.1
Economic services	5.5	36.3	50.2	17.9
Agriculture and fishery	2.7	1.4	0.3	2.2
Mining				
Industry	0.6	—	—	0.4
Transport and storage	1.7	25.2	49.9	12.2
Communications	0.1	7.5	—	2.2
Commerce and other	0.4	2.2	—	0.9
Financial services	0.1	11.9	35.1	6.2
Public debt	0.1	11.9	35.1	6.2
Total	99.8	99.8	100.0	100.0

| Function | 1966 | | | |
	Consumption	Subsidies	Investment	Total
General services	43.6	30.3	4.2	36.9
General administration	10.9	4.6	0.8	8.4
Defense	14.8	0.1	2.5	9.7
Justice	3.0	—	—	1.9
Internal security	9.7	—	0.7	6.3
Economic regulation	5.2	25.6	0.2	10.6
Social services	51.1	24.2	23.7	41.5
Education	34.9	0.8	17.3	23.9
Public health	14.1	3.6	5.3	9.8
Environmental hygiene	—	0.5	0.2	1.0
Social security	2.1	19.3	0.9	6.8
Housing	—	—	—	—

(Table continues on the following page.)

Table B-52 (continued)

Function	1966			
	Consumption	Subsidies	Investment	Total
Economic services	5.2	35.8	34.8	16.1
Agriculture and fishery	2.6	2.9	0.8	2.6
Mining	—	—	—	—
Industry	0.8	—	—	0.5
Transport and storage	1.4	25.6	33.7	10.7
Communications	—	6.0	0.2	1.8
Commerce and other	0.4	1.1	0.1	0.5
Financial services	0.0	9.7	37.2	6.2
Public debt	—	9.7	37.2	6.2
Total	99.9	100.0	99.9	100.7

Function	1968			
	Consumption	Subsidies	Investment	Total
General services	44.6	26.2	11.8	36.5
General administration	12.0	26.2	5.3	13.6
Defense	14.2	—	1.8	9.8
Justice	2.3	—	2.7	2.0
Internal security	12.4	—	1.1	8.5
Economic regulation	3.7	—	0.9	2.6
Social services	49.6	28.8	32.1	43.2
Education	35.5	0.8	24.0	27.4
Public health	12.3	0.1	6.7	9.3
Environmental hygiene	—	2.3	0.1	0.4
Social security	1.8	24.1	1.2	5.8
Housing	—	1.5	0.1	0.3
Economic services	5.7	32.3	37.8	15.3
Agriculture and fishery	3.3	7.6	3.4	4.1
Mining	0.1	—	—	0.1
Industry	0.4	0.3	—	0.3
Transport and storage	1.7	17.9	34.0	9.4
Communications	—	6.5	—	1.2
Commerce and other	0.2	—	0.4	0.2
Financial services	0.4	12.7	18.2	5.0
Public debt	0.4	12.7	18.2	5.0
Total	100.3	100.0	99.9	100.0

— Not available.

Source: Banco Central del Uruguay, Cuentas Nacionales, 1968.

Table B-53. *Uruguay: Sectoral Classification of Budgetary Programs, 1974–82*
(percent)

Sector		1974	1975	1976	1977	1978	1979	1980	1981	1982
Resources										
Human resources		36.99	39.67	39.81	42.18	40.29	—	—	—	—
1.1.1. Culture and education	(01)	15.98	17.29	15.71	16.28	16.12	16.07	14.84	14.77	10.98
1.1.2. Health	(02)	8.28	7.44	7.17	6.84	6.64	7.57	6.04	6.53	4.51
1.1.3. Labor and social security	(03)	12.39	14.57	16.53	18.32	17.46	17.57	24.98	25.67	28.95
1.1.4. Housing	(04)	0.34	0.37	0.40	0.74	0.07	0.04	0.03	0.06	0.05
Subtotal 1.1		—	—	—	—	—	41.25	45.89	47.03	44.49
Natural resources	(05)	0.56	0.65	0.46	0.91	1.64	1.27	1.27	1.39	0.84
Total		37.55	40.32	40.27	43.09	41.93	42.52	95.58	93.75	45.33
Infrastructure										
Transport and communications		10.96	4.12	9.23	10.90	10.56	—	—	—	—
2.1.1. Transport	(06)	9.89	3.26	8.47	10.14	9.80	9.18	5.24	7.21	5.94
2.2.2. Communications	(07)	1.07	0.86	0.76	0.76	0.76	0.93	2.29	0.75	0.65
Subtotal 2.1		—	—	—	—	—	10.11	7.53	7.96	6.59
2.2.1. Energy	(08)	0.02	0.02	—	0.02	0.04	0.02	1.00	0.03	0.02
Sewerage	(09)	—	0.07	—	0.03	—	0.01	—	—	0.17
Urban development	(10)	0.82	0.28	0.50	0.23	0.26	0.18	—	—	—
Total		11.80	4.49	9.73	11.18	10.86	10.32	8.53	7.99	6.78

(Table continues on the following page.)

Figure B-53 (continued)

Sector		1974	1975	1976	1977	1978	1979	1980	1981	1982
Production										
Agriculture	(11)	1.49	1.98	1.65	1.69	1.52	1.88	1.70	1.67	1.09
Industry	(12)	0.27	0.23	0.13	0.13	0.14	0.11	0.43	0.11	0.07
Services										
3.3.1. Commerce and other services	(13)	3.01	1.20	0.45	0.26	0.08	0.08	0.07	0.10	0.10
3.3.2. Tourism	(14)	0.13	0.14	0.10	0.08	0.05	0.10	0.09	0.09	0.04
Subtotal 3.3		—	—	—	—	—	0.18	0.16	0.19	0.14
Other rebate certificates		6.19	6.75	11.28	—	—	—	—	—	—
Total		11.18	10.30	13.61	2.16	1.79	2.17	2.29	1.97	1.30
General services										
Legislation	(38)	1.03	0.84	0.60	0.59	0.53	0.45	0.38	0.38	0.27
General administration	(31)	6.93	5.42	4.70	5.02	5.44	5.79	4.74	5.00	3.98
Financial administration	(32)	2.78	3.38	2.58	10.77	11.13	9.10	8.09	4.57	5.48
Defense and police		22.11	26.50	20.55	20.99	21.87	—	—	—	—
4.4.1. Defense	(34)	14.39	15.45	12.10	12.94	14.06	16.56	14.43	16.06	10.82
4.4.2. Internal security	(35)	7.72	11.05	8.45	8.05	7.81	7.51	7.68	7.98	6.04
Subtotal 4.4		22.11	26.50	20.55	20.99	21.87	24.07	22.11	24.04	16.86
Justice										
4.5.1. Justice	(36)	2.04	2.59	1.83	1.83	1.81	1.28	1.21	1.20	0.92
4.5.2. Electoral justice	(37)	1.54	2.05	1.36	1.36	1.36	0.41	1.01	0.34	0.25
Subtotal 4.5		—	—	—	—	—	1.69	2.22	1.54	1.17

	Code									
Foreign affairs	(33)	0.94	1.02	1.11	0.98	1.03	1.39	1.28	1.17	0.85
Total		35.83	39.75	31.37	40.18	41.81	42.49	38.82	36.70	28.61
Financial services										
Banking and insurance		—	—	—	0.01	—	—	—	—	—
5.1.1. Banking	(51)	—	—	—	—	—	—	—	2.25	1.09
5.1.2. Insurance	(52)	—	—	—	0.01	—	—	—	—	—
Subtotal 5.1		—	—	—	—	—	—	—	2.25	1.09
Management of public debt	(53)	3.14	4.40	5.02	3.38	3.61	2.50	3.20	2.67	16.89
Total		3.14	4.40	5.02	3.39	3.61	2.50	3.20	4.92	17.98
Nonsectoral expenditures	(99)	0.50	0.74	—	—	—	—	—	—	—
Total		0.50	0.74	—	—	—	—	—	—	—
Grand total		100.00	100.00	100.00	100.00	100.00	100.00	100.00	100.00	100.00

— Not available.
Source: Elaborated with data from Contaduría General de la Nación.

Table B-54. Uruguay: Total Public Expenditure, by Function, Selected
Years, 1972–83
(percentage of GDP)

Year	Defense	Education	Health	Social security	Other	Total
1972	1.4	2.3	0.4	12.8	7.7	24.6
1975	2.7	2.6	0.9	10.4	6.4	23.0
1980	2.9	1.9	1.1	10.6	5.3	21.8
1983	2.8	1.6	0.8	13.0	6.7	24.9

Source: Based on International Monetary Fund 1980, 1983, table 5-7.

Table B-55. Uruguay: Social Security Expenditure, Selected Years, 1964–83
(percentage of GDP)

Year	Retirees	Compensation per child	Illness insurance	Unemployment insurance	Total
1964	9.3	0.6	0.1	0.4	10.3
1970	8.5	1.5	0.2	0.3	10.5
1975	7.5	0.6	0.2	0.2	8.5
1980	8.0	0.7	0.4	0.1	9.2
1983	10.7	0.6	0.5	0.3	12.1

Source: Vieytes 1984, p. 230.

Table B-56. Uruguay: Social Security Revenues, Selected Years, 1964–83
(percent)

Year	Taxes	Subsidies from central government	Total
1964	91.6	8.4	100
1970	93.4	6.6	100
1975	73.3	26.7	100
1980	64.8	35.2	100
1983	54.3	45.7	100

Source: Vieytes 1984, p. 234.

Table B-57. Uruguay: Rediscounts, 1955–71
(millions of pesos)

Year	Rediscounts Banco de la República	Rediscounts Private banks	Total	Issue	Percent
1955	50	197	247	474	52
1956	50	252	302	536	56
1957	50	302	352	578	61
1958	40	460	500	732	68
1959	—	339	339	910	37
1960	70	379	449	1,240	36
1961	398	341	739	1,569	47
1962	144	442	586	1,791	33
1963	506	166	672	2,215	30
1964	1,414	279	1,693	3,062	55
1965	4,411	365	4,776	6,085	78
1966	6,176	1,644	7,820	9,286	84
1967	13,412	780	14,192	18,013	79
1968	23,127	664	23,791	31,390	76
1969	—	562	—	50,573	—
1970	38,530	1,910	40,440	56,959	71
1971	64,551	4,442	68,993	84,408	82

— Not available.
Source: Banco Central del Uruguay, *Boletín Estadístico,* various issues.

Table B-58. *Uruguay: Special Rediscount Lines (Maximum Authorized at Year's End), 1970–76*
(thousands of new pesos)

Item	1970	1971	1972	1973	1974	1975	1976
Wool	700	700	4,000	8,000	8,800	17,000	35,000
Raw materials	450	450	450	600	1,500	1,500	1,500
Nontraditional exports	—	500	500	2,000	4,500	10,500	15,500
Cattle	120	120	120	120	1,200	1,200	1,200
Trade	—	—	—	—	10,000	10,000	10,000
Sackcloth	—	200	270	—	1,600	2,500	—
Year-end needs	1,200	1,000	1,400	3,500	5,000	—	—
Cotton	15	0	0	30	100	300	—
Oleaginous seeds	150	400	600	2,000	4,500	6,000	—
Hides	—	—	—	420	3,500	—	—

— Not available.
Source: Banco Central del Uruguay, unpublished data.

Simon Rottenberg

III Costa Rica and Uruguay

A Comparison of Economic Experience and Policy in Costa Rica and Uruguay

In both Costa Rica and Uruguay the state has been active in designing and enforcing policies that have raised the share of manufacturing in national output and have effected income and wealth transfers among segments of the population. Those policies have produced rents for some and have generated rent-seeking behavior. Over the years rent recipients and the larger community have come to regard the rents as entitlements.

The policies have also generated economic waste and distortion. They have skewed the structure of yields in diverse economic activities, causing underinvestment in some activities and overinvestment in others, and have frustrated the pursuit of activities in which the countries have a comparative advantage.

The trade policies of both countries have nourished industries and firms that produce consumer goods almost wholly for their small domestic markets. Trade policy has affected the structure of input prices in ways that have encouraged capital intensity in production and have enlarged the volume of imports of raw materials and intermediate production goods.

In both countries state policies have led to transfers of income from those with earnings from rural activities to those in urban areas. The influence of the electoral system on the direction of this movement has been intensified by the concentration of the population in urban areas—primarily in San José in Costa Rica and in Montevideo in Uruguay.

The strategies for achieving income transfers have varied over time, but the two countries have applied a more or less common pattern of transfer policies. These include state social security, health, and education systems; massive proportional employment in the public sector; food subsidies; and policies regarding foreign exchange and commercial protection that have worked to the relative disadvantage of rural activities.

Both countries have undertaken a large number of parastatal ventures. The motives have included keeping alive private ventures that had failed market tests and were threatened with closure; providing improved terms of employment for workers of previously private firms after prolonged and acrimonious labor disputes; and displacing foreign direct investment, especially in public utilities and transport. Parastatals have also been established to undertake activities that private entrepreneurs have avoided but that government officials nevertheless saw as viable. Not infrequently, the parastatal enterprises are grossly overstaffed, and some suffer continuous losses and add to the public debt. When they have not suffered losses, it is sometimes because of the monopoly rights that they have been granted by the state.

Chapter 14 summarizes aspects of the economic experience of Costa Rica, and chapter 15 does the same for Uruguay. Chapter 16 deals with the similarities and differences in the experiences of the two countries and sums up the findings derived from the study.

14 *Costa Rica*

Costa Rica was initially settled in the sixteenth century by a handful of Spanish agricultural colonists. There were few native Americans, and their numbers were reduced greatly by epidemics shortly after the arrival of the Spaniards (Fernández Guardia 1913). An *hacienda* economy did not develop. The population grew slowly; in the early eighteenth century, a century and a half after the arrival of the Spaniards, a population of only 3,000 occupied a small area of the central plateau. Land was relatively abundant, and property rights were acquired by grants or by exercising squatters' rights.

For the first three centuries of its history, well past the achievement of independence in 1821, Costa Rica's characteristic economic unit was the farm family that cultivated its own land and produced for its own consumption. In general, there was no wage-labor employment, and income distribution was more or less equal. Material standards of living were low, and Costa Rica is said to have been an agrarian democracy in the sense that there was an equal distribution of poverty.

Coffee introduced revolutionary changes (Seligson 1980; Gudmundson 1985). Experimental attempts in the colonial period to find commercial agricultural crops had failed. Cacao, planted in the tropical lowlands of the Atlantic coastal region in the eighteenth century, fell prey to pirate and Indian attacks. Tobacco, which was in any case vulnerable because it was labor-intensive, did not survive the constraining mercantilist policies of the Spanish metropolitan authority. The colonial government brought coffee seeds from Jamaica in the early nineteenth century, but development of the crop awaited independence, and the first export shipments occurred only in the 1830s. From then until the 1950s output and exports rose steadily, and for those years the growth rate of the volume of coffee exports was extraordinarily high.

In the nineteenth and twentieth centuries road networks were constructed, a railroad to the Atlantic was built, ox cart transport was replaced by trucks, techniques for processing coffee beans were improved, coffee-processing plants decreased in number and increased in scale, and competitive bidding for the growers' crops was introduced. Coffee-growing land was traded in a land market, and small plots were consolidated into more efficient larger parcels. As both land prices and wages rose, self-employed smallholders sold their land and opted for more secure wage employment. The risks associated with crop prices and climate were transferred to their employers. Competition for labor in the coffee regions ensured that workers would share in the increased prosperity of the country's coffee economy.

Early shipments of coffee to Europe were transported to the Pacific coast and around Cape Horn because there was no passage to the Atlantic. The government contracted for the construction of a railroad to the Atlantic, and the line was completed, after a long delay, in the late nineteenth century. Construction of the railroad was capitalized in part by the grant to the builder of 800,000 acres of land on the Atlantic coast. To complement coffee cargo for the railroad and to put this land to use, banana production was undertaken and flourished. West Indian workers who had been brought in to work on the railroad took up wage employment on the banana plantations. Costa Ricans also entered the banana sector as producers and as wage laborers. Costa Ricans living on the central plateau could choose wage employment in bananas as an alternative to working in the coffee harvest or as self-employed subsistence farmers.

Plant diseases on the Atlantic coast caused banana production to be moved to the Pacific side. Later, when disease-resistant banana varieties were developed, production returned to the Atlantic coast.

Over the decades, the North American firm that overwhelmingly dominated banana production and exporting was accused of offensive behavior by trade unions led by the Costa Rican Communist party, by Costa Rican banana producers unhappy about the prices they received for their bananas, and by the government, which wanted a larger share of the company's earnings. There was, furthermore, a generalized community preference for ownership of the country's resources by Costa Ricans—even if these investments were capitalized by borrowing from foreigners—over direct foreign investment. The company has now virtually abandoned banana production and is engaged mainly in banana marketing.

Political Developments and the Economy

Until about 1940 power in Costa Rica was in the hands of the descendants of the forty original families who came from Spain in the mid-sixteenth century. These families were the officeholders; they received tracts of land under diverse land distribution policies, and they became the relatively large producers and processors of coffee. As mechanization in coffee processing progressed and the railroad to the Atlantic was built, coffee culture became less labor-intensive, and a migration from the countryside to the cities occurred. By the first third of the twentieth century, political power had begun to shift to urban residents.

The gestalt of the nineteenth century had favored state reticence. The new holders of power—merchants, professionals, urban workers, and, later, industrialists and especially public servants—had a different outlook. They favored an aggressively interventionist state that could serve as an agency for transferring to themselves income that originated in rural areas. In 1940 the new tendency was initiated with the enactment of a social security system, a code regulating the terms of employment and social guarantees. The activity of the state was intensified.

The ideological construct that had its genesis in the 1940s has had a powerful influence on the design of policy (Bell 1971). In 1942 Rodrigo Facio, an economist, attacked what he perceived to be the noxious effects of the coffee economy. Facio wrote that a monocultural coffee economy had introduced inequality and political contention and that within that economy, large producers, dispensers of credit, and an oligopoly of coffee processors were breaking the smallholding peasant yeomanry. He proposed that the state intervene with reformist policies designed to restore the homogeneity and egalitarianism that anteceded coffee. He also expressed a nationalist dispreference for foreign investors, especially in the banana zones on the tropical coast (Facio 1947). Facio had a powerful influence on the reformation of public and intellectual opinion in Costa Rica.

Over time the output of the Costa Rican economy has become more diversified. The share of coffee and bananas in agricultural output diminished as those of beef, sugar, and other crops rose. The share of agriculture in total output has also decreased as the population has become more urbanized. The relative rise in the size of the urban population generated a conflict of interest between the rural and the urban sectors concerning public policy. This conflict was settled in the late 1940s when a small-scale civil war was won by those who fundamentally espoused the cause of urban interests, even if their rhetoric contained overtures to the rural peasantry (Arias Sánchez 1971, p. 118).

Since then, policy has systematically tended to transfer income and wealth from the rural to the urban sector. The open and liberal ideology that instructed public policy in the nineteenth century has been displaced by a nationalist, autarkic, and protectionist doctrine. Since the 1940s its most apparent expressions have been a massive increase in public employment and in the share of the gross product of the economy expended by the government (from World Bank internal documents) and an extensive enlargement of government assertiveness in both production and regulatory activity. The effects have been adverse to economic output, and since Costa Rican experience has shown a correlation between economic growth and equality in the distribution of income, they have predictably been adverse to the achievement of equity.

Costa Rica has pursued protectionist import-substituting policies mainly through selective tariffs on imports. High duties have been imposed on consumer goods, largely through the tariff system of the Central American Common Market. The production of manufactured consumer goods has expanded substantially. These goods are sold largely within the country, partly because of persisting impediments to commodity flows among the countries within the regional common market. Prices for these goods are higher than prices for comparable commodities in the international market. The protectionist policies for domestically manufactured goods have been coupled with incentives for the importation of raw materials, intermediate goods, and capital equipment for manufacturing industries.

Costa Rican policy has tended to induce suboptimal capital intensity in manufacturing. The relative prices of capital and labor have been distorted by the exemption of raw materials, capital equipment, and intermediate industrial goods from the high tariffs imposed by the Common Market on consumer goods; by a tax regime that has selectively favored capital investment; by an exchange rate that for a long period benefited capital imports; by the selective rationing of credit even when interest rates were negative in real terms; and by minimum wage laws and payroll taxes for social security and other public sector purposes. This generated inefficient factor combinations and diminished output. Since labor was made relatively more costly, employment in manufacturing rose much less rapidly than manufacturing output.

The Public Sector

The expansion of state activities in the fields of health, education, nutrition, social security, and family allowances, in the construction of physical infrastructure, in the employment of large numbers of personnel, and in the operation of state enterprises has been financed by the expansion of the public debt. Costa Rica's per capita external public debt is one of the highest among all low-income countries.

The high price of coffee on the international market in the mid-1970s increased public sector receipts and induced a spending spree. Government policy responded to the enlarged revenue as though coffee prices would always remain high and stable. Later in the 1970s it became clear that the high prices were an aberration. The price of coffee fell, but political expectations did not permit contraction of state activity, and the inflated expenditures were financed by external borrowing.

Costa Rican governments have engaged heavily in parastatal ventures. The state owns enterprises engaged in public transport, oil refining and distribution, cement and fertilizer production, sugar refining, the marketing of agricultural exports, insurance, and banking. A public investment corporation is increasingly important in manufacturing investment. In 1980 the public sector accounted for one-quarter of national output and four-fifths of gross investment and received two-thirds of increments in domestic credit. The public sector is clearly very large.

Nationalized commercial banks hold four-fifths of the assets of the financial system. The state is therefore substantially able to control access to credit. During much of the period 1950–85 real interest rates have been negative, and the nationalized banks have often rationed credit according to political criteria.

A large proportion of employed people in Costa Rica works for the government and the state institutions. In 1950 about one in twenty of all employed people was a public sector employee; by 1980 the proportion had risen to one in five. Several factors combine to account for the large quantity of public employment: a proliferation of public sector activity, a policy of reducing unemployment (especially of people with professional training) through public sector employment, and the political resistance offered by unionized public employees to the shrinkage of public employment.

Landownership

As in Uruguay, many in Costa Rica believe that too much of the land is held by a few landowners; that there are too many holdings that are too small to permit efficient economies of scale (partly because of the practice of dividing a farm among all the heirs); and that there are deformities in the system of land tenure. In contrast to the situation in Uruguay, a large fraction of the country's population resides in rural areas, and the landlessness of many rural residents, who are regularly or occasionally employed in wage work, is seen as a problem that public policy should address. There is a conviction that the land market is not an efficient instrument for achieving efficient landholding sizes.

Squatting on land in the public domain or on privately owned property is not uncommon (Seligson 1980, ch. 5). Since colonial times it has been a legal method of acquiring prescriptive rights to land. The response on the part of public policy and civil justice has varied between evicting squatters and entitling them to the properties they occupy.

Agrarian reform policy has included colonization schemes and the establishment of communally owned properties. It has had some, but not a significant, effect in altering tenure systems and the structure of the size distribution of land.

Manufacturing and Diversification

Costa Rica's entry into the Central American Common Market in 1963 had the perverse effect of closing, rather than opening, the country's economy (Lizano and Sagot 1984). The common market raised high barriers to the region's trade in import-substituting goods with the rest of the world while it nominally opened trade within the region. Large increases in intraregional trade were frustrated by poverty and political disorder among the countries of the region and by members' use of policy strategies that impeded free trade even among themselves. The highly protective barriers of the regional system fostered the establishment and growth in Costa Rica of manufacturing firms that mainly produced consumer goods for the domestic market. These were, for the most part, high-cost firms that could not compete successfully in rest-of-the-world markets and would be unable to survive without protection.

Proprietors of physical and human assets specialized to manufacturing activities have formed coalitions that have achieved considerable influence over the design of public policy (Arias Sánchez 1971). They have been able to transform privileges generated by public policy into entitlements and to make permanent policies that were initially intended to be transitory. Real resources are consumed in the systemic entrenchment of protectionist policies and in "game-playing" for manufacturing incentives that are not uniform among industries.

The urge to diversify the economy and to lessen reliance on coffee and bananas took the form, in Costa Rica, of the subsidization not only of manufacturing but also of other agricultural crops. This was partly because a large part of the Costa Rican population consists of a smallholding peasantry. Grains, dairy, cotton, and fishing were promoted. Export constraints and price controls were imposed on beef and sugar to benefit domestic consumers; prices of those products were lower in domestic markets than in export markets. The controls had adverse effects on output in those parts of the agricultural sector.

15 Uruguay

Overall, since 1950 public economic policy in Uruguay has led to the stagnation of economic output without bringing about much improvement in the average material condition of life of the Uruguayan people.

Uruguay's resource endowment is a powerful explanatory variable for understanding its economic performance and policy. Its climate, soil, and topography give Uruguay a comparative advantage in the production of livestock. The country has almost no mineral resources, and when the Spaniards arrived, they found the area thinly populated by fierce native Americans who were not a sufficiently large or tractable labor force for an *hacienda* economy.

Cattle were introduced by the Spaniards in the early seventeenth century. From then until well after independence (gained in the early nineteenth century), much of the land area was public domain, and cattle, running wild, were hunted and slaughtered mainly for their hides.

Gradually, the land passed into private hands as large grants were made to early settlers and to favorites of the civil authorities. Tracts tended to be subdivided over time in a secondary land market, but large properties appropriate for raising livestock remain the dominant form of land tenure.

For generations much of the land was in the public domain but was put to private use. Land titles were insecure, the boundary lines defining the limits of property were uncertain, and properties were unfenced. The country was a quasi commons.

Later, a market developed for beef, in addition to hides. Jerked beef was produced by *saladeros* to feed Cuban and Brazilian slaves. When refrigerated shipping facilities became available, chilled and frozen beef was exported to Europe and North America. Sheep, raised mainly for their wool, began to complement cattle in ranching output in the mid-nineteenth century.

With time, land titles became more secure. Markets for beef and wool expanded, and technological improvements in steel production reduced the relative price of wire fencing. These developments raised the return on investments in fencing and in genetic improvement and made possible the introduction of technological advances in livestock production.

Until the beginning of the twentieth century authority in the countryside was exercised by *caudillos* who ruled by coercion and violence. Competition for power among the *caudillos* sometimes reached the dimensions of civil war. This often led to expropriation or destruction of the assets of the ranchers and discouraged rural investment.

Livestock production is not labor-intensive. The Uruguayan countryside has therefore always been thinly populated, with a large proportion of the population concentrated in Montevideo.[1] The fencing of ranching properties in the late nineteenth century reduced even further the need for rural labor and accentuated the concentration of the population.

In the early twentieth century changes were successfully made in the form of political expression. Violence was displaced by periodic elections and political campaigning for office. To secure consent for this transformation required various arrangements to permit the sharing of spoils.

The replacement of the decentralized authority of the *caudillos* by the central authority of the state implied a large role for the state. This tendency was first informed by the values of José Batlle y Ordoñez and was later accentuated by the ideological vision of the country's intellectual classes.

The principle that spoils should be shared implied that the state would become a generator of spoils. In diverse ways, the state produced rents and rationed their distribution. The principle also fragmented the structural organization of the state and induced the formation of narrow special-interest constituencies that competed for rents.

Urban concentration and the development of a class of professional politicians whose livelihoods and futures depended on winning votes combined to give the urban population an advantage in the competition to influence public policy. The result has been that for a long time income and wealth have been deliberately transferred from those engaged in rural production to those engaged in urban economic activities. This has been done largely through macroeconomic policies—monetary, commercial, and exchange rate policies, the subsidization of manufacturing and of food staples, the operation of parastatal enterprises, and unproductive public employment. The explicit and implicit taxation of rural ventures and the distribution of their revenues among urban residents have discouraged investment and technological progress in the countryside, produced stagnation in the livestock sector, fostered questionable urban economic activity, distorted prices and the allocation of resources, and diminished the aggregate output of the economy and the real income of the population.

Political Developments

In the colonial period the Spanish colonial administrations were able to exercise authority in and near the centers in which they sat, but they were not able to control the interior hinterlands. All of Uruguay was "interior" to the viceregal capital in Buenos Aires. "Rules" governing relationships in the interior were defined by a combination of informal consensus, informal contract, and the exercise of coercive power. The system was generally characterized by order, but competitive claims were frequently settled by violence.

This system survived into the period of Uruguayan independence. Authority was exercised by a set of local and regional *caudillos* whose authority was generally recognized by the populations of their respective localities and regions and who enforced their authority by means of violence. Coercion and private power were in part inputs into production and in part constraints that economic agents dealt with through strategies of adjustment and avoidance. Coercion and violence were instruments of competitive strategy. Coalitions of *caudillos* formed.

The exercise of decentralized private power had a great effect on economic performance in Uruguay because the countryside was a quasi commons. Ranching properties were unfenced, titles were not secure, and livestock strayed. Property rights were defined by possession, and the work force in rural areas had both to carry out productive activities and to defend cattle against thievery. Conflicting claims to property and other rights were frequent, and judicial authority for the settlement of claims did not extend effectively to the interior. Private property rights in what had been public domain put to private use were legally defined for the first time with the adoption of the Código Rural in the late 1870s.

Wire fencing of rural properties was introduced in the 1870s. Fencing encouraged ranchers to improve their stock by importing pedigreed animals and practicing selective breeding.

To remedy the occasionally disorderly and violent competition for power in the countryside, decentralized authority had to be replaced with centralized authority, and adversaries who had been in violent confrontation for generations had to be reconciled. This was done by establishing centralized political institutions that would permit the sharing of power and spoils among onetime adversaries.

The extension of the rail and communication systems in the late nineteenth century facilitated the centralization of authority. Those developments were made possible, in part, by technological advances in the making of steel that diminished its real price.

The State and Redistribution

Centralization implied an active state that would do much, employ many people, and have large expenditures. An enlarged role for the state implied the growth of a class that would be mainly devoted to political work. Power sharing within the government implied that employment in the public sector would be an instrument for transferring income to those who were politically active or who had the proper political connections.

Full-time professional politicians are vulnerable to constituent pressures for the adoption of policies that generate rents. They do not have other sources of support, and their primary sources of income depend on their achieving victory in elections. The state became an instrument for transferring income and wealth. Rent seeking and special-interest pressure groups developed.

As the state created transfers of income and wealth and opportunities for capturing rents, narrow segments of the population exploited those opportunities at the expense of society as a whole. Output of commodities and services was adversely affected, and real household income diminished. Resources were put to suboptimal use.

There is a high degree of urban concentration in the spatial distribution of population and of voters. Today, less than 10 percent of the economically active population works in rural activities—a much lower proportion than in most Latin American countries. Transfers of income and wealth have almost always been from the rural to the urban sector, mainly through low domestic beef prices, explicit income transfers such as payments to pensioners and others, and policies that relatively benefited those with physical and human capital specialized in urban activities such as manufacturing. The result has been underinvestment in rural activities—in which Uruguay has a comparative advantage—and overinvestment in urban activities.

The Livestock Sector

The control and reduction of the domestic price of beef is an important component of Uruguayan policy for the transfer of income from rural to urban areas. Beef has been important in Uruguayan consumption for a long time. A few hundred cattle and horses were introduced in the early seventeenth century and were permitted to run wild. By the end of the first quarter of the eighteenth century millions of cattle were roaming on unfenced land with ill-defined titles. Cattlemen lived nomadic lives (Pendle 1963, ch. 7).

In the early nineteenth century it was reported that "the constant diet of the people, morning, noon, and night, is beef." Animals had other uses; furniture consisted of animal skulls and stretched hides, dwellings were made of hides, and dried animal carcasses were used for fuel (Street 1959, p. 9). Today, beef provides more than a third of Uruguayan caloric intake and accounts for a large fraction of food expenditures.

Uruguay has a comparative advantage in the production of livestock products and their processed derivatives. Its resource endowments are sufficient—if not frustrated by policy—to supply goods both for high domestic consumption and for an export trade that could finance imports and greatly improve the material standard of living. Public policy has, however, intensively taxed rural output, encouraged land-intensive resource combinations in the countryside, and severely depressed rural productivity and output. Uruguay's beef output has stagnated over the past several decades, while other important beef-producing countries have greatly increased their output.

Because the production of cattle and cattle by-products is a large fraction of total economic output, stagnation in the beef sector has generated stagnation in the economy as a whole. Real income per capita has remained constant in recent decades.

From the late nineteenth century until about 1930 the Uruguayan economy expanded, led by exports of livestock products. During the Great Depression of the 1930s the government strongly extended and magnified a policy of protecting domestic manufacturing industry, with the apparent intent of diversifying output to avoid the effects of price fluctuations in the international market for beef. This fostered the establishment and survival of high-cost firms that were unable to compete successfully in export markets but instead produced import-substituting goods for the domestic market. The protectionist policies that gave rise to these firms were perpetuated by the political pressures exerted by interested groups, whether owners or employees of the enterprises.

An important public policy instrument that has taxed the livestock industry has been tariff protection for manufacturing. This policy has raised the real wages of labor in relation to the price of meat, induced the use of labor-saving methods in the livestock sector, and contributed to low levels of investment and productivity in that sector. Tariff protection for manufacturing has effected income transfers within Uruguayan society; exporters of livestock products have lost and manufacturers have gained. Intensive consumers of imported goods have been losers, and consumers who spend a relatively large fraction of their incomes on meat have been gainers because policy has driven down the price of meat. The income transfers implied by tariff protection for manufacturing, however, have tended to diminish output and yields in the livestock sector.

Livestock is produced in Uruguay by labor-saving, land-intensive methods. Almost all land was brought into production in the nineteenth century, and so the supply of land has been fixed for a long time. The light, thin soils are more suited for grazing than for alternative agricultural uses. Fertilizers and seeded pastures are little used. Because the livestock sector has been heavily taxed, the price of land has been low in relation to the prices of other inputs with which it is combined (Sapelli 1985, pp. 173, 175). Taxation has prompted the intensive use of land in production and has discouraged the improvement of pastures. As a consequence, the animals are fed exclusively on natural pasture and receive inadequate nutrition. The result is that they gain weight slowly and take longer to raise to slaughter weight. The output of meat per animal and per acre is low, the age of heifers at first calving is high, and cows' fertility is low. By these measures, Uruguay is less efficient by far than other important beef-producing countries. This situation arises because the distortionary price structure has discouraged investment in the livestock sector.

Another effect of feeding cattle on natural pasture is a large variation in the seasonal pattern of slaughter. Slaughter rates are high in the months just preceding winter, when pasture is thin. As a consequence, the capacity of the meat-processing industry must be high in relation to the annual slaughter.

Uruguay's protective commercial policy in the two decades from the mid-1950s through the mid-1970s diminished by one-half the size of the cattle herd and the slaughter rate (Sapelli 1985, ch. 2). Those commercial policies, although distortionary and costly in real terms for the economy as a whole, persist because they lower the cost of meat for domestic consumption. A coalition of consumers presses for their retention.

Some sense of the depressive effect of public policy on Uruguay's beef sector can be gained by comparing the relative prices of steers on the hoof and of ranching inputs in Uruguay and other countries. In the mid-1970s in Uruguay the equivalent, in steers on the hoof, of a 35–40 horsepower tractor was five times as much as in the United States and ten times as much as in France. Phosphoric anhydride costs four times as much, in steers on the hoof, in Uruguay as in the United States and seven times as much as in France. For gas and oil the exchange rate, in steers on the hoof, was more than eight times higher in Uruguay than in the United States and France (Reca and Regunaga 1978).

Technical deficiencies and underinvestment in the Uruguayan cattle economy have often been ascribed to the failure of livestock proprietors to engage in maximizing behavior. According to Hanson,

> Lack of enterprise was characteristic of the *hacendados* [large landowners]. They were for the most part content with the easy enjoyment of their large properties. Nature had generously provided splendid conditions for a thriving pastoral economy and the *estancieros* [large ranchers] were loathe to abandon for more intensive operations their crude pastoral regimen in which mediocre animals were bred on natural grasses for low-grade markets. . . . The Uruguayan *estancieros* lagged behind even the similarly unenterprising Argentine stockmen. (Hanson 1938, p. 6.)

Similarly, Finch wrote that Uruguayan rural stagnation is believed to be the result of the "concentration of landownership among a small number of families . . . that has produced a class of wealthy and tradition-oriented agricultural producers who are not profit-maximizers, or who admit noneconomic considerations into their calculations of cost and profit" (Finch 1981, p. 114).

A large part of the intellectual community of Uruguay has come to believe that nonmaximizing behavior on the part of large landowners, the size distribution of land (much of which is held in very large properties),

and the prevailing forms of land tenure, including much absentee ownership, combine to explain the low productivity of rural Uruguay. There
are no significant differences in yields, however, when farms are differentiated by size and form of tenure. Rather, since public policy has
imposed heavy explicit and implicit taxes on the livestock economy, the
failure to invest more heavily in that sector is consistent with principles
of rational, maximizing behavior by landowners. In addition, there is an
active land market in Uruguay, and one would expect that if land were
inappropriately distributed among owners, or if parcels were inappropriate in size, or if forms of tenure were inappropriate, those deficiencies
would be corrected by land market transactions.

Under the circumstances—a large urban population, elected officeholders who depend on their political careers for their livelihood, and
the importance of beef in household consumption and expenditure—a
political imperative for officeholders is to stabilize and keep down the
level of domestic beef prices. The government intervenes actively to
achieve that objective. The relevant instruments of policy are export
taxes on beef, the manipulation of the foreign exchange rate, price
controls at various levels of the beef market, and quantity controls on
slaughter, exports, and consumption. The total effect of these policies has
been the subsidization of domestic beef consumption and heavy taxation
of beef production.

State Intervention and Public Enterprises

Throughout most of the nineteenth century Uruguay's public policy was
relatively noninterventionist, in part because the government was unable to exercise its authority in the countryside. Occasional civil disturbances interfered with the pursuit of productive ventures, but the
exercise of private power kept this disorder within tolerable limits. Real
income grew, and large numbers of immigrants were attracted to the
country. During most of the period a uniform, relatively low tariff was
imposed on imports to provide public revenues. In the third quarter of
the century it came to be widely believed that ranching could not provide
employment for a growing population, and policy began to change. In
the 1870s the tariff was made somewhat protectionist for domestic
manufacturing. Nonuniform tariffs were imposed, and duties were
raised on finished goods and diminished on raw materials and capital
goods.

The tradition of active government in Uruguay dates from the early
twentieth century when, for the first time, civil disorder was overcome
and real central governing authority was established in Montevideo. Its
main progenitor was Jose Batlle y Ordonez, a political journalist and
newspaper owner. Batlle served two terms as president, but he dominated politics even when not in office, and his influence continued to be
felt, through *batllista* factions in the political parties, long after his death.

His proposals—many of which were adopted—included state monopolies in insurance and in electric power, a labor code, unemployment compensation, a state mortgage bank, state railways, state monopolies in the production of alcohol and tobacco, protection for Uruguayan industry against foreign competition, old-age pensions, family allowances, a workmen's compensation system for injuries suffered on the job, and compensation for discharged workers. This system of welfare policies anteceded by decades those of other countries (Hanson 1938).

Batlle opposed inequality in the distribution of income and proposed state action to redress it. He opposed foreign investment in public utilities and in manufacturing and favored displacement of foreign investors by the state.

The Uruguayan government nationalized foreign meat-packing plants in favor of public plants, which became technologically inefficient. These plants would not have been able to survive in a market with no subsidization, open competition, and freedom of entry. But they were a source of public employment, and to ensure their continued operation without large open subsidies, the government administered price controls to enlarge the operating margins of all meat-packing plants, controlled entry into the industry, and gave one of the state plants a monopoly of the Montevideo market. When in the late 1970s free entry into meat packing was permitted, the public plants were closed.

In the late nineteenth century a state bank was established. Over time, the state took over or established ventures in power generation, railroad transport, insurance, telephone communications, petroleum refining, and cement and alcohol manufacturing. Protective labor legislation was enacted much earlier than in other countries, and a social security system was set up and was gradually broadened in scope.

A system of institutionalized wage boards, established by law, has distorted the relative prices of production inputs and fostered capital intensity. The system was set up in the 1940s with the intention of improving living standards for workers' families. Because the system determines nominal wages without addressing the phenomena that would cause real wages to rise, it has had perverse effects. Combined with that policy were others that imposed payroll taxes to provide annuities to retired persons and others who qualified and that treated capital imports preferentially with respect to tariffs and exchange rates. In sum, the policies raised the price of labor and lowered that of capital. Distorted factor combinations followed from the distorted factor prices.

Protectionism

Protection of manufacturing in Uruguay was sometimes explicit, sometimes the implicit consequence of policies intended for other purposes. The protectionism introduced in the third quarter of the nineteenth century was intensified by exchange controls applied in the Great Depression and was further intensified after World War II by exchange controls intended to slow the rate at which foreign currency reserves were being run down. Import substitution in manufacturing made great progress in the 1950s, but because of the small size of the Uruguayan market, opportunities had been exhausted before that decade came to an end (Anichini, Caumont, and Sjaastad 1978).

Note

1. Concentration in Montevideo dates from the beginning of settlement. Montevideo is a natural port superior to those in neighboring countries. In the nineteenth century it was an important entrepôt for goods in transit to Argentina and Brazil.

16 *The Comparison*

The sections below present some of the similarities and differences seen in the two countries discussed in this study and present its findings.

Similarities

Costa Rica and Uruguay are both small countries with small populations. (Costa Rica's mid-1985 population was 2.6 million and Uruguay's was 3 million; Tilak 1988, table 1.) Both have homogeneous populations of Western European descent. The proportions of people of native American or African descent are trivial, and the countries have escaped the troubles of ethnically based claims and counterclaims. Neither country has substantial mineral resources, and the prime endowments of both are land and the human capital that they have been able to develop.

The real incomes of both populations depend heavily on output and prices of agricultural or pastoral commodities, large proportions of which are exported to other countries. Prices of exported commodities have fluctuated with some volatility over time. Costa Rica, after unsuccessful experiments with tobacco and cacao, became a substantial producer of coffee in the mid-nineteenth century and of bananas from late in that century. From early in the period of European settlement, Uruguay has engaged in livestock raising, first for hides and later, in response to opportunities opened by technology, for beef. From the middle of the nineteenth century wool has been an important complement to cattle products. Both countries account for only a small fraction of world output and trade in their important export commodities.[1] Uruguay's share in the world export trade in meat has diminished over time; its proportions of world exports of canned meat and of beef and veal carcasses were sharply lower in the 1960s than in the years just before World War II.

When measured by the standards of their respective regions, the people of both countries are quite well off. Income is less unequally distributed in Costa Rica and Uruguay than in other poor countries (table

16-1). Infant mortality and illiteracy, which tend to be concentrated in the poorest segments of the population, can be read as indicators of the extent of poverty. Both countries come off well with respect to those measures.[2]

Measure	Costa Rica	Uruguay
Infant mortality, 1984 (deaths per thousand live births)	18.4	30.4
Percentage of population 15 or older who are illiterate (mid-1970s)	11.6	6.1

In Costa Rica, although the majority of the population is rural, the San José Metropolitan Area alone accounts for a large part of the population. In Uruguay, too, from the beginning of European settlement, a very large fraction of the population has resided in Montevideo. In 1985 the population of Costa Rica was 44.5 percent urban; in 1983 the population of Uruguay was 84.3 percent urban (United Nations 1988, table 6).

Both Costa Rica and Uruguay have exhibited a certain ambivalence about direct investment by foreigners. Although foreign investment has been acceptable in a formal and legal sense, foreign firms that have become large in scale have encountered formidable opposition, decade after decade. The rhetoric of the opposition has taken a similar nationalist form in both countries. In response, foreign firms have almost completely withdrawn from banana production in Costa Rica, and British and North American companies have withdrawn from meat-packing in Uruguay. British investors in public utilities in Uruguay were bought out after World War II by the Uruguayan government, which, to do so, drew down its sterling reserves in Britain that had been blocked during the war.

Table 16-1. GNP *per Capita and Percentage Shares of Income, by Population Quintile, Costa Rica and Uruguay, Various Years*

Gross national product per capita	Costa Rica	Uruguay
U.S. dollars, 1985	1,300	1,650
Average annual growth rate (percent), 1965–85	1.4	1.4

Percentage shares of income, by population quintiles	Costa Rica (1971)	Uruguay (Montevideo, 1984)
Bottom 20 percent	3.3	7.9
2nd 20 percent	8.7	7.7
3rd 20 percent	13.3	14.4
4th 20 percent	19.8	23.6
Top 20 percent	54.8	46.4

Source: GNP, Tilak 1988, table 1; shares, Tilak 1988, table 3.

Foreign investment has rendered services to the people of both Costa Rica and Uruguay. North American investment in railroad construction and banana production in Costa Rica greatly diminished transport costs for exported coffee and transformed the coastal lowlands, where virtual wasteland became the site for production of a thriving export crop. British and North American *frigoríficos* in Uruguay opened export markets for chilled and frozen beef and expanded marketing opportunities for the livestock industry beyond hides, grease, and jerked beef. British public utilities and railway investment provided essential infrastructural services. Since large-scale foreign investment is vulnerable to nationalistic pressures, the income streams they yield their owners must be discounted at a high rate, and this may explain what appear to be occasional "subsidies" to encourage these ventures.

Finally, Costa Rica and Uruguay are somewhat alike in their geographic isolation; that is, both are distant from the main centers of the world economy in Western Europe and the Pacific Rim. Although Costa Rica is closer than Uruguay to North America, the absence of transport facilities meant that for much of its early history as a coffee exporter it had to ship from the Pacific side around Cape Horn.

Differences

The topographies of the two countries are very different. Costa Rica is mainly mountainous and temperate, although there are important tropical lowlands on both coasts. Uruguay is flat and has a temperate climate. Costa Rica's concentration on tree crops and Uruguay's specialization in livestock derive from this difference. In Costa Rica land is held in small plots, especially on the central plateau; in Uruguay land is held in larger plots appropriate for stockraising.

The 1983 crude birthrate was 30 per 1,000 in Costa Rica and 18.2 per 1,000 in Uruguay. (In that year the natural rate of population increase was 26.1 per 1,000 in Costa Rica and 9 per 1,000 in Uruguay; United Nations, 1985, table 19.) The table below shows the percentage age compositions of the populations.[3]

Age	Costa Rica (1985)	Uruguay (1980)
14 years and younger	36.6	27.0
15–64 years	58.9	62.6
65 years and older	4.5	10.4

Thus, the rate of natural increase is much higher in Costa Rica than in Uruguay, and the median age of the population is much lower. This means that transferring income from the younger working-age population to elderly retirees through the social security system is much more feasible for Costa Rica than for Uruguay. The viability of the Uruguayan system will become more and more questionable with the passage of time.

Costa Rica and Uruguay differ in one other significant respect: Costa Ricans consume a trivially small fraction of the country's output of coffee and bananas, whereas beef is important in the Uruguayan diet and a very large proportion of the country's beef output is consumed domestically. These differences in domestic consumption patterns affect the prospects for export earnings.

Findings

Some salient conclusions can be drawn from the combined economic experience of Costa Rica and Uruguay.

Law and Policy

Both Costa Rica and Uruguay have developed intensive income transfer institutions and protective labor laws that have raised the price of labor. Both have subsidized the importation of physical capital. Thus, both have distorted the relative prices of inputs and have generated socially inappropriate factor combinations in production that have brought about an excess of capital intensity, at least in their manufacturing sectors. Both have favored their urban sectors at the expense of their rural sectors, thus impeding those sectors in which they have a comparative advantage. Both have installed selective policies of protection that have grossly expanded the domestic production of manufactured goods for domestic markets. Both have mismanaged their foreign exchange markets. Both have experienced large public fiscal deficits. Both have run up large public sector debts, implying intergenerational transfers that, if not somehow adjusted, will greatly burden their people in the future. Both have engaged in extensive public enterprise ventures that have been kept alive even when they have been clear failures, in response to political pressures not to dismiss the ventures' employees. Both exhibit inflated employment in their public sectors.

Economic growth is promoted by an open economy. The rise in the relative standard of living of the populations of both countries to levels substantially higher than those in other countries of their regions occurred mainly in periods when policy did not skew the structure of output. During these periods coffee and bananas in Costa Rica and livestock in Uruguay developed into their economies' major sectors, and the gains from the improvements in economic performance were spread widely among the people. When, in Uruguay, public policy began imposing burdens on those sectors through strategies that sought to alter the composition of output, "traditional" activities stagnated, as did the economy as a whole. Resources were wasted, rents and rent seeking were generated, and the real income of the people was adversely affected. In Costa Rica coffee output rose continuously despite similar policies because the cartelization of the international coffee market produced rents for coffee growers. The burden of rural taxation fell on rents, and the relatively untaxed residuum of payments for the services of coffee inputs made it feasible to continue expanding investment in coffee mainly by improving yields.[4] Nonetheless, it is likely that the real incomes of the Costa Rican people would have increased even more without the policies of rural taxation that were applied.

Almost invariably, policies that reduced the openness of the economies sought a relative rise in the resources allocated to the manufacturing sector. The policies were nonneutral in their effects within that sector, either intentionally or inadvertently. In Uruguay superficially uniform policies gave differential effective protection to different industries. In Costa Rica economic policies encouraged capital intensity in factor combination and favored capital-intensive industries. Policies often were not uniform across manufacturing industries. Industries were rank-ordered for the receipt of favored tariff and tax treatment and of rationed credit from nationalized banks when real interest rates were very low or even negative. Those industries that processed Costa Rican raw materials were given privileged positions. Price support policies favored rice over other crops.

The aggressive behavior of the state authorities has, in both countries, reflected the tradition of close control derived from the practices of the Spanish colonial administration—even though both countries were in the backwaters of their colonial administrative regions and escaped the full force of those controls. It also reflects the populist agendas of single powerful political figures—José Figueres in the mid-twentieth century in Costa Rica and José Batlle y Ordonez in the early twentieth century in Uruguay—and the powerful counsel of the national intellectual and academic communities and of the professional staffs of the international agencies. That counsel has been homogeneous in urging state action. Aggressive behavior reflects, in addition, the high discount rates of political officeholders who must stand for periodic elections in democratic systems. For most of their recent histories both countries have had electoral systems in which all adults are qualified to vote, many participate, several parties campaign, campaigns are active, majorities rule, and voting results are honored. Elections are usually contested by two main parties (or coalitions of parties), both of which tend to offer what are, in the political contexts of their countries, similar centrist programs. Left-oriented parties usually draw little support but have sometimes had disproportionate influence because they have engaged in demonstrative or violent behavior or have formed temporary ad hoc coalitions with another party to constitute a majority.

In both countries an earlier liberal ideology was replaced by the ideology of social democracy. With the altered outlook the state became aggressively interventionist and an instrument for producing rents and administering transfer payments. Whereas before the change advantage had been sought in markets, it was now sought by soliciting the favor of the state.

The high intensity of state activity seems to have persisted and expanded because of the consequent opportunities for the capture of rents. Rent-seeking segments of the populations have managed political affairs, broadly defined, so as to keep and enlarge those opportunities.

International Trade

The similarities in the public policy regimes of Costa Rica and Uruguay are striking. Both have a comparative advantage in the production of specialized agricultural or pastoral commodities that face import constraints in international markets. Neither is an important participant in those markets. But although their market shares are small, export markets are important to them; exports of their main agricultural products are large fractions of their economies' outputs.

Both Costa Rica and Uruguay face constraints in international markets in exporting their main agricultural commodities. West Indian producers and countries covered under the Lomé Convention have preferential access to the U.K. banana market. Coffee exports to the principal coffee-consuming countries have been subject to export quota constraints under the terms of the International Coffee Agreement, which has been renewed periodically. Sugar imports into the United States are subject to national quotas. Many European countries give preferential access to their markets to domestic and Commonwealth beef. The United States forbids the importation of unprocessed beef from countries in which certain animal diseases are endemic.

These constraints have generated searches for second-best market outlets. Costa Rica now sells its quota allowances of coffee to International Coffee Agreement countries and ships the surplus to Eastern European countries to be sold at lower prices than under the Agreement. Uruguayan beef is shipped to Brazil, the Middle East, and the Far East in larger quantities than previously.

Both countries, moved by the desire to minimize the costs of transport and transactions, have responded to some degree to opportunities for economic integration within their respective regions. Uruguayans emigrate to Argentina, and Argentines invest in Uruguayan properties. This is a "natural" response to opportunity. Costa Rica engages in a somewhat active commerce with other Central American countries, in large part because of incentives created by the formation of the Central American Common Market (CACM). The high barriers to trade with the outside world imposed by the CACM have mainly worked to increase Costa Rica's industrial production for the domestic market, partly because incomes are higher in Costa Rica than in other Central American countries and because individual member countries of the CACM still put barriers in the way of regional commerce across their borders. It is questionable whether the increased trade within the Common Market is welfare-maximizing.

Distribution

Policy in both Costa Rica and Uruguay has been explicitly redistributive in recent decades. Earlier, before redistributive policies began to be applied, improvements in living standards were achieved by permitting relatively unregulated play for venturesomeness. In both countries the explicit formulation of redistributive policies has had depressive effects on economic growth. A somewhat greater measure of equality in the distribution of income has been achieved at the expense of real output and income.

Both Costa Rica and Uruguay (Economic Commission for Latin America 1985a, p. 15) use social security systems as part of their redistributive policy. In Uruguay not only retired persons but also those dismissed without fault and women who withdraw from employment to have children qualify for lifetime annuities, even if the beneficiaries subsequently find employment. In both countries the systems are unfunded. Because of differences in birthrates and in the age composition of the populations, the social security system is a much heavier burden on the working population in Uruguay than in Costa Rica. In Costa Rica redistribution occurs informally, within the family. Since Costa Rica's birthrate is much higher, its population is much younger. Thus, the main redistributive burden on the producing segment of Costa Rican society is consensual, and the recipients are the young. In Uruguay the burden is coerced, and the recipients are older. The cost is sufficiently heavy in Uruguay that it has for decades been mitigated by postponing prescribed changes in benefits and by delaying the certification of applicants for social security benefits. This compensates somewhat for the traditional generosity in the administration of social security and for the systemic tendency to favor politically well-placed applicants in rationing pension rights.

In Uruguay the number of social security beneficiaries is one-half the size of the labor force. In a recent year public expenditures were one-quarter of GDP, and more than half of all public expenditures went for social security. Only half of social security revenues are derived from social security taxes, and the taxes are frequently evaded. The residuum is provided by subsidies from the central government, but payments are often long delayed and are sometimes not forthcoming at all. People are given an incentive to retire from work early in life, when they are still hale and productive, or to receive pension payments illegally while they are working in the black economy. Thus, Uruguay is heavily engaged in the income redistribution business in ways that generate inefficiency.

Costa Rica has recently begun to encounter the "Uruguayan problem" in the administration of social security as an institution for effecting transfer payments. The number of working contributors to the system, in relation to the number of pensioners, declined from 157 in 1960 to 17 in 1983. Between 1970 and 1983 the number of old-age pensioners increased by a factor of ten. Life expectancy rose by thirteen years during the same period, greatly expanding the pension payment liability of the system. The prospects of the social security system are not bright, and it is expected to confront, before too long, deficits that will have to be met by diminishing pension payments, by increasing contributions (thus raising the price of labor in relation to other inputs), or by augmenting the revenues of the system with contributions from the general revenues, which would further complicate public finances.

The comparative advantage of Costa Rica in the production of coffee and of Uruguay in the production of livestock meant that, at international prices for those commodities, many producers earned rents. Those rents could be taxed away, and they were—through export taxes, the management of exchange rates, and protectionist policies for manufacturing activities. Taxation of agriculture was redistributive in its intent and in its effect and was responsive to the political power of urban voting populations in both countries. The taxation of agriculture and the redistributive income and wealth transfers from rural to urban sectors were "safe" policies in that, since it was rents that were being taxed away, the burdened sectors would not shut down. In Costa Rica coffee output could be expanded through new plantings on land that had not been used for coffee production, as well as through increased yields. In Uruguay virtually all the land was already employed in livestock production as early as the nineteenth century. Further expansion of the area devoted to livestock was not possible, and taxation of ranching depressed the rate of return on investment to a level that foreclosed more intensive exploitation of ranchlands. Thus, the output experiences of the main commodities differed in the two countries; beef output stagnated in Uruguay, but coffee output rose in Costa Rica.

Stagnation

Beginning in the 1950s Uruguay experienced economic stagnation. Costa Rica followed some three decades later. In both countries stagnation was produced by the active pursuit of redistributive policies and of policies that sought to change the composition of economic output and production inputs in ways that flew in the face of the countries' comparative advantages. Those policies distorted relative prices and deformed systems of incentives.

The effects of badly designed policies are felt with lags. One reason is that it is not clear at first whether the policies will be short- or long-lived and whether they will be applied consistently. Another is that the effects of the policies are cumulative. It must be remembered that although similar policy sets were adopted in the two countries, they were initiated at different times—in the early twentieth century in Uruguay and four decades later in Costa Rica. This time difference partly explains the difference in the onset of adversity.

Rural-Urban Transfers

Over time, Costa Rica became more urbanized, and urbanization in Uruguay has been intense. These tendencies, when combined with democratic and majoritarian electoral systems, explain the existence in both countries of redistributive public policies. In both countries, although the forms of redistribution are somewhat different, income is transferred from rural to urban areas. Both countries have extensive social security, health, education, and welfare systems that are vehicles for those transfers. Since beef is a staple of the Uruguayan diet, keeping its domestic price low is an important instrument of income transfer in Uruguay, but there is no comparable political imperative in the case of coffee and bananas in Costa Rica.

In both countries the rural sectors are not without influence on policy, and they have institutional instruments for making their influence felt. But they are outnumbered by middle- and working-class urban dwellers, who use the political parties, as well as more specialized institutions, as vehicles of influence. The urban capacity to siphon off income produced in the countryside is somewhat more evident in Uruguay, which is more intensively urbanized than Costa Rica. Changes in governing party lead to only peripheral, not radical, changes in policy, partly because the parties strive to satisfy the greatest number of voters and partly because attempts to diminish rents encounter resistance when privileges come to be seen as entitlements.

Although the time trends and the degree of population concentration are different for the two countries, for the past several decades urban residents have been able to capture part of the wealth of the countryside. The countryside has responded to diminished incentives by producing less.

Protectionism

Protection of domestic industry from foreign competition is not new in Costa Rica and Uruguay. In Uruguay it dates from the middle of the nineteenth century, but in earlier periods it was mainly a means for raising public revenues, a large fraction of which was derived from import duties. In more recent decades its purposes have been different in both countries, the magnitude of protection has been enlarged, and the universe of intended beneficiaries has been less uniform and more selective. These changes were generated in part by a shift from direct to indirect taxation as the public service employees developed talents and skills. They were also generated by a flawed conviction that public servants had enough information and foresight to distinguish those economic activities that would survive, if protected in their infancy, from those that would fail when finally exposed to open, unprotected competition with foreign goods. The main genesis of the changes, however, was

in a set of ideas that came to dominate intellectual thought, were promoted by the academic community and the community of international
civil servants, and were seized on by some economic actors to tilt policy
design so as to produce rents for themselves at the expense of other
elements in the population. Those ideas included the notions that

- Comparative advantage does not explain the international division of labor
- Economic diversification is preferable to specialization
- The terms of international trade run persistently against primary
producers
- The only, or at least the most efficient, defense against fluctuating
prices for primary products in international markets is to diversify
economic activity
- Manufacturing is inherently preferable to primary production as
a vehicle for improving the material standard of living of the people
- If manufactured goods are being imported for domestic consumption, and if within the country there exists or can be constructed
the capacity to produce those goods, they should be produced domestically, even if their producers could not survive market competition
without very strong import constraints.

Costa Rica and Uruguay both adopted policy sets framed by those
prescriptions. (In Costa Rica constraints on entry of nonregional goods
were intensified by the formation of the Central American Common
Market.) In recent decades manufacturing output has risen as a fraction
of total economic output. That change in the composition of output has
been celebrated in both countries. The import constraints have tended
to survive longer than would seem appropriate for an infant industry
rule, and they have been selective and nonneutral in their effects. Those
who possess physical and human assets that are specialized for the
production of protected commodities have exerted political pressure to
ensure the survival of the policies and the enlargement of the rents they
generate. Aggregate economic output, however, has been adversely
affected by the policies, which have brought about income and wealth
transfers at the expense of other segments of the population and of the
communities as a whole.

In both Costa Rica and Uruguay there is a widespread expressed
preference for "nontraditional" over "traditional" products and exports.
Both countries have sought to change the structure of production and of
exports through combined systems of taxes and subsidies. The traditional export products—coffee and bananas in Costa Rica, beef and wool
and their derivatives in Uruguay—came to be traditional precisely because they were able to establish themselves and grow in open international competition. Clearly, therefore, trade experience demonstrated
that these were the products in which the countries had comparative
advantage. By intentionally seeking to diminish their relative impor-

tance, the Costa Rican and Uruguayan governments engaged in a process of moving resources from more to less productive uses.

The nominal defense for those policies was that diversification of output and exports was a hedge against the wide fluctuations of the prices of traditional commodities in international markets. Hedges with lower social cost—for example, appropriately timed sequences of saving and dissaving—were given insufficient attention. That exemplary hedge requires, of course, the ability to make sophisticated estimations of market prospects, but both countries had long and intensive international trading experience in their traditional commodities, and the avoidance of estimational error should have been within their grasp. The saving-dissaving hedge also requires the discipline to hold the reins on expenditure when prices and revenues are high, and it is here that such a hedging policy might have run into trouble.

To sum up, the particular redistributive policies of Costa Rica and Uruguay, as their governments pursued their perceived mission as welfare states, distorted incentives and adversely affected the progress of their economies and the mean incomes of their people.

Notes

1. In 1984 Costa Rica produced 2.4 percent of world coffee output. In that year Uruguay had 0.78 percent of the world's cattle and 2 percent of its sheep; in 1984–85 Uruguay produced 2.8 percent of the world's wool (United Nations 1985, tables 83, 86, and 89).

2. The illiteracy figures are for 1973 (Costa Rica) and 1975 (Uruguay). For infant mortality the source is United Nations 1988, table 9. For illiteracy the source is United Nations 1985, table 59.

3. The source for the table is United Nations 1988, table 7.

4. Costa Rica's coffee output increased from 80,000 metric tons in 1975 to 124,000 metric tons in 1984 (United Nations 1985, table 83). Coffee production has exceeded the quotas set by the International Coffee Organization for export to member countries of the Coffee Agreement. Exports to nonmember countries are sold at much lower prices.

Bibliography

Academia de Centroamérica. 1981. *Perspectivas de la Política de Población en Costa Rica.* San José.

Academia Nacional de Economía. 1984. *Contribución a la Historia Económica del Uruguay.* Montevideo.

Acevedo, Eduardo. 1933. *Anales Históricos del Uruguay.* Montevideo: Universidad de la República.

Achío, Mayra, and Ana C. Escalante. 1985. *Azúcar y Política en Costa Rica.* San José: Editorial Costa Rica.

Adler, Robert W. 1981. "Recent Costa Rican Economic History." Presentation to the Peace Corps, San José.

Aguiar, César. 1982. *Uruguay: País de Emigración.* Montevideo: Ediciones de la Banda Oriental.

Aguilar Bulgarelli, Oscar. 1983. *Costa Rica y sus Hechos Políticos de 1948. Problemática de una Década.* 2d ed. San José: Editorial Costa Rica.

Aguilar Bulgarelli, Oscar, ed. 1971. *El Desarrollo Nacional en 150 Años de Vida Independiente.* San Pedro: Universidad de Costa Rica.

Akiyama Takamasa, and Ronald C. Duncan. 1982. *Analysis of the World Coffee Market.* World Bank Commodity Working Paper 7. Washington, D.C.

Alisky, Marvin. 1969. *Uruguay: A Contemporary Survey.* New York: Praeger.

Allerger, Daniel E., ed. 1962. *Fertile Lands of Friendship.* Gainesville, Fla.: University of Florida Press.

Alonso, José M. 1981. *El Proceso Histórico de la Agricultura Uruguaya.* Montevideo: Fundación de Cultura Universitaria.

Altimir, Oscar. 1981. "La Pobreza en América Latina." *Revista de la CEPAL.* (April).

———. 1984. "Poverty, Income Distribution, and Child Welfare in Latin America: A Comparison of Pre- and Post-recession Data." *World Development* 12(3):261–92.

Ameringer, Charles D. 1948. *Don Pepe: A Political Biography of José Figueres of Costa Rica.* Albuquerque, N.M.: University of New Mexico Press.

Anichini, Juan, Jorge Caumont, and Larry Sjaastad. 1978. *La Política Comercial y la Protección en el Uruguay.* Montevideo: Banco Central del Uruguay.

393

Araya Pochet, Carlos. 1971. "El Desarrollo Económico y Social de Costa Rica a Partir de 1821." In Oscar Aguilar Bulgarelli, ed., *El Desarrollo Nacional en 150 Años de Vida Independiente*. San Pedro: Universidad de Costa Rica.

———. 1982a. *Historia Económica de Costa Rica (1821–1971)*. San José: Editorial Fernández-Arce.

———. 1982b. *Liberación Nacional en la Historia Política de Costa Rica, 1940–1980*. San José: Editorial Nacional de Textos.

Arias Sánchez, Oscar. 1983. *Grupos de Presión en Costa Rica*. San José: Editorial Costa Rica.

———. 1984. *Quién Gobierna en Costa Rica?* 3d ed. San José: Editorial Universitaria Centroamericana.

Asociación Nacional de Fomento Económico. 1968. *Seminario sobre el Mercado Común Centroamericano*. San José: Antonio Lehmann.

———. 1980. *El Modelo Económico Costarricense*. San José: INLISA.

———. 1984a. *El Modelo Político Costarricense*. San José: Trejos Hnos.

———. 1984b. *El Modelo Social Costarricense*. San José: Trejos Hnos.

Backer, James. 1978. *La Iglesia y el Sindicalismo en Costa Rica*. San José: Editorial Costa Rica.

Balassa, Bela. 1986. *Toward Renewed Economic Growth in Latin America*. Washington, D.C.: Institute for International Economics.

Baldares, Manuel de Jesús. 1985. *La Distribución del Ingreso y los Sueldos en Costa Rica*. San José: Editorial Costa Rica.

Banco Central de Costa Rica. 1976. *Costa Rica: 25 Años en Estadísticas Económicas, 1950–1974*. San José.

———. 1986. *Estadísticas, 1950–85*. San José.

———. Various issues. *Cuentas Nacionales de Costa Rica*. San José.

———. Various issues. *Principales Estadísticas sobre las Transacciones de Costa Rica en el Extranjero*. San José.

Banco Central del Uruguay. Various issues. *Boletín Estadístico*. Montevideo.

———. Various issues. *Cuentas Nacionales*. Montevideo.

———. Various issues. *Formación Bruta de Capital*. Montevideo.

———. Various issues. *Indicadores de la Actividad Económica Financiera, Producto e Ingreso Nacionales*. Montevideo.

Barahona Streber, Oscar, and others. 1980. *Los Problemas Económicos del Desarrollo en Costa Rica*. San José: Editorial Universidad Nacional Estatal a Distancia.

Barbato de Silva, Celia, and Carlos Pérez Arrarte. 1979. *La Ganadería Vacuna Uruguaya: Caracterización General*. Montevideo: Centro de Investigaciones Económicas.

Barrán, José Pedro, and Benjamín Nahum. 1967. *Historia Rural del Uruguay Moderno, 1851–1886*, vol. 1. Montevideo: Ediciones de la Banda Oriental.

———. 1971. *Historia Rural del Uruguay Moderno, 1886–1894*, vol. 2. Montevideo: Ediciones de la Banda Oriental.

Behm, Hugo, and José Miguel Guzmán. 1979. "Diferencias Socioeconómicas del Descenso de la Fecundidad en Costa Rica, 1960–1970." Proceedings of the 7th National Seminar on Demography, Centro Latinoamericano de Demografía, San José.

Bell, John Patrick. 1971. *Crisis in Costa Rica: The 1948 Revolution*. Austin: University of Texas Press.

Bensión, Alberto, and Jorge Caumont. 1979. *Política Económica y Distribución del Ingreso en el Uruguay, 1970–1976*. Montevideo: Acall Editorial.

———. 1981. "Uruguay: Alternative Trade Strategies and Employment Implications." In Anne O. Krueger and others, eds., *Trade and Employment in Developing Countries: Individual Studies*. Chicago, Ill.: University of Chicago Press.

———. 1983. *Alternative Trade Regimes and Employment*. Cambridge, Mass.: National Bureau of Economic Research.

Bermúdez, Vera Violeta, and Miguel Gómez. 1974. *Panorama de Costa Rica. 1973. Aspectos Demográficos y Sociales*. San José: Centro de Estudios de Población.

Bhagwati, Jagdish N. 1982. "Directly-Unproductive Profit-Seeking (DUP) Activities." *Journal of Political Economy* 90, no. 51:988–1002.

Biesanz, Mavis Hiltunen, Richard Biesanz, and Karen Zubris Biesanz. *The Costa Ricans*. New York: Prentice-Hall.

Blanco Segura, Ricardo. 1984. *1884. El Estado, la Iglesia y las Reformas Liberales*. San José: Editorial Costa Rica.

Bourguignon, François. 1986. "Income Distribution and External Trade: The Case of Costa Rica." OECD Development Centre, Paris.

Brannon, R. H. 1967. *The Agricultural Development of Uruguay*. New York: Praeger.

Bulmer-Thomas, Victor. 1983. "Economic Development over the Long Run—Central America since 1920." *Journal of Latin American Studies* 15, pt. 2 (November):269–94.

Camacho, Arnoldo R., and Claudio González Vega. 1985. "Foreign Exchange Speculation, Currency Substitution, and Domestic Deposit Mobilization: The Case of Costa Rica." In Michael B. Connolly and John McDermott, eds., *The Economics of the Caribbean Basin*. New York: Praeger.

Camacho, Daniel, ed. 1985. *Desarrollo del Movimiento Sindical en Costa Rica*. San Pedro: Editorial Universidad de Costa Rica.

Cámara Nacional de Comercio. 1986. "La Tasa de Retorno al Capital en el Uruguay." Montevideo.

Carcanholo, Reinaldo. 1981. *Desarrollo del Capitalismo en Costa Rica*. San José: Editorial Universitaria Centroamericana.

Cardoso, Ciro F. S. 1973. "La Formación de la Hacienda Cafetalera en Costa Rica (Siglo XIX)." *Estudios Sociales Centroamericanos* 6 (September–December):22–48.

Carranza Solís, Jorge. 1933. *Monografía del Café*, vol. 1. San José.

Castillo, Carlos M. 1966. *Growth and Integration in Central America*. New York: Praeger.

Centro de Investigaciones Económicas. 1982. *La Protección Efectiva en Uruguay*. Montevideo.

Cerdas Cruz, Rodolfo. 1975. *La Crisis de la Democracia Liberal en Costa Rica. Interpretación y Perspectiva*. 2d ed. San José: Editorial Universitaria Centroamericana.

———. 1985. *Formación del Estado en Costa Rica, 1821–1842*. 3d ed. San Pedro: Editorial Universidad de Costa Rica.

Céspedes, Víctor Hugo. 1973. *Costa Rica: La Distribución del Ingreso y el Consumo de Algunos Alimentos*. San Pedro: Universidad de Costa Rica, Instituto de Investigaciones en Ciencias Económicas.

———. 1979. *Evolución de la Distribución del Ingreso en Costa Rica*. San Pedro: Universidad de Costa Rica, Instituto de Investigaciones en Ciencias Económicas.

Céspedes, Víctor Hugo, and Ronulfo Jiménez. 1988. *Evolución de la Pobreza en Costa Rica*. San José: Academia de Centroamérica.

Céspedes, Víctor Hugo, Alberto Di Mare, and Ronulfo Jiménez. 1985. *Costa Rica: Recuperación sin Reactivación*. San José: Editorial Universidad Nacional Estatal a Distancia, for Academia de Centroamérica.

———. 1986. *Costa Rica: La Economía en 1985*. San José: Editorial Universidad Nacional Estatal a Distancia, for Academia de Centroamérica.

Céspedes, Víctor Hugo, Ronulfo Jiménez, and Eduardo Lizano. 1983. *Costa Rica: Crisis y Empobrecimiento*. San José: Editorial Studium, for Academia de Centroamérica.

Céspedes, Víctor Hugo, Alberto Di Mare, Claudio González Vega, and Eduardo Lizano. 1977. *Poverty in Costa Rica*. San José: Academia de Centroamérica.

Céspedes, Víctor Hugo, Claudio González Vega, Ronulfo Jiménez, and Eduardo Lizano. 1983a. *Costa Rica: Una Economía en Crisis*. San José: Editorial Studium, for Academia de Centroamérica.

———. 1984a. *Costa Rica: Estabilidad sin Crecimiento*. San José: Editorial Universidad Nacional Estatal a Distancia, for Academia de Centroamérica.

———. 1984b. *Empleo y Costos de Producción en una Zona Rural de Costa Rica*. San José: Editorial Universidad Nacional Estatal a Distancia, for Academia de Centroamérica.

Céspedes, Víctor Hugo, Claudio González Vega, Ronulfo Jiménez, and Thelmo Vargas. 1983b. *Problemas Económicos en la Década de los 80*. San José: Editorial Studium, for Academia de Centroamérica.

Chenery, Hollis, Montek S. Ahluwalia, Clive Bell, John H. Duloy, and Richard Jolly. 1974. *Redistribution with Growth*. London: Oxford University Press.

Churnside, Roger. 1985. *Formación de la Fuerza Laboral Costarricense*. San José: Editorial Costa Rica.

Clements, Kenneth W., and Larry A. Sjaastad. 1984. *How Protection Taxes Exporters*. London: Trade Policy Research Centre.

Cline, William R., and Enrique Delgado, eds. 1978. *Economic Integration in Central America*. Washington, D.C.: Brookings Institution.

Cobas, E., J. C. Dean, Vivian Laffite, and Elbio Scarone. 1985. *La Dependencia Económica y el Comportamiento de los Productores de Carne Vacuna y Lana en Uruguay*. Montevideo: Universidad de la República.

Collier Paul, and Deepak Lal. 1986. *Labour and Poverty in Kenya, 1900–1980*. Oxford: Clarendon Press.

Coronas, Angel, Daniel Quirós, Eduardo Calzada, Fernando Cañas, Froylán González, Santos Quirós, Carlos Sáenz, and Arturo Castro. 1943. *Ideario Costarricense. Resultado de una Encuesta Nacional*. San José: Editorial Surco.

Corrales, Jorge. 1981. *De la Pobreza . . . a la Abundancia en Costa Rica*. San José: Editorial Studium.

————. 1985. *Políticas de Precios y de Subsidios en Costa Rica*. San José: Editorial Universidad Nacional Estatal a Distancia, for Academia de Centroamérica.

Costa Rica, Dirección General de Estadística y Censos. 1963, 1973. *Censo Agropecuario*. San José.

————. 1950, 1963, 1973. *Censo de Población*. San José.

Costa Rica, Dirección General de Estadística y Censos, and Centro Latinoamericano de Demografía. 1976. *Evaluación de Censo de 1973 y Proyección por Sexo y Grupos de Edades*. San José.

————. 1983. *Costa Rica: Estimaciones y Proyecciones de Población 1950–2025*. San José.

Costa Rica, Dirección General de Estadística y Censos, and Ministerio de Trabajo y Seguridad Social. Various years. *Encuesta Nacional de Hogares, Empleo, y Desempleo*. San José.

Costa Rica, Ministerio de Agricultura, Oficina de Planificación Sectorial Agropecuaria. 1979. *Diagnóstico del Sector Agropecuario de Costa Rica, 1962–76*. San José.

Cuéllar, Oscar, and Santiago Quevedo. 1981. "Condicionantes del Desarrollo Sindical en Costa Rica." In Daniel Camacho, ed., *Desarrollo del Movimiento Sindical en Costa Rica*. San Pedro: Editorial de la Universidad de Costa Rica.

Dabène, Olivier. 1986. "En Torno a la Estabilidad Política de Costa Rica: Tres Paradigmas, Dos Conceptos, Una Fórmula." *Anuario de Estudios Centroamericanos* 12, no. 1: 41–52.

Davrieux, Hugo. 1984. *¿A Quién Beneficia el Gasto Público Social?* Revista SUMA. Montevideo: Centro de Investigaciones Económicas.

d'Elia, Germán. *El Movimiento Sindical*. Nuestra Tierra 4. Montevideo: Editorial Nuestra Tierra.

Denton, Charles. 1971. *Patterns of Costa Rican Politics*. Newton, Mass.: Allyn and Bacon.

Díaz, Ramón. 1979. "Siglo y Medio de Economía Uruguaya." *Búsqueda* 86 (November).

————. 1984. "Uruguay's Erratic Growth." In Arnold C. Harberger, ed., *World Economic Growth*. San Francisco: Institute for Contemporary Studies.

Economic Commission for Latin America. 1970. *La Distribución del Ingreso en América Latina*. New York: United Nations.

————. 1983. *Anuario Estadístico*. Santiago.

————. 1985a. *Evolución de la Sociedad y de las Políticas Sociales en el Uruguay, 1985*. Santiago.

————. 1985b. "Vivienda y Ambiente Urbano en el Uruguay."

————. 1987. *Antecedentes Estadísticos de la Distribución del Ingreso, Costa Rica, 1958–1982*. Santiago: Naciones Unidas.

Economist Intelligence Unit. Various issues. *Quarterly Economic Review: Nicaragua, Costa Rica, Panama*. London.

————. Various issues. *Quarterly Economic Review: Uruguay, Paraguay*. London.

Facio, Rodrigo. 1947. *La Moneda y la Banca Central en Costa Rica*. Mexico City: Fondo de Cultura Económica.

———. 1975. *Estudio sobre Economía Costarricense.* 2d ed., rev. San José: Editorial Costa Rica.

———. 1982. *Obras Históricas, Políticas y Poéticas.* San José: Editorial Costa Rica.

Fallas, Helio. 1984. *Crisis Económica en Costa Rica. Un Análisis Económico de los Ultimos 20 Años.* 2d ed. San José: Editorial Nueva Década.

Fallas, Marco A. 1972. *La Factoría de Tabacos de Costa Rica.* San José: Editorial Costa Rica.

Faraone, Roque. 1972. *El Uruguay en Que Vivimos.* 4th ed. Montevideo: Editorial Arca.

Faroppa, Luis. 1965. *El Desarrollo Económico del Uruguay.* Montevideo: Oficina del Libro del Centro de Estudiantes de Ciencias Económicas y de Administración.

Favaro, Edgardo. 1987. "The Effects of Price Instability upon Economic Growth." Paper presented to the Latin American Econometric Society, São Paulo, Brazil. August.

———. 1990. "A Dynamic Model for the Uruguayan Livestock Sector." Ph.D. diss. University of Chicago, Chicago, Ill.

Favaro, Edgardo, and Claudio Sapelli. 1986. "Schocks Externos, Grado de Apertura y Política Doméstica." Premio Banco Central del Uruguay de Economía 1986. Banco Central de Uruguay, Montevideo.

———. 1989a. *Export Promotion Policies and Economic Growth.* Montevideo: Centro de Investigaciones Económicas.

———. 1989b. *Promoción de Exportaciones y Crecimiento Económico.* San Francisco, Calif.: ISC Press.

Favaro, Edgardo, and Pablo Spiller. 1990. "The Timing and Sequence of a Trade Liberalization Policy." In D. Papageorgiou, Armeane M. Choksi, and Michael Michaely, eds., *Liberalizing Foreign Trade in Developing Countries: The Lessons of Experience.* New York: Oxford University Press.

Favaro, Edgardo, C. Grazziani, and C. Sapelli. 1987. *Tamaño del Estado y Crecimiento Económico.* Montevideo: Centro de Estudios de la Realidad Económica y Social.

Fernández, Aída. 1984. *Estadísticas Sociales.* Montevideo: Instituto de Economía.

Fernández Guardia, Ricardo. 1913. *History of the Discovery and Conquest of Costa Rica.* New York: Thomas Y. Crowell.

Fields, Gary S. 1980. *Poverty, Inequality, and Development.* Cambridge: Cambridge University Press.

———. 1988. "Employment and Economic Growth in Costa Rica." *World Development* 16, no. 12 (December):1495.

Figueres Ferrer, José. 1970. *La Pobreza de las Naciones.* San José: Imprenta Nacional.

Finch, Henry. 1980. *Historia Económica del Uruguay Contemporáneo.* Montevideo: Ediciones de la Banda Oriental.

Finch, M. H. J. 1981. *A Political Economy of Uruguay since 1970.* New York: St. Martin's Press.

Fitzgibbon, Russell H. 1966. *Uruguay: Portrait of a Democracy.* New York: Russell and Russell.

Franco, Rolando. 1984. *Democracia a la Uruguaya. Análisis del Período Electoral, 1925–1984.* Montevideo: El Libro Libre.

Gantz, David A., and Lorin Weisenfeld. 1969. *The Costa Rican Industrial Encouragement Law of 1959*. San José: Proyecto de Derecho Agrario.

García, Norberto, and Victor Tockman. 1985. *Acumulación, Empleo y Crisis*. Santiago: Oficina Internacional del Trabajo, Programa Regional de Empleo para América Latina y el Caribe.

Gil Pacheco, Rufino. 1985. *Ciento Cinco Años de Vida Bancaria en Costa Rica*. 4th ed. San José: Editorial Costa Rica.

González Flores, Luis Felipe. 1933. "El Desenvolvimiento Histórico del Desarrollo del Café en Costa Rica y su Influencia en la Cultura Nacional." In Jorge Carranza Solís, *Monografía del Café*, vol. 1. San José. Reprinted in Héctor Rojas, *El Café en Costa Rica*. San José: Oficina del Café, 1972.

González García, Yamileth. 1984. "La Producción de Alimentos en Costa Rica (1575–1821)." *Anuario de Estudios Centroamericanos* 10:125–42.

González-Vega, Claudio. 1984. "Fear of Adjusting: The Social Costs of Economic Policies in Costa Rica in the 1970s." In Donald E. Schulz and Douglas H. Graham, eds., *Revolution and Counterrevolution in Central America and the Caribbean*. Boulder, Colo.: Westview Press.

———. 1985. "Health Improvements in Costa Rica: The Socioeconomic Background." In Scott B. Halstead, Julia A. Walsh, and Kenneth S. Warren, eds., *Good Health at Low Cost*. New York: Rockefeller Foundation.

González-Vega, Claudio, Eduardo Lizano Fait, and Robert Cross Vogel. 1970. *The Marketing of Agricultural Products in Costa Rica*. San José: Associated Colleges of the Midwest, Central American Field Program.

Graceras, Ulises. 1970. *Los Intelectuales y la Política en Uruguay*. Cuadernos de El País 3. Montevideo.

Grompone, Antonio Miguel. 1967. *La Ideología de Batlle*. 3d ed. Montevideo: Editorial Arca.

Ground, Richard L. 1986. "Origen y Magnitud del Ajuste Recesivo en América Latina." *Revista de la CEPAL* 30 (December).

Gudmundson, Lowell. 1983. "Costa Rica before Coffee: Occupational Distribution, Wealth Inequality, and Elite Society in the Village Economy of the 1840s." *Journal of Latin American Studies* 15, pt. 2 (November):427–52.

———. 1985. *Costa Rica before Coffee: Society and Economy on the Eve of the Export Boom*. Baton Rouge: Louisiana State University Press.

Gutiérrez, Carlos José. 1979. *El Funcionamiento del Sistema Jurídico*. San José: Ediciones Juricentro S.A.

Handelman, Howard. 1981. "Labor Industrial Conflict and the Collapse of Uruguayan Democracy." *Journal of Inter-American Studies and World Affairs* 23.

Hall, Carolyn. 1982. *El Café y el Desarrollo Histórico-Geográfico de Costa Rica*. 3d ed. San José: Editorial Costa Rica.

———. 1985. *Costa Rica. A Geographical Interpretation in Historical Perspective*. Boulder, Colo.: Westview Press.

Hanson, Simon G. 1938. *Utopia in Uruguay: The Economic History of Uruguay*. New York: Oxford University Press.

Harberger, Arnold, and David Wisecarver. 1978. *Private and Social Rates of Return to Capital in Uruguay*. Montevideo: Banco Central del Uruguay.

Herrick, Bruce, and Barclay Hudson. 1980. *Urban Poverty and Economic Development: A Case Study of Costa Rica*. New York: St. Martin's Press.

Herschell, Federico. 1977. *Incidencia Fiscal y Distribución del Ingreso en Costa Rica*. San José: CEPAL and Ministerio de Hacienda.

Hicks, J. R. 1979. *Causality in Economics*. Oxford: Blackwell.

Holdridge, L. R., and others. 1971. *Forest Environments in Tropical Life Zones: A Pilot Study*. Oxford: Pergamon Press.

Hunter, J. Robert. 1976. *The Forest Resources of Costa Rica: The Biological Approach*. San José: Associated Colleges of the Midwest.

Indart, Susana. 1981. *Rentabilidad de la Educación en el Uruguay*. Montevideo: Instituto de Economía, Universidad de la República.

Instituto de Economía, Universidad de la República. 1969. *Estadísticas Básicas*. Montevideo.

———. 1971. "La Distribución del Ingreso en Uruguay." Montevideo.

———. 1982. "Estructura Salarial en la Industria." Montevideo.

International Monetary Fund. 1980, 1983, 1985. *Government Finance Statistics Yearbook*. Washington, D.C.

Jarvis, Lovell S. 1985. *Livestock Development in Latin America*. Washington, D.C.: World Bank.

Jiménez Castro, Wilburg. 1986. *Génesis del Gobierno de Costa Rica: 1821–1981*. 2 vols. San Pedro: Editorial Alma Mater.

Jones, Chester Lloyd. 1935. *Costa Rica and Civilization in the Caribbean*. New York: Russell and Russell.

Kakwani, Nanak C. 1980. *Income Inequality and Poverty: Methods of Estimation and Policy Applications*. New York: Oxford University Press.

Lal, Deepak. 1986. *The Political Economy of Industrialization in Primary Product Exporting Economies: Some Cautionary Tales*. World Bank Development Research Department Discussion Paper 215. Washington, D.C.

Láscaris, Constantino. 1983. *Desarrollo de las Ideas Filosóficas en Costa Rica*. San José: Editorial Studium.

———. 1985. *El Costarricense*. San José: Editorial Universitaria Centroamericana.

Lederman, Esteban, and others. 1979. "Trabajo y Empleo." In Chester Zelaya, ed., *Costa Rica Contemporánea*. San José: Editorial Costa Rica.

Lindahl, Gore. 1971. *Batlle*. Montevideo: Editorial Arca.

Lindo Bennett, E. 1970. "La Actividad Cacaotera en Costa Rica." Licenciatura thesis, University of Costa Rica.

Lizano Fait, Eduardo. 1971a. *Comentarios sobre Economía Nacional*. San Pedro: Editorial Universidad de Costa Rica.

———. 1971b. *El Mercado Común y la Distribución del Ingreso*. San José: Editorial Universitaria Centroamericana.

———. 1975. *Cambio Social en Costa Rica*. San José: Editorial Costa Rica.

———. 1980. *Agricultura y Desarrollo Económico*. San José: Editorial Universidad Nacional Estatal a Distancia.

———. 1982. *Escritos sobre Integración Económica*. San José: Editorial Costa Rica.

———. 1987. *Desde el Banco Central*. San José: Editorial Universidad Nacional Estatal a Distancia, for Academia de Centroamérica.

Lizano Fait, Eduardo, ed. 1975. *La Integración Económica Centroamericana*. Mexico City: Fondo de Cultura Económica.

Lizano Fait, Eduardo, and Minor Sagot. 1984. *Costa Rica y la Integración Económica Centroamericana*. San José: Editorial Universidad Nacional Estatal a Distancia, for Academia de Centroamérica.

Lom, Helen. 1975. *Salarios Mínimos en Costa Rica*. San José: Universidad de Costa Rica.

MacLeod, Murdo J. 1973. *Spanish Central America: A Socioeconomic History, 1520–1720*. Berkeley: University of California Press.

Martínez Lamas, Julio. 1930. *Riqueza y Pobreza del Uruguay: Estudio de las Causas que Retardan el Progreso Económico*. Montevideo: Palacio del Libro.

Meléndez, Carlos. 1981. *Historia de Costa Rica*. San José: Editorial Universidad Nacional Estatal a Distancia.

———. 1982. *Conquistadores y Pobladores. Orígenes Históricos Sociales de los Costarricenses*. San José: Editorial Universidad Nacional Estatal a Distancia.

Meléndez, Carlos, and Quince Duncan. 1985. *El Negro en Costa Rica*. San José: Editorial Costa Rica.

Melgar, Alicia. 1982. *Distribución del Ingreso en el Uruguay*. Montevideo: Centro Latinoamericano de Economía Humana.

Méndez, Estela. 1985. *Ocupación en el Uruguay 1985*. Montevideo: Facultad de Ciencias Económicas, Universidad de la República.

Millot, Julio, Carlos Silva, and Lindor Silva. 1968. *El Desarrollo Industrial del Uruguay de la Crisis de 1929 a la Postguerra*. Montevideo: Facultad de Ciencias Económicas, Universidad de la República.

Monge Alfaro, Carlos. 1980. *Historia de Costa Rica*. 16th ed. San José: Librería Trejos.

Monge González, Ricardo. 1987. *La Reforma Arancelaria. El Caso de Costa Rica*. San José: ProDesarrollo.

Moore, R. 1978. *Soldiers, Politicians, and Reaction: The Etiology of Military Rule in Uruguay*. Tucson: University of Arizona Press.

Mourat, Oscar, Alba A. Mariani, Raúl Jacob, Adela Pellegrino, Rosanna Di Segni, and Silvia Rodríguez Vallamil. n.d. *Cinco Perspectivas Históricas del Uruguay Moderno*. Montevideo: Fundación de Cultura Universitaria.

Myint, Hla. 1971. *Economic Theory and the Underdeveloped Countries*. London: Oxford University Press.

Novak, Michael, and Michael P. Jackson. 1985. *Latin America: Dependency or Interdependence?* Washington, D.C.: American Enterprise Institute.

Oduber Quirós, Daniel, José Miguel Alfaro Rodríguez, Rodolfo Cerdas Cruz, Armando Vargas Araya, Arnoldo Ferreto Segura, Sergio Erick Ardón Ramírez, and Román Arrieta Villalobos. 1981. *Los Problemas Socio-Políticos del Desarrollo en Costa Rica*. San José: Editorial Universidad Nacional Estatal a Distancia.

Ortuño Sobrado, Fernando. 1963. *El Monopolio Estatal de la Banca en Costa Rica*. San José: Trejos Hnos.

Patrón, María del Rosario. 1986. *La Reforma Cambiaria y Monetaria y el Proceso Económico Uruguayo 1959–1962*. Montevideo: Banco Central del Uruguay.

Piaguda, Miriam, and Máximo Rossi. 1982. *Estructura Salarial de la Industria*. Montevideo: Instituto de Economia, Universidad de la República.

Pendle, George. 1963. *Uruguay.* 3d ed. London: Oxford University Press.

Piñera, Sebastián. 1978. *Medición, Análisis y Descripción de la Pobreza en Costa Rica.* Santiago: Proyecto Interinstitucional de Pobreza Crítica en América Latina.

———. 1979. "¿Se Benefician los Pobres del Crecimiento Económico?" E/CEPAL/Proy. 1/2. Santiago: Economic Commission for Latin America.

Pollack, Molly. 1987. "Poverty and Labor Market in Costa Rica." Santiago: Oficina Internacional del Trabajo, Programa Regional de Empleo para América Latina y el Caribe.

Pollack, Molly, and Andras Uthoff. 1985. "Wages and Price Dynamics in Costa Rica, 1976–1983." Santiago: Oficina Internacional del Trabajo, Programa Regional de Empleo para América Latina y el Caribe.

ProDesarrollo. 1984. *Estructura de la Protección al Sector Industrial en Costa Rica.* San José.

Quesada, Ricardo. 1983. "Política Cambiaria de Costa Rica del 1 de Enero de 1974 al 30 de Junio de 1983." Banco Central de Costa Rica, San José.

Rama, Carlos M. 1972. *Historia Social del Pueblo Uruguayo.* Montevideo: Editorial Comunidad del Sur.

Ramírez Arango, Julio Sergio. 1985. "The Political Role of the Private Sector Associations in Central America: The Cases of El Salvador, Nicaragua, and Costa Rica." Ph.D. diss., Harvard University, Cambridge, Mass.

Rapoport, Alan I. 1978. "Effective Protection Rates in Central America." In William R. Cline and Enríque Delgado, eds., *Economic Integration in Central America.* Washington, D.C.: Brookings Institution.

Real de Azúa, Carlos. 1971. "Política, Poder y Partidos en el Uruguay de Hoy." In Luis Benvenuto, Nicolás Reig, José E. Santías, Carlos Real de Azúa, Angel Rama, and Carlos Martínez Moreno, eds., *Uruguay Hoy.* Buenos Aires: Argentina Editores S.A.

Reca, Lucio, and M. E. Regunaga. 1978. *Costos de Insumos en el Sector Agropecuario Uruguayo.* Montevideo: USAID.

Rial, Juan. 1984a. *Partidos Políticos, Democracia y Autoritarismo.* Montevideo: Ediciones de la Banda Oriental.

———. 1984b. *Elecciones, Reglas de Juego y Tendencias.* Montevideo: Centro de Investigación y Experimentación Pedagógica.

Rivera Urrutia, Eugenio. 1982. *El Fondo Monetario Internacional y Costa Rica, 1978–1982, Política Económica y Crisis.* San José: Departamento Ecuménico de Investigaciones.

Rodríguez, Héctor. 1966. *Nuestros Sindicatos.* Montevideo: Editorial Universitaria.

Rojas Bolaños, Manuel. 1981. "El Desarrollo del Movimiento Obrero en Costa Rica. Un Intento de Periodización." In Daniel Camacho, ed., *Desarrollo del Movimiento Sindical en Costa Rica.* San Pedro: Editorial Universidad de Costa Rica.

———. 1986. *Lucha Social y Guerra Civil en Costa Rica, 1940–1948.* San Pedro: Editorial Alma Mater.

Rosenberg, Mark. 1983. *Las Luchas por el Seguro Social en Costa Rica.* San José: Editorial Costa Rica.

Rosero Bixby, Luis. 1980. *La Situación Demográfica de Costa Rica*. San José: Asociación Demográfica Costarricense.

———. 1985. "Infant Mortality Decline in Costa Rica." In Scott B. Halstead, Julia A. Walsh, and Kenneth S. Warren, eds., *Good Health at Low Cost*. New York: Rockefeller Foundation.

Ross, John A., Marjorie Rich, Janet P. Molzan, and Michael Penzak. 1988. *Family Planning and Child Survival in 100 Developing Countries*. New York: Center for Population and Family Health.

Rossi, Máximo. 1982. *Distribución del Ingreso y Pobreza*. Montevideo: Instituto de Economía.

Rovira Mas, Jorge. 1983. *Estado y Política Económica en Costa Rica, 1948–1970*. 2d ed. San José: Editorial Porvenir.

———. 1987. *Costa Rica en los Años '80*. San José: Editorial Porvenir.

Rovira Mas, Jorge, ed. 1984. *Costa Rica Hoy: La Crisis y sus Perspectivas*. San José: Editorial Universidad Estatal a Distancia.

Sáenz Pacheco, Carlos J. 1969. "Population Growth, Economic Progress, and Opportunities on the Land: The Case of Costa Rica." Ph.D. diss., University of Wisconsin, Madison.

Salas Marrero, Oscar, and Rodrigo Barahona Israel. 1973. *Derecho Agrario*. San Pedro: Editorial Universidad de Costa Rica.

Sapelli, Claudio. 1985. "Government Policy and the Uruguayan Beef Sector." Ph.D. diss., University of Chicago, Chicago, Ill.

———. 1987a. *Crecimiento Económico y Salario Real en el Uruguay*. Montevideo: Centro de Estudios de la Realidad Económica y Social.

———. 1987b. "Exportaciones, Integración y Productividad." Montevideo: Centro de Estudios de la Realidad Económica e Social.

Sapelli, Claudio, and Gaston Labadie. 1987. *Causas de la Emigración a la Argentina*. Documentos de Trabajo 3. Montevideo: Centro de la Realidad Económica y Social.

Sciandra, Eduardo. 1979. "Transferencias de Ingreso y Barreras Arancelarias en Uruguay: Un Enfoque de Equilibrio General." Unpublished monograph. Universidad de la República, Facultad de Ciencias Económicas, Montevideo.

Seligson, Mitchell A. 1980. *Peasants of Costa Rica and the Development of Agrarian Capitalism*. Madison: University of Wisconsin Press.

Semino, Miguel. 1984. *Partidos Políticos y Elecciones en el Uruguay*. Montevideo: Fundación de Cultura Universitaria.

Singh, Shamsher, Jos de Vries, John C. L. Hulley, and Patrick Yeung. 1977. *Coffee, Tea, and Cocoa*. Baltimore, Md.: Johns Hopkins University Press.

Sojo, Ana. 1984. "La Trayectoria Financiera de la Corporación Costarricense de Desarrollo, 1975–1982." Universidad de Costa Rica, Instituto de Investigaciones en Ciencias Económicas, San Pedro.

———. 1985. *Estado Empresario y Lucha Política en Costa Rica*. San José: Editorial Universitaria Centroamericana.

Solari, Aldo E. 1958. *Sociología Rural Nacional*. Montevideo: Universidad de Montevideo, Facultad de Derecho y Ciencias Sociales.

———. 1967. *El Desarrollo Social del Uruguay en la Postguerra*. Montevideo: Alfa.

Soley Güell, Tomás. 1947. *Historia Económica y Hacendaria de Costa Rica*. 2 vols. San José: Editorial Universitaria.

Stewart, Watt. 1964. *Keith and Costa Rica*. Albuquerque, N.M.: University of New Mexico Press.

Stone, Samuel. 1976. *La Dinastía de los Conquistadores. La Crisis del Poder en la Costa Rica Contemporánea*. 2d ed. San José: Editorial Universitaria Centroamericana.

Street, John. 1959. *Artigas and the Emancipation of Uruguay*. Cambridge: Cambridge University Press.

Taylor, Philip B., Jr. 1960. *Government and the Politics of Uruguay*. Tulane Studies in Political Studies 7. New Orleans, La.: Tulane University Press.

Thiel, Bernardo A. 1902. "Monografía de la Población de la República de Costa Rica en el Siglo XIX." *Revista de Costa Rica durante el Siglo XIX*.

Tilak, Jandhyala B. G. 1988. *Comparative Development Indicators*. Washington, D.C.: World Bank. Processed.

Trejos, Juan Diego. 1983a. "La Distribución del Ingreso de las Familias Costarricenses: Algunas Características en 1977." Universidad de Costa Rica, Instituto de Investigaciones en Ciencias Económicas, San Pedro.

————. 1983b. *Las Políticas de Distribución y Redistribución del Ingreso en Costa Rica en la Década de los Años Setenta*. San Pedro: Universidad de Costa Rica, Instituto de Investigaciones en Ciencias Económicas.

Trejos, Juan Diego, and María Laura Elizalde. 1985. "Costa Rica: La Distribución del Ingreso y el Acceso a los Programas de Carácter Social." Universidad de Costa Rica, Instituto de Investigaciones en Ciencias Económicas, San Pedro.

Trejos Escalante, Fernando. 1963. *Libertad y Seguridad*. San José: Trejos Hnos., for Asociación Nacional de Fomento Económico.

Trejos Fernández, José Joaquín. 1973. *Ocho Años en la Política Costarricense. Ideales Políticos y Realidad Nacional*. 4 vols. San José: Editorial Hombre y Sociedad.

Trías, Vivián. 1970. *Imperialismo y Rosca Bancaria en el Uruguay*. Montevideo: Ediciones de la Banda Oriental.

United Nations. 1980. *Compendium of Social Statistics*. New York.

————. 1985. *Statistical Yearbook, 1983–84*. New York.

————. 1988. *Demographic Yearbook, 1986*. New York.

Uruguay, Dirección General de Estadísticas y Censos. 1968, 1979. *Censo Económico Nacional*. Montevideo.

————. Various years. *Anuario Estadístico*. Montevideo.

————. Various years. *Censo Nacional de Población y Vivienda*. Montevideo.

————. Various years. *Encuesta de Hogares, Ocupación y Desocupación*. Montevideo.

————. Various years. *Encuesta de Vivienda*. Montevideo.

————. Various years. *Indice de los Precios de Consumo*. Montevideo.

Uruguay, Ministerio de Economía y Finanzas. Various years. *Estadísticas de la Gestión del Gobierno Central*. Montevideo.

Uruguay, Ministerio de Ganadería y Agricultura. Various years. *Censo General Agropecuario*. Montevideo.

————. 1965. *Proyectos de Leyes de Promoción Agropecuaria*. Montevideo.

Uruguay, Oficina de Planeamiento y Presupuesto. Various years. "Datos Estadísticos sobre el Sistema Tributario y Paratributario de Uruguay." Montevideo.

Uthoff, Andras, and Molly Pollack. 1985. "Análisis Microeconómico del Ajuste del Mercado de Trabajo de Costa Rica, 1979–1982: Lecciones para un Modelo Macroeconómico." *Revista de Ciencias Económicas* 5, no. 1:17–36.

Vanger, Milton I. 1963. *José Batlle y Ordóñez of Uruguay, The Creator of His Times, 1902–1907.* Cambridge, Mass.: Harvard University Press.

Vargas, Thelmo. 1987. "Informe sobre CODESA." San José.

Vega, Mylena. 1982. *El Estado Costarricense de 1974 a 1978: CODESA y la Fracción Industrial.* San José: Editorial Hoy.

———. 1984a. *La Política de CODESA durante el Gobierno de Carazo, 1978–1982.* San Pedro: Universidad de Costa Rica, Instituto de Investigaciones en Ciencias Económicas.

———. 1984b. *La Política de CODESA durante el Gobierno de Monge. Análisis de la Gestión de Junio de 1982 a Diciembre de 1983.* San Pedro: Universidad de Costa Rica, Instituto de Investigaciones en Ciencias Económicas.

———. 1985. *Perspectivas del Estado Empresario Costarricense: El Caso de CODESA.* San Pedro: Universidad de Costa Rica, Instituto de Investigaciones en Ciencias Económicas.

Vega Carballo, José Luis. 1968. *Hacia una Interpretación del Desarrollo Costarricense: Ensayo Sociológico.* 5th ed. San José: Editorial Porvenir.

———. 1981. *Orden y Progreso: La Formación del Estado Nacional en Costa Rica.* San José: Instituto Centroamericano de Administración Pública.

———. 1982. *Poder Político y Democracia en Costa Rica.* San José: Editorial Porvenir.

Vegh Villegas, Alejandro. 1987. *Economía Política: Teoría y Acción.* Ediciones Polo.

Vernazza, Francisco. 1987. "El Sistema Electoral Uruguayo y el Descenso de la Representatividad de los Diputados, 1925–1984." Unpublished paper. Montevideo.

Vieytes, Humberto. 1984. *Análisis Económico de la Seguridad Social en Uruguay.* Montevideo: Instituto de Economía.

Vogt, William. 1946. *The Population of Costa Rica and its Natural Resources.* Washington, D.C.: Pan American Union.

Weisenfeld, Lorin. 1969. "The Costa Rican Industrial Encouragement Law. Legislative History." University of Costa Rica, Agrarian Law Project, San José.

Wesson, Robert. 1984. "Costa Rica. Problems of a Social Democracy." In Robert Wesson, ed., *Politics, Policies, and Economic Development in Latin America.* Stanford, Calif.: Hoover Institution Press.

World Bank. 1980. *Costa Rica. Trade Incentives and Export Diversification.* Washington, D.C.

Zumbado, Fernando, and Carlos Raabe. 1976. *Evolución de la Distribución de la Población en Costa Rica.* San José: Oficina de Planificación Nacional.

Index

Gross domestic product (GDP) in Uruguay, 188, 270, 272, 287; comparisons with Costa Rican, 388; economic conditions and (1959), 232–33, 236; economic growth and, 190, 194–97, 198–200; economic policy and, 305–06; external influences and, 279–81; historical background to, 209–10, 220–21; manufacturing and, 283–84; oil shock and, 267–68, 275, 282; political change and, 289–90; political economy and, 253, 256, 258; stagnation and, 243, 245, 249

Gross national income in Costa Rica, 29–31

Gross national product (GNP) in Costa Rica, 29–31, 33

Growth-with-equity in Costa Rica, 6, 59, 64, 125–28

Guatemala, 62, 84, 87, 91

Guerra Grande in Uruguay, 205

Guerrillas in Uruguay, 242, 263, 301–02

Haciendas (Costa Rica), 65–66, 69

Health (Costa Rica), 16, 32, 36, 56, 370; comparisons with Uruguayan, 365, 390; economic progress and, 126–27, 139–40; modernization of state and, 77–78, 81–82; protectionism and, 103–04

Health (Uruguay); compared with Costa Rican, 365, 390; oil shock and, 290; social indicators and, 200–02; stagnation and, 228, 231, 236

Hernández, Alfredo, 102

Herrera, Luis Alberto de, 228–29, 238–39

Hess, Raúl, 91

Hidalgos in Costa Rica, 62

High-income households in Costa Rica, 54, 56–57, 83, 103

Home ownership in Costa Rica, 56–57

Honduras, 87

House of Representatives in Uruguay, 205, 215

Housing: in Costa Rica, 57, 77–78, 135, 140; in Uruguay, 196–97, 202–03, 280

Human capital (Costa Rica), 9–10, 32–33, 71; comparisons with Uruguayan, 382; economic progress and, 126–27, 132, 140; fiscal crisis and, 110, 118

Ideology in Uruguay, 374, 386; oil shock and, 265–66; stagnation and, 231–32, 241

Illiteracy in Costa Rica, 77, 108, 136, 140, 383

Immigration in Costa Rica, 17, 62

Immigration (Uruguay), 187, 296; historical background to, 206–07, 209, 211, 218, 379; stagnation and, 230–31

Imports (Costa Rica), 24, 28, 31, 370; comparisons with Uruguayan, 365, 390–91; development and, until 1950, 62–63, 67; economic progress and, 133–36, 140, 144; fiscal crisis and, 110–12, 117; modernization of state and, 76, 86, 89; openness and, 33–34; protectionism and, 95–99

Imports (Uruguay), 188, 286, 288; comparisons with Costa Rican, 365, 390–91; economic conditions and (1930–55), 219–20, 226; economic growth and, 190, 192–96; economic policy and, 298–301, 303, 305; historical background to, 209–10, 212, 226; historical perspective on, 377, 379, 381; manufacturing and, 283–85; oil shock and, 267, 272, 274, 279–82; political economy and, 253–54, 256, 258; political events and, 237–38; stagnation and, 231–33, 235, 244–47, 249

IMPROME in Uruguay, 272

Incentives in Uruguay, 272, 389, 392

Income (Costa Rica), 3, 5, 10, 23, 99; comparisons with Uruguayan, 385–86, 390, 392; economic progress and, 131–32, 135, 139, 143; fiscal crisis and, 106, 110, 113, 121; growth and, 28–31, 33, 42, 125, 127; modernization of state and, 78, 83, 86, 88

Income distribution (Costa Rica), 43–44; alleviation of poverty and, 57–58; comparisons with Uruguayan, 365, 382, 385, 388–89, 391; earnings inequality and, 52–53; economic progress and, 126, 128, 130, 138, 144; fiscal crisis and, 108, 113–14; household income (1960s) and, 44–45; household income (1970s) and, 48–50; household income (1980s) and, 50–52; historical perspective on, 367, 369; redistribution of wealth (1970s) and, 140, 142; standard of living and, 54–57; structural transformation and, 45–48; taxation and, 53–54

Income distribution (Uruguay), 188–89; comparisons with Costa Rican, 365, 382, 385, 388–89, 391; economic growth and, 190, 194, 197–99; economic policy and, 296, 306; historical background to, 210, 216, 226; historical perspective on, 374, 376–77, 380; oil shock and, 266, 275–77, 286–87, 290; political economy